Venture Capital Investing

The Complete Handbook
for Investing
in New Businesses

In an increasingly competitive world, it is quality
of thinking that gives an edge—an idea that opens new
doors, a technique that solves a problem, or an insight
that simply helps make sense of it all.

We work with leading authors in the various arenas
of business and finance to bring cutting-edge thinking
and best learning practice to a global market.

It is our goal to create world-class print publications
and electronic products that give readers
knowledge and understanding which can then be
applied, whether studying or at work.

To find out more about our business
products, you can visit us at www.ft-ph.com

Venture Capital Investing

The Complete Handbook for Investing in New Businesses

David Gladstone
Laura Gladstone

FT Prentice Hall

FINANCIAL TIMES

An Imprint of PEARSON EDUCATION
Upper Saddle River, NJ • New York • London • San Francisco • Toronto • Sydney
Tokyo • Singapore • Hong Kong • Cape Town • Madrid
Paris • Milan • Munich • Amsterdam

www.ft-ph.com

Library of Congress Cataloging-in-Publication Data

A CIP record of this book can be obtained from the Library of Congress.

Production Supervisor: *Faye Gemmellaro*
Manufacturing Buyer: *Maura Zaldivar*
Cover Design Director: *Jerry Votta*
Interior Design: *Gail Cocker-Boguss*
VP, Editor-in-Chief: *Tim Moore*
Editorial Assistant: *Richard Winkler*
Developmental Editor: *Russ Hall*
Marketing Manager: *John Pierce*

 © 2004 Pearson Education, Inc.
Publishing as Financial Times Prentice Hall
Upper Saddle River, New Jersey 07458

Financial Times Prentice Hall offers excellent discounts on this book when ordered in quantity for bulk purchases or special sales. For more information, please contact: U.S. Corporate and Government Sales, 1-800-382-3419, corpsales@pearsontechgroup.com. For sales outside of the United States, please contact: International Sales, 1-317-581-3793, international@pearsontechgroup.com.

Company and product names mentioned herein are the trademarks or registered trademarks of their respective owners.

Printed in the United States of America

First Printing

ISBN 0-13-101885-X

Pearson Education Ltd.
Pearson Education Australia Pty., Limited
Pearson Education Singapore, Pte. Ltd.
Pearson Education North Asia Ltd.
Pearson Education Canada, Ltd.
Pearson Educación de Mexico, S.A. de C.V.
Pearson Education—Japan
Pearson Education Malaysia, Pte. Ltd.

FINANCIAL TIMES PRENTICE HALL BOOKS

For more information, please go to www.ft-ph.com

Business and Technology

Sarv Devaraj and Rajiv Kohli

The IT Payoff: Measuring the Business Value of Information Technology Investments

Nicholas D. Evans

Business Innovation and Disruptive Technology: Harnessing the Power of Breakthrough Technology...for Competitive Advantage

Nicholas D. Evans

Consumer Gadgets: 50 Ways to Have Fun and Simplify Your Life with Today's Technology...and Tomorrow's

Faisal Hoque

The Alignment Effect: How to Get Real Business Value Out of Technology

Economics

David Dranove

What's Your Life Worth? Health Care Rationing...Who Lives? Who Dies? Who Decides?

John C. Edmunds

Brave New Wealthy World: Winning the Struggle for World Prosperity

Jonathan Wight

Saving Adam Smith: A Tale of Wealth, Transformation, and Virtue

Entrepreneurship

Oren Fuerst and Uri Geiger

From Concept to Wall Street: A Complete Guide to Entrepreneurship and Venture Capital

David Gladstone and Laura Gladstone

Venture Capital Handbook: An Entrepreneur's Guide to Raising Venture Capital, Revised and Updated

Erica Orloff and Kathy Levinson, Ph.D.

The 60-Second Commute: A Guide to Your 24/7 Home Office Life

Jeff Saperstein and Daniel Rouach

Creating Regional Wealth in the Innovation Economy: Models, Perspectives, and Best Practices

Finance

Aswath Damodaran
The Dark Side of Valuation: Valuing Old Tech, New Tech, and New Economy Companies

Kenneth R. Ferris and Barbara S. Pécherot Petitt
Valuation: Avoiding the Winner's Curse

International Business

Peter Marber
Money Changes Everything: How Global Prosperity Is Reshaping Our Needs, Values, and Lifestyles

Fernando Robles, Françoise Simon, and Jerry Haar
Winning Strategies for the New Latin Markets

Investments

Zvi Bodie and Michael J. Clowes
Worry-Free Investing: A Safe Approach to Achieving Your Lifetime Goals

Harry Domash
Fire Your Stock Analyst! Analyzing Stocks on Your Own

D. Quinn Mills
Buy, Lie, and Sell High: How Investors Lost Out on Enron and the Internet Bubble

D. Quinn Mills
Wheel, Deal, and Steal: Deceptive Accounting, Deceitful CEOs, and Ineffective Reforms

John Nofsinger and Kenneth Kim
Infectious Greed: Restoring Confidence in America's Companies

John R. Nofsinger
Investment Blunders (of the Rich and Famous)…And What You Can Learn from Them

John R. Nofsinger
Investment Madness: How Psychology Affects Your Investing…And What to Do About It

H. David Sherman, S. David Young, and Harris Collingwood
Profits You Can Trust: Spotting & Surviving Accounting Landmines

Leadership

Jim Despain and Jane Bodman Converse
And Dignity for All: Unlocking Greatness through Values-Based Leadership

Marshall Goldsmith, Vijay Govindarajan, Beverly Kaye, and Albert A. Vicere
The Many Facets of Leadership

Marshall Goldsmith, Cathy Greenberg, Alastair Robertson, and Maya Hu-Chan
Global Leadership: The Next Generation

Management

Rob Austin and Lee Devin
Artful Making: What Managers Need to Know About How Artists Work

J. Stewart Black and Hal B. Gregersen
Leading Strategic Change: Breaking Through the Brain Barrier

William C. Byham, Audrey B. Smith, and Matthew J. Paese
Grow Your Own Leaders: How to Identify, Develop, and Retain Leadership Talent

David M. Carter and Darren Rovell
On the Ball: What You Can Learn About Business from Sports Leaders

Subir Chowdhury
Organization 21C: Someday All Organizations Will Lead this Way

Ross Dawson
Living Networks: Leading Your Company, Customers, and Partners in the Hyper-connected Economy

Charles J. Fombrun and Cees B.M. Van Riel
Fame and Fortune: How Successful Companies Build Winning Reputations

Amir Hartman
Ruthless Execution: What Business Leaders Do When Their Companies Hit the Wall

Harvey A. Hornstein
The Haves and the Have Nots: The Abuse of Power and Privilege in the Workplace... and How to Control It

Kevin Kennedy and Mary Moore
Going the Distance: Why Some Companies Dominate and Others Fail

Robin Miller
The Online Rules of Successful Companies: The Fool-Proof Guide to Building Profits

Fergus O'Connell
The Competitive Advantage of Common Sense: Using the Power You Already Have

W. Alan Randolph and Barry Z. Posner
Checkered Flag Projects: 10 Rules for Creating and Managing Projects that Win, Second Edition

Stephen P. Robbins
Decide & Conquer: Make Winning Decisions to Take Control of Your Life

Stephen P. Robbins
The Truth About Managing People...And Nothing but the Truth

Ronald Snee and Roger Hoerl
Leading Six Sigma: A Step-by-Step Guide Based on Experience with GE and Other Six Sigma Companies

Susan E. Squires, Cynthia J. Smith, Lorna McDougall, and William R. Yeack
Inside Arthur Andersen: Shifting Values, Unexpected Consequences

Jerry Weissman
Presenting to Win: The Art of Telling Your Story

Marketing

David Arnold
The Mirage of Global Markets: How Globalizing Companies Can Succeed as Markets Localize

Michael Basch
CustomerCulture: How FedEx and Other Great Companies Put the Customer First Every Day

Jonathan Cagan and Craig M. Vogel
Creating Breakthrough Products: Innovation from Product Planning to Program Approval

Al Lieberman, with Patricia Esgate
The Entertainment Marketing Revolution: Bringing the Moguls, the Media, and the Magic to the World

Tom Osenton
Customer Share Marketing: How the World's Great Marketers Unlock Profits from Customer Loyalty

Bernd H. Schmitt, David L. Rogers, and Karen Vrotsos
There's No Business That's Not Show Business: Marketing in Today's Experience Culture

Yoram J. Wind and Vijay Mahajan, with Robert Gunther
Convergence Marketing: Strategies for Reaching the New Hybrid Consumer

Public Relations

Gerald R. Baron
Now Is Too Late: Survival in an Era of Instant News

Deirdre Breakenridge and Thomas J. DeLoughry
The New PR Toolkit: Strategies for Successful Media Relations

CONTENTS

INTRODUCTION XXVII

CHAPTER 1   KEYS TO SUCCESSFUL INVESTING 1

WHAT ARE THE BASIC ITEMS TO LOOK
FOR IN A BUSINESS PROPOSITION? 2

1. THE NUMBERS SHOULD BE
   PROPERLY PRESENTED 2

2. THE DEAL MUST MAKE LOTS OF MONEY 3

3. THE ACID TEST OF A DEAL IS MANAGEMENT 4

4. THE SITUATION SHOULD BE UNIQUE 7

5. THE PROPOSED VENTURE SHOULD BE ORIENTED
   TOWARD THE MARKET 8

6. THE DEAL MUST HAVE AN EXIT 9

IT'S NOT AN INVESTMENT, IT'S A PARTNERSHIP 9

PREPARE A WRITTEN SUMMARY BEFORE YOU
BEGIN TO INVEST 10

WHAT ARE YOU INVESTING IN? 11

WHO IS YOUR CONTACT AT THE BUSINESS? 11

SUMMARIZE THE BUSINESS SITUATION 11

WHO IS THE MANAGEMENT TEAM? 12

WHAT ARE THEY SELLING? 12

HOW MUCH MONEY ARE THEY RAISING AND HOW
MUCH ARE YOU CONSIDERING INVESTING? 12

IS THERE ANY SECURITY FOR YOUR INVESTMENT? 13

ix

How Will the Money Be Used? 13

What Is the Past Financial Performance? 13

What Are the Projections? 14

How Will You Cash In? 14

How Much Can You Make? 14

What Do You Like About This Situation? 15

What Do You Dislike About This Situation? 15

What Does A Summary Look Like? 15

Company 15

Type of Business 16

Company Summary 16

A Second Summary 18

Company 18

Type of Business 18

Company Summary 18

What Makes It Exciting? 20

Some Words about Franchising 22

Sound Concept 22

Well-Financed Franchisor 22

How Does the Franchisor Make Money? 22

Good Relations 23

Summary—Quick Standards
of Venture Capital Investing 23

CHAPTER 2 ANALYSIS OF MANAGEMENT 27

The Study of Entrepreneurs 28

Characteristics of Entrepreneurs 30

Need for Achievement 30

High Need for Autonomy and Power 31

High Degree of Self-Confdence and Need
for Control 32

High Tolerance for Ambiguity 32

Need to Assume Only Moderate Risk 32

High Degree of Determination 33

High Degree of Resourcefulness 33

Sense of Urgency 34

Knowing What Is Real 34

High Level of Energy 35

Mental Stamina 36

Strong Communications Skills 36

High Degree of Integrity 37

Seeking Partnership Status 39

Seeking Fair Play 39

How We See Entrepreneurs 40

How We Make Judgments 41

Analytical Approach to Evaluations 42

Interviewing Entrepreneurs 43

Be Prepared 44

Clear Mind 44

Conducive Environment 44

Be an Effective Listener 45

Keep on Your Toes During the Interview 45

Types of Interviews 46

Document Your Work 46

Assessment of Entrepreneurs 47

Intellectual Effectiveness 49

Work Approach and Style 50

Personal Relationships 50

What Venture Capitalists Look
for in Entrepreneurs 52

The Entrepreneur's Individual
Characteristics 52

Experience of the Entrepreneur 54

Characteristics of Small Business
Managers versus Entrepreneurs 55

Conclusions on Entrepreneurs 57

Developing Background Information 57

Personal References 58

BUSINESS REFERENCES 58

CREDIT REPORTS 60

PRIVATE INVESTIGATIONS 60

PSYCHOLOGICAL ASSESSMENT TESTS 61

WRITTEN INFORMATION 61

INFORMATION FROM THE ENTREPRENEUR 63

LOCAL PEOPLE 64

PUBLIC INFORMATION 64

CUSTOMERS 64

INVESTORS 65

EMPLOYEES 65

MANAGEMENT TEAM 65

ORGANIZATION STRUCTURE
    AND DECISION MAKING 66

DOCUMENTATION 66

STRENGTHS AND WEAKNESSES 66

FINAL JUDGMENT 67

CHAPTER 3   REVIEWING PERSONNEL
AND COMPENSATION 69

HOW IS THE COMPANY ORGANIZED? 69

CORPORATE ORGANIZATIONAL CHART 70

OFFCERS AND DIRECTORS 71

STOCKHOLDERS 72

CHARACTERISTICS OF MANAGEMENT 72

HOW ARE PEOPLE COMPENSATED? 73

EMPLOYEE COMPENSATION 73

COMPENSATION SYSTEM 74

PENSION PLAN 76

PROFT-SHARING PLAN 77

BONUS PLAN 77

STOCK OPTION PLAN 78

OTHER BENEFTS 79

WHAT EMPLOYMENT CONTRACTS EXIST? 80

  EMPLOYMENT CONTRACTS AND SPECIAL
    COMPENSATION ARRANGEMENTS 80

  NONCOMPETE AGREEMENTS 81

  NONDISCLOSURE CONTRACTS 81

WHAT IS THE WORK FORCE STRUCTURE? 82

  UNIONS 82

  WORK STOPPAGE 83

  TRAINING PROGRAM 83

  MORALE OF THE WORK FORCE 83

WHAT PERSONNEL RECORDS ARE MAINTAINED? 84

  MAINTAINING INTERNAL RECORDS 84

  PAYROLL RECORDS 84

  EMPLOYEE BOOKS AND MANUALS 85

  REPORTS FROM THE PERSONNEL DEPARTMENT 85

  HIRING PROCEDURES 85

  MOTIVATING EMPLOYEES 86

  PERSONNEL FILES OF MANAGEMENT 86

  EMPLOYEE LITIGATION 86

  REGULATORY AGENCIES 86

  PERSONNEL CONSULTANTS 87

  OTHER EMPLOYEE BENEFITS 87

  HEALTH INSURANCE 88

  SUMMARY 88

MAJOR STRENGTHS AND WEAKNESSES 89

  RATIO ANALYSIS 89

  CHECKLIST 90

CHAPTER 4   ANALYSIS OF MARKETING AND SALES 91

WHO ARE THE PEOPLE WHO MARKET
  AND SELL? 91

  PERSONNEL 92

  SALESPERSON ANALYSIS 92

  OUTSIDE REPRESENTATIVES 93

Motivation 93

Terminations of Employees 94

What Are They Selling? 94

Products 94

Product Descriptions 95

Seasonality of Products 95

Product Literature 96

Product Development 96

Who Buys the Product or Service? 96

Customers 97

Contracts with Special Customers 97

Loss of Customers 98

Customer Complaints 99

Order Backlog 100

Customer Credit Approval 101

Customer's Credit Terms 101

Disputed Invoices 101

What Is Said to the Customer? 102

Public Relations 102

Advertising 102

Formal Advertising Program 103

Advertising Budget 103

Questions for the Advertising People 103

What Is the Marketplace
for the Product or Service? 104

Market Size 105

Competitors 105

Market Growth 106

Market Information 106

Substitutes in This Marketplace 107

Marketing Objectives 107

Marketing Strategies 107

How Is Price Determined? 108

Pricing Policies 108

Pricing Process 109

PRICE CHANGES 110

PRODUCT WARRANTY 110

WHAT INTERNAL REPORTS ARE MADE? 111

MARKETING REPORTS 111

SALES PROJECTIONS 112

PROCEDURES MANUALS 112

WHAT EXTERNAL INFORMATION IS AVAILABLE? 113

INDUSTRY ASSOCIATIONS 113

TRADE SHOWS 113

TRADE PUBLICATIONS 114

BASIC INFORMATION 114

RATIO ANALYSIS 114

WHAT ARE THE STRENGTHS
AND WEAKNESSES? 115

CONCLUSIONS ON MARKETING 116

CHECKLIST 116

CHAPTER 5   INVESTIGATING PRODUCTION 117

THE FACILITY 118

PLANT MOVES 119

EQUIPMENT 119

THE NEED FOR NEW EQUIPMENT 120

SURPLUS EQUIPMENT 122

CAPITAL EXPENDITURES 122

PRODUCTION CAPACITY 123

PRODUCTION EMPLOYEES 123

MOTIVATING EMPLOYEES 124

UNIONS 125

RETIREMENT PLANS 125

STAFF MEETINGS OF PRODUCTION PEOPLE 126

REGULATORY AGENCIES 126

SUBCONTRACTING WORK 127

INVENTORY 128

QUALITY CONTROL 129

PRODUCTION COSTS 129

PRODUCTION LEVELS 130

BACK TO CAPACITY 130

STRENGTH AND WEAKNESSES OF THE PRODUCTION
    PROCESS 130

PURCHASING PROCESS 131

    SUPPLIERS 132

RECEIVING 132

SHIPPING 133

CUSTOMER SERVICE 134

RESEARCH AND DEVELOPMENT 135

    RESEARCH AND DEVELOPMENT STRENGTHS
        AND WEAKNESSES 137

BASIC INFORMATION 137

    PRODUCTION REPORTS 137

    RATIO ANALYSIS 137

CONCLUSIONS ABOUT PRODUCTION 139

    CHECKLIST 140

CHAPTER 6   ANALYSIS OF THE FINANCIAL STATEMENTS AND PROJECTIONS 141

PERSONNEL 141

ANALYSIS OF THE NUMBERS 142

    FINANCIAL ANALYSIS 142

    CASH FLOW ANALYSIS 145

    ANALYSIS OF THE BALANCE SHEET 146

BUDGETING AND CONTROL 148

PAST FINANCINGS 148

    PAST BANK FINANCINGS 149

    ENTREPRENEUR'S INVESTMENT 150

ENTREPRENEUR'S OWNERSHIP 151

PARTICIPATION WITH OTHER INVESTORS 151

USE OF PROCEEDS 152

PROJECTIONS 153

BASIC INFORMATION 155

RATIO ANALYSIS OF THE FINANCIAL STATEMENT 155

PROFITABILITY RATIOS 155

LIQUIDITY RATIOS 156

LEVERAGE RATIOS 156

CASH RATIOS 157

FINANCIAL REPORTS 158

CONCLUSIONS ON THE FINANCIAL AREA 158

CHECKLIST 158

CHAPTER 7 REFERENCE INFORMATION 161

CORPORATE IDENTIFCATION 161

CORPORATE STRUCTURE 162

MANAGEMENT QUESTIONS 163

STOCK QUESTIONS 164

PROFESSIONAL REFERENCES 167

QUESTIONS FOR BANKERS 167

OTHER INSTITUTIONAL LENDERS 168

ACCOUNTING FIRM 169

QUESTIONS FOR LAWYERS 171

SUIT SETTLEMENT 172

QUESTIONS FOR INSURANCE AGENTS 172

QUESTIONS FOR LANDLORDS 173

QUESTIONS FOR MANUFACTURERS'
REPRESENTATIVES 174

QUESTIONS FOR THE ADVERTISING PEOPLE 175

QUESTIONS FOR SUPPLIERS 176

QUESTIONS FOR CUSTOMERS 176

QUESTIONS FOR COMPETITORS 178

QUESTIONS FOR SUBCONTRACTORS 178

CREDIT INFORMATION 179

CONCLUSIONS ON REFERENCE
INFORMATION 179

CHAPTER 8   NEGOTIATING THE DEAL
AND COMMITMENT LETTER 181

PRICING THE DEAL 181

RISK/REWARD 181

REMOVING RISK BY STRUCTURE 182

RETURN ON INVESTMENT 183

TYPES OF DEALS 184

USING PROBABILITY 185

PROBABILITIES AND DEVIATION 186

RETURN 187

RETURN TO INVESTOR 188

PRESENT VALUE 188

INTERNAL RATE OF RETURN 189

NET PRESENT VALUE 189

INVESTOR'S STANDARD 190

COMMITMENT LETTERS 190

1. TERMS OF THE INVESTMENT 191

2. COLLATERAL AND SECURITY 195

3. CONDITIONS OF THE LOAN 198

4. REPRESENTATIONS 204

5. CONDITIONS OF THE COMMITMENT LETTER 208

AN INVESTMENT MEMORANDUM 209

1. TERMS OF THE INVESTMENT 210

2. COLLATERAL AND SECURITY 211

3. CONDITIONS OF THE INVESTMENT 211

4. REPRESENTATIONS 211

5. CONDITIONS OF THE COMMITMENT 211

OTHER ITEMS 211

CONCLUSIONS ABOUT THE COMMITMENT
LETTER 212

CHAPTER 9   THE LEGAL CLOSING 215

FIRST TYPE OF CLOSING: LOAN WITH OPTIONS 216

DOCUMENT ONE: THE LOAN AGREEMENT 217

DOCUMENT TWO: THE NOTE 223

DOCUMENT THREE: THE STOCK PURCHASE
OPTION 223

OTHER DOCUMENTS: EXHIBITS 224

SIMPLE IS GOOD 225

SECOND TYPE OF CLOSING: LEGAL DOCUMENTS
FOR THE PURCHASE OF STOCK 226

STOCK PURCHASE AGREEMENT 226

LAWYERS AS INVESTORS OR BUSINESS
OWNERS 229

EXPERIENCED LAWYERS ARE BEST 230

PROCEDURES FOR REVIEWING DOCUMENTS 230

LEGAL FEES KEEP GOING UP 231

HOW LAWYERS RUN UP YOUR LEGAL BILL 232

DISAGREE ON LEGAL POINTS 232

REWRITE SECTIONS 233

RESEARCH POINTS OF LAW 233

LEGAL STYLE 233

ARGUMENTS 233

SYNDICATIONS AND LAWYERS 234

THE CLOSING: A MOMENT OF TRUTH 235

LAST-MINUTE CHANGES 236

CLOSING FEES 236

WHAT TO REMEMBER ABOUT LAWYERS 237

DOCUMENTATION 238

CHAPTER 10   MONITORING THE INVESTMENT 239

INVOLVEMENT 239

MAJOR POLICY DECISIONS 240

MONTHLY REPORTS 240

  MONTHLY WRITTEN REPORT 242

BOARD MEETINGS/INVESTOR MEETINGS 243

OTHER DISCUSSION ITEMS 244

MAINTAINING GOOD RECORDS 245

  LEGAL RECORDS 245

  CORRESPONDENCE FILE 246

  FINANCIAL RECORDING FILE 246

  BOARD MEETING FILES 247

  TRACKING FILE 247

WARNING SIGNS 248

  LATE PAYMENTS 248

  LOSS OF PROFTS 249

  LATE FINANCIAL REPORTS 249

  POORLY PREPARED FINANCIAL REPORTS 249

  LARGE CHANGES IN BALANCE SHEET ITEMS 250

  UNAVAILABLE ENTREPRENEUR 250

  LARGE THEFTS 250

  MAJOR ADJUSTMENTS IN FIGURES 251

  SIGNIFCANT CHANGES IN MANAGEMENT 251

  MAJOR CHANGES IN SALES
    AND ORDER BACKLOGS 251

  INVENTORY CHANGES 252

  LACK OF PLANNING 252

  CHANGES IN ACCOUNTING METHODS 253

  LOSS OF A MAJOR CUSTOMER, SUPPLIER,
    OR LENDER 253

  LABOR PROBLEMS 253

  CHANGES IN PRICES AND MARKET SHARE 254

  EXTERNAL WARNING SIGNS 254

  TECHNICAL CHANGE 254

General Industry Decline 254

Government Changes 255

Ratio Analysis as a Warning Indicator 255

Our Personal Favorites of Early Warning
Signals 255

Why Entrepreneurs Have Financial
Problems 258

The Financial Control Problem 258

The Undercapitalization Problem 259

Why Entrepreneurs Have People
Problems 259

Poor Job Defnition 260

Poor Selection Process 260

Poor Incentives to Management 260

Poor Review Program 261

Poor Development Program 261

What to Do with Problems 261

What Is Your Next Step? 263

Secret of a Successful Relationship 266

Degree of Involvement by the Venture
Capitalist 268

Amount Invested 268

Need for Assistance 268

Management's Willingness
to Accept Advice 268

Experience in Certain Areas 268

Lead Investor 269

Distress of Company 269

Relationship with the Entrepreneur 269

Time Availability 269

Tips on Monitoring 270

Pitfalls of Monitoring 272

Venture Capitalist Objectives 273

CHAPTER 11 THE EXIT 275

EXIT ONE: GOING PUBLIC 276

WHEN TO GO PUBLIC 276

UNDERWRITER'S FEES IN THE PUBLIC OFFERING 277

SELECTION OF A BROKERAGE HOUSE FOR A PUBLIC OFFERING 278

EXIT TWO: SALE TO A STRATEGIC OR FINANCIAL BUYER 279

SELLING THE STOCK IN THE COMPANY FOR CASH 280

SELLING STOCKS FOR NOTES 280

SELLING STOCK FOR STOCK 281

SELLING ASSETS FOR CASH 281

SELLING ASSETS FOR NOTES 282

SELLING ASSETS FOR STOCK 282

OTHER FORMS OF PAYMENT 283

EXIT THREE: SALE BACK TO THE COMPANY 284

PURCHASE BY EMPLOYEE STOCK OWNERSHIP TRUST 285

EXIT BY PUTS AND CALLS 286

EXIT FOUR: SALE TO ANOTHER INVESTOR 290

CORPORATE PARTNER 290

NEW VENTURE CAPITAL PARTNER 291

EXIT FIVE: REORGANIZING THE COMPANY 291

EXIT SIX: LIQUIDATION 292

WHEN YOU ARE IN A WORKOUT 294

QUICK STUDY 295

THE BUSINESS PLAN 295

TURNAROUND EXPERTS 296

LIQUIDATION ANALYSIS 296

SAVE YOUR INVESTMENT 296

CHAPTER 12 FINDING GOOD INVESTMENTS 299

DEVELOPING AN INVESTMENT OBJECTIVE 299

    PURPOSE OF INVESTING 300

    THE TYPE OF MONEY YOU HAVE TO INVEST 300

    STAGE OF DEVELOPMENT 301

    SPECIALTY INVESTING 302

    TIMING OF YOUR INVESTMENT EXIT 302

    SIZE OF YOUR INVESTMENT 303

    GEOGRAPHIC PREFERENCE 303

    LIQUIDITY PREFERENCE 304

    RISK PROFILE 304

    ACTIVITY LEVEL 304

    TIMING OF RETURN 305

ORIGINATING INVESTMENT OPPORTUNITIES 305

    BANKS 306

    ACCOUNTANTS 307

    ATTORNEYS 307

    INVESTMENT BANKERS/STOCKBROKERS 307

    BUSINESS BROKERS/FINANCIAL BROKERS 308

    CONSULTANTS 308

    CONVENTIONS 309

    ECONOMIC DEVELOPMENT ORGANIZATIONS 309

    INDUSTRIAL AND PROFESSIONAL TRADE
      ORGANIZATIONS 309

    LOCAL CHAMBERS OF COMMERCE 310

    FRIENDS AND ASSOCIATES 310

    VENTURE CAPITAL COMPANIES AND LBO FUNDS 310

    COLD CALLS 310

    ADVERTISING AND DIRECT MAIL 311

    SUPPLIERS 311

    OTHER GROUPS 311

PROACTIVITY 312

HANDLING INVESTMENT OPPORTUNITIES 312

USING BROKERS 314

QUALITIES TO LOOK FOR IN A BROKER 314

AGREEMENT WITH BROKER 315

SOME TIPS ON DEALING WITH BROKERS 317

FINAL WORD 317

CHAPTER 13 QUESTIONS USED IN VENTURE CAPITAL INVESTIGATIONS 319

I. MANAGEMENT AREA 320

BASIC INFORMATION YOU NEED TO COLLECT 327

II. PERSONNEL AREA 329

BASIC INFORMATION 335

III. MARKETING AREA 337

MARKETING PEOPLE 338

PRODUCTS 340

CUSTOMER DESCRIPTION 343

CUSTOMER SERVICE 345

COMPETITIVE ANALYSIS 346

INDUSTRY ANALYSIS 347

MARKETING STRATEGY 353

DISTRIBUTION OF THE PRODUCT 355

BASIC INFORMATION 356

IV. PRODUCTION AREA 358

PRODUCTION PROCESS 361

PURCHASING, SUPPLIERS, SHIPPING,
AND RECEIVING 370

BASIC INFORMATION 373

V. RESEARCH AND DEVELOPMENT 376

BASIC INFORMATION 379

VI. FINANCIAL AREA 380

BASIC INFORMATION 380

ANALYSIS OF FINANCIAL OPERATIONS 386

FINANCIAL STATEMENT ANALYSIS 390

OTHER ASSETS AND LIABILITIES 395

TAXES 397

OTHER SECTIONS 400

ANALYSIS OF PROJECTIONS 402

BASIC INFORMATION 405

VII. REFERENCE AREA 408

CHAPTER 14   ACTUAL DOCUMENTS 417

WHAT DO ACTUAL COMMITMENT LETTERS
AND LEGAL DOCUMENTS LOOK LIKE? 417

COMMITMENT LETTER 418

LEGAL DOCUMENT 1 424

LOAN AGREEMENT 425

I. PARTIES 425

II. LOAN 425

III. USE OF PROCEEDS 425

IV. COLLATERAL 426

V. REPRESENTATIONS AND WARRANTIES 427

VI. AFFRMATIVE COVENANTS 430

VII. NEGATIVE COVENANTS 433

VIII. INVESTMENT COVENANT 434

IX. FEES, EXPENSES, AND INDEMNIFCATION 435

X. UNLOCKING 435

XI. "PUT" RIGHTS 436

XII. DEFAULT 436

XIII. NOTICE 440

XIV. ENTIRE AGREEMENT 440

XV. CONTROLLING LAW 441

XVI. HEADINGS 441

PROMISSORY NOTE 441

$3,000,000 441

INTEREST 442

PAYMENTS 442

MATURITY 442

PREPAYMENT 442

DEFAULT AND ACCELERATION 442

DEFNITIONS 445

SEAL 445

LEGAL DOCUMENT 3 446

STOCK PURCHASE WARRANTS 446

LEGAL DOCUMENT 4 453

STOCK PURCHASE AGREEMENT 454

LEGAL DOCUMENT 5 462

SCHEDULE A: EXHIBITS TO STOCK PURCHASE
AGREEMENT 462

APPENDIX A LIST OF TRAITS FOR ANALYSIS
OF PEOPLE 465

APPENDIX B EVALUATION OF AN ENTREPRENEUR
BY AN INDUSTRIAL PSYCHOLOGIST 469

INDEX 477

INTRODUCTION

This book has been great fun to write, and with this revision it is ready for another 15-year run. More than 500 venture capital, buyout, and mezzanine funds are using the book to enlighten their new investment officers, associates, and analysts. When the book was written 15 years ago, there was no prediction that *Venture Capital Investing* would become so widely used by professionals in the industry. However, with the tremendous increase in venture capital and the many new employees, the book has benefited by filling that need. Please note that throughout this book, we use the term *venture capital* to cover the areas often called *private equity investing*. Under this general term, *venture capital*, we are lumping investing in leveraged buyouts, investing in startups, and providing growth financing (mezzanine finance).

The chief strength of the book is that it is a "nuts-and-bolts" approach on how to invest in venture capital and should illustrate to you the pragmatic process of investing in venture capital. The style is plain English about the basics and does not have a lot of theory or war stories. It shows you how to win at the game of investing in venture capital.

It has been gratifying to see the book become so useful to so many people in the venture capital industry. Some people have claimed to have gained great insight into a particular investment and helped the venture capital fund make extraordinary returns. (We are waiting for some of those big winners to send us the commissions!) It would be fun to know how many billions of dollars have been made from venture capital firms by using this book.

We know the book is having an impact because some of our venture capital friends make comments to us about "giving away the secrets of the business." It seems that we have made it more difficult for them to gain the advantage over some of the new funds that have been entering the venture capital marketplace.

In addition to professionals, more than 60 business schools use the book in their classes on either investing or entrepreneurship. It is wonderful that there are so many business schools that use the book today. It is gratifying to know that people are studying how to invest in venture capital.

BACKGROUND ON THE AUTHORS

For this new edition, David has teamed up with his daughter, Laura Gladstone, to rewrite this edition. We are authors by night, but both of us have day jobs as managers of a fund we created, called *Gladstone Capital Corporation*. Our website is www.gladstonecapital.com. Come visit our website and learn about our fund and some more about venture capital.

We have one warning to readers about the authors. Every person is the total of his or her experiences. Each of us brings to every situation intellectual "baggage" in the form of prejudices and preferences, inherited and learned from past experiences. Therefore, to understand what this book is about, you need to know something about the background of the writers.

All of the experience of the writers has come from lending to and investing in small- and medium-sized businesses. Neither of the writers of this book have been a professional in any other area, such as the arts and letters or politics. David Gladstone's experience has come from investing in small- and medium-sized businesses since 1973. He has invested in all stages of the process, from startup to later-stage and, in some cases, small public companies. He is the past chairman of the group of companies that are now consolidated under the name of Allied Capital Corporation, which is listed on the New York Stock Exchange (ALD). As the chairman of that company, he gave investors an annual return of 22.4 percent compounded per year for 15 years. That company increased dividends and distributions to shareholders every year while he was in charge of its investments. He invested in more than 500 companies and had more than 400 successful exits while running that fund.

In 1997, David became chairman of American Capital Strategies, which is listed on NASDAQ (ACAS). Under his direction, that company grew from a tiny, private investment bank to a publicly traded buyout company with over $1 billion in market capitalization. During his four-year tenure at American Capital, David gave investors over 25 percent return per year and increased dividends every year for the four years he was head of the firm.

Although Laura's background is all in business, her experience has three distinct segments—and it all relates to lending or investing in businesses. First, she was head of the marketing department at Allied Capital Corporation (NYSE: ALD) for three years, with responsibility for finding new venture capital investments. In that capacity, she found new investments for the fund all over the United States. She has seen thousands of new business proposals and met hundreds of entrepreneurs. She has spent most of her time looking at leverage buyout opportunities and some of her time in early stage ventures.

Next, Laura worked for HSBC, a large multinational bank, where she made loans to many different types of businesses in various industries both in the United States and in Latin America. In this area, she developed her credit skills and approached business from a lender's perspective. She looked at them with a view for their ability to generate cash flow, one of the most critical elements of any business.

Finally, she worked on the sell side on Wall Street as an associate analyst covering the telecommunications industry for two of Wall Street's largest brokerage houses. In this job, she developed her ability to pick stocks and analyze equity situations. At these three different types of jobs, Laura learned financial modeling, analyses of companies, and the all-important due diligence in many different types of scenarios.

In 2001, Laura helped found Gladstone Capital Corporation, where she is a principal, making loans and investments in small- and medium-sized businesses.

David Gladstone and Laura Gladstone are the authors of their first book, *Venture Capital Handbook*, which helps a small business entrepreneur understand the basics of raising capital for a new idea or business. This second book, *Venture Capital Investing*, is not a sequel but instead takes a look at investing through the eyes of the venture capitalist. This book seeks to give understanding about investing in a successful entrepreneur and how to weed through endless business proposals to find the gem of all opportunities. What does it take to find a successful business venture and how does one invest? That is what we hope to answer in this book.

The structure of the book is sequential, that is, it begins with the due diligence process and proceeds through the closing, monitoring of the investment, and finally the exit.

ACKNOWLEDGMENTS

Many people made this book possible. Most of them are friends we have in the venture capital industry. Many are our friendly competitors. We wish there were enough pages to list them all here. However, if we tried to do that, we would most likely miss some. So we are just going to say thanks to all of you for giving us the help to make this book a success.

To all of you, the readers, best wishes and good luck with all your investments!

David Gladstone
Laura Gladstone
August 2003

1 KEYS TO SUCCESSFUL INVESTING

We are all presented with numerous opportunities to invest in businesses. If you are a professional working for a venture capital or leverage buyout firm, you are being bombarded with "opportunities" from professional money raisers known as *investment bankers*. If you are an "angel" investor, you are being flooded with new business plans from friends and business associates. In the introduction, we discussed how we all have biases toward everything, including what we like to invest in. Now we move from biases to gathering hard facts about the business, the industry, and the team running the business. This part of the investing process is know as *due diligence*.

This chapter starts the beginning of what venture capitalists (VCs) call the *due diligence process*. That is, it describes the steps that an investor should take in researching an investment opportunity. This is a detailed process that takes weeks—sometimes months—of work. It begins when an investor is confronted with a business proposal and must decide whether the idea warrants further investigation. If the investment does make it past this initial decision process (explained in this chapter), Chapters 2–8 go into further detail of the extent the due diligence process must take.

What Are the Basic Items to Look for in a Business Proposition?

There are six critical components to look for in this first stage of evaluation.

1. The Numbers Should Be Properly Presented

Everybody in the investment business lives and dies by "the numbers." This means that the investor cannot proceed without accurate figures on a company's past performance. Anything less than accurate and detailed (and in most cases, certified financial statements) will lead the investor into a business risk that is probably not worth the business opportunity. To repeat—no investor should make an investment without accurate historical figures.

In addition, current financial statements are an absolute must. All too often, investors are given old financial statements that are ancient history. The older numbers do not reflect how the company is doing at that current moment. You should not accept any statements older than two months. Make sure the entrepreneur gives you current (either monthly or quarterly) interim financial statements or don't invest. Any entrepreneur who sends you poorly prepared or stale financial statements does not deserve financing.

Another thing to look for is the entrepreneur's knowledge of the financials. You must make sure that your entrepreneur is able to explain the numbers in detail. If that cannot be done, it is a sure sign that the entrepreneur does not live and die by the numbers and, therefore, will be a poor match for you. As an investor, you must live and die by the numbers.

If an entrepreneur cannot produce accurate financial projections, he or she should hire an accountant to prepare them. However, even if hiring an accountant, the entrepreneur should still know most of the numbers by memory if he or she intends to live and die by the numbers. If you ask the entrepreneur about the financials and the answers is, "these financials were put together by my accountant and I cannot tell you why certain projections do certain things," the small business person does not understand the numbers. This is a clear sign that you will have problems in the future unless a new member of the team is brought in to handle that side of the business.

In addition, the entrepreneur must provide accurate and detailed projections for at least five years. As an investor, you cannot assess how much money you can make without good projections. An engineer was once asked for some projections on his small business, and the VC was told that he couldn't supply them because this involved "sheer speculation" and that engineers don't guess about things; they only report what is known. Needless to say, the VC did not invest in his company. Projections are important because they reflect the company's financial plan. A company without a financial plan is a company without direction.

Another point is that if the company has not reached the point where cash from sales is equal to expenses—the "breakeven"—the entrepreneur should provide you with a month-by-month financial analysis indicating when the company will reach breakeven. An investor needs to know when a company will finally reach cash flow breakeven and no longer require more investor money.

Accountant. As investors, we prefer not to deal with entrepreneurs who do not understand the financial projections for their companies. A good entrepreneur must know the operating plan and the financial plan. A good manager has a deep appreciation of accounting. Managers know that, without accurate and timely information, a manager cannot manage a company. This sounds obvious, but many entrepreneurs are "concept people." An entrepreneur who lives by the numbers is the one you want to back.

2. THE DEAL MUST MAKE LOTS OF MONEY

Usually, no one has to tell an entrepreneur that the projections must go up. Every set of projections that we have ever received from entrepreneurs has the infamous "bell curve," with everything on the income statement and balance sheet improving. If they didn't show improvement, no one would be interested in investing. Unless the projections go up significantly, no VC is going to be interested in investing. VCs look for a return on investment of at least 25 percent, and in many situations they expect to see as high as 50–100 percent return on investment per year.

When you look at the company's projections, you should be asking the question, What will the company be worth in three to five years? Using that projection and the earnings and cash flow of the business, one can put a value on the business at the end of that time period. Using that expected value of the company in the future, you can as the potential investor calculate how much of the company you will have to own in order to receive a return on investment that will compensate you for the risk. If the projections don't go up significantly, the investor will have to own a very large share of the small business in order to make a significant return. Years ago, a VC did this calculation on a potential investment, and it was determined that, to make the type of return that was commensurate with the risk, an investor would need to own 150 percent of the company. It was a nice little business on a slow growth pattern, but there was little possibility of a high return for an investor. Obviously, no one can own 150 percent of anything!

3. THE ACID TEST OF A DEAL IS MANAGEMENT

Recently, there was an industry seminar in which some very well known VCs were asked what attributes of a potential investment opportunity would indicate that the investment was going to be successful. There were 10 slots on the blackboard, and within a minute, the first six slots were filled with some phrase that had the word *management* in it. Over and over again, VCs say that the acid test of any deal is its management. You may have heard a real estate executive describe a good real estate investment as based on the three attributes of good real estate: location, location, location. Well, in the venture capital world, the three attributes of a good venture capital deal are management, management, management.

But what exactly does good management mean? It is very easy for an investor to blame poor management for a loss, but the reverse is also true. You can make a lot of money when management is good. Well then, what management qualities should an investor look for? Here are a few.

Honesty and Integrity. One criterion that every investor uses to test management is honesty. If the entrepreneurial team is not honest, almost "honest to a fault," it is unlikely that the lender or VC will invest. One VC tells about touring a plant with a group of VCs and stopping for a moment to watch a lady at a drill press. He happened to ask her what she was making. She replied, "Oh, nothing. I was hired just for the day. I was told there were some big shots coming through and that I should look real busy." At that moment, management's credibility (and that of others in the plant) was gone. As a result of that one incident, the company never raised the money it needed. The news of its actions went flying through the venture capital community and killed all hopes of raising cash.

Experience. Every VC wants to back an entrepreneur who has extensive experience in the industry in which the business is operating. If the entrepreneur is a white-collar government worker who is going to buy a meat-packing plant, for example, the investor should have serious reservations about that person's qualifications for work in the industry. Would the entrepreneur know how to run a meat-packing plant? I remember one of the questions that a VC asked a man who owned a meat-packing plant when the VC was fresh out of business school and filled with a new concept called *management by objective* (MBO). The VC asked the owner whether he used MBO to run his plant. He was a fairly burly fellow, puffing on a big cigar, and he quickly informed the young VC, "No, I don't use MBO in my plant. I use MBI." "Oh," asked said the VC, "What is MBI?" This husky fellow replied, "management by intimidation." This gruff entrepreneur knew how to work in his business. He knew that objectives were best left in the office and that MBO would not work inside his meat-packing plant. He had the experience necessary to operate the plant.

Achievement. Solid achievements in the entrepreneur's background are a big plus. Every investor should look for achievements. The chances of success increase when the entrepreneur is an achiever. Look at the entrepreneur's background. What did the entrepreneur achieve in college or in business? Achievers are what make the world go 'round.

During the 1950s, a social scientist studying achievers and nonachievers made some interesting discoveries about their backgrounds. The background factor having the highest correlation with the achievers was Eagle Scouts. The lowest correlation was between achievers and pipe smokers. There is a lesson here for anyone looking at an entrepreneur trying to raise money: Bet on high achievers. They have the spark that will light the fire. They want to win. They have achieved in the past and most likely will continue to achieve.

High Energy Level. What most investors look for in a management team is a high level of energy. Being an entrepreneur is tough. Every VC has the greatest respect for all entrepreneurs. Entrepreneurs work long hours. Most of us have worked only a few 70-hour weeks, and there are few people who like them. Your entrepreneur will have to be one who can accept the long hours and the grinding pace. Creating a great business is 1 percent inspiration and 99 percent perspiration.

Your entrepreneur must, therefore, be in good health and of sound mind. The entrepreneur's health will be put to the test as the daily stress and physical exhaustion mount. Make sure your entrepreneur is a strong person with plenty of energy. The entrepreneur must have the energy to be successful. Good management will not only possess the strength to work long hours, but also will actually put in the long hours to make the business successful.

Motivation. Many entrepreneurs work long hours, week in and week out. So some of the questions a VC should ask an entrepreneur are, Why do you want to do all of this, knowing it is going to take time out of your life. Why is it you want to get involved in this difficult situation?

The wrong answer to this question is, "I want to be my own boss. My current boss doesn't understand me. I just want to get out on my own." Investors should not be solving the personal or psychological problems of entrepreneurs. The right answer to this question is, "It is a great opportunity for us both. If you will invest in the company, we can make a lot of money."

Of course, there are plenty of greedy people in the world who want to make money. But it is my experience that the winners are rarely just plain greedy! Business profits are a way of measuring one's success. Every achiever selects some standard to be measured by. A doctor measures success by the lives saved or the diseases cured; a clergyman measures success by the souls saved; and an inventor measures success by the useful inventions created. When one selects a business career, one accepts as the ultimate measure of success a very successful, going concern with strong profitability for all parties at stake. You want to back an entrepreneur who measures success by profits.

4. THE SITUATION SHOULD BE UNIQUE

One basic question every VC asks is, Why is this situation special? Every investor knows that in the business world, big businesses "beat up" little businesses. Therefore, if a small business is to survive, it must have something special, such as a patent, a proprietary process, a two-year lead time on the competition, or a good location (for example, in the case of a restaurant). What does the small business bring to the marketplace that will make people want to buy its product or service? The business must have something unique if it wants to win in the competitive environment.

At the same time, most VCs have an aversion to products that are *too* unique. The product or service should not be revolutionary; rather, it should be evolutionary. I suspect that most VCs would not have backed Edison's new invention, the electric light bulb, because it was too revolutionary. Revolutionary products change the way human beings live on Earth. As a result, they take many years to gain public acceptance, and the return on investment is stretched out over such a long period of time that the annualized return on investment is too low for most investors. VCs don't want to wait 20–25 years. Their normal time horizon is five to seven years. So the product cannot be revolutionary; it should be a follow-on product.

5. THE PROPOSED VENTURE SHOULD BE ORIENTED TOWARD THE MARKET

Every successful business must take its direction from the marketplace it addresses. Emerson wrote, "If a man can...make a better mousetrap than his neighbor... the world will make a beaten a path to his door." Obviously Emerson was not a venture capitalist! Good entrepreneurs do not introduce a product because it is a nifty product. They introduce a product because their analysis of the marketplace shows that a new product will sell and that there is a demand for the product.

Some people praise Henry Ford for creating mass production. He should be given more credit for his market analysis. He believed that the average person would purchase a cheap, stripped-down car if it were available. Instead, most cars were like the high-priced and beautifully made Stanley Steamer or Pierce Arrow. His market analysis concluded that people would buy a low-cost, shaking, rattling, "tin lizzie." That contraption made marketing history. It changed the way we live.

A good entrepreneur starts not with a product idea but with a vision of what the marketplace needs and wants. A market division entrepreneur loves the action of making sales. He or she is not in the lab to create a new product but to find a solution to a problem or to develop a product that people will want. Make sure you back a market-oriented company.

6. THE DEAL MUST HAVE AN EXIT

The final element of a business proposition that every investor should look for is the exit. This refers to the way to get one's money back, or how to cash in on the investment. All VCs look at cash flow (sometimes known as EBITDA) and how the money will come back. VCs spend a great deal of time reviewing a business situation to make sure that they will get their money back, as well as turn a good profit. The event when a VC gets the investment back with a big capital gain is called a *liquidity event*.

There are only three basic ways to get your money out of a small business:

1. It can go public (this is one of the most common ways VCs reach liquidity).
2. A business in the same industry (a strategic buyer) or another investor group (a financial buyer) may want to buy the entire business, pay off its debts, and give the existing stockholders a good return on investments.
3. The company can simply buy out the VC by refinancing the company out of cash flow.

Although this last exit is an unusual way for VCs to make money, it happens more often than most VCs will tell you. The point here is this: Make sure there is a way out of the deal (a liquidity event) before you get into an investment.

IT'S NOT AN INVESTMENT, IT'S A PARTNERSHIP

Every person who reads this book, and especially those who intend to put money into a small company, should be absolutely sure that the relationship between you, the investor, and the entrepreneur is a strong partnership—in reality, a "marriage." It must be a trusting relationship in which neither party is trying to get the upper hand. Both parties must be working together to make money. Therefore, every investor should get to know the management of the company before investing any money in it. I usually try to spend extra time with members of the management team so that I feel comfortable with them.

There is the story of the VC who was talking to a group who had three "Doc-in-the-Boxes." This is slang for a medical delivery system. In place of a Jack-in-the-Box where one goes for a quick meal, you have a Doctor-in-the-Box, which refers to an accessible unit that provides quick, efficient, and cheap medical service. In this case, three individuals owned three Doc-in-the Boxes and wanted a large investment so they could continue to expand. After meeting with them for a full day and after being convinced that the VC should make the investment, the VC joined them for dinner. After a few drinks, they began to tell the VC how they really operated the business.

First they described (in their terms) how they were going to "screw" the IRS and not pay their taxes; then they described how they were going to "screw" their suppliers and not pay them, "screw" Medicare and Medicaid to get higher payments, and "screw" a few of their patients by overcharging them. The VC knew before that dinner was over that if the VC made the investment, someday in the future, one of those "screws" would have the VC's name on it.

PREPARE A WRITTEN SUMMARY BEFORE YOU BEGIN TO INVEST

We firmly believe that every investor should prepare a written summary before formally investigating the situation. A summary of one or two pages can crystallize your thinking about why this is such a great investment opportunity. It will also put in a concrete form what you want to discuss with your friends, your banker, your accountant, and others. All of them can help you to determine whether it is a good investment opportunity. After reading this book, you should be able to prepare such a summary. This summary should be a response to the following questions:

WHAT ARE YOU INVESTING IN?

Here you are trying to define the entity that you are investing in. For example, specify whether it is a partnership, a subchapter S company, a limited liability company, or a corporate entity. Also, it's a good idea is to have the name, address, and telephone number of the business. It is also helpful to describe in 10 words or less the type of company you are investing in. Describe the industry and describe its stage of development, such as a start-up. Try to pinpoint the kind of business you will be investing in. Often, this information does not appear in a conspicuous place on the proposal. Before you go any further, you should wade through the proposal to understand who and what you will be investing in. This information will also be handy in the future when you want to talk to the company's people.

WHO IS YOUR CONTACT AT THE BUSINESS?

Many proposals list a number of contact people in the firm, but as an investor you need to know who you will be dealing with directly during the due diligence process and during the monitoring after you have invested in the company. Usually, it is the president of the company, although sometimes the vice president of finance will be your contact. Find out immediately who this person is and make sure you have a clear channel for gathering information from this person. If your initial contact is a broker, you should ask the broker to introduce you to the person who is going to be your contact at the business. Don't let all of the information filter through the broker. Get it from the "horse's mouth."

SUMMARIZE THE BUSINESS SITUATION

Prepare a thumbnail sketch of the company's situation. Emphasize the strong points that draw you toward this investment. You should be able to do this in one paragraph, perhaps two. But it should be brief, and it should crystallize in your mind the business situation that you are getting involved with. If you cannot do this in a few words, ask yourself whether you really know what you are investing in.

WHO IS THE MANAGEMENT TEAM?

Although management is the most important section in the entire analysis, you don't need to cover entire backgrounds of the individuals involved in the investment you are considering. Do hit some of the highlights that make you want to invest, such as the entrepreneurs' experience, past achievements, and "go-power." Make sure you put down the names and the credentials of the top two or three people. You need highlight in only two or three sentences what aspect of their backgrounds set them apart from other management teams that you have seen and why their backgrounds are pertinent to this investment situation. Remember, you are investing in a team. If you don't have a good team at the top, it will be hard to win.

WHAT ARE THEY SELLING?

In a very brief paragraph, describe the product or service the company is selling. State why the product or service is unique, and if it is not unique, explain why this product or service will succeed over other products and services that are offered by the competitors. You need not discuss the competition in detail, but it is important to differentiate the company in summary form from others in the industry. More than a paragraph here would be too much.

HOW MUCH MONEY ARE THEY RAISING AND HOW MUCH ARE YOU CONSIDERING INVESTING?

Every business proposal tells you how much money its principals are looking for, but the amount should not be expressed in ranges. For example, the business proposal should not say $5 million to $10 million. The company should know how much money it needs to do the job and should state that figure. In addition, you will want to know the type of money that the business is raising. Is it selling common stock, preferred stock, convertible debentures, subordinated debentures, junior loans with warrants? What structure and format will be used in raising this money? You should know exactly what the deal involves on all levels of the balance sheet.

IS THERE ANY SECURITY FOR YOUR INVESTMENT?

Every banker looks for collateral when making a loan to a company. Even though you are an investor, your investment can be in the form of debt with collateral security (sometimes referred to as *second liens*). You may take a second mortgage on the assets of the business or you might have outside collateral, such as a mortgage on the person's house. Venture capital takes many forms, but whatever the form, your prime consideration should be how to lower your risk. Collateral is one way to lower your risk. However, most VCs who invest using stock options and warrants are the furthest down on the balance sheet and usually never see any type of security, which is why they demand such high returns.

HOW WILL THE MONEY BE USED?

The proposed use of proceeds is not always set out in great detail in the business plans. However, after investigating and discussing these plans with the entrepreneur, you should have a good idea of how he or she is going to spend the money. You should be able to state in one short paragraph where the money is going. You should not have to use such broad terms as *working capital* but should be able to specify where the funds are to be used. A detailed explanation of sources and uses is essential.

WHAT IS THE PAST FINANCIAL PERFORMANCE?

In this section, you want to summarize the sales, earnings, assets, liabilities, and net worth of the company. In three or four columns, you should be able to sketch out where the company has been and what kinds of trends it is setting. You may be surprised by what you can learn by dredging through the business plan and placing these items in your summary.

WHAT ARE THE PROJECTIONS?

As a VC taking a long-range view of the situation, you should look at the five-year projections for the company. Even though the fifth year is highly speculative, it gives you a clear idea of how the company will grow and in essence how much money you stand to make if it meets the projected goals. Without a summary projection in the same format as the financial history, you will not be able to develop a basic understanding of the company.

A word from the wise: Always make your own projections and do it with your own model. We know how easy it is to use someone else's model, but don't. Building your own model will give you much deeper insights into the business than you can ever get from reviewing someone else's model. You need to look at the business from your perspective.

HOW WILL YOU CASH IN?

As we mentioned before, no venture capital company wants to remain a stockholder in a company forever. Every VC must realize the capital gains on the fund's investment in the business. Even though your horizon may be three to seven years, you must have a clear perception of how you are going to get out of the investment before you go into it. You should be able to state in three or four sentences how you plan to get out of this situation.

HOW MUCH CAN YOU MAKE?

The expected profit is the final test of a promising business proposal. If you own a certain percentage of the company, what will it be worth when you cash it in? We like to set out in a tabular format the cash that we will be expected to be put into the company over the next seven years and the cash that we can expect to receive back. This format enables us to summarize clearly the cash in and cash out. There are probably a thousand ways to determine this, but I use a calculator that gives me internal rate of return. If a company can't show a strong internal rate of return and the situation entails all of the typical risks of a venture capital investment, it doesn't deserve any more of your time.

WHAT DO YOU LIKE ABOUT THIS SITUATION?

List in point form three to five reasons for making the investment. What is it that you like about the situation and is compelling you to invest? If you can't express it now, you probably will never be able to do so.

WHAT DO YOU DISLIKE ABOUT THIS SITUATION?

No investment opportunity is perfect. Every one of them seems to have some "warts." You should be able to explain those dislikes in three or four lines. You should know exactly what you don't like about the situation. If it goes bad, you will know what to avoid in the future.

WHAT DOES A SUMMARY LOOK LIKE?

What follows is a useful summary format. This format is a composite of many that I have seen. The figures are based on an actual investment, but the numbers and names of the people involved have been changed. The investment made a tremendous amount of money for everyone.

COMPANY

Electronic Press, Inc.
8888 Avenue of the Americas
New York, NY 10005
Telephone: (212) 555-1212
Contact: JB Entrepreneur, President

TYPE OF BUSINESS

Online preparation of camera-ready copy and printing of materials requiring quick turnaround.

COMPANY SUMMARY

A new company has been formed to purchase the assets of an ailing printing company. The existing company is a quick-turnaround, standard printing company for company documents. The company's team will write computer programs to receive standard formatted information over the Internet and convert it to the format for printing. Then it will be sent back to the customer in camera-ready copy, ready for editing. This will continue back and forth until the customer is ready to print.

All existing customers will be serviced with the current business people until the new system is ready.

Management. JB Entrepreneur, president, has been in printing for 12 years. JB has worked in all phases of the business and has been working with computer programs to do this job for the past year. JB has a BA in accounting from a university in New York. JB is 32 years old.

Jim Operator, vice president and COO, has been in the computer field for eight years. He has been a programmer, systems analyst, and management consultant on computer applications. He has been working on a computer program to set type for one year. He has an engineering degree from a large Boston college. He is 31 years old.

As far as product/service and competition, Electronic Press will be continuing to offer conventional typesets and printing. Once the computer can be used to set type, the company will offer the customer five-hour turnaround or better for typesetting and printing. Customers can use the actual camera-ready copy for corrections and make corrections quickly.

Janet Accountant, vice president and CFO, has been with the company for six years and is responsible for the financial planning side of the business. She is a CPA and is age 28.

Funds Requested. $10 million in common stock for a 40 percent ownership.

Collateral. None.

Use of Proceeds. $2 million for new inventory purchases; $2 million to pay off accounts payable; and $6 million to carry the company's research and development budget to develop the computer program. The purchase price of the business is $16 million (or 6 × earnings before interest, taxes, depreciation, and amortization [EBITDA]): $2 million in cash; $4 million in a five-year, 8 percent note; and $10 million in equity.

Financial History.

ITEM	ACTUAL 2 YEARS AGO ($)	ACTUAL 1 YEAR AGO ($)	ACTUAL LAST YEAR ($)
Revenue	5,109,000	9,989,400	12,460,500
Net Loss	(70,000)	(43,100)	(11,600)
Assets	5,279,000	7,700,000	9,870,000
Liabilities	4,238,000	6,420,000	8,601,000
Net Worth	1,041,000	1,280,000	1,269,000

ITEM	PROJECTED THIS YEAR ($)	PROJECTED NEXT YEAR ($)	PROJECTED 2 YEARS OUT ($)
Revenue	18,000,000	26,000,000	42,000,000
Net Income	10,000	1,600,000	5,000,000
Assets	12,000,000	18,000,000	22,000,000
Liabilities	1,000,000	4,000,000	3,000,000
Net Worth	11,000,000	14,000,000	19,000,000

Financial Projections Exit. The company will go public in three years. If the company does not go public in five years, the investors can exchange their ownership for three times their investment and be paid out over three years.

A SECOND SUMMARY

To give you more food for thought, here is a second summary (again, the information is disguised).

COMPANY

TT5 Corporation
123 Main Street
McLean, Virginia 22101
Telephone: (703) 555-1212
Contact: JB Entrepreneur, Chairman

TYPE OF BUSINESS

Manufacturer of switching gear for telephone equipment.

COMPANY SUMMARY

TT5 Corporation was founded three years ago by JB Entrepreneur, an individual with seven years' experience in the communication and switching-gear industry. The company's first product was a multipurpose switching unit attached to telephone systems that permits the buyer of the unit to use several low-cost telephone services. The company will reach profitability in one year, and estimates show that it will be very profitable in three years.

Management. JB Entrepreneur, with seven years' experience in manufacturing PBX and related equipment, founded the company and has served as president. He previously worked for a large communications network conglomerate and several other corporations in the communications field. He is a graduate of a Boston technological university with a degree in electrical engineering and is 32 years old.

Joe Operator, vice president and COO, has been with the company for one year. He has 17 years of experience in the field of telephone equipment for businesses and related equipment. He has written two books on the subject and has been granted six patents for work in telecommunications. Currently, he guides the company in all of its marketing operations. He has an MBA degree from a large university in Maryland.

Jane Accountant, vice president and CFO, has been with the company for two years and has a work history in communications. She worked for two public companies for a total of six years and is a CPA.

Product/Service and Competition. TT5 Corporation manufactures a unique electrical switching box that can be adapted to all forms of PBX and telephone equipment. At present, no companies other than TT5 Corporation are in the business of manufacturing these add-on communication boxes. It is doubtful that anyone will enter the business in the next two years. If competitors do enter, TT5's patents should give it a monopoly on certain types of installations.

Funds Requested. $15 million convertible subordinated debentures at 13 percent cash interest, 5 percent noncash and convertible into 20 percent ownership of the company.

Collateral. Second secured interest in the assets of the business, subordinated to a local bank debt of $35 million.

Use of Proceeds. The company has currently outstripped its line of working capital at the bank and its low equity base prevents the bank from increasing the line of credit beyond the current status. Initially, the company will use the $15 million to pay down the bank loan and negotiate a larger line of credit ($50 million) with the bank so that more working capital will be available to the company.

Financial History.

Item	Actual 2 Years Ago ($)	Actual 1 Year Ago ($)	Actual Last Year ($)
Revenue	100,000	450,000	2,450,000
Net Loss	(226,000)	(443,100)	(62,600)
Assets	443,000	1,002,000	1,200,000
Liabilities	232,000	1,402,000	9,876,000
Net Worth	211,000	(400,000)	324,000

Financial Projections.

Item	Projected This Year ($)	Projected Next Year ($)	Projected 2 Years Ago ($)
Revenue	8,000,000	26,000,000	82,000,000
Net Income	1,000,000	3,600,000	15,000,000
Assets	19,000,000	28,000,000	32,000,000
Liabilities	15,000,000	23,000,000	23,000,000
Net Worth	4,000,000	5,000,000	9,000,000

Exit. The company will attempt a public offering on the basis of earnings in three years. If there is no public market and no prospect for a public market in the near future, the company will offer to buy back the stock owned by the fund.

WHAT MAKES IT EXCITING?

There are three reasons why such summaries excite the VC. First, the product is unique. As mentioned, the product is manufactured only by this company, and there appears to be no potential competition on the horizon. The second bit of information that is music to the VC's ears is the fact that the individuals have had previous experience in this area, as well as long experience in the industry. This background usually makes the VC more comfortable about the operation and about the prospects for the future. The crowning touch is the financial projections. Not only has the company turned the corner from its actual financial statements, but it is now projecting strong earnings. Obviously, the VC will be led to believe that, in the years ahead, the company will go public or be sold to a large company. When the public offering occurs, the investor (as well as the entrepreneurs) will reap huge capital gains.

Whether or not you wish to use the format suggested here, you must try to summarize and crystallize your thoughts about why you are making this investment. If some nonmonetary items begin to creep into your thinking, it is the first sign that you are making a mistake.

For example, if you are making the investment to help a friend, why not just help him or her find a bank loan instead? Are you making the investment so that you will be famous and recognized as the person who backed this great investment? You may turn out to be famous for backing a crazy idea that failed. Are you making the investment because the entrepreneur is the same race, religion, or sex? These are very poor barometers for success. Are you making the investment for some social goal? Why not make a cash gift to some charity instead? That will look better than an investment in a failed company. Are you investing so you can be on the board of directors? Being on the board of directors will carry some substantial liabilities beyond your investment—you might find out one day that the IRS is looking to the directors for past-due payroll taxes.

Finally, if you are making the investment because you will get some free merchandise, it would be much cheaper to go out and buy the products you want. Too many people have ended up losing a great deal of money this way, and the product has turned out to be far from free. In your summary, you should keep coming back to the key points, that is, good management, good profit potential, unique product, and great exit opportunity. If these things keep popping into your mind while you are writing the summary, you are on the right track.

Once you have finished your summary, you should show it to a few friends and let them read it. An accountant should definitely look at it, and so should your banker. Both are very conservative people and would probably advise you not to invest, but make sure they understand what you see in the business and why you are interested. If your summary churns up their desire to invest in the business, you know you are on the right trail.

Some Words about Franchising

Just because someone is starting a franchise that at first glance looks like the next great fast-food concept in your area, don't automatically jump at the idea. Franchising is just another means of operating a business. Before you invest in a franchise, you have to be sure that some very important characteristics are present.

Sound Concept

When you look into the history of a franchise, investigate the uniform franchise agreement that it must file in many of the states. In that filing, you will find the failure rate of the franchisor. If you discover that the number of failures exceeds 3 percent, the franchise that you are about to invest in is above the national average. You may want to read the entire uniform disclosure agreement to learn about the franchisor.

Well-Financed Franchisor

One of the things that you will be looking for when you review the uniform disclosure agreement is the financial statement of the franchisor. If the franchisor is not well financed and is living hand-to-mouth, it is not going to be able to give your franchisee a great deal of help. Study the franchisor as well as you do your franchisee. Unless the franchisor has the wherewithal to give a great deal of assistance to your franchisee, in all probability, the franchisee that you are investing in will fail.

How Does the Franchisor Make Money?

Every franchisor has an orientation in one direction or another toward the franchisee. By this I mean that the franchisor is either trying to make a great deal of money out of the franchising fee or it is content to break even on the franchise fee and make its long-term money on the royalties. It is by far better to select a franchisor that is oriented toward long-term royalty payments than one who is betting on a quick up-front fee from the franchisee. The franchise fee should not exceed the amount of the service that is being given to the franchisee. In good franchisor relationships, the franchisor charges a fee sufficient to cover its expenses for delivering the training and other assistance to the franchisee.

GOOD RELATIONS

You may want to call a large number of the franchisees of the franchisor in question to see whether they are happy with their relationship with the franchisor. If after a few phone calls you find a group of unhappy franchisees, you may want to invest elsewhere. If the chain of franchisees is unhappy with their franchisor, in all probability, your franchise is not worth what you are being charged.

SUMMARY—QUICK STANDARDS OF VENTURE CAPITAL INVESTING

Using some simple standards can help you make a quick decision to go forward or say no. People use various "quick-look" criteria when making decisions about venture capital investing. Although everybody has their own ideas about what to look for, here is some sound advice from individuals in the business:

1. Look for people who are hard-working and honest.
2. Look for a growth industry with strong growth opportunities.
3. Make sure the company has an adequate capital base.

Those three simple rules have helped us sort through hundreds of proposals and work on opportunities that make a great deal of money. If it passes this quick screening, move on to the next four that the opportunity must pass.

First, is there a barrier to entry in the business? That is, each company has some kind of unique product or placement in the market that others are unable to have. It may be a proprietary situation or a patent. Each business has a competitive advantage, and you need to know how the business will defend its market.

Second, is the company leverageable? That is, the company is able to borrow money on the assets of the business so that it need not have an inordinate amount of equity capital in the business. Leverage is like buying stock on margin. You put up only part of the equity and the rest you borrow on the assets of the business. If a business is so risky that it cannot borrow money, it will have to use equity to grow. This is an expensive way to grow a business. At some point, it needs to be able to tap into the debt financing market.

Third, the venture is repeatable. That is, if you have only one location or one situation in which this business opportunity works, it is basically a one-time shot. Major venture capital firms look for things that can be done over and over again as a basis for a business. Repetition is a key trait of a good business. This concept has also led many VCs to conduct "roll ups" or "buy-and-build" strategies that we will mention later in the book.

Fourth, the venture has the ability to generate internal capital. The profits of a company must be great and its tax rate low if it is to generate its own capital to grow.

So look at the cash flow being generated by the company. If it is strong, you probably have a winner. And if you are banking on a "growth" story, its ability to generate cash in the near future is essential.

These four are the keys to success. The harder you work at analyzing and learning as much as possible about your investment opportunity and the industry it operates in, the easier it will be to identify the keys to success in the investment.

Chapters 2–7 of this book explain how in further detail the due diligence process of investigating a business. Obviously, investigating a new idea for a business is entirely different from investigating a business that is already thriving and needs growth capital. Do remember that you will have to adjust the questions you ask to the stage of development of the business in question.

2 ANALYSIS OF MANAGEMENT

This part of the job is so important that we have devoted both this and the next chapter to the subject. In analyzing management, the investor has one basic objective—to determine whether the management team is entrepreneurial enough to execute the business plan profitably. There are virtually hundreds of thousands of small- and medium-sized businesses in the United States today. Some have management that is entrepreneurial; most do not. But first, let's understand the term *entrepreneur*.

This term has undergone a change in meaning since the late 1800s, when it was used to refer to "the director or manager of a public musical institution." *Entrepreneur* derives from the French verb *entreprendre* (to undertake), which, had already entered English earlier as *enterprise*. *Enterprise* first appeared around 1430 and was commonly used to refer to an undertaking of a bold and arduous nature. The person carrying out the enterprise was known as the *enterpriser* but this term eventually lost ground to *entrepreneur*, the primary meaning of which became "one who organizes, manages, and assumes the risk of a business or enterprise." The term *enterpriser* remained primarily as referring to persons taking up a cause, usually warfare for personal gain.

In most instances, the enterpriser was someone who led a small band of men, perhaps a small army, in an attack on a town, usually to pillage. Enterprisers were also known for their ingenuity. Interestingly, some of these original meanings have not been lost. Today's entrepreneurs set out to capture markets, to beat the competition, and to obtain profits. Not everyone has the passion and smarts to win. An entrepreneur does. Does the team you are going to invest in have that entrepreneurial spirit?

THE STUDY OF ENTREPRENEURS

Entrepreneurs have been studied at some length over the past 30 years. However, researchers have been hard-pressed to differentiate between small business owners and entrepreneurs. They have had difficulty in differentiating managers in large companies and entrepreneurs. Indeed, researchers have had difficulty in identifying the characteristics of a successful entrepreneur at all. One book (which shall remain nameless) has described entrepreneurs as people who are of small physical stature and who have experienced some kind of physical illness in their childhoods, had acne as adolescents, and grew up poor and without good educations. The book in question strained desperately to name people who were short and had suffered physical illness but had overcome all of these in order to build great businesses. Although it is wonderful to read about those entrepreneurs who have overcome their physical problems, it does not necessarily mean that all entrepreneurs have to have these attributes in order to be successful. We found that book very entertaining but we found very little in the book on which to base future judgments for selecting entrepreneurs. How would you apply this "new knowledge" if you were an investor? Think how silly it would be to measure your entrepreneur's height, to ask whether the entrepreneur had a history of personal problems, or to ask about that person's physical health as a child, and to use all of that as a selection process for backing an entrepreneur. Nothing could be further from good investment management.

Another book (it shall also remain nameless) sees entrepreneurs as being loaded with guilt and having experienced great deprivation. These entrepreneurs are also said to identify strongly with their mothers. We always enjoy reading these psychological evaluations; they make us have a good laugh. This same book described entrepreneurs as mostly divorced people. In addition, the writer described their wardrobes and indicated that entrepreneurs would only be happy with shirts that did not have button-down collars and shoes that had very thin soles. Those individuals who wore wingtip shoes with very thick soles could not be entrepreneurs, or so the book hypothesized.

Imagine then, how you would analyze the entrepreneur from the investor's point of view. First you would need to do some psychoanalysis to determine whether the entrepreneur is loaded with guilt for not accomplishing the goals that the entrepreneur's parents or peers seemed to expect. Also, you would need to determine the degree of deprivation that the entrepreneur has undergone to decide whether that person had risen from sufficiently low ranks. Finally, you would need to know whether the individual identified closely with his or her mother. After you analyzed the "inner being" of the entrepreneur, you would be ready to look at the entrepreneur's clothes to see whether the entrepreneur had the proper attire, that is, thin-soled shoes and shirts without button-down collars. How ridiculous this approach is for an investor of serious money.

All of these descriptions of entrepreneurs are disastrous simplifications. If anyone used them as investment guidelines, the investor would soon be quite poor. Such oversimplifications will only lead you down the wrong trail. Your best bet is to develop your own knowledge base and apply it to the people you meet who have succeeded as entrepreneurs. First, determine what characteristics you think are important for an entrepreneur. Lets look at a few that practicing VCs have used.

CHARACTERISTICS OF ENTREPRENEURS

Many scientific studies of entrepreneurs have been conducted by social scientists. Most of this work has been reported in the trade press. Despite their problems, these studies have produced some very interesting results coupled with our experiences, we believe make sense. The characteristics that they have discovered are the ones that we believe you should look for in the individual you are backing in an enterprise. These are broad characteristics.

In general, social scientists study two sets of characteristics:

1. Mental characteristics (such as the need for achievement, need for power, belief that one is in control of one's own destiny, and risk preferences)
2. Behavioral characteristics (such as determination, resourcefulness, a sense of urgency to get things done, and a realistic approach to facts)

Generally speaking, mental characteristics have been studied more than behavioral traits. This is unfortunate because the average investor will find it easier to identify the behavioral traits than the mental ones.

Certain physical attributes of entrepreneurs are important as well, such as physical energy level, a better-than-average ability to speak and communicate, and mental stamina. Finally, there are some other characteristics that you as an investor will want in an entrepreneur, such as honesty, partnership orientation, and a desire for fair play.

Now let us turn our attention to the attributes most studied because they seem to be present in successful entrepreneurs that we have encountered over the years.

NEED FOR ACHIEVEMENT

Every study of entrepreneurial individuals has demonstrated that entrepreneurs need to achieve. They are competitive to a fault. They must be first. This basic trait makes it very easy to identify entrepreneurs in a business. Start by looking at their backgrounds. Does the entrepreneur have past achievements? Where has this entrepreneur been spending the past few years? Has the entrepreneur been trying to accomplish something? What accomplishment is the entrepreneur proud of? Go through the personal background in detail and try to determine what achievements have been made. Ask references whether the entrepreneur is an achiever and a self-starter. If you cannot demonstrate to your satisfaction that the so-called entrepreneur meets your definition, it's time for a quick dump.

HIGH NEED FOR AUTONOMY AND POWER

One of the universal characteristics of every entrepreneur is the drive to be independent. The entrepreneur wants to be autonomous. The typical entrepreneur doesn't need the support of any group, club, or clique. Most entrepreneurs do not need any nurturing by a mentor. Entrepreneurs need to dominate the situation, need to be in control and to direct others. As a result, some entrepreneurs may have poor personal skills. There are some that believe that everyone is motivated in the same way and that employees and associates do not need the kind of personal motivation that most skilled managers recognize they must instill in others. You need to be careful of those types of managers because they may alienate their employees and have a difficult time motivating people. Most successful entrepreneurs, of course, have excellent people skills. These entrepreneurs know how to be in control and at the same time motivate people to do their best for the company.

It will be difficult for you to see the entrepreneur's drive for independence without knowing something about that entrepreneur's past performance. That is why it is important to talk to the people acting as references and the employees of this new company. Also, if you continue to talk with the entrepreneur and see how he or she has behaved in the past, you will soon get a clear fix on whether the individual you are talking to has a strong desire for autonomy.

HIGH DEGREE OF SELF-CONFDENCE AND NEED FOR CONTROL

Most entrepreneurs are very confident about what they are doing. They seem to be emotionally stable and have very high self-esteem. Sometimes this is confused with self-centeredness, but most often their high self-esteem is merely an outward manifestation of their personal self-confidence. Because of this, most successful entrepreneurs exhibit good leadership skills and have the ability to set goals and work toward them.

In addition, entrepreneurs strongly believe that they can control their own destinies. They believe that fate is responsible for little in their lives. Although they may say that luck played a part in their success, they will also state that they took advantage of an opportunity. Some people believe fate will determine who they are and what they will be. This is not how entrepreneurs think. The responsibility for their destiny rests squarely on their own shoulders.

HIGH TOLERANCE FOR AMBIGUITY

Most tests of entrepreneurs have shown that they have a high tolerance for ambiguity. As a result, they are nonconformists by nature and have no strong aversion to change, as long as it suits their objectives. Most entrepreneurs are creative when measured on any creative scale, and they are generally curious and interested in almost everything. They are able to judge risks accurately and, thus, are perceived as risk-takers. Whereas most people would perceive something as a high risk, most entrepreneurs would have the good sense and analytical skill to see through the high risk to a safer way of accomplishing the goal. In doing your background work on the entrepreneur, you should look at the entrepreneur's ability to judge risk and the ability to take seemingly ambiguous situations and make sense of them.

NEED TO ASSUME ONLY MODERATE RISK

In fact, entrepreneurs are not high risk takers. That is, given the opportunity to (a) take no risk whatsoever and have a small gain, (b) take moderate risk and have a moderate gain, or (c) take a high risk with high gain, entrepreneurs will opt to take moderate risk. It might seem more natural to you to equate entrepreneurs with high risk takers. However, many researchers have noted that entrepreneurs are moderate risk takers. Those researchers who have classified entrepreneurs as high risk takers fail to understand that entrepreneurs are analytical by nature and, thus, are usually able to perceive risk better than most people. This means that where an average person might see high risk, an entrepreneur might perceive only moderate risks. When you are studying your entrepreneur, try to determine the entrepreneur's risk profile. If you sense that the entrepreneur is a gambler, don't bet any money on the deal or you will usually have a loss. If you are interested in high risks, you may as well go to a gambling casino and place your money on the red 13 on the roulette wheel.

HIGH DEGREE OF DETERMINATION

Entrepreneurs are a determined lot. They all seem determined to succeed. They want to accomplish things, and their desire to do so is strong. They are able to fix on a goal and reach it. This attitude can be seen in athletes who become "psyched up" on winning. A sports competitor will imagine that he or she has won an event and will put his or her mindset into a winning orientation. Entrepreneurs also exhibit this sense of determination and ability to see a clear win for themselves. Make sure that your entrepreneur is a determined person.

HIGH DEGREE OF RESOURCEFULNESS

Entrepreneurs are very resourceful. When problems occur, they are geniuses at finding solutions. When a situation presents itself, they become the consummate problem solver, looking at every area and finding a way to win. They are resourceful to the point of making the rest of us look silly. With their creativity and inquisitiveness, they won't rest until they find a solution. Make sure you know how resourceful the entrepreneur is.

SENSE OF URGENCY

Most studies of entrepreneurs indicate that they have a strong sense of urgency. They are constantly trying to beat the clock. They try to squeeze as many things as possible into each hour of the day. They seem to be in a race against time. They must achieve such-and-such by a certain deadline. Some entrepreneurs are driven to squeeze so many things into a single day that they end up being late for meetings and don't accomplish everything. These entrepreneurs are out of control, and you should avoid them. Any entrepreneur who can't be on time for meetings is most likely "out of control" and is not efficient at managing his or her time or accomplishing goals. Make sure you have an entrepreneur who is realistic about his or her own limits but who also has this sense of urgency to get things done.

KNOWING WHAT IS REAL

One of the striking characteristics of entrepreneurs is their sense of what is reality. Entrepreneurs rarely fool themselves into accepting bad situations. They know they have a marketing program and a sales job to carry out, and they do it. However, they are not caught up in their own sales hype or their own promotional fever. They know that the real facts will determine the outcome of events. They have a keen understanding of what is real and what is fabricated. As a result, they can get to the bottom of an issue very quickly.

When you are discussing projections with entrepreneurs, see whether they are blowing smoke or have their feet on the ground. A good long discussion about their projections will demonstrate whether they are in touch with reality or are on "cloud nine."

You can usually differentiate an entrepreneur from a dreamer. Dreamers hope a lot. They hope that what they want will happen. There have been studies of intelligent people who make poor decisions. These studies have tried to determine why smart people make mistakes. Time and again, the answer is simply because they want to. Sounds incredible that a smart person would intentionally make a mistake, but that is the conclusion. In the entertainment business, one refers to the people in the audience who can "suspend disbelief." That is, they know what they see is not real but they suspend that disbelief and accept it as real so they can enjoy the show. The same thing is true for intelligent people. Even though they know some piece of data is incorrect or that doing something is not best, they do it anyway. They have suspended disbelief and accepted an incorrect fact so that they can do what they want to do. Make sure your entrepreneur does not like to suspend disbelief when it comes to looking at the facts. As my mother used to tell me, "Reality is real."

HIGH LEVEL OF ENERGY

Successful entrepreneurs must have a high level of energy in order to succeed. Being an entrepreneur involves enormous amounts of time and energy. Every successful entrepreneur that I have financed has had tremendous energy. If the person you are looking at doesn't have a high energy level, you may not want to be the backer. Therefore, the health of the individual is important. If the person is not healthy, that person may break under the stress of being an entrepreneur. To determine the state of the entrepreneur's health, ask whether he or she is insurable. Ask how healthy the entrepreneur is and how many times the entrepreneur has been sick in the recent past. You can easily determine the health of your entrepreneur by inquiring about a life insurance policy. The entrepreneur will need a physical to have the insurance. What you will have trouble determining is the energy level of the entrepreneur. This is another point to check with your references.

One of the things that we routinely do is to call entrepreneurs early in the morning. We call to see whether they are at work early. We also call late at night to see whether they are still working. Being an entrepreneur takes many hours of the day, and if your entrepreneur is a late riser or an early quitter, it will be difficult for the company to be successful.

MENTAL STAMINA

Along with physical energy, most entrepreneurs have tremendous mental stamina. Usually, they can think about problems for hours on end without getting tired or giving up. It is not unusual for an entrepreneur to work long, long hours on problems. This mental stamina is a key skill of entrepreneurs, and it is used to their advantage. You will soon have an idea of the entrepreneur's mental stamina after you have "interrogated" the entrepreneur about the many issues of the business. If, at the end of the day, the entrepreneur is physically exhausted and is unable to give you satisfactory answers, you will have your answer. If there is sluggishness, then this one may not be the type of entrepreneur you will want to back.

STRONG COMMUNICATIONS SKILLS

Most entrepreneurs have good social skills and are adept at persuading and conversing with people. You can spot these skills in conversations with the entrepreneur. If the entrepreneur is able to explain the business proposal in a simple style, this will be an outward manifestation of self-confidence and social persuasiveness. If the entrepreneur seems to have an outgoing personality and good presence, this, too, will indicate great self-confidence.

Also, if the entrepreneur seems to be emotionally stable, this will be evidence of strong self-confidence. As mentioned previously, some writers think that entrepreneurs come from broken families, are riddled with guilt about things in their past, come from divorced families, and usually end up divorced themselves. According to my own perception of the world, as well as the reports I've read on entrepreneurship, none of this is true. It is a common myth that an entrepreneur is so driven that the entrepreneur inevitably destroys the marriage and the family. In reality, divorce among entrepreneurs is no greater than in corporate America.

As far as guilt is concerned, the successful entrepreneurs we have backed have not appeared to be guilt-ridden or to feel that they had to achieve to satisfy their parents. They did not seem bent on overcoming some past problem in their lives. All of the successful entrepreneurs I have known have had different reasons for their own success, and it's usually been something that comes from within, not been based on some incident in their childhoods.

HIGH DEGREE OF INTEGRITY

Most entrepreneurs are honest in their approach to the world. Of course, a number of entrepreneurs have cheated and lied their way through life. As an investor, you want to make sure that your entrepreneur is honest and straightforward. If you invest in a dishonest entrepreneur, somewhere along the way you will pay for it; the entrepreneur will get rich but not the investor. To determine an entrepreneur's honesty, during your interview you can ask the same question twice but at different times and in a slightly different way to see whether the entrepreneur answers the same way both times. Sometimes an entrepreneur who lies will trip up in answering the same question. Also during the interview, you may find that an entrepreneur is avoiding a question. Question avoidance is a sure sign that the entrepreneur is hiding something.

In checking the references of entrepreneurs, one of the questions you should always ask is, Do you think the person is honest? Although the more conservative references will avoid answering the question directly if they think the individual is dishonest, you can usually tell whether the reference is giving the entrepreneur an unqualified recommendation in the area of honesty. Credit records, too, will reflect his honesty. If the entrepreneur has a history of not paying his bills, what makes you think he's ever going to give you any money back? As an investor in a venture capital situation, you can never be too careful with entrepreneurs. It is much better to have an entrepreneur who is honest than one who cheats and lies.

However, it's not unusual for an entrepreneur to use what business schools call "constructive deceit" during negotiation.

This means that the entrepreneur and you as the investor have the right to "tell white lies" in order to advance your negotiation position. In negotiations with an entrepreneur, you may not want to give the real reason why you aren't going to proceed with a certain situation, because you might destroy the relationship between you and the entrepreneur. So as a negotiating position, you use constructive deceit. That is, you tell the entrepreneur that your board of directors would not approve something and that you can't go forward for that reason. In this way, you can avoid a confrontation with the entrepreneur and maintain your personal relationship.

You should also expect the entrepreneur to use the same kind of constructive deceit to protect the his or her position. Don't be surprised when you find that the entrepreneur hasn't been honest to a fault and that you have caught the entrepreneur in a little white lie. It is usually harmless and not worth mentioning. Studies have shown that telling white lies does not prove that the person is a thief or a crook. The facts and circumstances are needed to make a jump from using constructive deceit to being a liar.

Another term used in this regard is *intellectual honesty*. This means that the person expresses only views and examples that the entrepreneur believes in. There are, of course, those who will say or do things in order to sway your opinion. For example, a car salesperson may tell a potential buyer that the buyer looks terrific in a red car when the salesperson doesn't think so. Or the salesperson may say that a product is the most beautiful ever made, when the salesperson really believes it is quite ugly. In our society, we *expect* salespersons to be intellectually dishonest when they offer subjective opinions. We know they must sell a product to earn a living, so we expect them to be intellectually dishonest when giving their opinions on the product they are selling. You should expect your entrepreneur to be intellectually dishonest about his or her business. The entrepreneur's product may not be judged the best product by others, but the entrepreneur will "believe" it is the best.

Intellectual dishonesty becomes a more serious matter when it applies to the performance of the product or to facts that can be proved. For example, the car salesperson who tells a prospective buyer that a six-cylinder engine is as good as an eight-cylinder engine can be proven wrong. Sure, it may be just as good in stop-and-go traffic but not on the freeway. The entrepreneur who tells you the performance of his or her product is as good as that of a competitor's product in the face of objective evaluations that say otherwise lies. Don't fault your entrepreneur for trying to convince you of the worth of the product, but do avoid those people who can't accept the reality of the effectiveness of their product.

SEEKING PARTNERSHIP STATUS

The entrepreneur you are backing should see you as a partner and not as an investor. You can do this by spending a good deal of time with the entrepreneur so that you become friends and establish that you are both seeking the same goal—to make money for the both of you. In this partnership, your side of the equation is as important as the entrepreneur's. You must do your part in the partnership and not try to sandbag the entrepreneur with some special legal provision that reduces the entrepreneur's equity or places the entrepreneur in a weak position. You need to maintain your relationship as partners and work with the entrepreneur. Make sure your entrepreneur wants to be a partner. It is the best kind of relationship in venture capital deals.

SEEKING FAIR PLAY

Also make sure that your entrepreneur is seeking fair play from you and that the entrepreneur knows that you are seeking fair play in return. Explain any problems that arise or any situations that come up that might suggest you are not playing fair. If you pull a surprise on the entrepreneur along the way, he or she will believe that you are not working in good faith. If you ever find yourself pitted against the entrepreneur, remember that the entrepreneur has most of the advantage and that after you try to pull a fast one, you will from that moment on have a hard time working with the entrepreneur. Seek out the entrepreneur who has a high sense of fair play and honesty, and you'll be on stronger ground.

In reviewing an entrepreneur's background, it will be hard for you to determine whether the entrepreneur has all of the characteristics mentioned above. To get a proper perspective of the entrepreneur, you will have to adopt a special way of thinking.

How We See Entrepreneurs

The problem with the venture capital business is that when we analyze people, our perceptions of others are usually wrong. Perhaps not entirely wrong, but at best the judgments we make of entrepreneurs are vague and unverifiable. Unfortunately, we tend to tag people with traits that summarize past behavior or current observations that we believe will predict future behavior. The problem is that specific behavior may not necessarily be repeated and cannot be used to generalize or to predict future behavior in other areas. We observe a single incidence of a person's behavior and try to generalize from that. We try to place a general "trait tag" on an individual after observing only a few specific instances.

The classic example of a trait that people are often tagged with is honesty. We say a person is honest or dishonest on the basis of a few observations. The label implies that the person will be honest or dishonest in all future relationships. Trying to determine whether an entrepreneur is honest is difficult because there are so few opportunities for us to observe the entrepreneur's behavior. We dig into the entrepreneur's background and references, looking for clues. But most often we lack enough data to determine whether an entrepreneur is honest or will be in the future. We assume that because the entrepreneur has been honest in the past, he or she will be honest in the future.

Even when you do have more data, there is usually conflicting evidence. The problem with trying to test someone's

honesty is that, according to most studies, we all h̷
things that could be used to tag us as dishonest. Mos̷
are not honest to a fault. They do some things that could be
considered dishonest but will not do other dishonest things.
For example, a person might keep an article lost by someone
and found on the street, but that same person might not lie
about athletic achievement. Some people might lie about their
athletic achievements but might not cheat on exams. In the
retail trade, there are employees who might take store merchandise home but might not take cash from the register. How
many people take their employer's paper and pencils home for
personal use? How many people actually give the company a
full eight hours of work (not goof-off time) every day? So who
is completely honest? How can we judge anyone to be honest?
How can we predict that they will be honest in the future?

Other traits, such as persistence, dependence, conformity,
aggressiveness, and so on are just as difficult to measure as
honesty. Furthermore, some traits we decide to look for in
entrepreneurs don't have much predictive value at all. In our
own description of entrepreneurs we might think in terms such
as "good," "kind," "fair," and "nice." With these vague words
we are not describing the person; rather we are expressing our
approval of the person, saying that we like him or her. This
type of personal opinion doesn't have much predictive value.

How We Make Judgments

When we judge people, we are indicating what standard of
behavior we expect or the standard that we live by. We develop
these ideas about how people should behave through years of
experience. In making our judgment, however, we do not analyze the pros and cons of someone else's behavior at great
length. Normally, we react spontaneously and depend on intuition to be our guide. But intuition is fallible. Still, it is the way
most of us apply traits to various people. In essence, intuition
is a skill that has been so thoroughly learned that we use it
unconsciously. Thus, when people lie about their athletic
skills, we judge them to be dishonest. When another person
keeps a lost pen without asking who lost it, we may approve

that action and not brand that individual as dishonest. All of us subconsciously consult a particular list of behavior traits to test honesty, and we apply it intuitively, without questioning our underlying assumptions.

Intuition rapidly evaluates the data that we receive and allows us to form an opinion. Some people require more data than others before they are ready make a judgment; others are quick to reach a decision, sometimes on the basis of only one event (a snap judgment). Most people take written information, references, interviews, and any other information they pick up, and feed it into their minds, where they match it against the set of tests that they use in judging people.

The problem is that as we learn more facts about an entrepreneur, it is unlikely that all of these facts will point in the same direction. For example, some information may suggest the person is honest, whereas a small amount may indicate dishonesty in certain situations. So we begin to weigh each piece of information for its predictive value. Intuitively, we set up a checklist and put pluses and minuses alongside each item, according to whether it's a good point, an irrelevant point, or a bad point. Then we add the points to see whether the entrepreneur has passed our test. We may even use a very complex system wherein certain items are given much more weight than others on the grounds that they are much more important to the prediction of behavior or for this investment situation. We use these pluses and minuses intuitively because we have done it many times in our daily interaction with others. Although intuition may be a reliable guide for someone who has interviewed thousands of entrepreneurs, we also need to approach our evaluation of entrepreneurs analytically.

ANALYTICAL APPROACH
TO EVALUATIONS

What makes evaluation more complex is that every VC has a unique system of judging entrepreneurs, based on personal experience. One VC may decide that a certain entrepreneur is honest, whereas another might not give the entrepreneur the tag "honest" because the entrepreneur failed on one point that the VC considered critical. The way to handle this situation is simple. After you have investigated and interviewed an entrepreneur a number of times, you should make a list of items that you have observed about the individual and see whether you can use them to reach a logical conclusion about the traits reflected by these items. Appendix C lists examples of traits that a VC would be concerned about.

Look at the traits in Appendix C and decide whether you agree or disagree that each is descriptive of the entrepreneur. Make sure you have a basis for tagging the entrepreneur with each trait; question each judgment. Once you do this, you will better understand the individual. If two VCs have interviewed the entrepreneur, compare trait lists. Talk about the entrepreneur to get a good feel for the individual. As soon as you think you understand the entrepreneur, try to answer the following three sets of questions:

1. How will the entrepreneur treat you and your venture capital company? How will he or she treat you if the company is in trouble? How will he or she treat you if the company is going to make a ton of money? Or will he or she be happy that you are making money too?
2. Are the traits of the entrepreneur the ones needed to be successful in the relevant industry? How will the industry react to this person? Do these traits match up with the keys to success in the industry?
3. Are these traits the ones that will make this specific business successful? Will these traits be accepted by employees? Will they be accepted by professionals such as lawyers, bankers, and accountants?

This approach should help you put some thought into the judging of entrepreneurs. It is not scientific, but it is a logical approach that is bound to be more reliable than snap decisions.

INTERVIEWING ENTREPRENEURS

One of the VC's greatest sources of information is the interview with an entrepreneur. However, interviewing won't produce much in the way of information unless it's done correctly. Here are a few pointers on how to improve your interviewing skills so that the interview will yield more information.

BE PREPARED

Make a list of the information you want to learn from the entrepreneur during the interview. What precisely are you looking for? An interview that rambles through a person's background and business situation won't reveal nearly as much as one that has a specific focus. So make notes as you read the materials supplied to you by the entrepreneur and organize your questions around these notes before you meet with the entrepreneur.

CLEAR MIND

All good interviewers approach the interview with a clear mind. Research shows that an individual who has a clear idea of what he or she is trying to determine and whose mind is not cluttered with other problems or situations will come away with a great deal of information.

So enter the interview with a clear mind. If you are worried about missing a plane or another meeting, or if you have other things on your mind, your questions will be less effective and the answers less informative than if you are "tuned up" with sharp questions and "tuned in" to each answer.

CONDUCIVE ENVIRONMENT

An interview should not be constantly interrupted or conducted in an environment of distractions. Hold telephone calls, stop people from barging in, and don't interrupt the interview yourself to do something else. Don't hold the interview in a public place, such as a restaurant. An uninterrupted interview will yield much more than one punctuated with interruptions. Likewise, if the entrepreneur is constantly being interrupted, it could be a negative sign.

Always go into an interview with more than enough time. One long interview per day is about all that anyone can accomplish, so don't plan more that. An interview can't be completed well if you are in a hurry or have something else on your mind. Also, make sure the entrepreneur has plenty of time and has scheduled the interview as the major event of the day. Plan your interviews well, and they will yield golden nuggets of information.

BE AN EFFECTIVE LISTENER

Effective listening means encouraging the candidate to talk openly about his or her situation. Candidates who feel encouraged will provide better information than those who do not. Also, an interviewer who can see a candidate accurately can encourage him or her in the proper direction. During the interview, try to establish an atmosphere in which both you and the entrepreneur are in the right frame of mind. Be sure you have enough time to get to know each other.

One common mistake often seen with investors is interrupting when the entrepreneur is talking. Don't try to show how smart you are; let the entrepreneur show you how smart he or she is. Talk just enough to get the entrepreneur to open up and tell you what he or she really means. A nice joke will often show that you are friendly and let the entrepreneur "open up."

Use silence constructively; that is, don't feel you have to keep the air full of questions. Let the room fill up with silence, and usually the entrepreneur will volunteer more information. When the entrepreneur talks, pay attention, and *look* as though you are paying attention. If you aren't listening, it will show, and the entrepreneur will say less.

KEEP ON YOUR TOES DURING THE INTERVIEW

A very unusual process takes place when you interview an entrepreneur. You carry out several mental tasks simultaneously and switch from one to the other. A good interviewer focuses on specific points and has a rational approach to things. At times, an interviewer might let intuition come into play in order to pick up on some nuances or rationalizations made by the entrepreneur and bring those back into the question-and-answer session.

At other times, you might need to step back and see the whole interaction to determine whether additional questions are needed and where holes need filling in. You may ask the same critical question twice in an interview just to see if whether is answered the same way both times. Inconsistency may be a sign of dishonesty or lack of knowledge.

Interviewing is tough work. It can be a tremendously complex event marked by both strain and exhilaration as you push forward, looking for information.

TYPES OF INTERVIEWS

There are two types of interviews. The first type is a panel or group interview. For example, a group of VCs may interview one entrepreneur or two or three of the top management. In the latter situation, the entrepreneur is facing several interviewers at once and may be more formal and less open. On the other hand, when a group of questions is being asked, the interviewers tend to be sharper and more focused, and are able to probe into the situation due to the interaction of the panel members.

The second type is the individual interview. It can be more intimate and offers the entrepreneur an opportunity to open up and provide personal information that isn't normally talked about in groups. Usually you can get more personal information in a one-on-one interview.

Both of these types of interviews are useful, but the individual interview is a must. It is the only way to really get to know that person.

DOCUMENT YOUR WORK

After every interview, you should document your discussion. Keep a piece of paper handy while you are interviewing and make notes to yourself. Later, you may want to dictate a memo for the file. Make copious notes during the interview, although you will probably find it advisable to keep the paper on which you're making notes out of sight of the entrepreneur. When people see you taking notes, they tend to be more formal.

In summary, you should enter an interview with a clear and extremely alert mind. You can't have distractions. Also, you've got to review the entrepreneur's material beforehand so that you will know what you're looking for. You should have read the business plan and looked through the person's resume. You have to be prepared. Walking in and wandering through the business situation is a very inefficient use of time.

The cardinal rule for an interviewer is to be an effective listener and to encourage candidates to continue to talk.

ASSESSMENT OF ENTREPRENEURS

In assessing the abilities of an entrepreneur, you can gain information about the effective techniques from some of the industrial psychologists. For your enjoyment, Appendix D includes a psychological assessment of the current president of a major company. Most of us do not have the skills of industrial psychologists, but we can learn from the things they do.

The industrial psychological approach does not try to tell you why people act the way they do; it tries to tell you how able a person is. The industrial psychologist tries to avoid relying on many of the outward appearances of the individual. There is a considerable body of evidence holding that in some situations people are motivated either consciously or unconsciously to present themselves in what they believe to be a favorable light. This kind of "play acting" can lead you to misread a person. Therefore, industrial psychologists try to identify factors that truly reflect the individual's character. For example, an expert will not automatically rate a lively, outgoing conversationalist higher than the shy introvert or consider the highly educated person to be more clever than one who may not have had the same educational opportunities. Likewise, a successful business record is not taken at face value by a probing expert. Like the industrial psychologists, investors need to hone their techniques so that they are not misled by outward appearances.

The aim of the industrial psychologists is to discover not only how intelligent a person is but also how effective that person is in applying his or her abilities in various contexts. They try to construct an overly simplified model of the person that can be used to predict how he or she will behave in doing the required work. In applying this model, industrial psychologists are not trying to discover the causes of any particular behavior but are simply hoping to predict behavior. In essence, they are trying to predict how the person (in the most important job in the company) will react to various situations.

Industrial psychologists usually administer a large set of written tests to an entrepreneur. Although such tests have been used by some VCs, they are not fully accepted and are probably not something that VCs can use to any extent. This leaves you with the interview and conversation with the entrepreneur. An important point to remember is that people normally speak at 125 words a minute, but you can think and comprehend conversation at 500–600 words per minute. This means that you have ample opportunity during interviews and discussions with the entrepreneurs to pick up many of the subtle clues and basic information that will lead us to a sound decision about the person.

The first thing to do when you are spending the day with an entrepreneur is to outline what you expect to do during the day. This may put him or her at ease and give you more information about his or her approach to life. One of the things industrial psychologists ask the entrepreneur to do is to describe his or her life history. Initially the entrepreneur may be a little slow, but after a little encouragement, most people enjoy talking about where they grew up, their parents, their outlook on life, and how they arrived at the position they find themselves in now.

Most people will give you a detailed history of their business experience. It is very important to listen. You must stop yourself from interrupting an entrepreneur while he or she is talking. Industrial psychologists frequently use open-ended questions and encourage the entrepreneur to talk freely. In this kind of open and friendly interview, attitudes and opinions of the entrepreneur will inevitably emerge, as will many facts about the person's behavior. If you are a good listener, evidence in the form of recurring themes and patterns of behavior will reveal themselves. For example, the person who has consistently made major decisions for himself or herself in the past is likely to continue to do so in the future, and the person who has always led an essentially solitary life is unlikely to change into a highly gregarious person.

The industrial psychologist usually concentrates on three basic areas that will help you with some of the things you should be looking for.

INTELLECTUAL EFFECTIVENESS

Here you are trying to compare the manager with the entire management population you've ever known in order to determine whether this manager is in the top 5 percent of those you have worked with. The following questions will help you establish his or her intellectual effectiveness:

- Is the entrepreneur a quick learner?
- Is the entrepreneur a conceptual thinker?
- Can the entrepreneur work quickly and accurately with numbers?
- Does the entrepreneur have good verbal skills?
- Does the entrepreneur have the ability to communicate verbally, as well as in writing?
- Is the person an objective thinker or is the entrepreneur strongly influenced by personal emotions? There is now a considerable body of evidence that successful executives are able to be more logical and objective than are the less successful ones.
- Is the entrepreneur really a critical thinker or does the person let preconceived notions set the pace?
- Is this person able to produce original ideas?
- Is the entrepreneur imaginative or strictly conventional?

WORK APPROACH AND STYLE

- Is the entrepreneur a generalist or is the entrepreneur detail-minded?
- Does the person believe in having a thorough knowledge of minor matters or does that person dismiss detail items as irrelevant?
- Does the entrepreneur recognize priorities and know which things are important and should be put first?
- In the decision-making approach, is the entrepreneur impulsive or cautious, slow or confident?
- Just how does the entrepreneur go about making decisions?
- What kind of strategist is the entrepreneur?
- Is the entrepreneur a long-term planner or a short-term tactician?
- How energetic is the entrepreneur?
- Is the person restrained or explosive?
- Is the entrepreneur vigorous, efficient?
- How does the person tolerate pressure?
- Is the entrepreneur stable, or is this person easily pushed off the edge?
- How would the entrepreneur react to emergencies?
- Is this person calm or frustrated?
- How would you measure this person's ambitions, and how important is success to the entrepreneur?
- Will the entrepreneur sacrifice the interests of others?
- Will this person sacrifice investors' interests to make the objectives?
- Are this person's aims realistic?
- How flexible is the entrepreneur?
- Can the entrepreneur handle a number of tasks at once?
- How adaptable is the person?
- Can the entrepreneur adjust to different environments?

PERSONAL RELATIONSHIPS

- What kind of relationships does the entrepreneur have with supervisors and upper management?
- Is the entrepreneur frank, stubborn, loyal, and amenable?

■ What relationship does the entrepreneur have with peers?

■ Is the entrepreneur friendly, cooperative, tolerant, a team person, highly competitive, a loner?

■ What relationship does the entrepreneur have with subordinates?

■ Is the entrepreneur domineering, protective, decisive, and sensitive?

■ Is the entrepreneur willing to delegate responsibilities?

■ What relationship does the entrepreneur have with outsiders?

■ Is the entrepreneur confident, careful, courteous, or disdainful?

When an industrial psychologist is finished, the psychologist usually summarizes the person's traits and lists the positives and the negatives as they relate to this job opportunity. For example, the psychologist might say that the person is industrious and energetic, that the entrepreneur is flexible and can adapt to change, that the person is decisive, above average in ability to communicate clearly, and imaginative, and that the person makes a good first impression.

The psychologist might also list the individual's limitations. For example, the psychologist might say that the entrepreneur's basic intellectual power is a little below average, that the entrepreneur's judgment of emotionally toned situations is suspect, and that person's analytical skills are below average; the psychologist may say that the entrepreneur is unstable and insecure, hypersensitive and quick to take offense, unable to sustain a seemingly cheerful and friendly manner, and would not be a good team member.

This does not suggest that you should employ an industrial psychologist or that you should try to become an amateur industrial psychologist. However, it is interesting to see how professionals go about their tasks. All VCs can learn something from these situations that will help them become better at judging entrepreneurs. Although industrial psychologists can give us a general understanding of the individual, they cannot determine whether that individual will perform well in that person's chosen field or executive position. They are guessing, just as any investor is. You can look for general characteristics in entrepreneurs, but by themselves these will not indicate whether the individual is going to be successful in a chosen field. What you have to do is determine the keys to success in the business situation and in the industry you're looking at and whether the individual has the matching personal traits. Entrepreneurs should have certain general traits. However, some specific traits are also required for success in each industry.

WHAT VENTURE CAPITALISTS LOOK FOR IN ENTREPRENEURS

Generally speaking, the answers of entrepreneurs fall into two categories. The first category concerns individual characteristics and the second the experience of the individual.

THE ENTREPRENEUR'S INDIVIDUAL CHARACTERISTICS

The following is a list of characteristics that come up frequently.

1. **Staying Power.** VCs want an entrepreneur who is capable of intense effort over a long period of time. VCs know that 90 percent of every venture success comes from perspiration, not inspiration. They know that if a small business is to succeed, the management team is going to have to work long hours to compensate for the lack of employees at the company.

2. **Ability to Handle Risk.** VCs look for an individual who has the intellectual power to evaluate risk and knows what to do after the evaluation. Every small business twists and turns many times during its life, and the early years are the most traumatic. An entrepreneur must be capable of analyzing situations, evaluating the probability of success, and implementing a plan. Unless they are able to evaluate risk and analyze complex situations, small businesses usually remain small businesses.

3. **Verbal Ability.** VCs need an entrepreneur who can artic-
ulate an idea. Many people have tremendous minds but
lack the ability to explain their thoughts to the outside
world. Without an accurate and convincing voice, most
small businesses will fail. In the early years, an entrepreneur must persuade vendors to give the small business
credit, persuade banks to make loans to the business,
persuade employees to work long hours, and persuade
government authorities to stay off them. It is this verbal
ability that sets most entrepreneurs apart from scientific
inventors. If your entrepreneur lacks the ability to persuade, you are probably making a mistake by investing
in a business run by him or her.

4. **Detail Orientation.** Some find it almost contradictory
that VCs want an entrepreneur who knows the details.
Most of us think that good entrepreneurs worry about
the big picture and hire other people to handle the
details. This perception couldn't be further from the
truth. Entrepreneurs must carry an inordinate amount
of detail around in their minds and be able to use it all
to the best advantage of the company. Details about
numbers as well as the situation will need quick reactions and an individual with the ability to do it. Without this attention to detail and knowledge of the
specifics, most small businesses can't grow.

5. **Compatible Personality.** Believe it or not, VCs most
often invest in an entrepreneur who has a personality
that is compatible with their own. Compatible person-
alities may not be at the top of anyone's list, but entrepreneurs are not financed unless they are compatible
with their venture capital source. It is indeed like a
marriage. Most people don't get married unless they
like each other. VCs don't "marry" entrepreneurs
unless they like them. Even if an entrepreneur is capable of meeting many of the problems in a situation, a
VC will not invest unless the VC can stand "living
with" the personality of the entrepreneur.

One VC, for instance, was considering a restaurant situation, which the VC would have invested, but the VC found the

entrepreneur obnoxious. The VC said, "I knew I would not be able to stand working with this obnoxious ass over the ensuing years; therefore, I didn't make the investment."

EXPERIENCE OF THE ENTREPRENEUR

The following are a few items that you may want to look for in an entrepreneur's experience.

1. **Market Knowledge.** VCs don't have the time to learn about a marketplace in detail. For this reason, VCs want to know above all that the entrepreneur has a thorough knowledge of the marketplace. It is rare that a VC will back an entrepreneur who has little or no experience in a business area. It is common knowledge that an individual needs at least five years to understand an industry. No one wants to finance on-the-job training for an entrepreneur.

2. **Track Record.** Along with market knowledge, VCs would like to back people who have a track record, especially a track record relevant to the situation. Ten years ago, we were about to back an entrepreneur who wanted to buy a business that was a "turnaround." The individual seemed to have the proper background, in that the entrepreneur had turned around several businesses and made a substantial profit for the investors. The difficulty was that the entrepreneur had not been involved in a turnaround in this particular industry; therefore, we felt we should not invest. The track record of an entrepreneur is something that a VC will investigate time and time again. The VC will look for achievements in the individual's background and for achievements in the specific industry in which the VC is about to invest. This is a key point for every VC.

3. **Leadership.** Every VC is looking for a leader for the company. Any time a VC backs an entrepreneur without leadership, the VC has inevitably had trouble and has had to replace the entrepreneur. Therefore, VCs look for entrepreneurs who have been in leadership positions in the past and who have demonstrated their

abilities conclusively. Without leadership, the company is probably not going to go anywhere.

4. **Reputation.** VCs are looking for entrepreneurs with outstanding reputations. They want trustworthy people. They are about to give a great deal of money to a business run by the entrepreneur, and they want to be sure the manager of that business has a reputation that is above reproach. Every VC in the business can give you a long lament about some entrepreneur who took money out of the business illegally. If there is any hint that the reputation of the entrepreneur is not 100 percent solid, experienced VCs will not invest.

CHARACTERISTICS OF SMALL BUSINESS MANAGERS VERSUS ENTREPRENEURS

In trying to differentiate a small businessperson from an entrepreneur, one important aspect usually shines through. Although a small businessperson wants to build the business, he or she actually has a more immediate concern: to take as much cash out of the company as possible. The small businessperson will usually run the company as a subchapter-S corporation. The small businessperson will have a big car and a great many perks and other items of self-aggrandizement. All of these factors indicate that the individual is interested in taking money out of the company, rather than reinvesting it in the growth of the company. This usually means that, as soon as the business starts to grow, the company will run into a cash crunch. And it is at that time that the individual usually ends up on the doorstep of a VC, seeking additional capital to do the things that he or she should have been doing with his or her money in the first place.

In one situation, two individuals had come up with a unique line of cosmetics. It was a product that could be duplicated by others but this group probably had a two- or three-year jump on the competition. They enjoyed a great reputation after making this cosmetic discovery. Instead of using the huge profits that the company generated in the initial years to hire a chief marketing person, an outstanding sales manager, a good controller to keep the books accurately so that an audit could be taken, and a staff that could provide good quality control, these two entrepreneurs began to draw such enormous salaries that the company's main purpose became to pay their salaries.

At the end of three years, they approached a VC fund for investment capital. Having each taken over $5 million out of the business and invested it personally, they felt secure. The only problem was that by the time they had reached us, three major competitors were offering the same product, and a giant cosmetic company had just introduced a similar line. Instead of having a two-year time horizon in which to build the business into a great company, these two were stuck with a hopelessly small company with little or no chance of growth.

They were eagerly pawing over a registration statement that had raised $20 million for 25 percent of another small cosmetic company. The other company had started two years after they had begun their operation and had copied their concept completely about a year before. The difference was that the entrepreneurs behind this second company had plowed everything back into the business and built it into a money machine. Sales had more than tripled in three years, whereas in the company that had sought more investment capital from us, sales had remained flat. It is a sad sight to see two individuals who could have been worth $300–$400 million instead having only their nest eggs of $5 million locked away. They had missed a great opportunity.

In reviewing small business people and entrepreneurs and trying to differentiate between the two, you will find that the immediate need for cash and status is a sign of a small business person, whereas the desire to plow money back into the business and take a long-term outlook toward capital gain on sale of the stock at some future date is a characteristic of an entrepreneur. An entrepreneur builds a team to run a great business.

CONCLUSIONS ON ENTREPRENEURS

When you are analyzing the entrepreneur, you should first record five things you like about the entrepreneur and five things you dislike. As you begin your relationship, you will find the numbers in the "like" column adding up. Most of them should be in the areas outlined above. If you find a lot of comments in the "dislike" column, you should not make the investment. Every investment that our company has ever made in which we had reservations about the entrepreneur has turned into a very difficult situation for us. When you find something negative about the entrepreneur, try to understand the circumstances and ask yourself whether you would have done the same thing the entrepreneur did in that situation. If the answer is yes, you probably have to overlook it and continue your analysis.

If, however, you find a situation in which you don't believe you would have done the same thing as the entrepreneur, outline what you would have done differently. Then confront the entrepreneur with the situation and ask why the entrepreneur didn't go forward in that manner.

There is a good reason to make this confrontation. Sometimes in a relationship with an entrepreneur, you will uncover things that seem to be quite negative. If you don't ask about these negatives and just go your merry way without making the investment, you may have missed a great opportunity. You may face several situations in which potential negatives come out in the reviewing process. Appearances are not always what they seem. You need to dig behind almost everything, especially the negatives in an entrepreneur's background.

DEVELOPING BACKGROUND INFORMATION

Now you need to develop the background information on the entrepreneur in an organized fashion. To this end, we have the following areas to analyze and develop information. Every great VC has a system of getting information on entrepreneurs. You need to develop one, too.

PERSONAL REFERENCES

Ask the entrepreneur to supply references, beginning with personal references. These will be people who know the entrepreneur but are not part of the entrepreneur's business relationships. They are usually friends, relatives, and teachers. They may know a great deal about the individual but not much about his or her business.

These references should supply information about the personality of the individual and about the entrepreneur's personal habits. You are trying to discover whether the entrepreneur indulges in alcohol or drugs or is involved in asocial behavior that will be detrimental to your business. For example, in checking one personal reference, we determined that the individual was highly asocial. When we asked him about this, he admitted that he had a problem, and he was understanding when we declined the investment. This kind of risk was far greater than the expected return on this investment. Once you have finished a personal reference, you should prepare a written record of the inquiry, indicating how that person answered the questions you asked.

BUSINESS REFERENCES

You also want to ask the entrepreneur for a number of business references. These are people who have been in business situations with the entrepreneur and know how that person operates. There are three basic groups to consult for this information.

The first group consists of inside references. These are people such as superiors, associates, or subordinates in the entrepreneur's current business position or past business positions. Someone who was the entrepreneur's boss for 10 years may give you great insights into this individual's past. A cohort with whom the entrepreneur worked five years ago can also be helpful in determining the entrepreneur's business ethics. One person once asked for a business reference about an entrepreneur said: "I don't know why the little S.O.B. gave me as a reference. He worked for me for two years and did nothing more than ride around in his little sports car and got nothing done. He was a disgrace to my organization." It's not often that you will find such references, but every now and then even a good entrepreneur makes the mistake of giving a bad reference.

The second group of business references consists of outside references. These are people such as competitors, suppliers, or buyers of the entrepreneur's product. They are the ones who come into contact with the entrepreneur in a business relationship that is not inside the business. Quite often, the competition will know a great deal about the entrepreneur, especially if the entrepreneur has moved from one competitor to another. This kind of inside information can be very revealing, but always take it with a grain of salt, particularly if it is from the competition

The third type of business references comprises professional references. These are bankers, accountants, and lawyers who have worked with or for the entrepreneur in some business relationship in the past. Sometimes the entrepreneur will give you the name of a consultant the entrepreneur has used as a reference. Consultants can tell you whether an entrepreneur used their services efficiently or ignored their recommendations. This information will tell you whether an entrepreneur is willing to take advice from experienced people in the business.

Some references may not give all the information that you want but nonetheless will speak in reasonably positive terms about the entrepreneur. Therefore, you should ask each reference who else might know the entrepreneur well. In this way, you can generate other references on the entrepreneur and find out whether they think the same way as the primary reference. Sometimes an entrepreneur will use as a reference a boss to whom the entrepreneur merely reports but does not work for directly. If possible, you should try to determine who the direct supervisors are and seek them out. They may be left off the reference list because they have some good information that the entrepreneur doesn't want you to know.

CREDIT REPORTS

Credit reporting agencies can be used for obtaining additional information on the entrepreneur. Some, such as a credit bureau, specialize in personal reports. These give you information on an individual's personal credit. They can be quite interesting to read, especially if you find that the entrepreneur has amassed a large amount of debt and has been extremely slow in paying it back. Also, bankruptcies occasionally show up in these credit reports.

In addition, reports put out by agencies such as Dun & Bradstreet and Standard and Poor's can be used to evaluate entrepreneurs who have had previous small businesses. These can give you very insightful information on the payment history of the small business that the entrepreneur worked for. You can see how the entrepreneur ran the past small business from a financial viewpoint.

You can consider engaging hiring agencies, such as U S Investigation Services or Bishops Reports, to collect detailed information about entrepreneurs. These companies specialize in doing extensive background checks on people. They can even go to the county courthouses where the entrepreneur has lived and find all suits and court actions. They can verify whether the entrepreneur has attended the schools that he or she claims to have attended and do credit checks. Although this is a more expensive approach, it will provide you with a detailed credit history of the individual and will uncover criminal behavior.

PRIVATE INVESTIGATIONS

Private investigators usually are not hired to check out the background of an entrepreneur. However, from time to time one is forced to use this method of obtaining information. If you are thinking of hiring a private investigator to check out an entrepreneur, it most likely means that some basic things are wrong and that you probably shouldn't invest in the entrepreneur. However, private investigators can be used.

A private investigator once helped determine that the entrepreneur had had a drinking problem in a past job and that he had been fired for being an "alcoholic." However, when confronting the entrepreneur with the situation, he explained that at the time he was going through a divorce. It had been an extremely emotional and stressful experience, and he had turned to alcohol for a short period. He demonstrated conclusively that he was no longer alcohol dependent and had been involved in this life-style for only a short period in his career. This was an acceptable answer, and it checked out with later investigations.

PSYCHOLOGICAL ASSESSMENT TESTS

You earlier considered the issue of psychological tests and the hiring of industrial psychologists to conduct them. Some of these tests have proved quite fruitful in reviewing middle management in large corporations and even upper management to some degree. They have been used on a very limited scale by VCs. Basically, most VCs believe that they are adept enough at assessing entrepreneurs to do without psychological tests. It's also quite demeaning to ask entrepreneurs to take psychological tests to determine whether they are good entrepreneurs. However, this is changing, and it is more common today to hire such mental investigators. A good company in this field that has made investigating VC-backed enterprises is G.A. Smart & Company in Chicago. Goff Smart surveyed a lot of VC funds and inquired as to how they conducted their investigations. He later wrote his doctoral dissertation on the subject and founded a service to help VCs. He runs a great business.

WRITTEN INFORMATION

The entrepreneur will provide you with reams of written information, some of it containing details about the entrepreneur. There most likely will be brochures about the business and blurbs about the entrepreneur, along with copies of articles that have been published in newspapers and trade magazines; these articles will also describe the business and the entrepreneur. These sources contain information about the individuals that you should not overlook. Reviewing them will give you some inside scoop on the entrepreneur.

In addition, you should ask the entrepreneur to provide a detailed resume for each of the key people in the organization, including the entrepreneur. This resume will summarize the history of the entrepreneur and the other key principals in the company, from early schooling through the current period. The resume should lay out in chronological order where the entrepreneur has been. If the resume doesn't have all the years filled in, ask the entrepreneur to do a resume in that manner. This way, you can make sure there are no unexplained gaps in the entrepreneur's background.

A VC once told of an entrepreneur who presented the VC with a resume that hadn't covered three years of his background. All other credit references had checked out completely, and everything seemed to be in good order. However, as the VC pressed the entrepreneur for more information about this three-year period, the entrepreneur grew vague and said he must have put the wrong dates down. Because this was more than 10 years ago, he was not sure of the dates and would have to get back to the VC on that. This intrigued the VC, and the VC checked further on the individual's background.

After talking to a lawyer in a town where the entrepreneur had been located, the VC found that the individual had been involved in a fraud and had been sent to prison for three years. None of this information had been revealed in credit reports or any of the other references that the VC had checked. It was only by closely examining the entrepreneur's background year by year that the VC was able to detect this fact about the entrepreneur's background. The bad deeds had been committed over 10 years in the past and had been expunged from the entrepreneur's record.

Nor should you take the written information presented by the entrepreneur at face value. Entrepreneurs have been known to "exaggerate" their achievements. In telephoning colleges and universities to confirm an entrepreneur's credentials, most VCs have uncovered at least once that a claim to have graduated was false. This, along with other factors, helped to kill the deal.

There is also the story about an entrepreneur who presented a detailed resume to a group of VCs. Records at his high school and everywhere else indicated that he had graduated from that school and that he had gone to college in a good Midwestern town. Supposedly, he had also taken an advanced degree from that college and had worked for a good number of years at a solid Midwestern company. The VCs decided to invest in this new West Coast company. To their utter amazement, a few days after the money went into the business, the entrepreneur disappeared with the money they had placed in the business bank account. After checking with the FBI, they were told that the individual had been a two-bit mobster from New York who had ratted on organized crime and sent a number of them to prison. The authorities had provided him with a false background as part of its witness protection program. This crook had used his pristine background to lure VCs into his new business and took off with their money. He was never found.

INFORMATION FROM THE ENTREPRENEUR

In your conversations with the entrepreneur, you will be able to pick up things that will help you evaluate the entrepreneur's past performance and your ability to place your trust in the new business for the future. Encourage the entrepreneur to talk about the past, where the entrepreneur grew up, the type of parents the person had, whether the entrepreneur had a paper route, and what type of high school the person attended. All of these details provide background information that you should write down at your earliest convenience and put into your file. This kind of information will help you determine whether the individual has the characteristics that you are looking for in an entrepreneur for this business.

At some point in interviewing the entrepreneur, most VCs say, "Look, during the next days we are going to conduct a detailed check on your background and will specifically look for bad points. If there is anything out there that we are likely to pick up, would you tell us about it now so it won't come as a surprise?" By being candid with entrepreneurs about your background checks, you can often induce them to open up about their past. One individual once turned bright red when ask this question, then admitted that he had been arrested. When asked, "Oh, what for?" He looked back and said, "When I was in college, I was in a bar one night and got pretty drunk and tore up a piano." From the other details on his record, it looked as though he had sewn all his wild oats on this one night. It was an act that had no bearing on this person's ability to run the company.

Local People

Many times when investing in a small business that is not located in your area, you might call on a VC in the city in question or another contact in the area. Ask them to find out whether anyone has heard anything good or bad about this individual. It is generally easier for someone who lives in the same town to find the contacts who can tell you what kind of person you are dealing with. They may have heard something in their business dealings or they may have seen something about the individual in the local newspapers some years back. They can supply you with local information about the entrepreneur that you would otherwise be unable to obtain.

Public Information

If the individual you are investing in has been involved in a public company, the SEC files can provide additional information on the individual. If the person has been involved in radio or television, the FCC will have files on the stations that the individual has worked for, and there may be some information about the person in those files. This public information can usually lead you in the right direction.

Customers

Customer checks are an important part of due diligence, but they can also be important in assessing the entrepreneur's ability. When you are talking to the customers of the business, be sure that you ask about the entrepreneur. Many customers will know the entrepreneur because the he or she has been helping the company sell the product. They may give you some insight into the entrepreneur's personality, ethics, and reputation.

INVESTORS

Other investors in the company can also give you some background information on the entrepreneur. You will want to contact other investors and find out why they invested in the company and whether they are happy with their investment. Also ask them where there is anything they would want to change, what problems they have had with the entrepreneur, and what they liked about him or her. Get to know these investors and find out what they think about the entrepreneur you are investigating.

EMPLOYEES

Finally, ask employees of the company about the entrepreneur. What is it that they like about the chief executive officer? What is it they dislike? Don't despair if most of the employees say that they like the CEO and do not have any criticism. At some point, you will find the one who is willing to give you an earful. You will find the "mole" who will give you the inside information you need on the company and the CEO.

MANAGEMENT TEAM

Usually it takes more than one person to make a corporation go. You will want to investigate the number-two and number-three people in the firm almost as closely as you will investigate the CEO. It is important for you to know whether they can fill the shoes of the CEO if the CEO should die or become disabled. You will also want to determine whether there are any disagreements among the management team. Find out if any problems are brewing. Review the experiences of the management team to see how they fit together. Are they the same age, do they have the same background and experience, or do they have a diversity that will let them handle a multitude of problems? Do they work well together or is there constant bickering and conflict? Be sure to ask all of them how they feel about the chief executive officer. Also ask each one of them how he or she feels about the others.

ORGANIZATION STRUCTURE AND DECISION MAKING

It is very important to understand who exercises the authority. Is the CEO making the decisions or does the CEO share power with the board of directors and the management team? Does the board function as a committee or is it merely a sounding board for decisions that have already been made?

Determine the duties and responsibilities of each person on the management team. Who has defined these duties? Who has determined whether they are carried out correctly? Has there been sufficient delegation of authority? Have the authority limits been defined adequately? Does the organization depend on only one or two people on the team? Could it function without several of the key employees? Make sure you understand the decision-making process in the company. If the entrepreneur does not have control of the direction of the company, it may be a sign not to invest.

DOCUMENTATION

When you have finished asking questions, you should document in detail all the significant points you have uncovered. Also make sure that you have all of the items that you want or that management will be sending them to you. Appendix A contains a list of items that you should probably have on any company that you plan to invest in. What you may find particularly interesting are the reports used by management to manage the business. Once you have those, you can see the business the way the entrepreneur sees it. If you see it in that light, you will probably have a better understanding of the business.

STRENGTHS AND WEAKNESSES

At the end of the day, you should always try to list the strengths and weaknesses of the CEO and the management team. This helps you to assess the risk that lies behind every deal because the management team counts for so much. Management counts for at least 20 percent of the business, and in most circumstances 50 percent of the business. In essence, if you do not have a good management team, you will probably not succeed, no matter how good the product or the production process.

FINAL JUDGMENT

At the end of all your investigations, you are going to have to sit back and think about your entrepreneur. Is this person the type of leader who can make the projections that they presented to you come to fruition? This judgment is the final one. Good luck in making it.

3 REVIEWING PERSONNEL AND COMPENSATION

From an investor's viewpoint, a company is little more than the people who work for it. Companies succeed because the people make the company succeed. A company usually fails because the people fail. An entrepreneur alone cannot carry a company very far; there must be a group of people dedicated to the success of the corporation. The entrepreneur can be a quarterback and can call some extremely good plays, but without the complete team—all the employees working together—no entrepreneur can succeed.

One of the most important areas for an investor to investigate is company personnel. What is the true work ethic inside the company? What is the group culture? How do the company's personnel shape up in comparison with the competition? In this chapter we look more closely at the due diligence involved in checking out the personnel of a corporation.

How Is the Company Organized?

Academicians have studied company organizations for years. Academic and popular press have reported revelation after revelation regarding the corporate culture. Each season, a new group of buzzwords seems to appear to describe corporate organizations. If you are to understand the company and how it operates, you must understand how the company is organized.

CORPORATE ORGANIZATIONAL CHART

Organizational charts are necessary in even the smallest corporations in order to delineate the relationships between various people and to spell out each staff member's responsibilities. Organizational charts give a clear visual presentation of the corporation's hierarchy. Every organizational chart should indicate who is at the head of production, marketing, and finance. In the early stages of the company, one individual, usually the president, may play several of these roles, but it is understood that somewhere in the life of the company a person will be hired to perform each function.

Some small companies don't have organizational charts, and when they don't, you should construct one while talking to the entrepreneur. Draw a chart and put people's names on it. Determine who reports to whom and exactly who is responsible for what functions in the company. In turn, it will give you a very clear understanding of how the people interact and how the corporation functions. Although some academicians argue that organizational charts are not necessary or, at the least, that they rarely reflect the total interaction in the company (and we concur with the latter criticism), most investors think a chart is a good beginning. It may be that one individual reports to two people for certain jobs in which that individual is currently carrying out two functions. It is rare, however, to find that job functions have not been delineated in a larger organization. When they have been delineated, it's fairly easy to construct an organizational chart.

There was, for instance, one company in which the entrepreneur was adamantly opposed to having people's names on an organizational chart. The entrepreneur fervently believed that the team could work together to solve any problem and that, although certain people had certain jobs to do—for example, the accountant had to prepare the financial statements—it was a team effort, and everyone should work together. At the time, this seemed a fairly novel idea that might succeed. After the company failed, the appraisal of this entrepreneur's team approach to things had to be revised. There are a number of nitty-gritty jobs that need to be done in every corporation, and they should be assigned to specific individuals who have the ability to do them and are charged with completing them in a timely manner. These people should have someone to report to so that when those tasks are not completed on time the person responsible can be reprimanded and when they are completed on time the person can be rewarded. Any corporation that lacks this hierarchical structure is likely to experience growing pains, if not outright failure.

Many in the business world disagree about hierarchical organizations. Most critics question not the structure itself, but the height of the structure. In other words, an organizational chart that has a high pinnacle with one entrepreneur at the top and many people at the bottom will be less effective in the marketplace than one in which the pinnacle is less high and more spread out, and features a strong middle-management team. There are descriptions of organizations that have task force groups or associates with sponsors for each associate. These are almost the same as hierarchical organizations except that the hierarchy does not have a steep pinnacle. Decision making has been pushed down to lower echelons so that the employees on the floor are more involved in deciding how to get the job done. Regardless of whether the entrepreneur wants a hierarchical organization or not, at some point the entrepreneur will be involved in one, and every entrepreneur should be able to prepare an organizational chart for you to review.

OFFCERS AND DIRECTORS

In every company you study, always get a complete list of the officers and directors, with their names, addresses, and telephone numbers. You will want to talk to all of them. Also obtain a list of people who have over 5 percent ownership in the company, with their addresses and telephone numbers. It may be important to contact them and if you have the information in the file, it's easier than having to get that information later. In particular, anyone who owns a large block of stock should be contacted to determine why he or she made a large investment in the company.

STOCKHOLDERS

Have a list of all stockholders prepared for you. Ask that the list indicate the amount each person paid for their ownership and the percentage of ownership. Determine when each person purchased the equity. Call several of them to see what they know about the company.

CHARACTERISTICS OF MANAGEMENT

When you make a list of the officers, directors, and large stockholders, you should include the following information: the title or position of the person, age, years in present position, years with the company, prior business experience, education, compensation, and whether he or she has a written or unwritten employment agreement with the company. All of these details are important to the investor because they will say something about the management team. When you are looking at the management team, you will want to ask these types of questions: Is there a strong management team to carry out the plans? Or does everything depend on one key entrepreneur? What would happen to the company if one of the key employees were not available for an extended period of time? Is the group of key employees of the same age, experience, and background or does it consist of a blend of youth, experience, and different backgrounds? Does the key group of employees work together as a team? Are there identifiable lines of authority? Does management use an integrated approach to problems? Is there a great deal of bickering within the team?

Does the CEO dominate the operations of planning and projections or does the group decide where the company will go? Is there either a written or understood developmental plan for each of the key executives in the company to follow? How will they make a great deal of money if the company is successful?

One good question for the CEO is, "Who would run the company if—God forbid—something happens to you?" That way, you can understand the CEO's thinking and the confidence the entrepreneur has in the company's employees. And, if for some reason the CEO was incapacitated, you may want to understand how developed the management team is. For example, can the company develop from within the required middle-management people to carry out the business plan? What strategy does the group use to fill key positions? Do they use outside consultants or headhunters? What is the past experience of the company in filling key jobs?

How Are People Compensated?

For many years, sociologists and psychologists have been studying employees of large and small companies. They have determined that people work for companies for many reasons and that money is only one of the reasons. People look for many ancillary benefits when they work for a company, from the ambience of the offices to the camaraderie of the personnel. Each of these factors has some effect on how hard people work and how much they enjoy their jobs. Compensation in its broadest sense involves all of the rewards people receive in a work environment. Compensation as we know it is primarily the money and other material benefits received by employees for performing their duties. Ask yourself: Is the current compensation system for key executives designed to retain them and attract others to the company? Are these compensation levels in line with the industry norms?

Employee Compensation

Another part of the due diligence process consists of asking for a complete list of the payroll and W-2s for the preceding year. This will show you how much people are being paid and will also single out those who are being paid a great deal. You will want to find out why they are being paid so much. In addition, you should determine what kind of wage increases have occurred over the past years. If pay has risen dramatically in recent years, you will want to know why. If wages increase quickly, employees may expect salaries to continue increasing rapidly over the next few years. If the company is going to leverage itself with high debt or spend an additional amount of money in a new area, it may not have the cash to give employees the kind of raise that they have been expecting. As a result, employee morale may slump, and employees may not make the contribution to the company's progress that is needed to make the company a winner.

COMPENSATION SYSTEM

The compensation system that a company sets up for its employees is all-important. It must reward people for performance. You should study it to see how well it achieves this objective. Usually, one starts with written procedures for determining beginning salaries, raises, promotions, and dismissals. If the company has no written procedures, spend time with the management team asking questions about their procedures for determining these changes in employee status.

It is quite important for a small company to implement (early in its life cycle) a compensation scheme that rewards not only the top management team but all employees for their good work. The company should have an entrepreneurial spirit at the top and at the bottom. An employee at the bottom who makes an extra contribution to the company's growth and well-being should be rewarded. When these types of incentives are installed in a company, performance among the work force is more likely to improve. Some people don't work for money alone; however, money is a good motivating force for most people. In addition, it is a tool by which many people, both entrepreneurs and workers, measure themselves against other people. An hourly worker who makes 10 percent more than another will gain status and recognition among that worker's peers.

As part of the due diligence, you should determine the average salary of hourly wage employees, supervisors, and officers. Determine whether employees of this company are paid less than the norm for the area and for the competition. The less mobile, nonsupervisory personnel must have salary parity with others in their category in the same geographic area if the company is to keep its trained work force. Training an hourly worker is not cheap, and once an hourly worker has a skill that is marketable at an amount above the compensation the worker is receiving, the temptation to make another dollar per hour is usually more than the worker can resist. So compensation at the lower end must be on parity with the local organizations.

The pay rate of supervisors and management must also be commensurate with people in the same field in the general region and perhaps, for upper-level management, in the nation. Although management has become less mobile over the years, anyone who can get a 20–30 percent increase in salary would be a prime candidate for a headhunter or someone else wanting that manager to move to a different city. Good management is hard to find. Management that works long hours and achieves for the good of the company is even harder to find. Those managers who achieve for the company need to have "golden handcuffs" to prevent them from leaving the corporation.

There are myriad methods of compensating both management and supervisors. One of the most effective is a large salary, but there are others, such as pension and profit-sharing plans, retirement plans, stock options, time off with pay, and other perks that would give an individual a reason to stay with the company.

It's very hard for a small company to compensate management at the same rate that larger businesses can. However, small businesses have the tremendous advantage of being able to reward good management with a piece of the pie in the form of stock options. Direct ownership in the company is one of the strongest motivators and one of the best golden handcuffs that can be used in any small business. Part ownership in the company gives the manager an opportunity to make money if the company does well. In a small company, there is a direct correlation between the output of the general management team and

the success of the business. Any manager with an entrepreneurial spirit knows that a manager can make a significant
amount of money from the stock options if the manager does a
good job. As an investor, you should make sure that the key
managers, as well as those workers below the key managers,
have adequate incentive to stay with the company and make it
a success. If the compensation system of the company is not
adequate and doesn't look as though it's going to be changed,
one should probably not put money in the company. The compensation system is a key component of every company.

PENSION PLAN

In investigating a company, you should also review the pension plan. You should obtain a copy of the pension plan to
make sure it is adequate. In addition, you should determine
whether the plan has been fully funded for the past few years.
If the company has an unfunded liability to the pension plan,
this is like a debt owed to any other institution and could have
a direct impact on the cash flow of the company. A company
that is barely breaking even and has a huge unfunded pension
liability is a candidate for bankruptcy. At a minimum, it would
take a great deal of earnings to come out of this problem, and
future earnings would go to contributions to the pension plan,
rather than to building up the company's assets. In investigating the pension plan, find out who handles the pension side of
the business and whether it is fully funded.

Pension and profit-sharing plans are covered by the
Employee Retired Income Security Act (ERISA) under the
jurisdiction of the Department of Labor. You should ask the
expert who handles the pension and profit-sharing plan
whether he or she is aware of any ERISA violations. If the
plan needs to be updated, you should know when that is going
to happen. In addition to reviewing the ERISA plan, you
should determine what the contributions have been for the
last five years. This may give you an insight into the company's ability to generate cash. It also may show you, if the
contributions have been small, that the team running the

business now feels that it is getting a raw deal because its pension plan is not being funded.

Sometimes in reviewing pension and profit-sharing plans, you are suddenly greeted with a surprise. You may find that the company has overfunded its pension plan and that the company can take some money out of the plan for corporate purposes. This is a very exciting moment in the due diligence process; to find an overfunded pension plan is to find a hidden asset.

PROFIT-SHARING PLAN

If the company has a profit-sharing plan, obtain a copy of it and determine the formula for making contributions. A profit-sharing plan is a significant part of compensation in any company. If the company does well, a contribution is made to the profit-sharing plan, and all employees share in it. Nothing could be simpler in tying an individual's interests directly to those of the company. In reviewing the profit-sharing plan, find out whether all the contributions have been made for the past few years. If they haven't, find out why not. This may be another liability because the company must make contributions to the profit-sharing plan. You should determine what contributions have been made to the profit-sharing plan have been over the past five years.

In addition, ask whether the profit-sharing plan can be terminated or amended at any time. The plan may have been set up by a retiring management team and, thus, may have been designed to take the maximum amount of cash out of the company. Unless the profit-sharing plan is changed, some of the cash that may be needed to build the company will have to be set aside for profit sharing. It may be necessary to change the plan.

BONUS PLAN

Early in the investigation of compensation, one should determine whether the company has a bonus plan and, if so, how it is computed. Many companies have a Christmas bonus plan that offers employees goods, services, or actual cash. More often, the company's bonus plan for employees is based on its profits. If a performance-type bonus plan exists, you should obtain a copy and make sure you understand how it works. Again, a bonus plan that is based on the profits of the company, in which an individual receives a big bonus if the company does well, is a great plan because it directly rewards people who have made the company successful. It is central to every business operation. On the other hand, if the bonus plan rewards top management with outrageous amounts of money, it is a bad plan.

Sometimes an entrepreneur will set his or her sights on large bonuses. In the early years, as an investor, you should discourage top management that owns a large percentage of the company from taking large bonuses. The fact is that investors want to stimulate management's interest in making the stock worth a great deal, rather than taking cash out of the company. As an investor, you own stock in the company but do not get a bonus. Investors want the entrepreneur to be on the same footing and to be working for the company in a way that will build up the worth of the stock, as opposed to the size of the entrepreneur's bonus. For those individuals who depend on the company but who do not have large stock ownership, a bonus plan is definitely in order. In virtually every investment agreement, compensation is discussed in detail and is limited for those who have large stock holdings; for those who don't have large stock holdings, a strong incentive program is set up.

STOCK OPTION PLAN

Many companies have set up stock option plans to reward employees, especially key employees. If the company has a stock option plan, get a copy of it and determine whether the plan is effective in holding key employees. See how many options are available, how many have been awarded, and how people feel about the plan.

Other equity incentives available as rewards include "phantom stock option plans," in which stock is never really issued but management gets a bonus on the basis of how well the company's stock performs. These are most often used in large public companies, and as we have seen in many cases, this is not a very effective plan because some unethical managers will do just about anything to inflate its company stock price (look up some of the most recent companies in the headlines, if you need more clarity). It is more effective to reward managers based on hard numbers.

Stock incentives and stock options are some of the most important reward systems any small business can establish. You should make sure you understand how the small business you are reviewing is using its stock ownership plan to reward employees. What vesting policy does the company have? What happens to the option when the employee leaves? What happens to the stock that the employee has gained under the stock option plan if the employee leaves? If the company has the right to purchase the stock back, what price does the company use to repurchase the stock?

Sometimes companies become involved in stock ownership plans on the theory that employees who own a tiny bit of the company will feel like owners. Usually this is a myth, and management should pay no attention to it. Management should shut down the stock option plan for those employees further down the ladder and should institute a good profit bonus plan. This has much more effect than a stock option plan for employees who want to own a little bit of the company.

OTHER BENEFITS

Other benefits are also used to hire and retain employees. One entrepreneur was asked how he was able to hire a top engineer away from a major computer company. The entrepreneur explained that the engineer would not even take his telephone calls until he asked the engineer's secretary to put a note in front of the engineer with only two words on it: Laguna Beach. The big computer company had stationed the engineer in upstate New York, whereas the entrepreneur's company could offer to transfer him to its headquarters in Laguna Beach.

Look at the company you are investigating to see what other reasons might be used to hire and retain top employees.

WHAT EMPLOYMENT CONTRACTS EXIST?

In every medium-sized and large company, employment contracts exist between the top management team and the company it is running. Smaller companies usually do not use employment contracts. These contracts are becoming more commonplace as top managers try to make sure that the company treats them fairly and the company tries to make sure that the employees know what is expected of them. As an investigator of a company, you need to review all employment contracts.

EMPLOYMENT CONTRACTS AND SPECIAL COMPENSATION ARRANGEMENTS

Employment contracts can be extremely detrimental to companies. Some years ago, an investor tried to sell a company in which the president had a 10-year irrevocable employment contract that based his salary on his performance. The formula turned out to be ludicrous, and the company found it was paying most of its profits to the president. No one wanted to buy the company with such an onerous contract in place. Employment contracts that cannot be amended or changed under certain circumstances can spell disaster.

When you are investing in a company, make sure you understand the employment contracts for all individuals. In recent years, these termination agreements, sometimes called "golden parachutes," have provided ridiculously high payments to top management, regardless of the reason for their termination. Sometimes the agreements are negotiated when a person is hired; most often, they are put into place when the company becomes very profitable.

Employment contracts and termination agreements can also work to the disadvantage of the employee. Two young men once spent three years as virtual slaves because they had signed employment contracts that said they would have to give all their time and attention to the company's efforts as long as they were paid a specific salary. A new owner bought the company and made these two young men perform the most incredible jobs. They were threatened with lawsuits if they didn't comply. As a result, they wasted years of their lives doing things that most of us wouldn't do.

NONCOMPETE AGREEMENTS

Noncompete contracts are usually signed by key employees and those with special knowledge about the company. These agreements make it illegal for employees to leave the employment of the company and work for a competitor or to start up their own companies. The employee is thereby precluded from competing directly with the company.

However, in recent years, noncompete contracts have been voided by many state and federal courts on the grounds that an individual cannot be precluded from being gainfully employed. As a result, most noncompete contracts are good only in the city in which they are signed; an employee can go to another city and be gainfully employed, thus becoming a direct competitor with the company.

NONDISCLOSURE CONTRACTS

To avoid having a noncompete contract voided by the courts, many employers make their employees sign a nondisclosure contract. This means that the employee will not disclose proprietary information about the company to the new employer. Although the employee may go to work for another organization in another town, according to the nondisclosure contract, the employee will not use proprietary information to aid the new employer. Where possible, an investor should review both the noncompete and the nondisclosure contracts to see whether they have any teeth in them. Otherwise, you might find yourself with the entire sales team leaving one afternoon, joining a competing company down the street and destroying the company you have invested in.

WHAT IS THE WORK FORCE STRUCTURE?

The structure of a work force can determine how well the company operates. If the work force is primarily a blue-collar union work force, the company will be quite different from a white-collar nonunion company. You need to understand the structure of the work force.

UNIONS

Does the company have a union that represents the employees? If so, what is the name of the union? Who controls the membership, the national or the local union? How long has the union been in place? How many employees are covered? When does the contract expire? Describe the terms of the contract, including (a) escalation clauses, (b) regular rate increases, (c) promotions, (d) retirements, (e) production requirements, (f) hiring, (g) firing, (h) hours worked per week, and (i) other benefits. Get the name of the union head so you can talk to that person.

List the grievances filed and the arbitration awards that have occurred during the last five years. Are labor contract problems anticipated for the next time the contract arises? Are significant increases anticipated for the contracts as they come due?

Have there been labor strikes during the past 10 years? If so, give the date of the strike, the union involved, the duration of the strike, the cause of the strike, and the settlement involved in resolving the strike.

If the company does not have a union, has there been union activity in the past? Is there a pending election?

Like everything else in this world, there are good unions and bad ones. Some unions are bureaucratic and unchanging, whereas others are flexible and progressive. You need to understand the type of union that controls the work force at the company.

WORK STOPPAGE

It is important to determine whether the company has had a work stoppage of any kind. If the company has had strikes, find out why and get all the details, as mentioned above. It is also important to know whether work stoppages or work slowdowns have been due to equipment failure, inventory shortages, or other reasons during the past three or four years. Any work stoppage is serious, and it will tell you what operating problems the company is having.

TRAINING PROGRAM

Does the company have a formal training program for its employees? If it does, obtain a copy of the teaching materials and review them. If there is no formal program, describe the procedure for training new employees and for transferring employees. Every company should have a training program for bringing new skills into the company.

Determine who is responsible for ensuring that the company has well-trained employees. Spend time discussing employee training with this person. Determine how much money is spent on training each year, broken down by departments, if possible.

Determine whether any cross-training has occurred, that is, whether people have been trained to do different jobs so that if an employee is absent, someone else can step into that job.

MORALE OF THE WORK FORCE

What effort is expended by the company in trying to determine the morale and attitude of its employees? Has a consultant ever come in and discussed attitude and morale? Do employees believe in giving the company an honest day's work or do they try to do as little as possible for the company?

WHAT PERSONNEL RECORDS ARE MAINTAINED?

Most companies maintain personnel records regarding wages. However, quite often small companies keep poor personnel records. If there are personnel records, you should go through them to evaluate the way the company handles its personnel and its record keeping.

MAINTAINING INTERNAL RECORDS

Hiring and firing of employees is an important process, but keeping up with them while they are in the company and determining how well they are performing is also important. You should review the records created for hiring employees, as well as for evaluating, transferring, promoting, and demoting them; changing compensation; reprimanding them or taking disciplinary action; and for training, absenteeism, tardiness, and any terminations.

In today's litigious society, you should determine what procedures have been laid down by the company for building legitimate cases for employee termination. In addition, you should find out what requirements the union has imposed on the hiring and firing of employees. One good method of reviewing this area is to obtain a copy of each form used to monitor employees, and if possible, review several actual employee files to see how well they are maintained.

PAYROLL RECORDS

As a check on the other information you've been gathering about employees, obtain a copy of the weekly or monthly payroll records for all employees, both full- and part-time. Also get a copy of the annual salaries that were reported on the employees' W-2 forms for the previous year. This kind of information can give you an overall view of the general payroll and employment practices of the company. Divide the employees by their departments to see which departments have the most people expenses. It may be that you will determine an imbalance in one department or another, or a shortage in one department that is critical to the company. This can be an illuminating exercise.

EMPLOYEE BOOKS AND MANUALS

You should determine whether the company has a corporate policy handbook for employees. Usually it is a book that is given to each new employee to acquaint him or her with the company. If one exists, obtain a copy and read it. Also determine whether the company has an employee benefit handbook. If it does, get a copy and read it to see what benefits the company tells its employees they have.

Determine whether the company has a Standard Operating Procedures Manual for the various departments or job functions. If it does, obtain a copy of each one of the department manuals.

REPORTS FROM THE PERSONNEL DEPARTMENT

Get a copy of the reports the personnel department directs to other areas of the company and assess their value. Some memorandums and reports will give you an insight into the way the personnel department works.

In addition, determine what reports are generated from outside the personnel department and given to the personnel people, and see what they do with them. Assess the value of these reports.

HIRING PROCEDURES

Bringing in a new employee to a company is a serious step. Every time a new employee comes into the company, he or she brings a new set of values and goals. It is critical that the people hired strengthen the company's goals and aspirations. You should review in detail the procedures used for soliciting, interviewing, screening, evaluating, and conducting reference calls and credit checks in the hiring of new management personnel, as well as other employees. Determine what techniques are used in hiring people. A lie detector test? A written examination? Do industrial psychologists evaluate employees? How does the company screen candidates and determine who will best fit into the company?

MOTIVATING EMPLOYEES

In this section you are trying to determine what specific methods or techniques the personnel department has applied to motivate the employees. What motivation techniques does the company use, other than compensation?

PERSONNEL FILES OF MANAGEMENT

Quite often, the personnel files on management are kept in a different area and perhaps under the control of a different group. One of the things you should do as an investigator is review the personnel files of all the officers, directors, and department heads, as well as some of the supervisors, to determine what kind of people are running the company.

EMPLOYEE LITIGATION

In any organization with a substantial number of employees, an employee now and then files a lawsuit against the company. Get a copy of the litigation and determine what kind of accusations have been made. Determine whether there are any actions threatened or pending. How serious are the actions, and do they give any indication of how the company is operated?

REGULATORY AGENCIES

Numerous local, state, and federal agencies regulate the way employees are to be treated and how they are to be paid. The questions you must answer are: Has the company experienced any regulatory problems from these agencies in the last two or three years? Have any complaints been filed? If so, find out what they are. This may also give you an insight into the company's employee practices. In addition to the normal employment agencies, there are other agencies that regulate an employee's relationship with the firm. There are safety and health regulations, consumer product safety regulations, and environmental regulations pertaining to air, water, waste treatment, and land. Are there any actions threatened or pending? Have there been any actions along these lines during the last two or three years? If there have been any such actions, get as much information on them as possible to see whether they might create a problem in the future.

Obtain a summary of the company's rating for unemployment and worker's compensation. If the company has very large claims in this area, they will be a giveaway on how it treats its work force.

PERSONNEL CONSULTANTS

Sometimes a small business will hire a personnel consultant. Determine whether the company has hired an outside personnel consultant during the past two or three years. Get the consultant's name, address, and telephone number, and talk to him or her. Find out what problems the consultant was called in to solve and whether they were actually solved.

OTHER EMPLOYEE BENEFITS

Indirect benefits to employees are also of interest. You should describe the vacation and holiday policies, as well as the leave policies available to top management. You should understand the policies relating to travel and entertainment expense. Sometimes corporations are quite generous with travel and entertainment expenses, and an employee is permitted to buy all kinds of things on expense accounts. After all, historians will remember, George Washington accepted no pay in his leadership of the Continental Army. He asked that the Continental Congress pay only his expenses. Well, his expense account is a classic. He ran the expenses of feeding the Continental Army through his personal expense account. This included clothing, guns, and other necessities, such as food and military paraphernalia needed to fight the British.

Does the company pay for automobiles, airplanes, limousines, and boats? These kinds of off-the-balance-sheet perks can be enormously rewarding to management and can also be draining on the culture and income sheet of the company. One astute manager of a billion-dollar fund said he never, ever invested in a company that had a corporate airplane.

HEALTH INSURANCE

One of the largest line items on a major corporation's profit-and-loss statements is health insurance. General Motors pays more for health insurance than it does for any other single line item on its profit-and-loss statement, even more than it pays for steel and metal. You should review the medical and life insurance cost for the company. It may be that the company's health and life insurance costs are out of line with the norm in the industry.

SUMMARY

Hiring and retaining good employees is of paramount importance to the growth of any company. A company that doesn't hire the best will ultimately be unable to compete. A company that does not fire employees who are not performing well will ultimately have troubles. This has happened in many a small business that let "dear old Uncle Joe" or perhaps a spouse handle the financial records. Because of the family relationship, that person cannot be replaced, and no one can be hired over them. If this individual is not capable of doing the job, the company may suffer. This kind of favoritism will ultimately hurt the company and hurt your investment.

Another thing you should think about after you have gone through the personnel department and understand it thoroughly is whether you would like to work for this company. Is there some place in the company that you would like to work? Does it seem to be a pleasant place? Does it have the *esprit de corps* of a winning company? Is it an exciting and dynamic company in which employees are motivated to do their best? You need to concentrate on this item in order to come to a final judgment on the personnel area.

MAJOR STRENGTHS AND WEAKNESSES

You should determine the five major strengths the company has with regard to personnel. You should write these points down for future reference. In addition, you should identify its five major weaknesses in the personnel area, and you should confront management with these weaknesses to see how they plan to deal with them. If they don't have a solution, it may not be a good company to put money into.

When you are reviewing the company for its strengths and weaknesses, try to determine how the company must change or upgrade its benefits programs or its salaries to be on par with the competition and to be in a position where it can adequately compensate those people who are going to be needed to make the company go. It is extremely important that you understand what needs to be done to a company's compensation system before you invest.

RATIO ANALYSIS

A number of ratios in the personnel area can give you a good feeling of what is going on inside the company. These ratios can be calculated over time by using prior financial statements. Those for the future can be computed by using projections to determine what is happening with the company. These ratios will indicate how the company has performed historically and what it might be expected to do in the future.

- Calculate the **average salary** over time by dividing the total payroll by the total number of employees. This will tell you whether average pay has gone up or down per employee over a given period of time. If salaries are going up, can the company maintain its growth and have salaries increase at the same rate?

- Calculate the **average sales per employee by division,** such as the sales division or the production division. This ratio will show you which divisions have high labor costs. Calculate this by dividing total payroll expense for that division by the number of employees in that division.

- Calculate the **total payroll as a percentage of sales** by dividing total payroll and benefits by net sales. This can show you whether labor costs are going up, relative to sales. Over time, this ratio is a good gauge of an inflated work force.
- Calculate the **benefits as a percentage of payroll** by dividing benefits by total payroll. This will tell you whether benefits are going up as a percentage of payroll and whether the company is spending more than it should on benefits.
- Calculate the **employee turnover** by dividing the total number of employees who left in a year by the average number of employees. This will measure the stability of the work force and perhaps even reflect employee satisfaction. It is quite common in the fast-food industry to have a 100 percent turnover of employees in a year, but in other companies with a highly professional work force, the turnover is extremely low.
- Calculate the **sales per employee** by dividing net sales by the number of employees. This will give you a measure of the efficiency of the company. If, as the company goes forward, it has fewer sales for the number of employees, this will be a sign that the company is not getting as much out of its total labor force in terms of sales as it should. This could be a key indicator of inefficiency.

CHECKLIST

The checklist in Appendix A contains a number of questions to help you gain information about the personnel area. Pay special attention to the section on documentation. You should follow it in collecting information on all aspects of personnel.

4 Analysis of Marketing and Sales

Before you start with your due diligence on the marketing and sales functions, it's best to know the cast of characters who will be carrying out the marketing plan. This approach to the marketing area—to look at the people first—is a carryover from the investigation of people set out in Chapters 2 and 3. If there are some marketing people you haven't interviewed, do so as part of this section.

Marketing is a critical aspect of any company. Marketing-driven companies are usually high-growth companies. You should be trying to determine whether this company is market-driven. There are the people who set up the marketing plan and have a marketing strategy, and there are those who sell the product or service. We are working with both of these functions in this section. Both are critical to the success of the company in generating revenue.

Who Are the People Who Market and Sell?

The people who sell the product may run the gamut from someone selling directly for the company to an outside sales representative. All of these people help to move the product to the consumer. It is important to understand who these people are and how they sell. The people who determine the marketing direction are usually the senior executives in the company. This may be the president, or there may be an executive vice president of marketing. If there is a large sales force, there may be a vice president of sales. Each has his or her own area of expertise, and each should have strong input into the strategy to generate revenue for the business.

PERSONNEL

Study each of the key marketing people to determine what mental assets they bring to the company, what kind of experience they have in marketing this kind of product, and what knowledge they have of this particular industry. Without skilled marketing people, there is little chance that a product can make it. As mentioned in Chapter 1, you have probably heard the saying, "If a man can...make a better mousetrap than his neighbor... the world will make a beaten a path to his door." Nothing could be further from the truth. It should really be re-written as, "If you build a good marketing group, it will beat a path to the customer's door." Developing the strategy to market a product is key to the success of the entire business.

Once the strategy is set, the salespeople take over. With very few exceptions, products and services are sold, not purchased. It is the salespersons of the company who must convince the purchasers to buy. Therefore, you must perform exceptional due diligence on the personnel responsible for selling. This detailed analysis should follow the guidelines set out in Chapters 2 and 3.

SALESPERSON ANALYSIS

You should obtain a short resume for each of the salespeople. If there are too many salespeople, resumes for the top 10 will do. You should review the resumes and look for a pattern. Meet some of the salespersons and discuss how they sell the product. It is important to get to know the sales force and try to understand how they view the marketplace.

To assess the abilities of the salesperson, you should have a list of them and their dollar volume of sales for the last three years. In addition, find out what management expects them to sell in the future. Does this expectation exceed what the salesperson themselves are saying? This is an important point, because if management is setting quotas that the sales force cannot meet, management is probably being unreasonably optimistic. You are trying to understand all the aspects of a sale in order to judge the reasonableness of the sales projections being made by management.

OUTSIDE REPRESENTATIVES

Many companies do not have a direct sales force, or they may have a small sales force that calls on representatives or distributors. If this is the case, you need to find out who these outside representatives and distributors are. You need a list of these representatives by dollar volume sold and by unit volume sold for each product. You will need the names, addresses, and telephone numbers of these outside representatives so that you may call them and talk to them about the product. See Chapter 7 for the types of questions to ask manufacturing representatives.

MOTIVATION

Describe in some detail the technique and methods used by the marketing department to motivate its salespersons and the representatives of the company. Is monetary reward the only motivation? Or does the marketing department use other items to motivate employees and representatives? It is critical to find out what will make employees and representatives of the company sell more of the product. Motivation should not be treated lightly.

Once you understand the motivation being used, ask yourself whether this motivation is sufficient to sell the product. How does it compare with the industry or the competition? Do the salespeople feel sufficiently motivated? You are trying to determine whether the sales projections can be met. If you find the motivation of the employees quite low, you might begin to think that the sales projections being made by management cannot be met.

TERMINATIONS OF EMPLOYEES

Make a list of the salespersons or other representatives who have been terminated during the past three years. You will want to know how long they were with the company and the reasons they left. Frequently, you can get the names and telephone numbers of past salespersons and representatives to ask why they left or why they were terminated. Needless to say, some terminated employees may have an axe to grind, and they may tell you things that are untrue. On the other hand, they may give you some insight into the company that will not come through from loyal employees. It behooves you to track down several of these people and make sure you understand why they left.

WHAT ARE THEY SELLING?

The age-old question that every company asks itself is, What are you selling? This may seem obvious in a product-oriented company, but after some analysis you may determine that the product is not the only thing the company is selling. It may be selling service, a new idea, or a whole new approach to a problem. There are many items to be sold in addition to the product. Be sure you understand what the company is selling.

PRODUCTS

The best way to begin analyzing the marketing side of the business is to identify the products or services being sold by the company. List the products by category, and within each category make a specific list. This specific list should include the dollar volume in sales of each product and the number of units sold for earlier periods. You might consider going back three years in determining units and dollar volume. In addition, you need the same information for each of the products that are projected in the future, that is, the number of units to be sold in the following five years and the dollar volume for those units.

This will be discussed in greater detail in both the production section and the financial section, but for now remember that the marketing people should know their gross margin on each product. Beside each product, put down the percentage gross margin that the company will have, as indicated by the marketing people. It is important to check this with the information you get from others. Marketing people are normally optimistic on both gross sales and gross profit. When it comes to cutting prices and making the sale, the marketing people are most likely to cut the price and reduce the gross margin in order to make the sale. They do this because they are usually being paid on a percentage of gross sales and not on gross profit.

PRODUCT DESCRIPTIONS

Within each of the product categories (or, if the product list is not too long, each of the products), describe the product in detail and emphasize its distinguishing features. For each of the products, ask the basic question, What benefits will the user derive from this product or service? What makes this product or service different from the competitor's? These are key questions that you will spend more time on later, when we discuss the consumer.

SEASONALITY OF PRODUCTS

Each of the products should be analyzed as to seasonality. In both the historical data and the projections, one may be able to see evidence of demand seasonality. Seasonality is common in most industries, and if severe, it can be disastrous to the cash flow of a company. Obviously, a candy maker will have tremendous seasonality, particularly around Halloween and to some extent Christmas and Easter. You should look for the seasonality of the product to make sure you understand how it's being sold and what it does to cash flow.

PRODUCT LITERATURE

Also collect all the sales literature and sales brochures you can find on each of the products. This will help you become familiar with the product and the claims being made by the company concerning product quality or performance. You should also obtain a price list outlining what the company is charging for its products or services. Sometimes price lists are called by a different name. For example, in the radio and TV business, they're called *rate cards*. This tells you how much an advertising "spot" will cost on radio or TV.

PRODUCT DEVELOPMENT

What new products are being discussed by the marketing department? How is it planning to implement these new products? When does the staff think they might be available? What marketing studies have been completed to validate the new product? What marketing studies were completed for the existing products? Get a copy of each marketing study.

What product would the marketing department introduce into the market next if it had sufficient funding? Is the next product a "missing product," that is, one that is needed to fill out the product line? If so, ask the marketing department to describe this new product.

WHO BUYS THE PRODUCT OR SERVICE?

The customer has been studied extensively in business research. The marketing department should know its customers inside and out. It's important to understand who the customer is. Sometimes you will be surprised. For example, although men are the consumers of men's underwear, most often it is the wife who buys the man's underwear. Thus, the customer of the product is not the man who wears it but the woman who buys it for him. Many surveys have shown that some men wear only what their wives have told them to wear and that the wives have purchased it for them. That is why advertisements for underwear show the "Mr. Macho" male model. Every company should know who buys its product or service, and your research should confirm what management tells you.

CUSTOMERS

Now that you are acquainted with the product or service and how it's sold, you want to understand the customers. First, get a complete list of the customers, if possible. By all means, get a list of the 10 largest customers. You will want to make a list of the customers by sales volume and unit volume in order to understand which customers are buying the most units and represent the highest dollar value. The marketing management should have this list on hand. If it is a retail business, ask management to prepare a customer survey. You should know the demographics of the retail customer and who the product target is.

CONTRACTS WITH SPECIAL CUSTOMERS

You need to determine whether there are special arrangements with major customers. In some instances, the company will not sell its product outright but merely places it on consignment. Consignment is very popular in many businesses, such as clothing. Although the retail store "purchases" the product from the manufacturer, the contract may allow the store to return the merchandise for full or partial credit. Sometimes, to get a major account, a manufacturer will produce enough goods so that it can place them on consignment with the retail outlet. This places a tremendous burden on the manufacturing outlet because it must carry in its inventory the investment that is normally carried by the retail outlet.

You should get copies of any contracts between the company and its customers. If there are no contracts, get a detailed explanation of the relationship between the seller and customer.

A dress manufacturer we investigated once had tremendous sales, and each year at the New York City show, buyers
would come to New York to look at the new line. Orders would
be taken during a relatively short time each season. What we
didn't realize was that after all of the bookings were placed in
the company and the products were shipped, the company
still had not "sold" the merchandise. We had to wait until the
end of the season to see whether those clothes had actually
been sold by the retailer. If they hadn't been sold, the contract
between the manufacturer and the retailer allowed the retailer
to return the merchandise and get back 80 percent of what the
retailer had paid the manufacturer for them. In essence, there
was a huge contingent liability not recorded on the balance
sheet of the manufacturing company, and it was one that did
not go away for approximately six months. The frightening
thing was that if the dress manufacturer happened to produce
a whole line of "doggy rags," the company could become bankrupt. The company risked the entire operation every six
months. Make sure you know when a sale is a final sale.

LOSS OF CUSTOMERS

You should determine how many customers have been lost
during the last two years, and if any major customers have
been lost, you should get their names, addresses, and telephone numbers so that you may later contact them. In addition, you should ask the company why it lost those customers
and whether there is any opportunity to regain them.

Venture capitalists studying a small computer printer company learned from the marketing department that the company had lost several good customers. Upon contacting one of
the customers, the VC found that the printer product they had
been shipped had numerous problems. The printer had to be
returned many times, the input device did not work properly,
and the computer program itself had several "bugs." When the
VC confronted management with these problems, it maintained that this was unusual and that all problems had been
corrected. However, upon further analysis, the VC found

return slips from numerous other customers and realized that the computer system did not work. If it hadn't been for the one or two customers that had been lost by the company, the VC probably would not have uncovered all the other problems regarding their printer problems.

CUSTOMER COMPLAINTS

List the five most common complaints received from customers regarding the product or service. It is necessary to discover what customers are complaining about. Some may be minor problems and may be fairly random in nature, but if you see a pattern of complaints about the product, this shows a vulnerable point that the competition can jump on. It may also indicate why people aren't buying the product.

List the five most serious or costly complaints received from customers regarding the product or service. Here you are not worried about why people are complaining but what it is costing the company to overcome these complaints. It's important to know how much the company is spending to handle complaints. One such company had very strong sales for the first two years; however, it was spending an inordinate amount of money fixing the product so that it would meet its advertised attributes. This was a costly method of handling customer complaints. Ultimately, it dragged the company into bankruptcy.

You should determine who handles company complaints and how they formulate a strategy for handling such complaints. For example, is the customer always right, or does the company spend time and money proving the customer is wrong and that the product is okay? A skeptical or negative attitude toward all customer complaints is going to lose the company sales in the long run. Research has determined that a customer will spread the word of a bad experience with a product to fourteen other people, whereas a good experience with a product will only be related to three other people. This means that the company must hustle to avoid too many complaints in the marketplace. Ask the marketing people whether there is a set procedure for handling complaints. Is there a written description of how complaints are to be handled? If so, obtain a copy and find out how the company handles its complaints.

Is there a monthly or cumulative list of complaints? Are the complaints logged in so someone can follow them? There is one very large hotel company that mails all complaints to the chairman of the board. Some afternoons, the chairman of the board can be seen opening complaints and reading them. It's a very effective method. Every employee knows that all the complaints go to the chairman and that someone in full authority is reading them. This encourages employees to handle customers in an exemplary fashion.

ORDER BACKLOG

It's extremely important to determine the present backlog for each of the customers and for each of the products. This will give you a quick overview of where the company stands with its customers and products. For purposes of comparison, you should try to determine the company's backlog at the end of the last two years. This will enable you to see whether the backlog is actually building or whether the company is eating into its backlog and is not able to replace it.

It's also important to determine when the backlog can be produced and shipped so that it can be turned into an account receivable or cash. For each product, list the backlog and see when it is to be delivered and how many dollars are involved in the shipment. For example, you might list the current backlog by product, then look at the backlog for three months, up to six months, up to nine months, and up to twelve months or more. Within each of those categories you would look at the dollar volume for each of the products. If some of the products go into the distant future, you may want to discount the likelihood that they will ever be delivered. By aging the backlog, you can get a quick idea of how likely the company is to produce profits in the near term. If it has a tremendous backlog but most of it is not deliverable for over a year, you might start asking yourself what the company is going to do for the next

12 months. Verifying the backlog can be very important, especially if there is a large current backlog.

CUSTOMER CREDIT APPROVAL

One of the most critical elements of any business's selling program is the extension of credit to customers. This can facilitate sales but it can also be a disaster if customers don't pay.
You need to understand the credit facility in detail. Who establishes the credit limit for the customers? What is the credit
approval process? How do they go about determining whether
a customer is creditworthy? Do they run credit reports? What
special credit arrangements do they have with certain customers? Do they extend credit longer to some customers than to
others, and if so, why?

To understand the marketing department, you must understand how the company determines which customers qualify
for credit. If setting credit lines were left entirely up to the marketing department, almost everyone would get credit. After all,
the marketing people are paid on the basis of sales, rather than
on collections. If you are paid by sales, you want to extend
credit to the world so that everybody will buy the product.

CUSTOMER'S CREDIT TERMS

In understanding the credit terms given to customers, you
should try to understand what role the marketing department
has in collecting the accounts receivable. If intimately
involved with the credit collection and paid accordingly, it's
highly unlikely that it is going to extend credit indiscrimi-
nately. Nonetheless, you should establish the normal terms of
a sale and exactly how the marketing department fits into the
overall scheme of setting credit limits and collecting from
credit customers.

DISPUTED INVOICES

Determine whether there are any sales invoices with material
disputes. It is important to know why they're in dispute, and if
necessary, you may want to call the customers and discuss

why they are not paying their bills. That call may give you tremendous insight into the business. On the other hand, you may just end up talking to a deadbeat who should not have been shipped product on credit.

WHAT IS SAID TO THE CUSTOMER?

Public relations runs the gamut from the spunky ads we all watch on TV to the industrial manuals that are given to potential consumers of industrial products. Communicating with the outside world is a delicate part of the process of selling the product. It's important to understand what is being said to the customers about this product and this company.

PUBLIC RELATIONS

In general, all information about the company comes under the heading of public relations. What articles have been written about the company? What research has been done by industry analysts? Has the company or any of its competition been mentioned in any studies of the industry? All of these types of information should be gathered. Usually the company gathers articles that are flattering and will hand these out. The company doesn't give out the ones that aren't flattering. If possible, ask for the company's public relations file and go through it to see all articles that mention the company.

ADVERTISING

Some small companies don't have advertising or public relations agencies, but most large companies do. *Advertising agency* here means someone hired by the company to promote its product. You should obtain the name, address, and telephone number of the agency and the names of the individuals who work on the company's account. You will later want to call them and discuss in detail their relationship with the company.

FORMAL ADVERTISING PROGRAM

The company should be able to outline its formal advertising program and explain how it intends to inform the consuming public about its products or services. A fairly detailed media plan should be used to disseminate this information. It is important that the company gains recognition in the marketplace, and the advertising agency is supposed to be instrumental in gaining this recognition. If it has media samples, get copies of the print advertisements and be sure to listen to and watch the radio and television ads.

ADVERTISING BUDGET

You should determine what the advertising budget has been for the last three years. You should also determine what the company intends to spend for the current year and its projected advertising budget for the next five years. In addition to finding out how much money will be spent, you should try to learn what the money has been spent on in the past and what the money is earmarked for in the future.

One company once wanted $10 million (a nice round number). When asked what the company was planning to spend this amount on, the reply was "advertising." When pressed even further as to what it intended to spend the ad dollars on, the company representative said it would all be spent on TV advertisements. Needless to say, this seemed to be a fairly reckless approach to promoting the company's product, because TV is not the best medium through which to advertise all products, especially those of an industrial nature. You must understand in detail the advertising program being put forth by the company so that you can determine whether it is spending the money wisely.

QUESTIONS FOR THE ADVERTISING PEOPLE

When you talk to the people at the advertising or public relations agency that works for the company, you will want to ask some specific questions. First, find out how long it has been the company agency. If it's only been a short time, then obviously you are going to have to find out the name of the previous agency and why a switch was made.

In addition, you should determine how often the company advertises. Perhaps it has been rather spotty, and the advertising people may be able to explain why that is a good approach. Ask about the average size of its printed ads to get a feel for whether they are adequate. Does the advertising agency have a standing order to place certain ads in certain publications? If so, find out how much longer and why it will continue to advertise in that specific periodical. What is the cost of advertising, and what is the average amount the company is spending? How does that compare with others in the field?

Has the advertising agency always been paid on time? Has it ever had to contact the company for failure to pay? If the company is not paying the advertising people and you find this a persistent trait of the existing management team, it may mean that you will never be paid, either.

Will the advertising agency continue to run the ads for this company? Does it think the company is making the right moves in its marketplace? Who is the contact person at the company? If the agency deals with someone other than the person you've been talking to in marketing, you will want to talk to the agency's primary contact to see why that person thinks the agency is good. In addition, you should solicit any general comments from the agency regarding the company. How would it change the ads to make them better? What could the company do to capture more market share? These kinds of general questions can yield more information about the industry, the competition, and the company you're analyzing.

WHAT IS THE MARKETPLACE FOR THE PRODUCT OR SERVICE?

By defining the marketplace for the product, you can tell how much money the company can make. If the market is small, you cannot expect sales to go beyond a certain point. The size and strength of the competitors in the marketplace will also determine how much of the marketplace can be obtained by a company. It is very important to understand market growth, market size, and the strength of the competition.

MARKET SIZE

You must analyze the markets in which each one of the products is sold. You need to know the total dollars and the total number of units that are sold in this marketplace. Are there geographic limitations to the marketplace? You should determine the market share of each of the companies, or at least the market share of the major companies. For example, Competitor A might have 20 percent of the marketplace and Competitor B might have 10 percent of the marketplace. Your company, because it is new, may have only 2 percent of the marketplace. Make sure that the company and its competitors aren't making grand statements about their market share. For example, during the Internet boom, many companies made claims that they had the illustrious "25 percent market share." However, when there are hundreds of players in an industry, not all of them can have 25 percent market share. Be careful to ask how the company measures its share of the market.

It is very important to know the kind of market in which you're selling. If it is dominated by one financially strong competitor (e.g., one that has 70 percent of the marketplace), you must use a completely different strategy than when selling into a marketplace in which the largest competitor has 10 percent of the market. A highly fragmented market versus a highly segmented market means a different marketing strategy and different chances for success.

COMPETITORS

You must investigate the competitors thoroughly. You can often understand the company you are dealing with much better if you understand the competition. You should go through all of the products that you have listed and note the competition for each one. Next, gather information on the financial strength, the name recognition of the product, and the general standing in the marketplace for each one of the competitors. You should describe in detail the competition's strengths and weaknesses, and any significant differences between it and your company.

An important aspect to look for when investigating the competition is sales tie-in. Does it sell this product as part of a whole list of products? If it is selling brake systems in general and one of the components of the brake system happens to be the brake pad, how will your company, which manufactures only brake pads, compete with this fully integrated competitor?

MARKET GROWTH

You should study the market and determine its annual growth rate. Certainly, the marketing department should understand how fast its product market is growing. It should know how much the market grew for each of the last three years and should be able to project growth for each of the next five years. It is very important to establish whether you have a growing market or a stagnant market. For example, if you have a market that is stagnant and management is projecting growth at the rate of 15 percent per year, this means that it will have to take market share and sales away from competition. This is an entirely different marketing strategy from one that would be appropriate when the market is growing at 30 percent per year and your company is projecting a 20 percent growth rate. Understanding the growth rate of a marketplace is critical to any long-term projections and strategy.

MARKET INFORMATION

Be sure to ask where the market information is coming from. If someone says the market is growing at 35 percent per year, you will want to know the basis on which they are making those projections. Sometimes the information is merely based on hunches and guesses. On the other hand, some industries are studied in detail, and the information available on the market is very good.

SUBSTITUTES IN THIS MARKETPLACE

Many products have substitutes. In the food business, for example, when beef prices go high, people switch from beef to chicken or pork. Try to determine whether there are any substitutes for the product that the company is selling. If there are substitutes, the company will have to worry about not only the competition in its industry, but also the competitors who manufacture the substitute product. You must understand how substitution can work, who the substitute competition is, and how they can affect your product.

MARKETING OBJECTIVES

Ask the marketing people what the marketing objectives are in a general sense. Sometimes a marketing person will say the objective is to obtain a larger share of the market. At other times, marketing people say the objective is to gain geographic coverage, that is, to have the product sold nationwide. When they talk about market coverage, they often talk about their marketing rollout, as they roll out from one corner of the United States to the other. They may even talk about penetrating foreign markets. All of these can be important marketing objectives, and sometimes a short-run strategy to cut price and gain market share can be a great benefit to the company in the long run. However, market share and geographic distribution are not nearly as important as generating gross profits for the company. If the marketing people are interested in generating profit for the company, rather than pursuing goals that are not strictly related to profit, the company is more likely to be successful than it would be if they had other objectives in mind.

MARKETING STRATEGIES

In addition to obtaining a list of objectives, you need to ask the management team members to explain in detail their specific strategy for accomplishing the objectives. They may be relying on seven or eight strategies to achieve their basic objectives.

HOW IS PRICE DETERMINED?

The price of the product or service is directly related to the sales a company will make. It is important for an investor to understand how the price of the product is determined. The price of a product will determine its position in the marketplace with respect to products of a similar nature. Price is the single most important attribute in trying to define where a product or service fits in the marketplace.

Companies often talk about price points. These are the imaginary lines between the higher-priced and lower-priced items that determine the price category in which a product will be classified. Most companies talk about their high-priced, medium-priced, and low-priced lines. Each one of these particular items has a price point, and companies place their product in one of these price quadrants. For example, they may have a product that is priced on the high end of the mid-price range. You should find out why the company is pricing its products in this range and how it arrived at the various price points and positioning of its products.

PRICING POLICIES

This brings us to one of the most important questions for any company, that is, what price should it sell the product for? The pricing question has received little attention. As a result, some big mistakes have been made in pricing products. For some strange reason, entrepreneurs approach pricing in an unsophisticated fashion. One company's whole reason for being was to beat the competition's price. It ignored service, failed to have good salesperson, ignored good packaging techniques, and gave little attention to the distribution channels because its sole concern was to have the lowest price. It believed that the market was so price-sensitive that if a product could be sold for less, customers would demand it. This company's product was never accepted in the marketplace, and the company was soon liquidated.

Other companies seem to price their products according to the competition's prices. For example, in the computer industry, most hardware is priced according to the computer industry leader. The large market share being held by the leader is a pricing umbrella under which all of the smaller companies must price their products. It's important for an investor to determine whether a small business has arrived at the price of its product logically.

Of course, there are many products that are commodities. If you sell strawberries, you are stuck with the price the marketplace dictates. In times of plenty, the price will be low, and when the strawberry plants don't produce a lot of berries, the price is high. If you are working with a company that has a commodity, you had better understand the marketplace because that marketplace has a lot to do with determining the price and profitability of the company in which you are investing.

In a sense, all products can be analyzed as being somewhere on a continuum from commodities such as oil to a high-tech product that has a patent. Many products fall somewhere in the middle, that is, they have competition but their product can be differentiated from the competition. It is your job to understand the reason that one product is different from the other. If you cannot differentiate the company's product from the competition's, you are getting close to having a commodity for which the company has very little control of price. A company that has little control or the price of its product is a much higher risk than one that has some competitive advantage and can charge for that advantage.

PRICING PROCESS

You should ask the marketing people to describe in detail the pricing process they follow. Who establishes the price? Who has input into setting the price? How do they determine the proper price? Who is authorized to sell the product at a price that differs from the approved price list? Can any salesman cut the price? Who is in charge of setting the price?

A retail organization that we know has a basic floor price that no one can go beyond. However, its advertised prices are in excess of that amount. Snappy ads are used to entice customers into the showroom. The ads say, in essence, "Come in and make us an offer." This company allows a salesperson to sell the product for practically any price above the floor price. This often creates a rather bizarre approach on the selling floor, especially if two salespersons are selling the same product next to one another, and you can hear different groups haggling for different prices. It also leaves many customers disgruntled because they aren't sure whether they are getting a bargain basement deal or being ripped off. Prices float from high to low, and salespersons are compensated more as the price goes up. Their percentage of the total sale grows with the price. This company is flourishing!

PRICE CHANGES

How often does the company revise its prices? Does it change prices frequently or does it try to keep them more or less stable? Does it respond to the competition's price changes quickly? Or does it wait a while to see whether the price will stick? Is there a price leader in the industry that everyone else follows? Understanding how prices change and who changes them is of critical importance to every business operating in the industry and to you as an investor. Price changes can be an indication of a rapidly changing industry where one can have big losses.

PRODUCT WARRANTY

Does management describe in detail the present warranty policy? What kind of warranty actually exists? Get copies of the warranty for the product and review it, carefully.

What warranty expenses has the company had for each of the last three years? What warranty expenses does the company expect to have for each of the next five years? How did the company calculate the amount it expects to spend in warranty expenses?

What amount does the company have as a warranty reserve? That is, what amount of sales has been placed on the balance sheet as a reserve against future warranty claims? Is this warranty reserve adequate? Because the warranty reserve is basically an accounting entry, does the company have the cash or credit line it would need to honor a large warranty claim? Is a warranty claim one of the reasons it needs money from an investor?

WHAT INTERNAL REPORTS ARE MADE?

Every company should record its marketing and sales endeavors. This is one of the key activities of any business. You should be able to review the company's marketing reports and determine from them what is going on, both in the company and in the marketplace.

MARKETING REPORTS

Get a list of the reports generated by the marketing department and assess their value to the company. Try to determine how the marketing department uses them. Also review them for information about how the marketing department is being run and for details about the products and customers.

Determine whether any other reports from the company are shared with the marketing department. For example, does the marketing department know what is happening in the production area? Does the marketing department know what is happening in the financial sphere? Does the marketing department understand the problems in collecting accounts receivable? If it does not, it may be selling the product to people who don't pay. As a result, the finance department may be clogged up with an inordinate number of slow-paying or nonpaying customers. The marketing department should not allow this kind of situation to develop.

Is there a report that charts any of the activities in the marketing department? For example, does it have a sales chart showing monthly or weekly sales?

SALES PROJECTIONS

How often and for what forecast period does the marketing department project sales and expenses for its department? Get a copy of the marketing forecast and determine how it is put together.

Go through the marketing forecasts with the marketing managers and review how they are put together. What assumptions have been made? How often do the assumptions change and with what frequency are the projections changed?

Get copies of actual financials for the past three years and compare them with the sales department's projections for the past three years. If they diverge substantially, the new sales projections may be of little value in assessing the company's promise. In determining how accurate the sales projections have been in the past, you will obviously be making a statement about what degree of accuracy projections should attain in the future.

Discuss in detail the results for the company as projected by the marketing department for this year. Probe to determine how well it understands the marketing budget and sales projections. The marketing department that puts together sloppy projections probably does not understand the marketplace very well.

PROCEDURES MANUALS

Does the marketing department have a manual on procedures? If so, get a copy and review it. If not, ask why not. Determine from talking to people in the marketing department whether they follow the procedures manual or whether it's just an out-of-date binder that's never used. Determine when the last entries were made in the manual and the date it was last

reviewed. This will give you an indication of how well organized the marketing department is. The fact that a marketing
department does not have a procedures manual is not the kiss
of death, but it should have some kind of document that
encourages the people in the marketing department to work
together as a team.

WHAT EXTERNAL INFORMATION IS AVAILABLE?

By developing external information, you will have an opportunity to check the accuracy of the information being supplied
by the company. You will also be able to develop a clearer
understanding of how the industry views itself, as well as its
position in the overall marketplace. Trade associations and
trade publications are key information sources. Quite often,
research institutions supply this type of information.

INDUSTRY ASSOCIATIONS

Is the company a member of any trade or industry association? If so, get the names and addresses of the associations
and, if possible, the names of the managers of those associations. It will be important to contact the manager of the major
trade association for industry statistics and for other information on the industry. Many times, an association is small
enough to know the inside scoop on the activities of both your
company and some of the other companies in the industry.
You should also determine whether there are other ancillary
trade associations or perhaps some that are somewhat similar
in nature that could give you an understanding of the industry.

TRADE SHOWS

Does the company participate in any industry trade shows? If
so, list them and determine how this helps sell the product.

Does the company attend conventions that might enhance its stature in the industry? If possible, attend a convention and see what type of people attend.

TRADE PUBLICATIONS

Obtain a list of the names and addresses of the most important trade periodicals in the industry. Get recent copies and find out what the contributors consider to be the pressing issues of the industry. If you make an investment in a company, you should subscribe to one or two of the trade periodicals in order to follow the industry. Many trade periodicals are published by the trade association itself, and most trade associations have newsletters. Make sure you review past publications, and get on the mailing list if you invest money in the company.

BASIC INFORMATION

RATIO ANALYSIS

You will have to undertake a number of marketing ratio analyses if you are to understand the company's performance in the marketing area.

Calculate the sales per salesperson by dividing the total sales by number of salespersons out during the year. This will measure salesperson productivity in terms of their ability to produce sales for the company. If you see this figure declining over the years, it will indicate that the company is not producing per salesperson what it has in earlier periods and may indicate that there is a problem.

You should also calculate selling expenses as a percentage of sales by dividing total selling expense by sales. This will measure the cost related to obtaining each sale. If you see this cost going up, you should investigate why.

Another useful calculation is salaries and commissions as a percentage of sales. This can be calculated by dividing total salaries and commissions by total sales. Again, this percentage will give you an indication of what cost is incurred for each sale, that is, the human cost. If you see this human cost going up, you need to ask why.

Calculate gross profit per salesperson by dividing gross profit by the number of salespersons on the average during the past year. This will let you measure the ability of a salesperson to contribute to the gross profit of the company. If you see this number going up, you should be happy.

Also calculate the gross profit as a percentage of marketing expense by dividing gross profit by total marketing expense. This will measure the effectiveness of the marketing team with respect to gross margins per marketing dollar spent.

Another area of analysis is marketing expense as a percentage of sales. Here you divide the total marketing expense by the total sales in order to measure the total cost of the marketing programs, relative to the sales being generated. You should include all marketing expenses, such as advertising and promotion.

Another useful ratio to analyze is the returns as a percentage of sales. You may do this by taking the total dollar returns and dividing this figure by sales before returns but after any discounts. This will measure to some degree the customer satisfaction and the product's quality.

The final area to review is the discounts as a percentage of sales. You may calculate discounts as a percentage of sales by taking the discounts given and dividing by gross sales. This will indicate the amount the product must be discounted in order to gain sales. This is a key figure in the retailing business.

WHAT ARE THE STRENGTHS AND WEAKNESSES?

Once you've gathered as much information as possible about the marketing department, you should write down the five major strengths that you see in this corporation. In addition, you should identify the five major weaknesses in its marketing department. Once you've done this, you should assess how critical these five strengths and weaknesses are to the success of the business.

CONCLUSIONS ON MARKETING

Finally, you must formulate some basic conclusions about the marketing area. Is this the marketing team that can implement the marketing strategy? Can this marketing team make the company successful in this sales arena? Is this the marketing program that best fits this industry? Can this marketing strategy really work? At the end of the day, you should write down your conclusions on the marketing area before proceeding to other areas.

CHECKLIST

Appendix A contains a long list of questions to guide you in analyzing the marketing area. It also provides numerous documentation sections to refer to and suggests references to call with regard to marketing. Make sure to call them.

5 INVESTIGATING PRODUCTION

Every business involves production. Even a service company follows some production process in order to deliver the service to the customer. Every investor should understand the process by which the product or service is produced for the customer. Most of this chapter deals with the manufacturing process. However, the investor should become familiar with all the stages of production in order to understand this area.

The production process also includes purchasing. Here you will identify the suppliers for the business. In addition, there is usually a shipping and a receiving area; both of them need to be examined. Customer services usually pertain to the production area. That is, after the product has been shipped to the customer, if the customer complains, the production department has to make good on what it has shipped to the customer. Finally, research and development (R&D) is critical in every growing business and must be understood by the investor if he or she is to determine whether the investment is suitable for the long term.

THE FACILITY

You should also examine the facility where the production takes place, even if the property is leased or owned. A number of basic questions need to be asked. First of all, what is the exact address of the production area? If it is on the property, what is the square footage of the land? If it is owned, what is the cost of the land? Also, if it is owned, what is the assessed value for tax purposes and the fair market value today? If you have an appraisal, what is the date of the last appraisal and what was its appraised value?

The building size is another important item, along with the age of the building and any expansion that has been done. The condition of the building and the possibility for expansion should also be investigated. To understand the value of the assets, you should determine the assessed value of the facility for tax purposes, the fair market value from an appraiser, and the date of the last appraisal.

Here you are trying to determine whether the plant is adequate for the company. If it is not, a move in the near future may be necessary. Your analysis should also determine whether the facility is a "good deal" or is an albatross around the company's neck.

One nice little business was doing $5 million a year, but unless it could crank the operation up to more like $15 million in a year, the facility would remain too large. The company was investing a great deal of money into a huge facility in hopes that sales increases would soon fill up the plant. Sometimes entrepreneurs don't understand real estate. They take on far too much real estate and let it drag the company down. Entrepreneurs should also realize that they are not in the business of investing in real estate. Ownership of real estate may be nice for a mature company that needs to invest its money. However, for a start-up company, owning your own real estate is not nearly as important as having enough working capital to produce the product.

This is a good time to ask questions about the insurance coverage on the building. Does the company have fire and hazard insurance? Does it have insurance against floods and hurricanes?

Also, you should ask questions about the amount of the mortgage on the property and the monthly payments. If the property is leased, of course, you should make notes on the amount of the monthly payments, when the lease is to expire, and whether there are any renewal options.

PLANT MOVES

As part of your due diligence, you may determine that the company will have to move its plant. This is perhaps the single most traumatic event any company can experience. Moving a company will be extremely disruptive and will take up a great deal of management time in the planning process, the actual move, and the adjustment period. Many management groups can be hired to help with the move, so most entrepreneurs believe that a move is a fairly simple process and will not engage them. The truth is that moves usually cause considerable disruption in production, as well as in the overall management of the business. Many companies go through such difficulties when having to move, and you could witness your investment dwindle so rapidly in the process that you should avoid them wherever possible.

EQUIPMENT

Once you have an understanding of the facility itself, it's time to move on to the machinery and equipment. Ask some basic questions, such as the age of the equipment and current repair costs per annum. It is also important to know whether new replacement equipment is available, as well as spare parts.

A firm that was started in 1920s found that the very specialized equipment used by the firm was no longer being manufactured. This meant that every time a part was broken, the company had to make the replacement item itself. This is the type of very time-consuming process that could interfere with production for some time if a major piece of the machinery breaks.

As an investor, you should know what kind of new equipment appearing in the marketplace might make this company's equipment obsolete or put it at a competitive disadvantage. It's been reported that the new steel mills in Europe and other parts of the world are much more efficient and better able to utilize the new technologies than the old steel mills in America. As a result, American steel industry has suffered.

You should ask the production people what kind of production equipment is used by the competition and how efficiencies are gained, as compared with the company. Does the competition have more modern equipment or a better assembly-line process? Is its plant better laid out? What does the production process at the competition look like and how can it be emulated here? If the company has a poor process, perhaps a different method of production will have to be invented.

You should ask whether the company has a formal preventive maintenance program for repairing machinery on a regular basis. If so, investigate the program and determine whether staff are maintaining the equipment adequately or are just running it into the ground; also determine whether you can expect huge maintenance costs to show up as soon as you make your investment.

Be sure you meet the person who is in charge of preventive maintenance and talk to that person about what kind of reports are prepared on the maintenance of the equipment. Make sure to ask whether the company anticipates any major repairs or reconditioning work to the equipment in the next 12 months. Get an idea of what kind of repairs are going to be done in the future and see whether this amount corresponds to the figure being used by the financial side of the business in its projections.

THE NEED FOR NEW EQUIPMENT

Ask the person in charge of equipment whether new capital equipment or new production space is needed during the next

12 months. If the answer is yes, you should try to determine how much more space or equipment the company will need. You should review these items and amounts with senior management and compare them with the company's capital expenditure budgets for this year and several years to come.

Always ask people in production the following questions: If you had no money constraints, what pieces of equipment would you replace? What new equipment items would you add to improve efficiency? This usually gives me a pretty good idea of what items are needed in the production process.

Also ask which piece of equipment is responsible for the current bottleneck in the production process. Looking to the future, ask which area of the production process will need to be increased as the number of units produced increases.

Another factor to consider is what pieces of equipment can cause a production stoppage for any significant period of time, for example, anything over four hours. How many times has the production process been shut down in the past because of equipment failures? What plan exists if a certain piece of equipment fails and shuts down the production process? What will management do if production is shut down by this one piece of equipment?

It is important to know how easily production can be shut down. If it seems a likely event because the company has only one piece of critical equipment, this means that the risk in investing in this company is fairly high, because there is no backup.

One company was in the business of making jackets for records and CDs. As the company developed, it decided to purchase a special piece of equipment for making record and CD jackets from Germany. Although the company did spend a great deal of time making sure that the German equipment worked properly, it was not until the company had actually installed the equipment and began operation that it discovered a serious problem. To begin with, it took hundreds of hours to get the equipment to operate. Countless numbers of Germans flew to the company's plant to help the management team make the piece of equipment work.

After months of working on the equipment, it was found that the equipment was not much better than some of the existing machines already on the market. Even though the piece of equipment handled the entire operation from start to finish, it was no faster than two smaller, American-made machines operated by seven people. The savings in labor were not realized, because when all was said and done, it took seven people to keep the new German machine in operation, three in actual operation and four as a support group handling software tapes and other aspects of the machine after some months of operation.

SURPLUS EQUIPMENT

Here are some other important questions to ask about equipment: Do you have surplus equipment, and if so, is there a plan to sell off this equipment?" Do you have any surplus or idle building area that could be subleased? These kinds of questions should tell you whether the company is overcapitalized from the standpoint of machinery, equipment, and building. If there is a substantial amount of excess equipment, perhaps it should be sold off.

In this world of ever-changing technology, it is critical to understand that a company's equipment must be modern enough to prevent it from sinking to a competitive disadvantage. This may take some snooping among people (other than management) in the production area so that you can understand what they are thinking. If they constantly complain about not having the latest equipment, you can be sure that they are at a disadvantage.

CAPITAL EXPENDITURES

You should establish whether a formal procedure exists for approving capital expenditures. You should also determine whether equipment can be purchased just because the production crew wants to have the latest gadget.

At a company involved in high-technology video production, the management was in love with new equipment. They bought every new "gizmo" that came on the marketplace, and they were constantly changing every part of the production process. This wreaked havoc on the process itself and drained the company of the capital needed to do the marketing, even though it had the most modern, beautiful equipment. After the company failed and went into bankruptcy, the beautiful equipment was auctioned off for a few cents on the dollar.

In purchasing equipment, management should look at this as a return on investment. When the company is about to buy a piece of equipment, it should calculate the return on investment on the basis of the expenditure of funds. If the company buys a $60,000 piece of equipment and the return on investment is 10 percent, the company probably should not buy it. As an investor in the company, you will want to know how the company calculates the return on the money it invests in equipment or any other part of the business.

PRODUCTION CAPACITY

All of the questions above were oriented toward determining the capacity of the facility. It is important to know how much it can produce. If you are investing in a company that is near its capacity and none of the investment capital is going to be used to increase that capacity, obviously the company will have to obtain financing for new equipment before it can expand capacity.

You should also compare the capacity with the backlog. If the plant cannot chew up the backlog for several months or even a year, perhaps management should consider increasing its capacity so that it can catch up with the backlog for delivery to the customer.

PRODUCTION EMPLOYEES

Even though you have already spent a lot of time investigating the employees of the firm, you still need to look at another aspect of the employees. What you are looking for now are the really tough jobs in the production process. You need to identify the key production positions and determine what personnel backups you have for each of these key positions. If there is an extremely high-skilled job and only one person is doing it, what happens to the firm when that person is out sick?

You must recognize that the people involved in the production process can be a limiting factor. If it is extremely hard to find a critical person, such as a qualified machine operator to operate certain types of equipment, obviously the production process can reach capacity quickly and will be difficult to expand.

Training is the key to the growth of any company. You should review the company's training manuals and determine how it is training employees to help increase its capacity and its productivity. Find out how production management selects and trains individuals, as well as new supervisors. Determine who does the training and how it is carried out. Here you are looking for a logical approach that will show employees how to be highly productive and get the job done. A haphazard approach to production training will be a deterrent to growth.

MOTIVATING EMPLOYEES

Employees must be motivated, whatever the production process. You need to understand specifically how management measures employee productivity and efficiency. You also need to know whether the employee understands the importance of this productivity and efficiency. Try to get a handle on the specific techniques that management uses to motivate the employees.

If you have the opportunity, review several employee evaluation forms and see whether management is making a conscientious effort to spur the employees on through regular evaluations. In addition, ask for the amount of turnover in the production process every year and the average number of years that a full-time employee works in production. The number of years people work in a plant is very telling. Some production plants hire temporary labor, due to seasonality. You may want to find out how many are hired and whether they see the same people returning or whether they constantly have to retrain new temporary labor.

Review the written wage rate schedule for employee positions and determine the last date of revision. Try to determine whether the wage rates are high, low, or average in relation to the industry, the competition, and the area. Is the company training people, only to have them leave shortly thereafter for a higher-paying job down the street? These are all key things to know. If the turnover rate is high because the pay is not very high, you can be sure this company is going to have to increase its pay before it can grow. One question that we always ask is, Does the company have a formal procedure for reporting employee absences, reprimands, promotions, and transfers? There should be a file that follows employees, as well as the entire work force.

Ask production management to classify the production employees into production staff, supervising of shipping, quality control (QC), receiving, R&D, and management. Then break down the payroll by these categories. Ask management where people need to be added and where they need to be cut. Ask the head of production to name five major personnel problems at the present time. The answers may be revealing.

UNIONS

If you have an opportunity, make sure you talk to the production people about the union and its activities. Ask for their grievance log and talk to the labor lawyer for the company. It is important that the relations between the union and the company be one of mutual respect and harmony. If there is bitterness and constant disagreements, it will affect the competitive strength of the company. If the company does not have a union, ask what activities have been going on to bring in a union.

RETIREMENT PLANS

You should talk to the production people about the retirement plan to determine whether they are satisfied with it. If they are not satisfied, find out what they would like to change. Also, make sure that the retirement plan is treating the people well or whether people are afraid to retire because the plan is so poor.

STAFF MEETINGS OF PRODUCTION PEOPLE

Do the production people meet regularly with all the supervisors to determine what problems are going on in the plant? What regularly scheduled meetings does the company have for each of the department heads? The company should be holding meetings that allow the production process to learn from its many activities.

REGULATORY AGENCIES

Every production process seems to be regulated by a myriad of governmental regulations. The most prevalent of these emanate from the Equal Employment Opportunity Commission (EEOC). Ask management whether it has received any EEOC reports concerning discrimination based on age, race, or sex. What kind of grievances have been filed with federal regulatory or state regulatory agencies regarding equal opportunity employment?

The occupational safety and health laws are stringent in every state. The Environmental Protection branch of the state government usually handles the Occupational Safety and Health Administration (OSHA). Determine what kind of OSHA regulations are required of the company, whether OSHA has audited the company, and whether it is in compliance. Review the file from OSHA and make sure you understand what risks are involved with this company and OSHA.

Other federal, state, and local laws and regulatory agencies have an impact on companies. For example, for radio stations it is the Federal Communications Commission (FCC). In this regard, you should contact the agency directly and determine whether the company has any problems at that agency. With regard to the FCC, you can actually go to the agency and review the records on the company that are in the public reading rooms.

SUBCONTRACTING WORK

Determine whether part or most of the work is subcontracted out to other companies. If it is, get the names, addresses, and telephone numbers of the subcontractors so that you may contact them to determine what kind of subcontracting work is being carried out.

There are really two kinds of entrepreneurs when it comes to subcontracting work. Some entrepreneurs are marketing-oriented and subcontract out every piece of work possible. They have someone else make the product that they are selling. In doing so, they sometimes miss having the flexibility to control their own destinies. When they make big sales, they are unable to deliver the product because they don't have the ability to command the production process so as to meet the demand. They also miss some tremendous profits they could gain by producing some parts of the process themselves. These entrepreneurs loathe the production area and don't want to deal with the headaches. You need to make sure that subcontracting is the best strategy for the company.

The second type of entrepreneur is more manufacturing-oriented. This entrepreneur may be a scientist who loves dabbling in R&D and tinkering with the production equipment to make it work better. This type of entrepreneur wants to manufacture everything. He or she also wants to control the entire process, from the time it comes in the door until the finished product goes out. Some of these entrepreneurs are at a disadvantage because they often produce items that have no margins to speak of. For example, they might manufacture a product that could be purchased for 5 percent or 10 percent over its manufactured cost. These entrepreneurs are tying up their own time and working capital to make a very small profit.

In discussing the production process with management, you should determine why it has decided to make or buy each component in the production process. There is a very straightforward, simple analysis on making or buying that should be carried out by those in charge of production before they make a product and before they buy it. By performing such an analysis, it is very easy to determine whether one should be using subcontractors. (See Chapter 7 for the questions for subcontractors.)

INVENTORY

You need to ask the production people about the inventory levels. That is, is their current level of inventory at an optimum level? Is it too little or too much? Who establishes the optimum inventory level and who do they have to answer to if they increase inventory? Ask how they determine the optimum inventory level for finished goods and for raw materials, as well as work and process. You want to make sure that the production people are sensitive to the amount of inventory carried by the company. After all, a large amount of inventory means that capital is tied up in that inventory. Unfortunately, a company can't operate without inventory. You need to know that the production people are conscientiously trying to reduce the inventory level at all times.

Determine whether any of the company's inventory items require long delivery lead times. If anything has to be scheduled 60–90 days out, you need to find out who that supplier is. This will be discussed later, in the supplier section.

What inventory items, if any, have only one source of supply? You need their names, addresses, and telephone numbers because these suppliers are as critical to the company as any of the bottlenecks in the plant. If for some reason one of these suppliers were unable to deliver, the company could come to a standstill. You will want to investigate these sole sources to see whether they are stable businesses.

Find out whether any items in inventory are obsolete, outdated, out of style, subject to markdowns, or have become unsellable in any way. If so, make a list of them and determine their value. You will want to compare this with the value they carry on the balance sheet. Some companies try to carry obsolete inventory on their balance sheets. A good accounting firm will usually catch this, but sometimes they don't.

QUALITY CONTROL

Does the company have specific employees in charge of QC? You should determine who is in charge of QC and make sure you speak with them. What QC standards, if any, are followed by the QC department? Ask management to describe in detail the company's QC program and to provide to you with any procedures manual used by the QC people. A specification sheet for each product that is produced should also be available. The manufacturing process is like putting together tinker toys or cooking a pie. There should be a recipe for each product that is produced. It should be written down in straightforward language so that anyone can produce it. The QC people will use this book to measure quality. If it is not produced by the book, the quality is probably not good.

PRODUCTION COSTS

It's always intriguing to talk to the production people about cost. You will be surprised to learn how few production people know what money is involved in what they are producing. The production people should have a detailed worksheet for determining the direct labor costs, the indirect labor costs, and the labor content of each one of their products. If they don't, management will never know how much labor cost goes into producing anything.

Usually the production process involves a standard cost system. If it does, this will be all the more confusing to those who don't have an accounting background. It is essential to know that the standard cost program is frequently updated to ensure that it does not get completely out of sync with reality. You should know who is monitoring and controlling the various costs of production, especially the cost of labor. Frequently, reports are put together on the direct and indirect costs going into every product being produced. You should get a copy of any of these reports on costs.

PRODUCTION LEVELS

Is there a daily, weekly, or monthly production schedule? The production people should have a schedule, and you should know how they determine what will be produced and the quantity. There should also be a log of the production process that summarizes each of the production runs. In addition, records of the production stoppages should be available. Whenever the company experiences a shutdown for more than four hours, the reason should be documented so that it doesn't happen again. Always ask about production levels and why they are not higher.

BACK TO CAPACITY

Now you should be able to determine the production capacity of the firm. You have to determine how many shifts and days it is operating, and from that you should be able to walk through the production capacity, assuming that no new plant or equipment is being added. From that, you should calculate at what percentage of capacity the company is currently operating and how it can improve its capacity.

STRENGTH AND WEAKNESSES OF THE PRODUCTION PROCESS

You should make a mental note of three major strengths and three weaknesses in the production area of the company. Ask management to list them, then try to draw those conclusions from what you have seen, heard, and read.

PURCHASING PROCESS

In small companies, purchasing is usually handled by one person. As the size of the company grows, the purchasing work increases, and a team may be used. You need to analyze the purchasing process. Here you want to ask the purchasing people some questions to check on what you have heard before. Do they have any inventory items where less than two suppliers are available? In other words, do they have any sole-source suppliers?

Are there any contracts between the company and any suppliers? If so, obtain copies so you can find out whether they are locked into a high-cost supplier because of a stupid purchasing mistake. Determine the company's objective in maintaining inventory levels. How many months of production are they supporting in their inventory?

Ask the purchasing person whether any inventory items have delivery lead times in excess of 60 days. If any do, you should make a list of these items. It may be critical to have certain products in stock in large quantities, rather than having to order them frequently, especially if lead times are in excess of 60 days.

What are the normal credit terms that the company is getting from suppliers? Does the company take advantage of purchase discounts? If it doesn't, the company may well be losing a substantial amount of money by not taking the discounts offered.

How often is a physical inventory taken? Who takes the inventory and what procedure is used to take it? When an inventory is taken, are the numbers often incorrect?

Who establishes the specifications for the items to be purchased? Before something is purchased, what purchasing requisition or approval procedure is followed? Is there a procedures manual for purchasing items? If so, you may want to take a look at it to see whether it is actually a current working book.

How much theft goes on in the business? How much "shrinkage" is involved in the inventory area? What system is in place to reduce the possibility of theft, both internally and externally? What has been the company's experience in inventory shortages during the past few years?

When it comes to reordering, does the company have a formal reorder policy? That is, when a certain item that is to be used in the production process reaches a certain level, is it automatically reordered? Does the purchasing agent have to receive a formal command before he or she can reorder something?

SUPPLIERS

You need to obtain the names, addresses, and telephone numbers of the major suppliers to the company. You need to know the number of units purchased from them during the last time period, for example, the last 12 months. You should know the dollar volume of the products being purchased.

Once you have this list, you will need to begin calling suppliers. Questions to be asked of suppliers are found in Chapter 7.

RECEIVING

Once a product has been ordered, it will be received by the company and brought into inventory. Receiving goods should follow a regular procedure. Ask the people in receiving what procedure is followed for receiving products and what kind of procedures manual is available. They should be able to describe the procedure for receiving goods and services. There should also be a method for requisitioning and receiving tickets being reconciled so that those items that have been purchased are received. You should determine who is authorized to sign a receiving ticket. Is there a regular procedure for signing and completing a receiving ticket for every item that is received? You should understand how the company is handling its receiving because a great deal of money can be lost in the receiving process.

A common problem here is that the items received are improperly recorded from the company's records. Some items received are never logged into inventory and, therefore, aren't used until they are found. This could take a number of months. It is also important to determine what system is in place to reduce the possibility of internal theft at the receiving process area.

There should be a procedure for determining that the goods and services received meet the specifications and quality of those ordered. You should identify the company's three major strengths and three major weaknesses in the receiving area. Usually, management can name these very quickly.

SHIPPING

Once the product has been manufactured, it needs to be shipped. There should be some kind of shipping procedure and perhaps even a shipping manual. There should be someone to sign the shipping tickets to make sure the accounting department knows goods were shipped out the door. When the product is received by the customer at the other end, there should be some way of determining that the customer has signed your shipping ticket so that you can prove that the merchandise was received.

One company, for instance, had a computer failure and did not know which items had been shipped. Fortunately, there were notices indicating that the customer had received the items and the company could use them to reconstitute the accounts receivable and rebill the clients accurately. However, another company that didn't have a good shipping policy or keep good records went out of business because it couldn't reconstitute its accounts receivable.

As an investor, you need to know what checks and balances are in place at the company to reduce the possibility of theft at the shipping level. It is important to understand the method of shipping, as well. Is it by trucks, a delivery service, such as UPS, or by common carrier? In emergencies, what kind of air freight service does the company use?

CUSTOMER SERVICE

Frequently, customer service is placed in the marketing area, but for larger items, customer service becomes part of production. The customer service people are part of the production area and are responsible for making sure that customers get the product that they ordered. As part of your due diligence, determine how many employees are in the customer service department and who performs the customer service work. Sometimes, the employees of the firm prepare the product for reshipping to the customer. At other times, service reps in the field handle customer service. You need to delve into the customer service side to understand how the customer is kept happy.

You should ask staff to identify the most frequent customer service problems. List the top 10. This will give you a good idea of what the customer service people are up against. We remember one company that had to rework a complete order because of a production process, and this caused a great deal of overtime and an extremely frustrating working experience for the people in customer service. They did it, and the company saved face, even though it lost a great deal of money on the order.

The customer service people should be able to describe the product warranties and guarantees provided by the company, and the cost of these warranties and guarantees to the company. It is important to understand the customer service area because it will give you a sense of how the product is being accepted in the field.

Sometimes the company contracts out the customer service work. If it does, you need to know who is providing this customer service and what it is costing the company. You also need to have a copy of the customer service contract with this service agency. You should determine the names, addresses, and telephone numbers of any of these contractors.

Here are some questions to ask about customer service that is contracted out.

- How long have you performed the customer service work for the company?
- How many customer service calls do you have on a monthly basis?
- What is the basic nature of the customer service calls that you get?
- What specific items have you been asked to fix that pertain to customer satisfaction?
- If you could fix one item in the company, what would you want to fix so that it would make customer service easier?
- How much does the company pay you to perform customer service?
- On the amount that you are being paid, can you make a profit?
- Will you continue to do the new customer service in the future?
- How would you change your customer service contract if you could change it today?

You should ask management to identify the three major strengths and three major weaknesses in its customer service area.

RESEARCH AND DEVELOPMENT

The final section of this chapter is about R&D. It is extremely important to know what R&D goes on in the company. First, you should identify the people responsible for R&D. Are they tied in with production or separate from it?

What has the R&D budget been for the last five years? What kind of money is the company going to spend on R&D in the next five years? Once you have these figures, you can ask the following questions about financings.

What specific projects are in progress? Why were those projects chosen? Who made the decision to proceed on these projects? Usually the market where the products are to be sold has been carefully studied. Entrepreneurs in some of the smaller companies claim to have "intuitive" knowledge of what the market is looking for. Usually these intuitions are incorrect. Every product that is being brought to the marketplace should have been market-tested. You should look at the past to see what kind of formal research projects were completed by the company before it instituted R&D programs for those products.

Often, an outside consultant will be used to help the company determine what products it should go after or to evaluate products that the company has determined are the best. One of the critical aspects of the R&D area is secrecy. You need to determine how these projects are protected from being stolen by the competition. You should describe the company's procedure for capitalizing or expensing its R&D budget. If it is being placed on the balance sheet, this may artificially inflate the value of the company because the product has not proved itself.

Find out to whom the people in research and development report. If they report to the production area, R&D will most likely be enhancements in some minor way to the existing product line. If those in R&D report to the marketing people, you probably see all kinds of items being added to the existing product to make it sell. Many of them may be little more than bells and whistles. If R&D individuals report directly to the president of the company, the company is probably charged with a long-term vision and is coming up with good products for R&D.

Review any reports that are coming from R&D staff. If there are no reports, you may ask top management how they know that the R&D people are doing their job.

When reviewing a product that is being researched and developed, you should ask the company's management whether there are any patents or patents pending around the new product. Sometimes new products are produced under a patent license. If there is a license for the patented products, you should review it in detail. You may find that the patent license for a company is about to expire. Ask the company what it intends to do if the individual who owns the patent will not license it again. You may be stunned to hear that management hadn't even thought about it.

RESEARCH AND DEVELOPMENT STRENGTHS AND WEAKNESSES

You should identify the five major strengths and weaknesses of the company's R&D section. Management should be able to give you some help in this area.

BASIC INFORMATION

PRODUCTION REPORTS

Ask middle management to show you the reports they are generating and sending to top management. If they have no reports at all, ask them why not. What value does top management place on these reports? Determine who receives the production reports. Also determine whether reports are made at the change of each shift and whether a production log report is made out regularly to keep up with what is being produced.

RATIO ANALYSIS

Although a number of critical ratios need to be examined in a manufacturing company, we will mention only a few key ones. If you want to develop this further, obtain a good book on production processes and make sure you study the ratios used by manufacturing personnel.

You can determine hours needed to produce a unit by dividing direct labor hours by the number of units produced. This will measure the units of labor it is costing for each unit to be produced and indirectly will measure employee productivity.

Calculate labor cost as a percentage of total production cost by dividing labor cost by total production cost. This will give you a measure of the total labor cost to the total production cost and show the labor required to produce each item. If you see this labor content going up over the months and years, you need to determine why.

Material cost to total production cost can be determined by dividing cost of materials by total production cost. This, too, will show you the percentage of total cost going to materials. If you see the cost of materials going up, you should ask why.

Calculate manufacturing overhead to total production cost by dividing the total manufacturing overhead by total production costs. This will give you the percentage of total production costs that is consumed in overhead. If you see the overhead percentage going up over of periods of time, it will be a clear indication that something is wrong.

Determine idle time as a percentage of total time available by dividing the total idle time by the total available direct labor hours. This is often a hard number to get to, but if you can, it will measure the efficiency of the company in achieving and keeping all of its employees busy and productive.

An interesting but difficult calculation to make is the percentage of total factory hours taken up by direct labor hours. You can obtain this figure by dividing the direct labor hours of people on the production floor by total hours of all the factory personnel. This will measure the amount of support personnel needed to complete the production process and will also show you what percentage is direct labor. If you see direct labor going down and support labor going up, there may be a problem.

Calculating overtime as a percentage of total hours can also give you a measure of the company's costs. To calculate, divide the total overtime hours worked by the total hours worked. You will see how often people have to be brought in on overtime. If this number is large, it may mean that the company is having to schedule overtime to catch up with work that was not completed during the regular shift. You will need to investigate this in detail. Overtime hours are paid at a higher rate than regular hours, so it is costing the company considerably more to produce the product in overtime hours.

Machine utilization is another interesting figure. You can compute this by dividing productive machine hours used by total available hours on the machines. This will measure the efficiency with which the equipment is utilized and perhaps give you an indication of a scheduling problem. If the machines are not being used efficiently, it may mean that the company is buying excess equipment instead of getting the efficiency out of its existing machine base.

Finally, calculate the scrap rate by dividing the number of units scrapped by the total units produced. This will be a good measure of efficiency of the production process, as well as the quality control of the company.

Conclusions About Production

Once you have analyzed the production process in detail, you need to determine the efficiency of the overall plant. Does the company use its assets (such as land, building, machinery, equipment, employees, supervisors, etc.) efficiently? You need to come up with a general idea of whether the company is efficient or inefficient, or falls somewhere in between.

You also need to reach a basic conclusion about the management of production. Are these people able to manufacture the product efficiently? Are they able to meet the production schedule, as set forth in the business plan? Can they maintain the production process like a well-oiled machine? Are you confident that they will be able to achieve the production goals that they have projected?

As part of the production analysis, you should evaluate R&D. Do you think the company is engaged in the proper R&D? Is it on the forefront of technology or merely following the leader in the industry? Does it seem to know what it is doing in R&D? Do you believe management is capable of handling R&D? By the end of the day, you should have an overall feel for production management, the production process, and the R&D area. If you come out feeling uneasy or negative about this area, you definitely want to turn down the investment opportunity.

CHECKLIST

Appendix A contains a list of questions about the production process. You should ask yourself many of these questions. You will want to pay particular attention to the checklist provided under the documentation area and make sure that you receive many of the items listed.

6 ANALYSIS OF THE FINANCIAL STATEMENTS AND PROJECTIONS

Who are the people who count the beans? For many years, financial people have been known as "bean counters." Although the term is belittling, these people play an important role in the company. If the numbers are not correct, there is no way to manage the business. If the financial side is in the hands of incompetent people, the business is doomed to failure. The safety of your investment depends on these bean counters and how they keep the books of the company.

The procedure in analyzing this area is the same as it was for the areas already discussed. You will need to analyze the financial people before you analyze the financial area. You need to know the individuals who will carry out the financial plan. You need to know who has computed the projections for the company. If you haven't yet interviewed some of the financial people, you should do so now.

PERSONNEL

You should first concentrate on the background and experience of the people in the financial area. Obtain a short resume on each of the key financial people and look for experience in the small business area, specifically in helping small business companies grow and managing the financial function of small companies. These are key attributes of anyone in the small business area. You should analyze the financial people in depth, as you did with the personnel carrying out the marketing and production functions.

ANALYSIS OF THE NUMBERS

All of the qualitative analysis accomplished in the previous chapters now needs to be transferred into a financial analysis in this section. That is, all the qualitative data must be verified in its quantitative form. All the achievements of the marketing and production department must now be stated in terms of financial achievements. At this point of the analysis, you must turn all of your thoughts to numerical concerns. As most managers know, you have to "live and die by the numbers."

It is wise to start with the year-end numbers, then go to the interim financials. Usually, the year-end numbers will have been prepared by an auditor and should have been certified.

FINANCIAL ANALYSIS

The first place to begin the financial analysis is to study the historical financial statements of the company. One must first verify that these financial statements are accurate and current. Frequently, a small business will try to skimp on financial data by not preparing regular financial statements. This is a sure sign that the company is not being run by the numbers and should give you a clear indication that the company is not serious about using the financials to guide the management team.

Before you begin investigating the financial section of a company with old historical financial statements, you may want to have the accountants come in and review the situation. Accountants call this an *operational audit* of the numbers. Ask accountants to review companies with old financial statements, and be wary if the accountants come back with horror stories. Frankly, you should be down on companies that can't keep current financial statements, and you should not invest in such companies. Old or sloppy financials usually mean business problems.

Hundreds of books have been written about financial analysis, about how to "walk through" the balance sheet and profit and loss statement to determine whether the company is operating well or is in trouble. Anyone who is in the venture capital business should have been schooled in depth in financial analysis. Therefore, this book does not try to elaborate on the various areas of financial analysis. This kind of analysis is important, but you will also be concerned with the venture capital analysis, which should include the other items mentioned in this chapter. Before discussing these other items, let's consider some of the major items you should look for in the financial statements.

Analyzing the Income Statement. Begin by looking at the company's sales and try to understand how the company recognizes revenues. So many companies recognize sales in so many different ways that you can no longer trust a mere number in the sales column. You need to understand what is behind it. For example, in the publishing business, a book is sold by a publisher to a bookstore, and the revenues are recognized by the publishing company. However, the book can be returned by the bookstore to the publisher for full credit, so that a sale does not occur for the publisher until the retail store has sold the book to a retail customer. Recognizing revenue in the book-publishing business can be difficult because a company may have several of its books take off and make sales look extremely good until the reviews come in, then those books may be sent back to the publisher. Verifying the way sales are recognized is critical.

Nor can you rely on the accounting profession to give you everything. Recently, there was a public company that had contracts with companies that called for the services to be provided over several years. The accountants let the company recognize all the revenue from those contracts in a single quarter. This increased sales substantially and made the earnings look fantastic. Later, when the accounting trick was uncovered, the financials were restated, and the company was sued by it shareholders. Make sure you understand revenue recognition before you invest.

Percentage of Completion. In other companies, such as government contractors, large contracts are recognized on a "percentage-of-completion" basis. This means that the project can be half finished and the contractor can recognize half or maybe more than half of the contract as revenues, even though progress payments of cash to the business may fall behind the amount of the contract that has been completed. This is another way to "front load" sales of the contractor and make it look as though it is having a fantastic year when, in fact, it is experiencing a severe cash shortage.

Loss Leaders. In other situations, a contractor may bid on the initial part of a contract, and the bid may be so low that the contract constitutes a loss to the company. According to accounting principles, it can then bury those losses as investments in future contracts. That is, they never show up on the income statement. They are booked on the balance sheet as an asset to substantiate the theory that the government, after an initial contract, usually comes back for a larger follow-on contract. The loss that was incurred on the initial contract can be amortized over the second long-term contract. It was the small company's loss leader. Several companies you encounter may show losses of this nature on the balance sheet as an asset. In analyzing the company, you should become familiar with the way it recognizes revenues. The revenues will tell you how the cash flows of the company will occur.

Research and Development. Expensing research and development (R&D) can also give rise to assets on the balance sheet. The income statement may show no expense for R&D because the R&D expense is being capitalized. This new asset is then taken off the balance sheet and expensed through the income statement over a five- or ten-year period. The company has spent the money and run out of cash but the income statement may show that it had a profit!

Standard Cost. How the company recognizes its costs of production can also be tricky. Some companies measure costs on the basis of "standard costs." At the end of the year, they adjust the "standard cost" and bring in the real costs of production. However, standard costs do not recognize any reworking of the product. If the product doesn't meet the specifications of the client, more cost will be incurred in making the product right. This may mean that the company will produce an item, recognize a standard cost, show a profit on the product, then later in the year have to recognize either (a) an expense for reworking the product to make it sellable or (b) additional expenses to bring the standard cost in line with reality. Both of these can be extremely disconcerting to an analyst because it is not until the end of the year that things pop out.

One small public company always showed good revenues in its first, second, and sometimes even in its third quarter, only to have all of those profits taken back by the audit at the end of the year, which took into account the real costs. The audit had such large adjustments that the year ended with a huge loss. If this happens to you, you will be left wondering whether this was a deliberate deception by management or just the result of a poor accounting system. In any case, it is directly indicative of the management.

CASH FLOW ANALYSIS

The first thing to do in cash flow analysis is to check the cash in the bank. How much cash does the company have and how does it flow in and out of the company? Make sure you understand how the company gets its cash. Critical questions to ask are: How many collection points does the company have for its cash? How many depository bank accounts does it maintain? What kind of cash balances does each account have? Of the cash that is collected, what amount cannot be used because it is in the financial float? What procedure does the company have for minimizing the transfer time for collecting cash balances?

Also look at the number of disbursement points. Who authorizes payments from the company's funds and what amounts are they authorized to disburse?

What procedures are used to ensure the proper disbursements by authorized people? What procedures are used to transfer funds and ensure the timely payment of bills? Does the company take advantage of discounts when they are available? How does it avoid missing discounts when payments are late? If the company is missing discounts, what does this cost the company per year? Quite often, companies come to VCs asking for financing to take care of discounts. Obviously, if this is the only reason someone comes to you for venture capital, it is a mistake to put your money in. You will not get the kind of return on investment that you are looking for if the cash is going to be used only for making timely payments of bills in order to take advantage of discounts.

ANALYSIS OF THE BALANCE SHEET

Cash flow analysis naturally leads you to the balance sheet. One source of cash is accounts receivable. You need to understand how receivables are recognized and how frequently receivables are not paid. That is, the company may have a receivable booked and income recognized, but the buyer of the product owing the money may not have recognized it as a payable and may not believe it owes anything to the company at all. Looking behind accounts payable is a must.

You should determine what percentage of the company's sales is cash and what amount is credit that will be recognized as accounts receivable. What credit terms is the company giving its customers and how do those terms compare with those offered by the competition and the industry in general? What credit information is used to make the credit analysis and who in the company determines which customers will get credit? Is the procedure for extending credit coordinated with the sales activity? How frequently do the financial people update the customers' credit information? The small business world is strewn with failures from small companies that extended credit to non-creditworthy customers who did not pay their bills. Like any other assets, an accounts receivable is no good unless it can be turned into cash.

Inventory. What dollar amounts are tied up in inventory? How does management explain the money in inventory? How is this inventory coordinated with the management of production? What are the trade-offs between the flexibility of having a maximum inventory and the advantage of keeping a minimum inventory to reduce working capital? How is the responsibility for inventory control divided between the finance people and the production people?

Inventory can be a perplexing number. One VC walked through a plant once and saw a big pile of goods with a large tarp over it. After asking what was under the tarp, he was told, "spare parts." A look under the tarp revealed some rusty junk. When going over the inventory numbers, the VC found the spare parts sitting there at full value, just waiting for the auditor to write them off and lower earnings.

Fixed Assets. What capital budgeting procedure is used by the company, and who decides what production equipment and machinery to buy? What is the minimum acceptable return on investment used to determine which capital budget items to buy? Does the company consider leasing? Who does the analysis on lease versus purchase? What capital expenditures are budgeted for the coming years?

Liabilities. You must go through the liabilities in the same way that you walked through the asset side of the balance sheet. You need to determine the size of the accounts payable. Who are they owed to? How far back do they go? Accounts payable must be aged. You should determine whether the IRS is owed payroll taxes or whether any income tax bills have not been paid.

Usually, this section of the analysis shows the loans from stockholders, banks, and others. Make a list of all debts and confirm each later.

BUDGETING AND CONTROL

Sound budgeting and effective controls of the company are one key to a successful operation. Although budgets may be based on a shorter time period than the projections you will analyze, you should investigate how the company budgets and funds its day-to-day activity. How does the company control its operations? The basic question you need to ask is, What are the company's budgeting procedures? That is, how often are the budgets put together and are they modified on an interim basis? How are the budgets used to manage the company?

Some other key questions are as follows: How are the budget figures derived? What supporting schedules are available for these budgets? You need to understand how the corporation sets the budget objective. Does management set goals, then translate them into numerical budgets? How is the process carried out in the company? In your analysis of the budget, find out how well the company has met its budget in the past. What discrepancies, if any, show up in the past between its budget and its actual achievements? How often does the management measure performance in relation to budget figures? What kind of accountability is established for employees? Who is held responsible when there is a deviation from the budget, and what corrective procedures are followed to make sure that future budget numbers and performance are the same?

PAST FINANCINGS

During its lifetime, each company goes through a number of financings, from banks, insurance companies, VCs, individual investors, and so on. You should write down the past financings of the company chronologically and indicate how they came about and what value is placed on the company. You should establish the current status of these investments. That is, find out whether bank debts are being paid as agreed. Are individuals getting the dividends they were promised? Are past investors happy with the situation and willing to invest again? You should determine whether any personal guarantees were part of these earlier financings and what assets of the company were pledged. In other words, what outside assets belonging to individuals have been pledged for these financings?

You may find that past financings from previous VCs often contain onerous terms with respect to the personal signatures of entrepreneurs. In some cases, houses or other assets outside the business have even been pledged. Entrepreneurs are extremely anxious to have these types of financings paid off, and it's common for an entrepreneur to push hard for venture capital financing because the business is in trouble and he or she is trying to save his house by getting the bank loan paid off. You should keep an eye out for this type of financing.

Also, keep in mind that if the entrepreneur has guaranteed the bank financing and if the business gets in trouble in the future, the entrepreneur will be working hard to pay off the bank without regard to your investment or what is best for the business. In a workout situation, the entrepreneur will want to make sure the bank is paid off so that the guarantee is not called. The entrepreneur will not care about your investment. You could lose money in this type of situation, so be careful.

PAST BANK FINANCINGS

In reviewing the company's past bank financings, you should go through all the pieces of information about each loan, including the legal documents. You should determine what collateral has been used for these loans, such as deeds of trust and life insurance, as well as specific assets on the balance sheet. Have there been personal or corporate guarantees? What are the requirements of the loan? That is, are there current ratios, working capitals, milestones, and the like? Determine what things the company must do to maintain the credit line with the bank.

In one situation, a bank's requirements had not been met, but the bank was still willing to work with the VC portfolio company so that it could go forward. The day after the venture capital financing agreement was reached and the money was deposited in the bank, the bank offset its loan amount against the money newly deposited into the account to pay down the debt immediately. The bank claimed a default on the loan and demanded that all future cash payments be made to the bank. Needless to say, this left the VC in a very unhappy situation. But, because it was a winery, the venture capitalist took some solace in his plight by drinking several cases of the wine. Each case cost about $65,000, and it wasn't very good wine. But, somehow, a bitter wine suited the moment.

ENTREPRENEUR'S INVESTMENT

In reviewing past financings, you should determine how much money the entrepreneur has invested in this business and how much stock the entrepreneur received for it. Sometimes you will find that entrepreneurs have put very little in the company and have very little to lose if the company goes bust. This often makes us nervous because nothing keeps the entrepreneur's attention riveted on business like a substantial personal investment in the company.

In one situation, an entrepreneur had invested $500,000, but he had made $12 million out of his past company. He had used the money to invest in other venture capital deals and put only $500,000 in this second business. When the company got into trouble, the individual worked very hard to save it. No one will ever know whether, had the entire $12 million had been invested, he would have had the incentive to save the business. As it was, he lost his $500,000, but he was still able to walk around with a smile because he had over $11.5 million in other situations. As a VC, you want to make sure that 100 percent of the entrepreneur's time is committed to the business you are investing in. A large and significant financial commitment is one of the strongest indicators of the entrepreneur's desire to make the business a success.

When entrepreneurs don't have a great deal of money, it is best to get them to guarantee part of the venture capital investment to ensure that, if things turn sour, they won't walk away without a substantial personal loss. The fact that entrepreneurs will hock their houses by taking out second mortgages to buy stock in small businesses is one of the strongest signs of commitment that an entrepreneur can show a VC. You will hear all the other arguments—"My life and soul are wrapped up in this business" or "My reputation and prestige are on the line for this investment"—but none of these arguments carries any weight when compared with the words, "Everything that I own is invested in this company."

ENTREPRENEUR'S OWNERSHIP

Similarly, you should determine how much of the company the entrepreneur owns. No entrepreneur is going to work hard for the company if the entrepreneur owns little of it and has nothing to gain. At a small company in Atlanta, the entrepreneur had been diluted by individual outside investors to the point that the entrepreneur owned such a small part of the company that he was virtually a hired employee.

Always make sure that the entrepreneur has a substantial stake in the company (so that the entrepreneur can make lots of money). Otherwise, the entrepreneur might give the company no more attention than a hired employee would. In the financings in which you invest, insist that the entrepreneur have an increased ownership, to the detriment of prior investors, in order to ensure that the entrepreneur would be motivated enough to make the company successful.

It's the rare entrepreneur, indeed, who will work hard for less than approximately 20 percent of the small business. If it is a large business, 5 percent may be fine. With anything less, you probably won't have the entrepreneur's full time and attention. Most likely, the entrepreneur will be out looking for another company to jump into where he can own a substantial amount of the equity.

PARTICIPATION WITH OTHER INVESTORS

Investing with other venture capital companies or other individuals is always a benefit. However, those who have invested in the past and are now watching you invest your money have a vested interest in (a) not giving up much equity and (b) making sure you put your money in so that theirs will continue to be worth a great deal. The views, comments, and information gathered by a past investor who is now trying to induce you to make an investment are not nearly as valid as the analysis made by a current investor putting in new money for the first time, along with you. It is interesting to talk to these past investors, but one needs ask why they invested and what profit they expect to make in the future. However, it will be practically impossible to gain unbiased information from this type.

In analyzing these past investments, you should determine who invested, how much they paid, and what valuation is placed on the company. This will give you a good idea of how much they are stepping up the investment from the time they invested to the time they are asking you to invest. If the new value is substantially increased from the last financing, you need to ask the question, What has happened to the business since the last financing that would make the value increase so much?

Use of Proceeds

It is important to establish how past financings were used. If a company raised cash in the past, it is important to know where they spent it. This will give you a good indication of how well the company has been run and how far it will be able to run on the money that you are investing.

You should review the company's use-of-proceeds statement in detail to determine why the company needs money for each of the items listed. Vague comments on the use of proceeds, such as "working capital," should not be accepted. You need to know exactly where the money is going before you put it in. You need to determine whether the new money will make a difference in that company's future.

If a fee is to be paid to a financial broker, make sure it is listed on the use of proceeds. These fees have a way of being overlooked until the day before closing.

PROJECTIONS

Among the items that you and the entrepreneur will come back to many times are the entrepreneur's financial projections. These constitute the numerical forecast that you (as an investor) are buying. The entrepreneur is saying these projections are possible, and you are purchasing a part of the company on the basis of these projections. Your return on investment—the cash that you will receive back—depends on the company making these projections. Your analysis of these projections is one of the key aspects of your investigation of any business opportunity.

You will want to investigate the assumptions being made about the projections. How realistic are the margins being projected? How realistic are the financings? Go through all of the assumptions in detail with the management team to determine whether the projections are based on sound assumptions.

One of the main assumptions that you should always have difficulty accepting from entrepreneurs is sales growth. Entrepreneurs are extremely bullish individuals whose sales projections tend to go through the ceiling. It is not uncommon to see unrealistic entrepreneurs thinking that they will double sales every year for 10 years. Sometimes sales projections are prepared in a haphazard manner. This is usually the case when a sales projection has a lot of zeros. For example, the first year might be $1 million, even; the second year $6 million; and the third year $15 million. These round figures are a sure tipoff that the entrepreneur's projections are being shot from the hip, rather than coming from hard analysis.

With the aid of computer spreadsheets, it has become much easier to run sales and profits projections. However, computer spreadsheets can increase sales by whatever percentage per year the entrepreneur dictates. As a result, the computer programs cannot be taken as the strong evidence that the nonrounded financial projection is accurate, even though the computer carries out the projections with brutal numerical accuracy. For example, if sales are to increase 67 percent each year and sales in the first year have been

$1,253,000, the computer will show sales for the following year at $2,092,510. This means that your tipoff is not zeros but numerical accuracy. You will have to do much more digging into the rationale of the projections because you will no longer have the many zeros to tip you off that the entrepreneur is shooting from the hip. With the aid of the computer program, the entrepreneur is giving you a different type of projection, but this time it is based on a flat rate that he has assumed will be constant. You need to make sure you know how the entrepreneur has arrived at the projections and what degree of work has gone into formulating the assumptions.

In addition, you should be given projections of the balance sheet, cash flow, and the profit and loss statement. Without these three figures, you will be left out in the cold. You need all of them to make a valid judgment as to where the business is going and how it is going to get there.

The projections should include a breakeven analysis with respect to profit and loss and cash flow. That is, the entrepreneur should show you monthly projections up to the point where the company expects to break even in terms of profit and loss, meaning it is no longer losing money. However, because of growth in accounts receivable and inventory, some companies may show a profitable financial statement even when they are having negative cash flow. This is the reason that the entrepreneur should show you a cash flow breakeven analysis. You want to determine at what point the company will stop having to raise capital and be able to finance itself on bank debt and other conventional borrowings. Until the entrepreneur shows you this breakeven analysis, you will not have a good handle on the company.

Make sure you have a balance sheet before and after financing so you can see how the proposed financing will affect the company. It is necessary to trace the flow of funds into and out of the company, especially as company transactions. Without a transition balance sheet, you will not be able to follow the flow of funds.

Quite often, the funds flow statement will not include the brokerage fee that the entrepreneur must pay as part of the financing. Make sure the fee has been subtracted from the cash available to the company. In addition, look for any consulting fees to be paid going forward and make sure that these consulting fees—and of course your own fees—have been deducted from the cash flow statements.

The projections should be based in part on assumptions about the stage of growth, when prototypes will be completed from the amount being spent for R&D, when the first model will be installed, when the beta test sites will be finished, and so on. You also need to know when branches in new cities will be opened with marketing staffs and when new locations will come on line. The cost of these items should be in the projections.

Almost every VC has difficulty obtaining reliable projections. Quite frankly, most entrepreneurs know little about how to make projections and usually need help from an accounting firm.

BASIC INFORMATION

RATIO ANALYSIS OF THE FINANCIAL STATEMENT

There are numerous financial ratios to consider, each of which is significant. Generally speaking, the ratios in the financial area revolve around four areas: profitability, equity, leverage, and cash management. Each of these has its own slice of the financial numbers and can give you some indication of how well the company is doing.

PROFITABILITY RATIOS

Gross margin percentage can be calculated by dividing gross profit by sales. This will measure the margin that the company is achieving on sales. Over periods of time, it may reflect transit profitability.

Profit margin percentage can be determined by dividing net income before taxes by net sales. This indicates the profitability of the company on each sales dollar. Over a period of time, it measures the profit trend of the company.

Return on equity can be determined by dividing net income by total shareholders' equity. This measures the return on invested capital and can show you how hard management is making the equity in the business work.

Return on assets can be calculated by dividing net income by average total assets out during the year. This indicates the return on the average dollars of assets outstanding during the year.

LIQUIDITY RATIOS

The current ratio can be calculated by dividing current assets by current liabilities. This gives you some indication of the ability of the company to pay short-term obligations.

Quick ratio can be calculated by dividing current assets minus inventories by current liabilities. This is also a measure of the ability of the company to pay its short-term obligations without selling off its inventory to generate cash.

To calculate the working capital as a percentage of assets, divide working capital by total assets. This will indicate the due date of the assets, relative to the total assets of the company.

Liquidity ratio can be calculated by dividing total assets by total liabilities to measure the overall liquidity of the company.

LEVERAGE RATIOS

Debt equity ratio can be computed by dividing total debts outstanding by total stockholders' equity. This measures the degree to which the company has leveraged itself with debt.

A similar ratio to debt equity ratio is total liabilities to stockholders' equity. It can be computed by diving total liabilities by stockholders' equity. This will give you a feel for how much of the capital has been provided by the stockholders versus creditors.

The working capital to net sales ratio is also of interest. It can be computed by dividing net sales by working capital. This will measure how efficiently the company has been able to generate sales on the basis of working capital.

Debt coverage ratio is something bankers always compute. It is calculated by dividing earnings before interest and taxes by total annual debt service. This measures the ability of the company to see its debt obligations.

Cash flow debt coverage ratio is more difficult to compute. Here you must calculate earnings before interest and taxes plus depreciation, divided by interest and principal due on all of the company's debts. This will give you a more cash-oriented measurement of whether the company can meet its debt service.

Percentage fixed charges of earnings is another good calculation. Here you divide the fixed charges by earnings before interest and taxes, plus fixed charges. This will give you a measure of how far the earnings could decline before you would be unable to meet the fixed cost.

CASH RATIOS

Cash flow cycle can be calculated by dividing receivables plus inventory by the cost of goods sold. This gives a general measure of the number of days it takes to convert inventory and receivables into cash.

Calculate the receivables cycles by dividing net credit sales by average trade receivables. This will give you the time it takes to collect credit sales.

A similar index is the past due index. This is calculated by dividing total receivables past due by total receivables. This will give you a trend in the collection activity over a time.

Calculating the bad debt expense as a percentage of sales is a matter of dividing bad debt expenses by total credit sales. This calculation will give you a trend of the bad debts that the company is experiencing.

Inventory turns can be calculated by dividing cost of goods sold by the average inventory outstanding in a year. This measures the number of times the inventory is sold and replenished during a given period of time.

Another measure of cash flow is the percentage of cash flow to total assets, which can be calculated by dividing net cash flow by total assets. This will measure the cash-generating ability of the assets over a period of time.

FINANCIAL REPORTS

You need to determine which financial reports the financial management team uses in carrying out its tasks. The reports they use in day-to-day operations will give you a good indication of how they are managing the company. In addition, you should ask the financial people to give you copies of the reports that they provide to top management, and of course, you should find out how top management uses these reports to analyze the financial health of the company.

CONCLUSIONS ON THE FINANCIAL AREA

At the end of the financial analysis, it is important to evaluate this area as follows:

- What do you think the major problems will be over the next two or three years?
- Does this financial team have the wherewithal to tackle these problems?
- Can this team finance this company over the next two to three years?
- Can it manage the profitability and assets of the company in such a way that it will not have financial problems?
- Do you feel comfortable with this financial team negotiating bank debt and other credit lines?

At the end of the day, you will have to ask yourself the question, Can they do the job?

CHECKLIST

Appendix A contains a long list of items that you should look for in the financial area. It lists the documents that you should collect when you have made your analysis of the financial area. In addition, you should obtain as much information as possible about the numerical analysis of the company to satisfy yourself that you have all the reports that count.

7 REFERENCE INFORMATION

You have asked the management team lots of information about the business in which they want you to invest. You have spent time working on their answers. But there are two more important areas about which you need to get information. First is the corporation itself and second is what others know about the company. You will explore these two information-gathering aspects in this chapter.

CORPORATE IDENTIFCATION

It seems unusual that some business proposals don't contain basic information about an entrepreneur's corporation. However, entrepreneurs may be so taken up with the marketing of a new product or the firm's financial possibilities that they leave out the general information that you will need to understand the type of deal you are getting into. You will find yourself having to dig out some of this information from the business proposal because it won't all be in one place. Much of it will have to come from the entrepreneur during your questioning period.

Remember to ask the entrepreneur for the exact name, address, and telephone number of the company. You will also need to know where (in which state) and when the business was incorporated and the states in which the company is qualified to do business. Usually the lawyer will pick up this information, as well as some of the other items on this list. It is important to know the state in which the company is operating (or in some cases, the country), because business laws vary greatly from state to state, sometimes even for the most miniscule parts of the business that can affect the company's entire operations. If the entrepreneur is not cognizant of these nuances, you and your attorney need to be.

You will need to know the location of the minute books, the bylaws, and the certificates of incorporation. You will also need to know whether the organization has had any predecessor. By investigating this area, you may determine that your corporation has gone through several reincarnations to arrive at its current corporate organization.

Also, get the standard industrial classification code for the business. It will be needed some day when you put together statistics for your investments.

CORPORATE STRUCTURE

The corporate structure, with all its subsidiaries, divisions, and branches, needs to be detailed. You need to know the names and locations of these subsidiaries and what operations consist of in each location. It is quite tempting at times to lump everything into one big corporate pile, but most corporations have various operations. Even within a single location, you should understand exactly how all of these parts fit together. You may have a law firm work through all this for you and present it in a memo for your review.

If the company has subsidiaries, make a list of them with the exact names of the subsidiaries, where the stock for each one is located, who holds the minute books, bylaws, and certificates of incorporation, and in which states the subsidiaries are qualified to do business. You will also want to determine whether any of these subsidiaries have predecessors. This information on each subsidiary is important because you may be investing in only one or two of the entities.

Is the corporation a Subchapter-S Corporation? Is the stock 1244 stock? Are there any differences in the corporate structure from a standard corporation?

Is the company a limited liability company (LLC)? Is it operated as a corporation or a partnership? You just need to nail all this down. Most small businesses like to be set up as a LLC because it gives them more flexibility in paying out distributions without being taxed. As a VC you may not want all this operating income coming into your fund, because you will have to pay taxes on it. If you do not want the company's operating income to be on your tax return you will have to insist that the LLC file its taxes as a corporation so taxes are paid at the LLC level. So determining the tax status here may be very important.

MANAGEMENT QUESTIONS

You will ask some more questions about the company, and management should know the answers to all of them. You need to determine whether there are any actions, lawsuits, or proceedings pending or threatened against the company and any of its officers or directors. If there are any actions, list them and the dollar amount of the claims, and go over them with the corporate attorney. Your background checks will help you nail down this, and having management tell you first, then comparing their answers with the findings in the background check will give you some insights into the management.

Does the company or any of its officers own 10 percent or more of the equity of any company other than this company? If they do, you will want to make a list of their holdings. It may be that this company is doing business with the company in which an officer owns more than 10 percent and, thus, some special deals are going on.

Determine whether the company has any shareholder agreements. That is, certain shareholders will own certain amounts, or certain shares cannot be traded. You should make a list of these shareholder agreements and get copies of them.

Does the company have any management contracts? If so, you will want to get a copy of them. You should at least make a list of the terms and conditions of each of these contracts so that you will know exactly what is going on with regard to management's contractual relationships with the company you are about to invest in.

Is any broker entitled to a commission on this financing? If so, determine what the amount of the fee is and to whom the fee is to be paid. Determine whether the company has paid commissions in the past for financing.

Are there any restrictions on the company's common stock? Sometimes the minutes of the company will indicate whether a restriction is to be placed on the future sale of company stock and whether common stock can be sold to anyone outside of the company. Make sure you know the restrictions.

Determine whether any affiliated transaction exists between the company and any of its officers, directors, or relatives and whether it has been an arms-length transaction and not a sweetheart deal. Even if the company has been getting a sweetheart deal, this should concern you because at some point, sweetheart deals usually go sour. This would mean that if an officer's company has been selling the company an item below or near cost, when the price comes back to normal, the company you invested in will have less profit.

Determine whether the company has any patents, trademarks, copyrights, or licenses. If so, speak to the lawyer who handled the application to find out what makes these patents, trademarks, and copyrights unique. It is quite easy to get a patent but much harder to defend it if it isn't strictly unique.

STOCK QUESTIONS

There are a few questions you should ask about the stock of the company. You need a list of shareholders but also you need to know whether there are any voting trust agreements on any of the company's stock. Some entrepreneurs will agree to a financing and will place their shares in a voting trust to be voted by the financing group. You will want to make sure that no such agreements exist before you come in and require voting trusts so that you can control the company, should the entrepreneur make the wrong step. We discuss this point further when we look at the structure of the deal.

Do any preemptive rights exist on the company's stock? That is, does anyone have the right to buy certain stock of certain people or from the company for any reason? In addition, do these rights relate to the sale of new shares in the future? If so, what are the exact rights?

Is there an option or right outstanding of first refusal on the sale of any shares of the company's common stock? If so, you may want to have the company obtain a waiver from the person who holds this right to let you purchase the stock that you want to purchase. Without such an approval, you may go all the way to the end and find that you can't do the financing because somebody else has the right to handle the financing that you proposed.

Consider one effort to buy a group of franchised fast-food restaurants. At the last minute, the franchisor was asked to waive its right of first refusal to acquire the locations. The franchisor thought the purchase price was a bargain and bought the units. The entrepreneurs had wasted three months and a large amount of money doing due diligence, only to have the right of first refusal exercised by the franchisor. The VC did not get to buy the locations and wasted a lot of time working on the proposal, but not nearly as much as the entrepreneurs.

Does the company have more than one class of stock? If it does, make sure you understand the various classes and in which class the company wants to set the financing. Many entrepreneurs try to raise money by selling nonvoting stock to VCs. They usually do this because the entrepreneur believes that the "VC wants to take control." You will have to work through this with your entrepreneur, but purchasing nonvoting stock is not the way to go.

Does the company have any stock purchase warrants, options, subscriptions, convertible instruments, or any contracts or agreements for issuing common stock to anyone? If these exist, you will need to take them into account in determining how much of the company you should own. In addition, you want to protect yourself from dilution.

For example, there was one company in which the management team had an option to buy stock at a nominal amount to maintain their position of 51 percent of the company. This meant that no matter how much money anyone put into the company, they could not be diluted beyond 51 percent. This certainly prevents anyone from taking control of the company. However, from a VC standpoint, you don't want to sign anything that precludes you from putting up more money and diluting all stockholders.

Determine whether any puts and calls or other equity purchase or sale instruments exist. Sometimes in the sale of stock to new stockholders, an entrepreneur will agree to "buy back any shares at cost" in his or her company to prove to the unsuspecting stock buyer that there is no risk in buying shares in this company. These "puts" mean that the stockholder has the right to put the stock back to the company at any time and take cash out of the company for those shares. Make sure you know what puts exist in your company.

In addition, the company may have a call on the shares that are outstanding. This can make a deal even more attractive, because if the call is at a low price and if the company can later buy back a large amount of equity at a fixed price, this can limit the upside of some of the stockholders, giving you and the entrepreneur an opportunity to buy them out and not let them make a lot of money. It is very unusual to give a call, but sometimes it happens.

Determine whether the company has any treasury stock and if it does, determine why this treasury stock exists. Again, sometimes an individual will be bought out for any number of reasons, and the stock will become treasury stock. When stock is bought back, make sure you understand the full reason for its having been purchased. If necessary, contact the person who sold the stock back to the company to find out why he or she sold the stock.

In one company, the individual had treasury stock. On investigation, it was learned that he had purchased this stock from three or four individuals who were early investors. The contacted individuals indicated that they had been "screwed out of their stock by an unscrupulous entrepreneur." Needless to say, this should be enough to tell you what kind of future you might expect with this entrepreneur.

PROFESSIONAL REFERENCES

You will want to contact three groups of professionals when looking for references on this company: the bankers, the lawyers, and the accountants. Landlords should also be questioned.

QUESTIONS FOR BANKERS

You are primarily interested in finding out what the banker knows about the company that will give you greater insight into the operation of the business. The bank will be expressing a financial viewpoint, so make sure your questions are oriented toward that area, except for those about management.

How long has the company been dealing with the bank? If it has been only a short time, you will need to contact the former bank. You will notice that companies that have an unsatisfactory relationship with their bankers move frequently. When you find this is the case, you will also probably find a banker who has an unhappy relationship with an entrepreneur. Make sure you contact former banks to find out why the relationship went wrong.

How long has this particular bank officer dealt with the company? If it has been only a short time, you will have to contact others within the bank who have had a longer relationship. Banks are notorious for changing bank officers, and it won't be unusual for you to find a new bank loan officer servicing the credit of the company.

Determine the amount of credit the bank has with the company. That is, what is the total amount the company has ever borrowed from the bank, both the high and the low? What formulas have gone into determining what the highs and lows are for the company?

What collateral is there for the loan? Determine what collateral the bank can sell if the company does not repay the loan. Find out whether the company meets its payments as agreed. That is, has it been late on interest or principal payments?

Determine whether the bank has ever been in default on any of its loans to the companies. Has the bank ever called a loan in default and later reinstated the loan? What were the circumstances surrounding any defaults on the loan? Remember, if the company is in default on its loan, you can expect the same thing on your investment.

Has the company ever asked the bank for lines of credit and been denied? If so, how large was the requested credit line, and why was it denied?

Ask the bank officer whether he or she believes the company has operating problems. Although the company may be making its payments, it may have other operating problems that you missed.

Ask the banker whether the management is good. Sometimes bankers may lend money to the management because they have collateral, even though they do not like the entrepreneur. You can determine this after a few minutes of discussion. Also find out whether the banker thinks they live "too high on the hog." If they are high livers now, think how high they will be living once they have your money.

OTHER INSTITUTIONAL LENDERS

Sometimes other institutional lenders are lending money to the company. These include finance companies and leasing companies. You should ask each of them the same questions you have asked the banker to determine how they view the company. Make sure you understand who is financing the company and have asked all such lenders what they really think of the company.

ACCOUNTING FIRM

You will need the names, addresses, and telephone numbers of the accountants for the company. If the company has changed accountants, you will want to ask these questions of all prior accountants.

Verify the numbers in any audit or compilation. Call up the accountant and go through the numbers one by one to make sure that the accountant agrees with them. You may even want to do this with the tax return to make sure the accountant has signed off on the numbers in the return given to you by the company to determine whether it is correct.

In one situation, the entrepreneur was not satisfied with the audit that he received from a large accounting firm. He copied the top of the accountant's report in order to duplicate the letterhead on some blank pages. He then constructed his own audit, and the opinion in it showed that his company making a considerable amount of money when, in fact, the auditors said it was losing money. He presented these falsified accounting statements to his board of directors and various others in order to obtain financing. Needless to say, when checking with the accountants to determine whether the numbers were correct, VCs uncovered a tremendous fraud. The entrepreneur served three years in prison for this act.

Most accountants issue a management letter stating what they find wrong with the day-to-day operations and, specifically, the financial controls of the company. If the accountants have issued a management letter, you will want to make sure you get a copy and talk with the accountant about its content.

Ask the accountant whether the books and records of the company are in good condition and easy for them to audit or whether they need substantial improvement. If the accounting records are a mess and the accountant is making hundreds of adjusting entries, it will mean that the company is, in a financial sense, out of control. Ask the accountant whether there are adequate controls in place to foil any misuse of funds.

Ask the individual at the audit firm how long he or she has been handling the work of the annual audit and working with the company on its financial matters. If the individual you are talking to is a relative newcomer, you will need to talk to those who have worked with the company over the years and ask them many of the questions you are asking this new person.

Ask whether the financial officer for the company is a good one and whether that person can grow with the company to manage all of the company's financial needs in the future. Ask the accountant whether he or she thinks the management team is a good one and, if so, why. Sometimes and accountant will have a unique perspective on the management team.

Ask the accountant whether the company is having operating problems. If is the answer is yes, ask him or her to help you determine what they are. Many accountants are quite candid in their assessment of the financial operations of a company.

See whether the accountant has begun work on this year's audit. If so, you should ask him or her whether there are any material changes from the financial statements that have been prepared by the company previously.

One public company showed earnings for three quarters in a row, but when it came to the fourth quarter, the accountants would have to make so many adjusting entries that all of the profits for the previous three quarters were wiped out. The company had overstated its profits, and the stockholders would not get the sad news until the end of the year. Ask the accountant whether this has ever happened with the company. It is another red flag indicating that the company doesn't know how to manage its financial business. If it doesn't know how to manage its financial business, you should not invest.

Ask the accountant whether there are any significant changes in the numbers set out by management. When you review the audit, look for disagreements over the inventory values or disagreements between the goodness of accounts receivable. Ask whether there was a disagreement over the work in process or the cost of goods sold. Ask whether there have been any material differences between the audit and actual financial statements.

One of the key questions to ask the accountant is whether anything in the audit would indicate that the company is having operating problems. This is usually a standard question, and auditors always expect it.

QUESTIONS FOR LAWYERS

Another professional you will want to spend some time with is the lawyer for the company. Make sure the current lawyer has been around long enough to know all of the company's secrets. If this is a new legal group, make sure you go back and talk to past lawyers and find out why they were dumped.

The basic question for the lawyer is, What suits are against the company today? Ask what suits have been filed against it in the past and how were they resolved. Ask the lawyer whether any potential suits are brewing against the company. Also ask the lawyer whether the company has filed any suits against others that are still open. Ask the lawyer to enumerate suits that the company has filed against others during the last two years. Ask the lawyer whether he or she knows of any suits the company plans to file against others.

It is important to establish the litigation history of any company that you intend to invest in. Although it is becoming a way of life in business to solve many problems through the court system, any company that sues a great deal or has been sued a great deal is most likely to end up in a suit with you. Any company that is litigious will try to solve its relationship with you in a litigious manner at some point. Be careful to document all legal situations so that you understand them in detail.

Ask the lawyer about product liability suits or problems, as well as any union suits or legal problems regarding the union. Has this lawyer or any other lawyer helped the company file patents or defend patents in suits? Has the company been filed against because it is infringing on others' patents?

SUIT SETTLEMENT

If there have been suits and they have been settled, determine the following. First, what is the maximum settlement that has been assessed in each case? What is the most likely settlement for any suits that are outstanding now, and when will they be settled? What is the nature of any suit that is outstanding? Does the suit have merit? Why does the suit have merit? Again, make sure you understand the litigation history of the company.

You might end your conversation with a lawyer with the question, Are there any legal problems with this company whatsoever? Sometimes a lawyer will hem and haw in response. If the lawyer isn't being straightforward, ask him or her the point-blank question, Why are you being so hesitant about saying there are no legal problems with the company? Again, if you find reticence, you may want to visit the law firm and go through the complete file—with the permission of the company, of course.

You should ask the lawyers to give you their appraisal of management. Also, ask them whether they know of any nonlegal problems. All of these should be open-ended questions so that you can get the maximum information out of the lawyers.

You should ask the lawyers whether they know of any suits against the management team or any of the individual employees of the company. Have any suits been filed by trade creditors or customers? This will also give you a flavor for how the company treats its customers.

QUESTIONS FOR INSURANCE AGENTS

Interestingly enough, the insurance agent can be a bonanza of information about the situation at the company, especially in the areas of product liability and life insurance. You should ask the insurance agent to explain the company's fire and casualty insurance, the product and general liability insurance, and fidelity bonds and life insurance on the entrepreneur.

Ask the insurance agent how many claims the company has made. Ask the insurance agent whether the company has been dropped from any insurance in the past. Ask the insurance agent whether the premium being paid by the company is standard for the industry or whether the premium is based on a poor record.

Ask whether the company or the entrepreneur has been turned down for insurance. If so, why?

If the insurance agent hasn't had a long relationship with the company, you will want to find the insurance company that is no longer the carrier and determine why the association was terminated.

QUESTIONS FOR LANDLORDS

When a company rents space from landlords, you will want to ask what they think of the company. You will want to document the company name of the landlord, the telephone number, and the person you talked to, because usually you will not have access to the investor/owner of the real estate but will talk with the real estate agent who handles the situation. The following questions are appropriate.

How long have you been renting to the company? How many square feet do you rent to them? Sometimes this differs from what the company has told you, and you will want to determine why.

Nail down where the rental property is located. If the company has given you the name and address of two properties but the rental agent knows of only one, you may have a bamboozling entrepreneur on your hands.

What is the monthly rental on the property? How timely have their payments been? Have you ever had to contact them for failure to pay rent? Have you ever had to threaten to evict them in order to collect rent?

Do they keep the property up? Do they make sure the property is in good working order at all times? Do they constantly ask you for changes in the lease and assistance in maintaining the property?

Would you rent to them again? This is a key question that you should always ask.

Finally, you should probably ask for any general comments about the company or its management team.

QUESTIONS FOR MANUFACTURERS' REPRESENTATIVES

Ask the representative what products he or she represents for the company. It is important to know precisely which products the representative handles. Sometimes a representative will handle only one of the company's products.

How long has this person been the company's representative? Remember that representatives come and go in most industries. Nevertheless, it's important to know why a representative is no longer representing a product or why an existing representative continues to represent the product.

What products not made by the company does this person represent? With this question, you'll begin to get a feel for the representative and be able to determine whether this is an important product for this representative or just a sideline. What percentage of his or her sales does this product represent? Is this an important product for this representative?

Be sure to ask the manufacturer's representative how many of the company's products he or she has sold during the last 12 months and what the dollar volume was. This might not be the same as the numbers being given to you by the company. At any rate, it's a good check.

Ask the representative to predict the number of units he or she can sell in the next 12 months and what the future holds in the next five years for this product. These projections will help you substantiate the projections being made by the company.

Ask the representative whether the quality of the product is good and how it compares with competitors' products. Ask whether his or her customers like the product. How does he or she feel about it?

Does the representative receive many complaints about the product? If so, what kind of complaints? Is the company quick to respond to problems with the product? Does the company "make good" to the customer if there are problems?

Ask the manufacturer's representative to compare and contrast the company's product with those of competitors in the same market. Is the quality better? Is the delivery better? Is there a perceived name for this product? Is there good name recognition? These are all important questions for the manufacturer's representative.

The final question we usually ask is about price. Is the price right? Is it too high or too low? How does it compare with the competition? What price does the representative think the product should sell for? Pricing is one of the most revealing topics you can discuss with customers or manufacturers' representatives.

QUESTIONS FOR THE ADVERTISING PEOPLE

When you talk to the people at the company's advertising or public relations agency, you will want to ask some specific questions. First, find out how long the agency has been advertising for the company. If it's only been a short time, you must find out the name of the previous agency and why a switch was made.

In addition, you should determine how often the company advertises. Perhaps its advertising has been rather spotty. The advertising people may be able to explain why that is a good approach. Ask about the average size of the company's printed ads to get a feel for whether they are adequate. Does the advertising agency have a standing order to place certain ads in certain publications? If so, find out how much and why the company will continue to advertise in that specific periodical. What is the cost of advertising, and what is the average amount the company is spending? How does this compare with other companies in the field?

Is the advertising agency always paid on time? Has it ever had to contact the company for failure to pay? Remember, if the company is not paying the advertising people and this is a persistent trait of the existing management team, you may never be paid either.

Will the advertising agency continue to run the ads for this company? Does it feel the company is making the right moves in its marketplace? Who is the agency's contact person at the company? If the agency deals with someone different from the person you've been talking to in marketing, you will want to talk to the agency's primary contact to see why he or she feels the agency is good. In addition, you should solicit any general comments from the agency regarding the company. How would they change the ads to make them better? What could the company do to capture more market share? These kinds of general questions can prod the advertising agency into giving you more information about the industry, the competition, and the company you're analyzing.

QUESTIONS FOR SUPPLIERS

The leading questions are: What does the supplier supply to the company? What is the annual dollar volume that the company supplies? What credit limit do you have for the company?

Other important questions are: Do you anticipate any shortage of any items you supply to the company? How promptly does the company pay you? Has there ever been a problem with payment? Have you ever shipped to the company on a COD basis only? What do you like about the company? How would you describe your relationship with the company? Are you treated as a good supplier? Will you continue to supply the company in the future? Have you met the management team? What do you think of them?

QUESTIONS FOR CUSTOMERS

It is important to get a customer list and ask pertinent questions about the company. Although a company will say that their customers are very satisfied and extremely loyal, you will always find something that could be improved. Sometimes the answers are very significant, and sometimes it is just a good idea to learn more about the customer's thoughts, because it can improve the company's product. In any case, it is important to get a qualitative "gut feel" about the customers' satisfaction.

Some questions would be: What products have you purchased from the company during the last two years? How long have you been buying from the company? Here you are trying to establish how long the relationship has lasted with the company.

How long ago did you purchase the product from the company? Has it served you well? What are the current outstanding orders that you have with the company? Are you a repeat user, or is this your first time? What do you like about the product?

Has the company's product lived up to the quality that you originally perceived? Does the company's product perform as well as you expected?

Have you ever been shipped faulty goods? If so, what happened? Did the company make good on them, or was there a fight?

Has the company lived up to the service representations it made to you before you bought the product? Has it been responsive?

Did you find the product overpriced? Or was it a bargain? Would you pay more for the product?

Do you think that the product has brand name recognition? Is its brand name recognition strong or weak?

Have you purchased products from the competitors of this company or from other manufactured brand names similar to the one the company produces? How would you compare them with the company's product? When you compare the company's product with others, how does it rate on quality, price, and service?

Do you intend to buy from the company again? Could you estimate how much you will purchase from the company during the next 12 months?

What change would you like to see in the company? What changes would you like to see the company make in the product? What do you think of the people you have had contact with in the company? Have you met any of the management team? What do you think of them?

QUESTIONS FOR COMPETITORS

It is very difficult to call a competitor directly for information. However, under certain circumstances, you may be able to develop information on the competition. Certainly, credit reports and information surveys abound on industries and certain companies. It is also possible to hire an investigator to call the company's competitors and get information in this way. You will want to make sure that you cover the competition in detail to satisfy yourself that you know where your company stands in relationship to those competitors.

QUESTIONS FOR SUBCONTRACTORS

Learning information from subcontractors is important because they are working with your company and may know quite a lot about how the company works. In many instances, the business could not operate without the subcontractor, so if the subcontractor goes out of business, it could destroy the company you are about to invest in.

Some of the questions that you will need to ask the subcontractor are as follows:

How long have you been doing contract work for the company? What is the annual volume that you produce for the company? Do you provide subcontracting to others in the industry? What is the annual volume of subcontracting work you do for all others?

Is the business with the company an important contract to you? If you lost this contract, would it be detrimental to your business? Have you had any disagreements with the company over production? Has the company ever refused to pay you for products that you have produced? Has it returned products to you, and if so, what happened?

What kind of investigation of your production facility did the company perform before it chose you as a subcontractor? Do you plan to continue to do work for the company? Do you like working for the company? Is there any possibility that your company will be shut down by strike or other problems at your plant in the next 12 months? If your plant burned down, would there be another subcontractor that the company could go to for the same merchandise?

CREDIT INFORMATION

Information on various aspects of a company can be obtained from basic credit reporting agencies. Dun and Bradstreet and Standard & Poor's both provide such information, but information about the individuals will be available from credit reporting agencies. You should run the corporate reports on the company as a standard procedure to make sure that the company does not have a bad credit history.

There are numerous major investigation agencies that can help you find information about the company. You may want to hire one of these to gain more detailed information about the company. You may use the same agency to do background checks on each member of the management team. We make a point of running background checks on each member of the management team. If you don't, there may be a little surprise in the future as you learn that they have sexual harassment suits against them, have tickets for driving while intoxicated, or have been sued by others quite a few times. Find a good background-checking firm and use it.

CONCLUSIONS ON REFERENCE INFORMATION

In this section, you will have developed a tremendous amount of information from the questions that you have asked of the many who deal with the company. You will also have collected data from numerous trade journals and other areas to find industry information. Remember that investigation is a long and arduous process, during which you must leave no stone unturned.

8 NEGOTIATING THE DEAL AND COMMITMENT LETTER

In this chapter, you explore how to calculate your risk and return, how to structure deals, and what to put in the commitment letter. You need to know what risk you are taking and what the expected return will be. It's important to structure a deal to your advantage and to spell it out in business terms so that your lawyer can put it into legal terms.

PRICING THE DEAL

Pricing a deal is one of the investor's most difficult tasks. There are dozens of different critical aspects to pricing, and this chapter touches on some of them.

RISK/REWARD

The greater the risk, the greater the reward—supposedly, but how do you identify and define risk? And how do you quantify risk? What is the probability that an enterprise will succeed? There are just so many variables in every investment you review that it becomes extremely difficult to quantify risk in most business situations. This is why experience is so important. From experience one can get a "feel" for the situation and judge the likelihood of success. Statistics can help define the risk by using a large database of similar investments to estimate the probability of failure and success.

At the same time, you can rely on some obvious factors to judge the risk involved in a business. For example, a large business with a large amount of gross sales usually has less chance of going out of business than a smaller company. An existing business that has existing cash flow will be less risky than a new business that has not made its first sale. A business in a stable industry will be less likely to fail than one in a new industry or one that gyrates greatly. A company with a management team that has been around for many years will have greater likelihood of success than one with a new management team with less experience. That small partial list gives you the general idea of the way you differentiate risk in one situation from another one. Good, hard work during the due diligence process will reveal the strengths and weaknesses of a business and its management team. From the results of your due diligence, you can determine the risk.

REMOVING RISK BY STRUCTURE

You, as an investor can use the structure of the investment to reduce risk. You will have to give up something, but what you have to give up may be worth it. For example, you can set the investment up as a debt instrument or preferred stock, rather than as common stock, and secure the debt instrument as much as possible. Where possible, you can use debt to invest and take collateral to secure the loan. As a loan investor, you can file a security agreement or UCC-1s to move from being a general creditor to being a secured creditor. (Note: A UCC-1 is the document a lawyer files in the state records to let everyone know that the investor has a lien on the assets.) As an investor, you may want to avoid high-risk common stock and even preferred stock, both of which provide a disaster scenario when a company gets into trouble and must be liquidated or put in Chapter 11 bankruptcy.

Within the bounds of debt, you can refine the structure to an art form. You may prefer a loan with equity (sometimes equity is in the form of warrants or stock options), rather than a convertible debenture because the loan can be repaid in a deal that doesn't make a great deal of money in the early years. As time passes, you (as the investor) will have your stock options, which may cost little or nothing to purchase and which may be worth something someday. You can hold the warrants for a long time and have no great reduction in your return if you didn't pay much for them.

As a general rule on options, you should ask for less of a company's equity for a low price, rather than more of a company for a high price. For example, would you rather own 5 percent of a company for a payment of $10,000 or 35 percent for $5 million? This is your dilemma when you negotiate the terms of a warrant agreement. You may want to have the smaller ownership with the lower price because if the option runs out, you can afford to exercise the option at a low exercise price, and it doesn't cost very much to carry the resulting stock. You can hold onto low-cost stock forever and hope that someday it will be worth something. These structural approaches lower the risk.

Preferred stock too can move the investment from high-risk common stock to a level in which you have a preferred return. Preferred stock can be set up to let the investor control the board from the day of the investment or if there is trouble. If the owner of the business has common stock and the investor has preferred stock, there can be an agreement that the preferred stock gets a preferred return of, for example, 15 percent before the common stock gets any return. All these structuring approaches are to be used to reduce risk. The reduction of risk can benefit the investor if there is ever a problem with the business and may not harm the upside if the business is successful.

While you are structuring the deal and assessing the risk on a nonquantitative basis, it's time to start thinking about return on investment.

RETURN ON INVESTMENT

As a backdrop, remember that VCs can average very high returns of over 30 percent return on investments (ROIs). Obviously, you want to achieve this strong ROI. One method of looking at return is how many times you expect to multiply your initial investment. For example, if you get five times your money back in five years, it's a 38 percent compounded return on investment. In fact, a rule of thumb is if you can get one times your money back for each year that you are in the deal, it's an excellent investment.

If you looked at every one of your investments and thought that you could get on the upside a 25 percent return on investment, including interest (assuming everything worked right), you would be very lucky to exceed a 15 percent ROI. This is because most projections are optimistic, and this means that some of the investments will return more than you expect them to; however, most will give you less than you expect. On the average, you would probably have less than a 25 percent return. So the desired return on each investment should be higher than the average you want on all your investments.

Sometimes you may be tempted to go into a deal that has been referred to as a "safe deal," "no-brainer," "good collateral," and "no real downside." Every VC has heard these buzz words and been told that he or she should accept a lower return on investment because the opportunity is such a good one. Most experienced VCs don't believe that there is such a thing as a safe deal. Before you jump into any deal, you need to know what kind of investment you're really getting into. Deals can be stratified into categories that give you a hint of what to expect.

TYPES OF DEALS

In general, deals can be divided into six basic groups, as outlined below. Here we set aside the risk and talk just about return.

1. **Big Winners.** Here we are talking about a big winner for you, not whether the company is a big winner, although the two usually go together. In this situation you get three or four times the money you expected to get, or about a 90 percent or 100 percent ROI. These are outstanding deals. These are the exception to the rule. Normally on your best deal, you are looking for a 50 percent ROI and are surprised when the company gives you the big upside.

2. **Winners.** In this situation, you get what you expected—a solid 25–35 percent ROI, and everybody is quite happy. Unfortunately, there are not as many of these deals as we would all like to see.

3. **Sideways.** A sideways deal is one in which you get the principal and interest back plus a little on your equity for about a 5 percent or 15 percent ROI.

4. **Workouts.** You will have your share of workouts. In these situations, you normally get your principal back with little or nothing else.

5. **Losers.** Losers usually consist of a 50 percent hit. That is, you might put in $2 million and get $1 million back. You should pray that you have few losers.

6. **Wipeouts.** Although VCs rarely have wipeouts, they do occur now and then. This is where the investor loses all or practically all of the investment. As an investor, you must avoid wipeouts at all costs.

USING PROBABILITY

So what have you learned? Invest in more winners and less losers. Obviously! To quantify your risk/reward and help you price a deal, you should categorize your new investment opportunities by the three top categories discussed above. The deal you are considering will be in one of the following categories:

CATEGORY	ROI (%)	PROBABILITY OF MAKING PROJECTION (%)	WEIGHTED AVERAGE (ROI) PROBABILITY) (%)
Big Winner	100	10	10
Winner	30	50	15
Sideways	10	20	2
Workout	0	10	0
Loser	(50)	5	(2.5)
Wipeout	(100)	5	(5)
Total		100	19.5

In the next section, you explore two investments with varied results.

The weighted average of the investment is computed by multiplying the probability by the return and adding the columns. In the case shown in the table, it adds to 19.5 percent. If your ROI objective is 30 percent and if the weighted average is not in excess of 30 percent, you should not make the investment.

Here is an example of two companies that show the results of using the weighted average above:

CATEGORY	COMPANY #1 (%)	COMPANY #2 (%)
Big Winner	10	10
Winner	70	50
Sideways	10	20
Workout	5	5
Loser	5	5
Wipeout	0	0
Total	34.5	28.5

PROBABILITIES AND DEVIATION

When you set the probabilities in the return column, you are also establishing the *risk* of receiving it. You have established a standard deviation curve for the expected return. For example, compare the two deals set out below:

CATEGORY	COMPANY "A" CHANCES (%)	COMPANY "B" CHANCES (%)
Big Winner	20	70
Winner	30	0
Sideways	50	0
Workout	0	0
Loser	0	0
Wipeout	0	(30)
Total	34	40

Look at the difference between these two investments. Is the investment in Company B a better opportunity? Company B is more of a crapshoot, a big winner, or a wipeout, whereas Company A has a greater chance of making some money. Given the expected return, one would want both deals, but given an investor's bias toward lower risk, deal B's return may not be high enough because it is such a high risk. So how do you judge deals that are so far apart in risk? The answer is to look at the return. Is a 40 percent weighted average return enough to take the risk implied in Deal B? Is 34 percent enough return to take the lower risk implied in Deal A? This is the type of judgment you will have to make as an investor.

RETURN

Another point you need to consider concerns the term return. In the investment business, there are too many ways of defining return. You will hear talk about ROI, the internal rate of return (IRR), and how many times our money an investment. Some investors figure return before interest and with interest. There are optimistic, average, and pessimistic projections. This is a fine exercise, but when it's over, there should be only one scenario, and the return to the investor should be computed on only one scenario—the most likely scenario. As an investor, you should set up the situation as demonstrated below:

All numbers are in thousands of dollars.

INVESTMENT	1ST YR.	2ND YR.	3RD YR.	4TH YR.	5TH YR.	6TH YR.	7TH YR.
Invested	(1,000)						
Return of Capital				250	250	250	250
Interest Income	75	100	100	100	75	50	25
Capital Gains							10,000
Cash to Investor	(925)	100	100	350	325	300	10,275

By using this type of projected cash flow to the investor, you can call on various techniques to analyze the return. You should always set up investment projections like this so you can understand them more easily.

RETURN TO INVESTOR

Hundreds of techniques can be used to measure return on investment. Simple ROI is the amount of money invested divided into the amount returned. For example, a deal that pays interest of $150,000 per year on a $1 million investment has a ROI of 15 percent ($150,000/$1,000,000). You can adjust the ROI for multiple years by dividing the ROI by the number of years. So a deal that paid $150,000 in year one and $300,000 in year two would have an annualized ROI of 22.5 percent [($150,000 + $300,000)/$1,000,000/2].

However, this simple annualized ROI lacks the added dimension of time. ROI doesn't take into account the time value of money. We all know that a dollar you receive today is worth more than a dollar you will receive tomorrow. Why? Because you can reinvest the dollar you receive today and make even more money and because the dollar you receive in the future will have less buying power because of inflation. The technique of adjusting for the time value of money is called *present value*.

PRESENT VALUE

The term *present value* has been used to define the price you would pay today—the present value—with dollars to be received in the future. Present value achieves this by discounting future dollars to be received by a certain interest rate. Often the rate is the alternate rate at which one could invest the money. This alternate rate is referred to as the *discount rate*. For example, if you could leave your cash in a bank at 8 percent, a discount of 8 percent would be used to discount the receipt of future cash flows. Under your 8 percent discount rate, $1 to be received in one year is worth only about $0.92 in present value. This discounting of future income can become complicated when multiple years are involved and the discounting is compounded each year. This complex approach is embodied in a technique of analyzing investments called the *internal rate of return* (IRR).

INTERNAL RATE OF RETURN

IRR can add the time dimension. IRR is defined as the interest rate that equals the present value of the expected future receipts. Theoretically, by computing IRR one finds the interest rate at which one would have to invest the money to equal the cash flows generated by the proposed investment. If a proposed investment had an IRR of 20 percent computed on the cash flow to us, we can say that if we invested our money in a bank at 20 percent, it would give us the same return as the proposed investment. The present values are the same.

There is one flaw in using IRR. It assumes that you reinvest the money received in the early years at the same rate as the overall deal. So interest received in the early years is reinvested at the same rate. For example, if the IRR on a deal is 35 percent, the calculation assumes that interest received from the investment in the early years is reinvested at 35 percent! This is not true in most investment situations. Although this is a distortion of the basic situation, it is one that most analysts accept. There is one technique that lowers this reinvestment rate. It is called *net present value* (NPV).

NET PRESENT VALUE

NPV can correct this flaw in IRR. NPV assumes that the money received in the early years is reinvested at the discount rate used in calculating NPV. So if we used a discount rate of 8 percent, that same rate would be used for reinvesting the interest received in the early years. This is a more conservative approach to calculating return.

INVESTOR'S STANDARD

There is no clear consensus in the investment community on which type of return calculation should be used. As far as analysis goes, you should use either IRR or NPV and be specific when stating which technique has been used.

The more difficult question is, What is the minimum IRR or NPV you are willing to accept? Here are some suggestions on IRR from the venture capital industry by type of investment.

STAGE OF INVESTMENT	EXPECTED RETURN TO INVESTOR (%)
Seed Capital	100
Start up	50
Second round	40
Third round	30
Bridge to Public Offering	25
Turnaround company	50
Leverage Buyout	35

COMMITMENT LETTERS

All investors and venture capital companies have very different ways of making a commitment to finance an entrepreneur. Some venture capital companies will not issue commitment letters. They have a verbal agreement with a small business person, then they begin to draw up the legal documents and attempt to close on the investment on the basis of the verbal understanding.

Other venture capital funds use a one-page "term sheet" that spells out the high points of the deal, that is, those items that are most critical, such as amount of equity owned and type of investment. A term sheet does give the lawyer something to start with.

You may prefer more detailed commitment letters. There should be a good intermediate step between the verbal understanding and the legal documents. Although this means outlining in a commitment letter the bargain struck on each side, it lets two business people state in business language what they believe the deal may be.

Some banks use very short commitment letters to identify the terms and conditions of a bank loan. These are more akin to term sheets than the type of commitment letter that most VCs use.

In the commitment letter it will be important to specify why each item discussed is necessary in an investment. Every commitment letter should cover five basic points:

1. The terms on which the loan is being made to the company and the equity options (this is the fundamental point of any deal)
2. The collateral for any loan or any external aspects to the loan that will be picked up by the investor
3. The conditions of the investment, both negative and positive
4. The representations made by the entrepreneur to induce the investor to invest in his company
5. The conditions on which the commitment was made to the entrepreneur.

An example of what you may see on a commitment letter is set forth below:

1. TERMS OF THE INVESTMENT

In the section of the letter dealing with this point, the investor needs to state clearly the terms and conditions on which the investment is being made.

> 1.01 The venture capital company will make a junior subordinated loan ("the Loan") of $10 million for eight years at an interest rate of 12% per annum, paid monthly on the first of each month.

This sentence is self-explanatory. In essence, the company has a $10 million infusion of cash at 12%.

> **1.02** The loan shall have payments of interest only for the first 36 months with no principal amortization, and beginning with the 37th month, the Company will pay principal and interest sufficient to fully amortize the loan over the remaining 60 months. All principal and interest outstanding at the end of eight years shall be due and payable in full.

The investor is abating principal repayment during the first 36 months and after that period, the investor expects the loan to be amortized over the next 60 months.

> **1.03** The loan may be prepaid in whole or in part, at any time, with no prepayment penalty.

Here the investor is allowing the small business to repay the loan. In some situations where the interest rate is high, the investor should add that the company cannot prepay the loan at any time. Otherwise, at some strong moment the company will prepay the loan and cut down the ROI that the investors were counting on with the high interest rate. On the other hand, if the investors have a large equity ownership in the company resulting from the loan, investors will want to encourage the entrepreneur to prepay the loan quickly.

> **1.04** Disbursement and takedown of the loan shall be 100 percent of the loan at closing.

The investor has invested the entire amount of money at one fell swoop into the company. It is much more common for the investor to require the entrepreneur to jump certain hurdles in order to draw down the money. For example, disbursement at closing might be only 25 percent of the amount being invested, with the rest coming in when the company has achieved certain milestones, such as sales of a certain amount or completion of a research and development project.

> **1.05** In connection with this financing, the venture capital firm shall receive at the closing separate stock options to purchase stock in the company. The cost of the options to the venture capital firm will be $100. When exercised, these options will provide 20 percent stock ownership in the com-

pany. The exercise price will be $20,000. The options will expire 10 years from closing. The venture capital firm will share pro rata in any redemption of stock by the company in order to expand its pro rata ownership.

In this situation, the venture capital firm is receiving a large amount of cheap options in the company. Once this piece of paper is signed, even if the loan is repaid, the investor has an option to buy the stock in the company for a significant amount of time. If the investors are the type who like to invest in a company and receive warrants, their basic objective is to run the investors' money through the company as quickly as possible in order to pick up as many pieces of options as possible. Sometimes, rather than using a percentage of ownership, it will actually state the number of shares and the price per share. If so, there will also be an antidilution clause stating that if the company sells additional stock and it is below a certain price, the VC will be issued additional shares so as to maintain the equity ownership. This is standard in most deals.

> 1.06 There shall be an "unlocking" provision whereby, if there is a bona fide offer to purchase the company and the VC wishes to accept the offer but the company does not, the company will be required to purchase the VC's interest on the same terms and conditions as the bona fide offer. If the company does not buy out the VC, it must be sold according to the terms of the bona fide offer.

The "unlocking" provision gives the VC an opportunity to exit from the company if there is a bona fide offer to purchase the company. In essence, if someone offers to buy the company and both the entrepreneur and the VC believe it should be sold for that price, the company will either (a) buy out the VC at the price per share indicated by the offer or (b) be sold on the terms and conditions made by the bona fide offer.

> 1.07 There shall be a "put" provision whereby anytime after five years, the venture capital firm may require the company to purchase its stock options or the resulting stock from the options at the higher of the following

1. $500,000 cash
2. 120 percent of book value times 20 percent ownership
3. Five times net pretax earnings for the year just ended, times 20 percent ownership
4. Ten percent of sales for the year just ended, times 20 percent ownership
5. Ten times cash flow, times 20 percent ownership
6. Appraised value times 20 percent ownership.

Most entrepreneurs will not agree to a put position, especially if it is at a reasonable price. As a negotiator, you as the investor will probably have to convince the entrepreneur that a put is in everyone's best interest because if for some reason the company does not do what the entrepreneur says it will do, you as an investor want some way of cashing in and going on to the next deal. Usually at this point, the argument revolves around the price of the put. In most instances, an entrepreneur will give in if the put is at a low price that just gets the VC out but not at any big ROI.

> 1.08 There shall be a "call" provision for a period of three years whereby after five years from closing and after the VC's loan has been paid in full, the company can purchase the stock options or resulting stock from the options on the same terms and conditions as 1.07 above.

As an investor, you should avoid call provisions if at all possible, even at astronomically high rates, because the only time the entrepreneur is going to exercise the call provision is when the company has made tremendous strides and all you're doing is capping your ROI. Certainly, if a 40 percent ROI is built into the call provision, it's nice to have but you're going to be called out and capped in your ROI only when the company is doing very well. You should as an investor avoid call provisions.

> 1.09 Any time after five years from closing, the VC may require a registration and public offering of the shares owned by the VC at the company's expense.

Demand registrations, as they are known in the business, are standard procedures for people investing in small companies.

It is rare that a VC will require a small business to register, but most often the VC and the entrepreneur are ecstatic with the idea that they can register the shares and make some money for themselves and for the company. However, although it is standard procedure for the VC investor to ask for a demand registration clause, entrepreneurs are usually not keen on this provision, usually giving it reluctantly.

> 1.10 The VC shall have full "piggyback" rights to register his or her shares whenever the company or its management is registering shares for sale, and such registration of the VC's shares shall be paid for by the company.

This paragraph enables you as an investor to ride on the coat-tails of any registration that goes on for public sale of the company. It means that when the stockbroker is going to take the company out for public offering, you as an investor have the right to offer and sell some of your shares in the public offering. Generally speaking, the brokerage house will not permit inside investors to sell more than 10–20 percent of their holdings in the public offering, but it's nice to have this opportunity so that you can sell some of your stock in any public offering. This piggyback right is a standard paragraph for investors in the venture capital situation.

2. COLLATERAL AND SECURITY

In this section of the commitment letter, you as an investor must set out what is collateralizing the loan that you are making to the company. Which assets of the corporation will be yours in case the company has problems? What personal assets will the entrepreneur pledge? You must enumerate these in detail.

> 2.01 The VC will have a second deed of trust on the land and building of the business, subordinated as to collateral to a first mortgage of $2 million from a bank on terms acceptable to the VC.

According to this paragraph, the VC will have a second deed of trust on the land and building owned by the company, and it will be subordinated to a $2 million first mortgage by the bank. There may be no equity left in the land and building at this time but as time goes on, it's amazing how the equity in the land, building, and other assets will build up. As an investor, you need a secured position on assets whenever you can it.

> 2.02 The VC will have a second secured interest in all the tangible and intangible assets of the company, including but not limited to inventory, machinery, equipment, furniture, fixtures, and accounts receivable, subordinated as to collateral to a first secured bank loan of $10 million on terms acceptable to the VC.

In this situation, the VC investor has a second secured interest in all the tangible and intangible assets of the company and is subordinated to a secured interest of a term loan from a bank of $10 million. A VC will frequently try to secure these loans in order to remove him- or herself as a general creditor of a company. This gives the VC some protection in case the company falters and goes into bankruptcy. It's not a sure-fire thing, however, because many times the equity built up in secondary collateral is not very much. However, a second or third secured interest in the assets of the company is better than being among the general creditors because you are higher up in the distribution of assets by the bankruptcy court.

> 2.03 The company will pledge and assign all the stock of the company and assign any and all leases of the company to the VC.

In this situation, the VC asks the entrepreneur to pledge the entrepreneur's stock or the stock of the entire investor group as collateral for the VC's investment. This will give the VC the ability to foreclose on the stock of the company and then to own it, should trouble come along. It is unlikely that a VC would ever do this, and it's probably more of a psychological thing to have the entrepreneur pledge personal stock to the VC than will be meaningful in a workout situation. You can imagine a scenario where a company is having a great many problems and the VC forecloses and owns the stock of this company. Now the VC can replace management but will still have all the problems that the previous management created.

> 2.04 The entrepreneur will give his or her personal signature and guarantee (and that of his or her spouse) to the loan.

Most VCs ask for and receive the personal guarantee of a small businessperson on a loan to the company. It is not quite as common on later-stage investments or leveraged buyouts. Sometimes the personal guarantee is used to make up for the entrepreneur's having little or no money to invest. It makes the entrepreneur think twice about doing something, knowing that he or will personally be wiped out if the company is liquidated.

> 2.05 The VC will obtain a life insurance policy for the amount of the loan outstanding, with the VC listed as the loss payee to the extent of the loan.

It is becoming standard practice in the venture capital business to require a life insurance policy on the life of a key entrepreneur or on several members of the management team. If the key entrepreneur dies, the policy will pay back the VC some or all of the money invested in the company and cancel any debts due from the company to the VC. This helps both the VC and the entrepreneur because the entrepreneur's estate will be the major benefactor of the company, which is practically free of debt.

> 2.06 The company will obtain adequate hazard and business insurance, which shall include flood insurance if the business is located in a designated federal flood area. All such insurance shall be assigned to the venture capital firm, which shall be listed as the loss payee to the extent of its interest. In this regard, the company will supply the venture capital firm with a list of all business insurance, and such insurance and coverage shall be acceptable to the venture capital firm.

Business insurance is an absolute requirement of any venture investment in a company. In today's litigious society with huge awards being given to people for very routine suits, it has become absolutely necessary to protect the assets of the business by having a large insurance policy.

3. CONDITIONS OF THE LOAN

In this section of the commitment letter, the investor should enumerate all the conditions of the loan. This will let the entrepreneur know up front what is expected in order for the investor to be able to invest in the company.

> **3.01** The company will provide the VC with internally prepared, monthly year-to-date financial statements, in accordance with generally accepted accounting standards (including a profit-and-loss statement and balance sheet) within 30 days of the end of each month.

This section is fairly self-explanatory, but it means that the investor will be kept apprised of the financial status of the company through monthly financial statements.

> **3.02** The company will provide the VC with a monthly one- or two-page summary of operations, to be submitted with the financial reports detailed in 3.01 above.

Every investor needs to know what is going on with the company beyond the numbers covered in 3.01 above. Most investors will require that the company prepare a brief summary of the major things that have happened to the company during the preceding month. This will accompany the financial statements as they go out to the investor. Sure, the investor should be in touch with the company frequently and should know what's going on, but it's also good to have management record on paper exactly what's happened in the last 30 days.

> **3.03** Within 90 days after the year end, the company will provide the VC with an annual certified audit from an independent certified public accounting (CPA) firm acceptable to the venture capital company.

A certified audit from an independent CPA is absolutely mandatory in these days of complex financial statements. As an investor, you should require every company that you invest in to give you certified financial statements. If a company can't do that, it is normally in deep trouble, and without audited certified financial statements it will be impossible to sell that company to someone who thinks that they can turn it around and fix it or attract good management to replace the existing management. Always insist on having certified financial statements.

> 3.04 Within 30 days of the year end, the company will provide the VC with projections for the next fiscal year in the same format as the financial statements.

Projections that you as the investor receive now while you're making your investment will go stale within a few months; certainly within a year, they will be worthless. It is important to have the entrepreneur prepare new financial statements each time the company goes through a big change and to receive new projections at least once a year.

> 3.05 Within 30 days after they are filed, the company will provide the VC with a copy of all material documents filed with government agencies such as the Internal Revenue Service, the Environmental Protection Agency, and the Securities and Exchange Commission.

An entrepreneur can easily provide information about the company by sending copies of government agency filings to all investors. This is not a great hardship for the small businessperson, and these documents will enable you to get a better view of how the company is doing. Tax returns, in particular, contain a wealth of information.

> 3.06 The president of the company will provide the venture capital company with a certificate each quarter, stating that no default has occurred in the terms and conditions of this loan.

It's also good to have an entrepreneur submit a monthly progress report indicating that all of the things you asked the entrepreneur to do in the legal documents are being done. This is something of a positive statement that everything is going well, and it can be presented simply. Entrepreneurs don't usually argue about this.

> **3.07** On a quarterly basis and within 30 days of the end of the quarter, the company will provide the venture capital firm with a list of inventory, accounts receivable, and other collateral to be compared with certain ratios.

The venture capital firm will often ask for certain levels in the business to be maintained, the reason being that if the company falls below these certain levels, the business will be worth much less. It's important to include such items in a commitment to a small business.

> **3.08** In accordance with generally accepted accounting principles, the company will maintain:

1. A current ratio of one to one
2. Accounts receivable to loan balance of one to one
3. Inventory to loan balance of 50 percent
4. Sales of $20 million per year
5. Net worth of $3 million

In this section, you as the investor will have dreamed up some ratios that you want the entrepreneur to maintain. These things make the agreement more like a bank loan, but usually you put them in for only certain critical items. For example, in the radio business, radio stations sell at a multiple of sales. It's not uncommon in legal documents for a radio financing to specify that the investor's loan will be in default if the radio station falls below a certain amount of gross sales per month, per quarter, or per year.

> **3.09** There will be no change in control or ownership of the company without the venture capital firm's express written approval.

Under the terms of this section, you as the VC will not permit any change in control of the company. To the small business person, this means that you have debt on this person and you do not want the people you invest in to be changed in midstream without your permission. Most entrepreneurs do not have a problem with this because they think they will be in control forever.

> **3.10** Management will not sell, assign, or transfer any shares it owns in the company without written approval of the venture capital firm.

Here again, the VC as an investor is trying to make sure that the small business person will not sell, assign, or transfer his or her shares in the company without the investor's approval. You want to make sure that the person you have bet on stays with the company and continues to work for it and will reap no benefit by leaving. Again, most entrepreneurs don't have a problem with this section because they are intent on making their fame and fortune in this situation.

> **3.11** The company will have board meetings at least once each quarter at the company's business offices. Although the venture capital firm's representative will not serve on the board, its representative will have the right to attend each meeting at the company's expense, and the venture capital firm shall be notified of each meeting at least two weeks before it is to occur.

By setting up a paragraph such as this, you as the VC investor have given yourself an opportunity to come in and see how the company is run, not at the management level but at the board level. You may even want to consider taking a seat on the board of directors; however, being a board member of a small company carries with it a tremendous amount of liability. Only those who can stand the liability of suits from IRS for nonpayment of payroll taxes and other suits from suppliers and disgruntled investors should sit on the board of directors. You can gain just as much information by attending board meetings without being on the board.

> **3.12** The company will pay no cash dividends and will not sell any assets of the business that are not part of the regular course of business without the venture capital firm's approval.

The venture capital company is usually very intent on making sure that a small business does not waste its assets. As an investor you want to make sure the small business doesn't pay out cash needed to run the business in dividends but rather reinvests in the business that you've invested in and goes forward and prospers. You also want to make sure it doesn't sell off pieces of the company to keep itself afloat, especially if those pieces are needed to make the company run as originally envisioned. This paragraph is a standard requirement and one that most small businesses don't have a problem with.

> 3.13 The company will not expend funds in excess of $2 million per year for capital improvements without written approval of the venture capital firm.

This is a general restriction on the amount of money that will be spent for capital improvements. You'll have a lot of fistfights with entrepreneurs over what the amount will be, and some will even say, "If you don't like the way I'm running things, you should vote me out as management, rather than restricting each and every item that we might make a decision on." But in this area of capital improvements, it is important to make sure you have some restrictions over management. If you don't, you'll build a palace with no income. This is one way to keep restrictions on an entrepreneur who wants to build a palace to the entrepreneur.

> 3.14 The management team, including you, will live in the metropolitan area where the business is located. The business will not be relocated without the express written permission of the venture capital firm.

Most investors want to make sure that the management team remains with the company and continues to live and work in the same area. It is practically impossible to run a small business from a distance, so restricting an entrepreneur to a geographic region should not cramp his or her style. It also keeps you from having to chase an entrepreneur who has moved out of town, because doing so will be in default of the agreement giving you the right to foreclose and take over the business if necessary.

> **3.15** The company will not pay any employee or loan or advance to any employee money that in total exceeds $250,000 per year without the written approval of the venture capital firm. If the company is in default for nonpayment on its loan to the venture capital firm or in default on any senior lien, or if the company is not profitable for any calendar quarter, the company will not pay any employee or loan or advance to any employee money that in total exceeds $300,000 without written permission of the venture capital firm.

Every VC will want a ceiling on the salary of the entrepreneur, and you should be no exception. It is not hard to understand and to make the entrepreneur understand that you don't want to invest your money if it is going to be drawn out as salary by the entrepreneur. If you put $500,000 in and the entrepreneur takes a salary of $500,000 out, what have you done except finance the entrepreneur's salary for the first year? Although arguments over the amount of salary will be long and heated, it is of paramount importance that you have some kind of provision preventing the entrepreneur from taking a great deal of money out of the company.

> **3.16** The company will not pay any brokerage fees, legal fees, or consulting fees in excess of $300,000 per year without written approval of the VC.

This paragraph is meant to prevent the entrepreneur from hiring a bunch of hangers-on who are not necessary to the business. It gives you some control over how many people outside the company are going to be paid. It is not a very big provision, and you may want to trade it for something else when bargaining.

> **3.17** The company will pay all closing costs and recording fees, which include all attorneys' fees, even those of the VC's attorney. The VC investor will select an attorney to draw up the legal documents; however, the documents must be reviewed and approved by the company.

One of the conditions in almost every deal is that the entrepreneur's company pays for all of the legal and closing costs. This is becoming a standard practice in the investment world. Just make sure that you have a professional drawing up the documents so the entrepreneur cannot complain about legal costs.

4. REPRESENTATIONS

In this section of the letter, you will state the representations made by the entrepreneur that induced you to invest in the company. If any of these representations are not true and the entrepreneur signs this agreement and takes your money, you have the prerogative to declare the investment violated and demand your money back. It may also give you leave to sue the entrepreneur for fraud.

> **4.01** The company is a corporation in good standing in (your state). It will provide the venture capital firm with a certificate of good standing and a copy of the charter, the bylaws, and the organizing minutes of the company.

This is a standard certificate the company will have to provide; usually the company's attorney can do it.

> **4.02** The company is primarily engaged in the business of (type of business).

Here you want the entrepreneur to state exactly what business the company is in so that if it gets off the straight and narrow and tries to get into another business, you will be able to invoke this representation the company has made, namely, that it is in a certain business, and one of the conditions of the loan is that it won't change the business it is in.

> **4.03** There are no lawsuits against the company, its directors, or its officers, nor does the entrepreneur know of any that may be contemplated. If there are any suits outstanding or contemplated, the entrepreneur's attorney will provide the venture capital firm with a letter stating the nature of

such suits and a copy of such suits at least 30 days prior to closing. The company will provide the venture capital firm with a copy of all lawsuits it has filed against others.

This is a fairly standard representation made by every small business, and you should make sure it is correct through your due diligence, but here you are also requiring the entrepreneur to state that it is true.

4.04 The company is current on all taxes owed; in this regard, the company will provide the venture capital firm with a copy of the last three years' tax returns and a copy of the receipts for payment of the last four quarters of payroll taxes.

Again in this section, you should have verified that the company is current on these kinds of things, but as final evidence that everything is all right, you are asking the entrepreneur to state something that he or she has already told you.

4.05 The entrepreneur has presented financial information, business information, and a business proposal that he or she represents to be true and correct.

This is a more difficult paragraph to get the entrepreneur to sign. What you are trying to do is get the entrepreneur to say that the prospectus the company has given you is true and correct. This means that if any of the information presented to you during the first year is found to be incorrect, under securities law you will be able to ask the company to rescind the financing and give you your money back.

4.06 The entrepreneur's personal financial statement showing a net worth of $5 million is true and correct.

In this paragraph you make the entrepreneur represent his or her personal net worth but only if he or she is a guarantor of your loan.

4.07 The entrepreneur will invest an additional $500,000 of cash in the company as equity on or before the closing of this loan on terms acceptable to the venture capital firm.

Here the entrepreneur will provide the venture capital firm with written information on the terms of this investment. If the entrepreneur is going to invest additional money, it needs to be covered here.

4.08 A group of investors will invest $1.5 million in the business as equity on terms acceptable to the venture capital firm. The company will provide the venture capital firm with written information as to these investments.

If a group of investors is going to invest additional money that too needs to be placed in the commitment letter.

4.09 The money borrowed will be used as follows:

1. Pay accounts payable $1 million
2. Pay bank debt of $3 million
3. Provide working capital of $8 million
4. In this section you cover in more detail the company's use of the proceeds. Don't be surprised to see changes made at the last minute here.

4.10 Upon closing of the investor's loan, the company will have approximately the following assets:

1. Cash, $8 million
2. Inventory, $2 million
3. Accounts receivable, $1 million
4. Machinery and equipment, $5 million
5. Land and building, $3 million
6. Other assets, $2 million

In this section, a VC will look for representations made by the company and if there have been no audited financial statements, the venture firm will select items that the company has represented to be critical to the operation of the company.

> 4.11 With regard to all material leases, the company will pro-
> vide the venture capital firm with a copy of each lease.

Here the VC will want copies of leases and other items that the
entrepreneur has represented as being in his or her ownership.

> 4.12 The company will pay no brokerage fees, legal fees, or
> other fees in connection with this loan without the venture
> capital firm's written approval; in addition, the company will
> indemnify the venture capital firm against all such fees.

Here the venture capitalist, like the entrepreneur, wants to
make sure that neither the VC nor the company has to pay
any brokerage fees. If certain fees are due, the VC wants to
make sure they are to be paid by the company and not by the
venture capital firm. Almost everybody who's been in the
investment business realizes that a broker often pops out of
the woodwork somewhere near the end of the deal, asking for
a fee. A representation by the company early on will prevent
this from happening.

> 4.13 During the past 10 years, none of the directors, officers,
> or members of management has been arrested or convicted
> of a material crime or a material matter.

Every investor needs to know that there are no crooks in the
company, and this type of representation is standard.

> 4.14 The company has a commitment from a bank or other
> financial institution to borrow $2 million on terms accept-
> able to the venture capital firm. With regard to this commit-
> ment, the company will provide the venture capital firm with
> a copy of its commitment and closing documents.

If the company has a commitment from a bank, make sure
you put it into the commitment letter and certainly into the
legal documents to assure yourself that the commitment
from the bank exists. As an investor, you should have already
developed this during the due diligence process, but it is just

another way of making sure the representation is carried forward in the legal documents.

5. CONDITIONS OF THE COMMITMENT LETTER

A number of conditions will not be contained in the legal documents. These are the conditions of the commitment letter. If any of these conditions don't go forward, the commitment letter is rendered void.

> 5.01 In connection with this financing, the venture capital firm will receive a $200,000) fee. Upon acceptance of this commitment letter, the company will pay the venture capital firm $50,000 of the fee and the remainder at closing. Should closing not take place through the fault of the venture capital firm, the fee in total will be returned. Otherwise, the paid portion of the fee will be forfeited and the unpaid portion of the fee will be due and payable immediately. Acceptance by the company of this commitment letter and the return of one copy of this letter to the venture capital firm fully executed by the company with the fee must be received before (date).

It is becoming more common for investors to receive one or two percentage points when the deal closes. This usually covers some of the out-of-pocket expenses involved in due diligence and investigating companies. Although most entrepreneurs hate to pay fees up front, it is good to get something paid up front.

> 5.02 Closing must take place on this investment before (date).

Every investor needs to have a date by which the commitment is rendered null and void if the investment hasn't been closed with the legal documents.

> 5.03 All legal documents must be acceptable to the venture capital firm.

As an investor, you need to know that the legal documents will be acceptable to you. It is conceivable that a lawyer might draft legal documents that don't follow the document precisely. That would not be acceptable to you. In this area, you protect yourself by inserting this paragraph.

> 5.04 The venture capital firm must complete a "due diligence" report reflecting favorably on the company, its management, and its industry. This will include a favorable credit check of the management and the business, and no adverse material occurrences before closing.

Every investor should run good credit checks and other reference checks on entrepreneurs. Many times, the commitment letter is signed before all this is finished. This paragraph will protect the investor from bad news that could be uncovered after the commitment letter is signed.

> 5.05 A favorable visit to the business operation by the venture capitalist must take place.

Sometimes the commitment letter is signed before a visit is made to the firm. In this case, again, a proviso that the investor likes the company when he or she visits it is in order.

> 5.06 The entire funds set forth in this commitment letter must be raised. The venture capital firm will invest only 50 percent of the amount set out in this commitment letter and will use its best efforts to assist the entrepreneur in raising the remaining funds stated in this commitment letter.

Often, the commitment letter will be for less than the amount needed by the company. In this case, an escape clause should be added for an investor who has committed early so that he or she can drop out in case the full amount is not received. This section is for the VC's protection.

AN INVESTMENT MEMORANDUM

Equity investments by VC firms often use investment memoranda or term sheets rather than commitment letters. This is a more shorthand method than the commitment letter, but almost all of the terms in an investment memorandum or term sheet are the same as those set out above in the commitment letter. However, consider the equity section of the term sheet below so that you can see what a typical commitment looks like if you are involved in an equity investment using a term sheet.

1. TERMS OF THE INVESTMENT

In this section of the memorandum, you are trying to state exactly what you intend to do with this investment.

1.01 The venture capital firm will purchase 100,000 shares of common stock in the company at $30 per share.

1.02 All shares will be purchased at closing.

1.03 If any stock of the company is sold by the company for less than $30 per share at any time within five years from this sale, there shall be antidilution for the ownership of these 100,000 shares.

1.04 If the company has not had a public offering of its stock within five years from the closing date, the venture capital firm will have a put provision whereby the venture capital firm can require the company to redeem the shares resulting from this purchase at the higher of the following:

1. Book value per share
2. Earnings per share times 10
3. $6 per share, fixed price

1.05 At any time after five years from closing, the venture capital firm may require a registration and public offering of the shares owned by the venture capital firm at the company's expense.

1.06 The venture capital firm will have full piggyback rights to register shares any time the company or its management is registering shares for sale, and such registration of the venture capital firm's shares shall be paid for by the company.

2. COLLATERAL AND SECURITY

Usually there is very little collateral or security except life insurance or hazard insurance on the business, but sometimes a venture firm will put in a liquidation preference, especially if it is preferred or common stock, to be sure that the investor gets out first if the company is liquidated. The paragraph dealing with this point looks like the following.

> 2.01 Should the company be liquidated, it is agreed that the shares being issued to the venture capital firm shall have priority in liquidation to the shares owned by anyone else. This means that any funds remaining after all creditors have been paid will first be paid to the venture capital firm to the extent of its investment of $3 million, and the remainder shall go to other stockholders, who are assumed to be management, until the cost of the shares is repaid. If any funds remain, they shall be divided pro rata.

3. CONDITIONS OF THE INVESTMENT

Almost all of the conditions of the investment are the same as those for a commitment letter and don't need to be repeated here.

4. REPRESENTATIONS

Again, representations for an equity investment are very similar to those of a debt investment and therefore don't need to be outlined here.

5. CONDITIONS OF THE COMMITMENT

Almost all of these are the same as in a commitment for debt money and don't need to be repeated here.

OTHER ITEMS

A number of items emerge from an equity investment. One of these is a consulting agreement. To get income, an investor may set up a consulting arrangement whereby he or she buys stock to obtain funds, rather than setting it up as a debt. This is better for the entrepreneur because the equity doesn't have to be repaid. Moreover, if the company gets in trouble, the consulting arrangement can be stopped because it has no collateral security in the company. A typical consulting arrangement will be stated as follows.

> 1.11 The company will enter into a consulting arrangement a with the venture capital firm whereby the venture capital firm will provide consulting services to the business for $100,000 per month. This consulting agreement will be in effect for the first 12 months subsequent to closing on the investment.

Another item connected with equity investments is the voting trust. This means that the entrepreneur will place all of his or her shares in a voting trust to be voted by the venture capitalist. Therefore, if the company misses its projections or somehow gets in trouble, the venture capitalist will be able to vote the shares owned by the entrepreneur and elect a new management team. This can be put into your commitment letter is as follows.

> 1.12 All shares of the company will be placed in a voting trust. The trustee shall be an officer of a bank acceptable to both you and the venture capital firm. If the company's sales are less than $500,000 in any month, the venture capital firm may name two additional trustees to the trust. A majority vote of the three trustees may vote the shares placed in the voting trust.

CONCLUSIONS ABOUT THE COMMITMENT LETTER

Both you and the entrepreneur should remember that the commitment letter is not a legal document. Its main purpose is to define in writing the business deal and the terms of the agreement between the venture capital firm and the entrepreneur's company. When you ask a lawyer to help you go through a commitment letter, it often turns into a very long legal document (an example of a complete commitment letter is in Appendix B). You will probably end up paying a substantial legal fee and not achieve the objective that you are seeking, which is good business letter.

Good business judgment on your part is probably worth more than a legal review of the commitment letter, although if you are novice at the business, it is wise to have a corporate lawyer go through the commitment letter with you and point out items that may give you some problems. However, you should remember that you have one more shot at formulating the business structure when your lawyer and the lawyer for the entrepreneur draw up the legal documents. The legal document will take each paragraph of the commitment letter and expand and clarify parts of it. However, if you do not understand the clarification proposed by your lawyers, you should help them understand the true business meaning of the commitment letter.

It is vitally important that the commitment letter spell out the business deal and not the legal deal between the entrepreneur and the investor. If it doesn't clearly state the business deal, you should revise it until it does. Once a commitment letter is signed, it is ready to be given to the lawyers so they can draw up the legal documents.

9 THE LEGAL CLOSING

Now that you have completed all of the important steps from the initial review to the due diligence process to signing a term sheet or commitment letter, it is time to bring in the lawyers. This may be the entrepreneur's first exposure to a closing, so some "handholding" may be needed along the way. The lawyers for both sides should be competent in venture capital transactions. One of the most painful processes is to try to educate a new lawyer in venture capital financing. Avoid amateurs if at all possible.

As an investor, you will want your lawyers to draw up the legal documents for closing. They should follow the commitment letter very closely. When they are completed, copies for review should be forwarded to you, to the entrepreneur's attorney, and to the entrepreneur. As an investor, you should read the legal document to determine whether it agrees with the business deal. The legal document should contain standard paragraphs—sometimes called *boilerplate* paragraphs—that lawyers need to put into these kinds of legal documents and that are not part of the commitment letter. Make sure the lawyer for the entrepreneur explains these boilerplate paragraphs so that the entrepreneur doesn't think you are trying to pull something over on him or her. An example of legal documents with these boilerplate paragraphs is provided in Appendix B.

In this chapter you explore two types of closings: a loan with an option to own stock (warrants) and an agreement to purchase common stock.

FIRST TYPE OF CLOSING: LOAN WITH OPTIONS

It would be truly be wonderful if an entrepreneur could simply sign an IOU to an investor and get the money for the business. Unfortunately, neither party would be well served by such an approach as an IOU type of investment. There must be adequate legal documentation before any investment can be closed and the proceeds disbursed. Any investor who puts up money before the legal documents that accurately reflect the deal are complete and signed by all parties has made a big mistake. Three fundamental legal documents are involved in a loan with an option to buy stock

1. The loan agreement
2. The note
3. The stock purchase option

Each document has specific objectives, and each covers separate ground.

It is important for every investor to realize that these documents will govern the legal relationship between the entrepreneur and the investor. As the investor, read the legal documents carefully. There is nothing frightening about legal documents. They are written in English and not a foreign language. As you read them, make sure they say precisely what you and the entrepreneur had in mind. There can be only two reasons why they may not. Either the entrepreneur has changed his or her mind and has instructed the lawyer to make changes in the documents or there has been a mistake. In either event, you should discuss the changes with the entrepreneur and make sure that he or she is not trying to back out of the deal. This will head off an expensive argument between your lawyer and the entrepreneur's lawyer.

Now let's review the three basic legal documents of our first closing.

DOCUMENT ONE: THE LOAN AGREEMENT

By far the largest document in this trio will be the loan agreement. It will contain 50–200 pages and possibly more if the investment is a complicated one. To some extent, the loan agreement will include the items in the commitment letter plus items standard for such loan agreements. A loan agreement contains 10 sections, each of which is discussed below.

1. Purchase and Sale. In this section, the lawyer will use specific language to describe the loan with all its terms and conditions. The lawyer also will describe the equity option with all its terms and conditions. This section will describe in detail the securities to be purchased and will specify the following:

- The interest rate per annum
- When repayment of principal will begin and over what period it will be repaid
- Dates on which payments are to be made, such as the first day of each month
- Delivery date of the funds by the VC
- Description of the VC's stock option
- Ownership in the company by the VC
- Cost of ownership

Also, this section will establish that the company has authorized and empowered its management to enter into the sale. It will discuss any other venture capital participants and the amount that they will be purchasing in your company.

2. Collateral Security and Subordination. This section will describe the collateral for the loan in great detail, and it will refer to a collateral security agreement that will be an exhibit to this agreement. Normally, the lawyer will describe each piece of collateral as set forth below:

- A second mortgage on specific land and buildings
- A third secured interest in machinery and equipment of the company
- Personal guarantees of certain individuals
- Assignment of certain leases
- Assignment of life and casualty insurance

3. Affirmative Covenants. This section covers all the items the entrepreneur agrees to do as long as this loan or option to own stock is outstanding. The company will do the following:

- Provide the investor with detailed financial and operating information on a monthly basis.
- Provide the investor with any documents filed with the Securities and Exchange Commission or other government agencies.
- Provide an annual budget by a specific date each year.
- Advise the investors of any adverse changes in the company's status.
- Maintain certain current ratios, working capital amounts, or net worth amounts.
- Maintain life insurance on certain executives of the company.
- Maintain property and liability insurance in sufficient amounts.
- Notify the representative of the venture capital company when board meetings will occur so that the venture capital representative may attend the meetings.
- Provide access for the VC to the premises and to the books and records of the company.
- Keep all equipment and property in good repair and in working order.
- Comply with all applicable laws and regulations
- Pay all taxes and other levies of taxes against the company.
- Maintain its corporate existence and other business existences.

- Give the venture capital firm the right of first refusal on new financings in the future.
- Maintain a standard system of accounting in accordance with generally accepted accounting standards.
- Notify the VC if it is in default on any loans or leases.

The items above will be spelled out in separate paragraphs in the affirmative covenants section of the loan agreement. Be sure you understand each covenant because once you sign the agreement, this will be the only thing the entrepreneur must do to keep the loan out of default. If a new covenant is brought up as a "standard" covenant, discuss it with the entrepreneur, not the entrepreneur's lawyer.

4. Negative Covenants. As you can imagine, this section specifies what the entrepreneur does not agree to do. Some typical negative covenants are as follows:

- There will be no change in control of the company.
- Management will not sell, assign, or transfer its shares.
- The company will not change the basic business it is in.
- The company will not change its current business format, that is, change from being a corporation to a partnership.
- The company will not invest in other companies or unrelated activities.
- The company will pay no cash or stock dividends.
- The company will not expend funds for capital improvements in excess of certain amounts.
- The company will not pay or loan to any employee money in excess of a certain amount per year.
- The company will pay no brokerage fees and the like in excess of a certain amount.
- The company will not transact any business with members of the board of directors, management, or its officers or affiliated individuals.
- The company will not dissolve, merge, or dispose of its assets.
- The company will not change its place of business.
- The company will sell no additional common stock, convertible debt, or preferred stock.

Each item above will be covered by a short paragraph in the legal documents. Violation of any of the above items will be considered a default, as set out below. Each item should have been discussed with the entrepreneur. If a new item appears, you need to discuss it with the entrepreneur because it will have an impact on the way you conduct business. If substantial new covenants appear in this section, you may have to meet with the entrepreneur to negotiate the terms in the legal documents.

5. Events of Default. This section describes items that will cause a default of the loan. A default may mean the company will have to repay the loan in full on the day of default. A default is usually called on any of the following items:

- If the company does not carry out the affirmative covenants
- If the company violates any of the negative covenants
- If the representations and warranties made in the legal documents are not true
- If the company does not make the loan payments on time
- If the company does not pay other debts as they come due
- If the company has any other loan called in default
- If the company has any lease called in default
- If a final judgment is rendered against the company by a creditor
- If bankruptcy or reorganization of the company should occur.

In this section, the lawyer will also specify what remedies are necessary to remove the default. As an example, suppose a default is called because the company has not made a payment; making the payment within 10 days of written notice of the default may be the solution to remove the default. Some defaults can happen easily, as in the case of a payment that is not made on the due date. If the company misses the payment date by only one day, the investor can call the loan in default. A grace period should be provided in the legal documents. This refers to the amount of time the company has to correct a default, once notified. In granting grace periods, remember that the longer they are, the worse it is for the investor.

6. Equity Rights. Here the agreement may cover a wide range of items relating to the equity of the company, the equity of the investor or VC, or option to own equity held by the investor or VC. These items include:

- The right of the VC to force the company to register the VC's shares in a public offering, free of charge
- The right of the VC to include his or her shares in any registration of the company's shares, free of charge
- Any restriction on the transfer of the shares being received by the VC
- A section referring to certain Securities and Exchange Commission regulations to which everyone must conform
- An indemnification of the venture capital company against any violations on issuing of stock
- Representations on the VC's part about the number of shares and options outstanding
- Any rights the VC may have to require the company to repurchase the shares held by him or her (this is the put)
- Any rights the company has to repurchase the shares at a later date (this is the call).

This section covers all the equity rights that the investor will have. This part of the document should cover all matters that you and the entrepreneur have agreed upon with regard to the equity rights in the company. These equity rights are the mechanism whereby the VC will someday realize a profit on the equity position. It is the investor's exit. Be sure you understand how you will realize a profit on this equity. This section is particularly critical to you. You want to exit from your deal someday, and these equity rights will be the mechanism for doing so.

7. Representations and Warrants. This section constitutes a warranty from the company that the representations in the legal documents are true.

- The corporation is in good standing.
- The company is in compliance with all laws.
- There is certain capitalization of the company.
- There are no subsidiaries.

- The financial statements are correct.
- There have been no material adverse changes since the last financial statements.
- There is no litigation going on, or if there is, a description and amount of potential payment is attached as an exhibit.
- The company is in compliance with all government regulations.
- There are no defaults on current borrowings.
- The company is current on all taxes.
- The company has rights to any patents that the entrepreneur owns.

Paragraph after paragraph of these types of representations and warranties can be expected in the legal documents. Each one has a specific focus and meaning. Your lawyer should be able to substantiate most of the claims. Read each one and be sure that on the closing date, all representations made by the company are the ones you expected.

8. Fees and Expenses. This section will explain who pays the lawyers for drawing up the documents, who pays for filing any legal documents at local courthouses, who gets notices, and so on. Normally, the entrepreneur's company will pay all the lawyers' fees and closing costs.

9. Definitions. In this section, the lawyers will define every technical or legal term appearing in the document. You should understand the definitions because they are an integral part of the entire document.

10. Conditions of Closing and Miscellaneous. This last section includes items such as indemnification, waivers, notices, and addresses. In this section, too, the lawyer will list the conditions for closing. Condition-of-closing items are things such as:

- Certificate of incorporation
- Copy of bylaws
- Certificate of incumbency
- Opinion of entrepreneur's lawyers
- Certified audit

- Certificates from Secretary of State
- Copies of all corporate action taken by the company to authorize its execution of these documents
- Copy of letter from senior lender consenting to this transaction

There will also be a final page for your signature, the entrepreneur's signature, and the signatures of any guarantors.

This is a general overview of the loan agreement. You should find that the loan agreement follows closely the terms and conditions set forth in the commitment letter. If it does not, something is wrong.

DOCUMENT TWO: THE NOTE

Usually the note will be written on one to five pages. The note will be an in-depth, detailed statement of the terms of the loan. It will specify:

- How much money is being loaned
- When it is to be repaid
- The interest rate
- What day of the month payments are to be paid
- Guarantors
- Conditions of prepayment of the loan
- Collateral for the loan
- Subordination of the loan to other loans
- References to covenants in the loan agreement
- A complete list of defaults
- Waivers and amendments

The note will be signed by the president and usually the secretary of the corporation, as well as any guarantors of the note. The corporate seal will usually be affixed to the last page.

DOCUMENT THREE: THE STOCK PURCHASE OPTION

Finally, you can expect a four- to ten-page document describing the stock options to purchase stock in the company. It will provide details such as the following:

- Duration of the stock option
- Any covenants of the company during ownership of the stock option
- The mechanism for surrendering the option in exchange for stock
- The exact price that must be paid when the option is exercised
- Adjustments to the exercise price (that is, the formula that will be used in case shares are sold at a low price or additional shares are issued by the company)
- The availability of shares owned by the company to be issued if the option is exercised
- Any written notices that must be given
- A definition of common stock
- Expiration date of the stock option
- Transferability of the option

Normally, this option will be signed by the president and the secretary of the company on the final page of the stock purchase option.

OTHER DOCUMENTS: EXHIBITS

Anywhere from five to ten exhibits will be attached to every financial agreement. Most of these were listed in our discussion of the sections of the loan agreement. Be sure you understand what each exhibit states because you will be agreeing that it is true and correct. Some typical exhibits listed for a closing are:

- Security agreement describing the collateral security for the loan (be sure the collateral agreed upon has been given)
- Financing statement that includes UCC-I forms that will be filed in the records of the courthouse (this statement will let all creditors know who has a claim on assets of the company)
- Opinion of the company's counsel on the validity of the transaction

- Copy of all corporate actions taken by stockholders to effect the transaction
- Copy of certificate of incorporation
- Copy of the bylaws of the company
- Certificate from the Secretary of State evidencing good standing
- Copy of a certified audit from accounting firm for the company
- Any forms necessary for government-related financing

The description above is a simple overview of the documents and exhibits. Appendix B contains a set of documents from an investment made by a venture capital company. When you receive the real documents, you should read each one in detail to make sure you understand what you are signing. Not all investors read the legal documents. Some investors ask their lawyers whether everything is all right, and if the lawyer nods yes, the investor signs it without reading the legal documents. The lawyer's nod means only that the legal documents are fine. It does not mean that the business deal is correctly presented in the documents. Only you can determine that. Some entrepreneurs do not read the legal documents. That is a mistake. Be smart; read your legal documents. Ask questions if you do not understand the legal descriptions.

SIMPLE IS GOOD

The complexity of legal documentation has baffled American investors and business owners for decades. The simpler the legal documents are, the better it is for all parties. If there is a simple way to say something in a legal document so that everyone will understand it, that should definitely be the order of the day. Some lawyers are carried away with a great deal of verbage that many people call "legalese." You should ask lawyers to refrain from following this practice. In legal documents, simple is good.

The best legal documents are those that you never refer to after the closing. If during your relationship with the entrepreneur, you never have to look at the legal documents, the deal has worked well. If you or the entrepreneur are constantly referring to the legal documents and questioning the meaning every word, something is wrong. This is a signal that you and the entrepreneur have a problem.

SECOND TYPE OF CLOSING: LEGAL DOCUMENTS FOR THE PURCHASE OF STOCK

You would think that the purchase of stock would be a simple transaction—that an investor could write a check and the company would issue the investor some stock certificates. As it turns out, that is far from the truth. There will not be a stock option (unless options are an additional part of the stock purchase), but there will be a fairly lengthy stock purchase agreement. An example of a stock purchase agreement is given in Appendix B. The stock purchase agreement will be similar to the loan agreement described above, but let us discuss the points again from the perspective of a stock purchase.

STOCK PURCHASE AGREEMENT

The stock purchase agreement has 10–12 sections. Many of the sections will be similar to the ones covered below.

1. Purchase and Sale. In this initial section, the lawyer will describe the sale of stock and the price being paid, as in the corresponding section of the loan agreement above.

2. Affirmative Covenants. Many of the affirmative covenants that were covered above in the loan agreement will be set forward in this section.

3. Negative Covenants. Again, many of the same negative covenants will appear in this section for the sale of stock.

4. Equity Rights. In this section, the lawyer will carve out the liquidation rights of the stock:

- Are the shares being sold to the investor on the same basis or do the shares get preference in liquidation?
- What dividends do they receive?
- What rights do they have to elect directors?

It is typical for the VC to have the right to elect one to three directors, as long as he or she does not elect a majority. Although the VC may have the right to elect as many as three directors, the VC often elects only one. This single director will follow the company, attend the board meetings, and if things become critical, will ask the company to elect two additional directors who will then have more to say about the operation of the business. However, often VCs do retain a majority ownership through the equity of the business from the outset.

Covered in this section are the many equity rights of the VC, including the right to register his or her shares in any public offerings and the right to require registration of shares free of charge. These equity rights are the primary exit for the VC. Be reluctant to change any of these equity rights.

5. Representations and Warranties. A full set of representations and warranties similar to the ones in the loan agreement will appear here.

6. Fees and Expenses. Again, this section explains who will pay all the legal fees; usually it is the seller of the stock.

7. Definitions. There may be a short section on definitions, but usually there is none.

8. Restrictions. Some restrictions may be placed on the entrepreneur's operation of the company. The entrepreneur may have to operate under certain guidelines as long as the VC owns shares. This section will describe any operating restrictions.

9. Voting Trust. A voting trust may be involved in a sale of stock. If so, this section will discuss the voting trust in detail. Here is how a voting trust works. Usually a trust is set up at a bank trust department with a bank trust officer as trustee. Shares of the entrepreneur and the shares of others are put in the trust. The venture capital firm controls the voting trust, but only under certain conditions can the venture capital firm vote the shares in the trust. This section will give the precise details on the voting trust.

10. Employment Agreement. Many times the venture capital firm will want to ensure that key employees continue to work for the company, at least for a specific period of time. The VC may therefore ask key employees to sign one-way employment contracts ensuring that the key people will be with the company as long as the VC is an investor. As part of the agreement, the employee may be asked not to reveal confidential company information if he or she is permitted to leave the company.

The employment agreement can be turned around, of course, to the advantage of the entrepreneur. It can ensure that the entrepreneur's job is secure during a period in which the venture capitalist firm may have an opportunity to take over the company. Usually this security is overshadowed by the one-sided nature of the contract.

A VC told us of three young MBAs who signed employment contracts. The contracts provided that these gentle souls to be paid a reasonable sum despite their brief experience in the business world. However, the contracts were for five years. As fate would have it, the business failed. Among the "assets" of the business were the three employment contracts. The institutional investor who had invested the funds foreclosed on all the assets of the business and picked up the employment contracts of the three MBAs. For the remaining four years of their contract, these men were virtually the slaves of this corporate giant.

11. Consulting Contract. Many venture capital firms play an active role in the management the company in which they invest. They may help the company to establish marketing or financial controls or to address any number of problems that may arise in a new or small, growing company. They want compensation for the time and attention their consultants take to help the new business get the ground. Compensation is usually arranged through a contract with the venture capital firm for management consulting services. This agreement will describe the services to be rendered and the terms and amount of payment that will be made to the venture capital firm for these services.

12. Conditions to Closing. Again, there will be a section on indemnification, waivers, and notices. There will be a list of items that must be completed before closing can occur. At the end there will be a page for you, the VC, and other parties to the agreement to sign.

LAWYERS AS INVESTORS OR BUSINESS OWNERS

Many lawyers will take it upon themselves to tell a client not to enter into a business arrangement because it is a bad business deal.

All clients want to know whether something is wrong from a legal perspective, but most business people become upset by lawyers who jump into the business fray in order to "save" their clients from signing a bad business deal. Some good lawyers are certainly good business people. However, very few practicing lawyers are good entrepreneurs or VCs. It's difficult for anyone to carry on two professions successfully. Every VC can tell you about a lawyer who killed a business deal because the lawyer felt the client was not getting a good deal.

You should encourage your lawyer to refrain from trying to renegotiate the deal for you. If your lawyer tries to renegotiate the deal, the entrepreneur will assume that you have directed your lawyer to do so. The entrepreneur will believe you are trying to change the deal or find a way to get out of it. Needless to say, this will take the entrepreneur's attention away from closing the deal and may start the relationship off on a sour note. Be very careful before you instruct your lawyer to negotiate openly with the entrepreneur. If there is something you do not like about the legal documents, go to the entrepreneur and negotiate yourself. Do not use a surrogate who is not familiar with the business deal.

EXPERIENCED LAWYERS ARE BEST

A lawyer experienced in drawing up legal documents for venture capital investments is worth a ton of gold. A lawyer trying to bluff through this type of investment agreement will destroy your chances of a quick and successful closing.

Be economical in your use of lawyers; they are expensive. Usually, you will be better off having your lawyer complete the first draft of the proposed legal documents, then letting the entrepreneur's lawyer review them. If you start with your lawyer, the document will have all the things you need in it, and you will not have to argue with the entrepreneur's counsel to put language in the agreement. This way can save significant time and expense.

One of the main factors to slow down the legal process is the lack of time that lawyers have to work on legal closings. Legal documents sent by a VC's attorney to the entrepreneur's attorney can sit on the desk of the entrepreneur's lawyer for weeks before the lawyer gets around to reviewing them. Tell your entrepreneur to remind his or lawyer daily, if necessary, that there can be no closing until the lawyer reviews the documents. Do not let the entrepreneur put you in charge of riding herd over the entrepreneur's lawyer.

You may not realize it, but your lawyer may incur liability by not performing quickly and reasonably. Any lawyer who does not close a deal that should have closed could be held liable for whatever damages are caused. Certainly a lawyer who does not act on legal documents sent to the lawyer for review within five days is courting disaster.

PROCEDURES FOR REVIEWING DOCUMENTS

When you get the first draft of the legal documents, be sure to read them very thoroughly. Too many people do not read the legal documents. Read the legal agreement for the basics of the deal, not for the meaning of every word. Compare your commitment letter with the legal documents. Make sure each point in the letter is covered in the legal document. Lawyers sometimes make mistakes.

LEGAL FEES KEEP GOING UP

Legal fees are rarely low. In fact, of all the fees that business people complain about, legal fees probably top the list. The question is not whether legal fees are too high but whether a specific legal fee is fair, in view of the work that has been performed by the lawyer. Some attorneys are unethical in their billing practices. They think nothing of padding a legal bill with 10 or 20 hours of work, then mailing the bill to the client without a great deal of explanation. Most legal bills consist of a single line, "for services rendered," followed by a dollar amount.

Because legal bills have become such a large part of business life, most business people are attempting to manage the fees. The most common method of managing legal fees was introduced by large corporations: They all now require a detailed legal bill. The bill must include hours worked, the specific project on which the time was carried out, the billing rate of the individual working on it, and the name of the individual authorizing work on the project. In addition to these detailed bills, many smaller businesses are requiring the law firms to give them advance estimates of the time it will take to complete a project. They ask the lawyer to call them once the lawyer reaches a certain amount of time expended. By doing this, the small business keeps track of the law firm's hours and does not let it run up a big bill.

If the small business has agreed to pay the legal fees for both your lawyer and its lawyer, it is incumbent upon you to help the small business manage the legal fees. This means contacting your lawyer and discussing fees. You must discuss the procedure for working on your deal and how the bill will be rendered. Do not let yourself be surprised when you arrive at the closing table and see the legal bill. If you are surprised by the amount of the legal bill, you have not been managing your lawyers very well. All too often, entrepreneurs receive a shock at the closing table. As an investor, you may be in a poor position to help the small business negotiate fees. If your lawyer is a close friend, you will have a hard time questioning him or her about legal fees, even if they seem too high. Although an investor cannot be expected to manage the small business legal fees, it is important that you manage all your own legal fees so you are satisfied with the amount that is being charged at the closing table.

How Lawyers Run up Your Legal Bill

Besides the unethical padding mentioned above, watch for the many methods employed either intentionally or unintentionally to run up your legal fee. Listed below are five of them.

Disagree on Legal Points

Your lawyer or perhaps even the small business lawyer will often disagree on many points. This means that they will have to spend innumerable hours discussing these points and working each one out to their satisfaction. Remember that when these two lawyers disagree, you are paying the bill on both sides of the table, even as they argue about minuscule points. There is a fairly simple way to cure this problem. When your lawyer has reviewed the papers drafted by the small business lawyer, tell him or her to mark each item in the documents seen as problem. Before discussing these points with the small business's lawyer, ask your attorney to discuss each one of them with you. Many of them may have no material business significance; therefore, you will be willing to let the small business lawyer put them into the agreement. Each time you knock out one of these small points for discussion, you save legal fees.

REWRITE SECTIONS

Some lawyers increase their fees by rewriting sections of the documents over and over again. Suppose the small business's lawyer presents a written version of the document. Your lawyer may rewrite the documents completely, running up secretarial and drafting time in order to redo entire sections. You should instruct your attorney from the beginning that there is to be one writer of the documents and one commentator on the documents. Your lawyer should be the writer and the small business lawyer should be the commentator. This arrangement will reduce legal fees.

RESEARCH POINTS OF LAW

Often, lawyers will disagree vehemently over points of law. The disagreement will send them scurrying to the library or to other research sources to clarify various points of law. This research can burn up many hours of time. Each lawyer is trying to show which one is the best legal scholar. You should instruct both lawyers that you do not wish them to research various points of the law without your permission and that you will not pay for such research.

LEGAL STYLE

Lawyers will correct each other on usage, style, grammar, and even spelling. They will use up your time for the purpose of "clarifying the language." Tell the lawyers that you are not interested in matters of style. Stress that you want a clear document and that is all.

ARGUMENTS

Most lawyers are by nature argumentative. They spend three years in law school arguing points back and forth. Once they enter the real world, they continue to argue with one another. You should remember that you are paying for all of these arguments. If you have two lawyers arguing with each other and they are each billing you at the rate of $350 an hour, you are paying $11.66 per minute to hear them eloquently debate the merits of a legal point. Act as a moderator and get to the heart of the argument. Ask your lawyer what the consequences will be if you agree to the words being proposed. If these consequences are quite modest or if the consequences are extremely unlikely, you may wish merely to sign the document, rather than fight to remove the words. On the other hand, if the consequences appear to be drastic, you must adjourn the legal meeting and call a business meeting with your entrepreneur partner to iron out the problem.

SYNDICATIONS AND LAWYERS

When you are dealing with a syndication of investors, each investor's lawyer may want an opportunity to review legal documents. There should be only one fee—for the lead investor's lawyer, not for each participant's lawyer who wants to look at the documents. If the small business agrees to pay for all the lawyers and if four or five investors' lawyers look at the documents, the small business is opening up the cash register. When you let the lawyers take out what they need to cover their time in reviewing the documents, the "review" may go on indefinitely.

Some lawyers tell a story about the young lawyer who began working in his father's law firm right out of law school. His father took a much-needed vacation to Europe and left his son behind to continue the legal practice. The first case the young lawyer worked on was a railway right-of-way case. The young lawyer noted that his father had been working on the case for almost 20 years. In several days, the young lawyer assembled the parties in a room and negotiated a settlement. The case was closed. When the father returned from his vacation, the young lawyer explained with glee that he had settled that long-outstanding railway right-of-way case. Needless to say, the father was extremely upset as he explained to his son that the railway case sent all of the young lawyer's brothers and sisters to college and the annual fees from the case had even sent the young lawyer himself to law school.

Remember, lawyers receive fees while cases are open. They do not receive fees from cases that are closed. Another factor to watch for in syndications is the tardiness with which other investor's lawyers may review the documents. Invariably, one of the lawyers will be slow and not get around to the documents for days. You must obtain the names of all the lawyers and constantly put pressure on each lawyer to submit his or her comments so that closing can take place. You can help manage this process. The lead investor needs to lead the lawyers to a closing.

THE CLOSING: A MOMENT OF TRUTH

Once the lawyers have drawn up and examined the documents and once the businessmen have ironed out the business problems, a big pile of legal documents will be ready for signing. Normally, three to ten copies of each document will have to be signed. The closing usually takes place in a conference room. Every closing seems to have its crisis. Usually the entrepreneur's lawyer will bring some documents, such as incorporation papers or life insurance, that are not in the proper form. If not all of the required documents are present at closing, your lawyer will not be able to close the investment. In large deals, the lawyers will get together the day before the closing date to see whether all the papers are in order and whether it is possible to close the investment. An inexperienced lawyer for the entrepreneur or VC may try to have a closing without reviewing all the documents beforehand. To simply pick a date and show up for a closing is almost a sure way to abort the closing.

A closing is an extremely exciting moment because it is the moment when the VC parts with money and the entrepreneur's business gets an infusion of capital. However, the physical process can take hours and be extremely boring. Documents are signed, shuffled around the table, looked at by lawyers, and verified by lawyers. It is, to say it most simply, a lawyers' environment.

LAST-MINUTE CHANGES

You can always expect last-minute changes. Generally these are minor items, but occasionally they are material. My recommendation to you as an investor is not to waive any major items. This is the only time the entrepreneur will be fully motivated to get everything done. Once it is closed and you have invested your money, the items you needed at the closing are less urgent. The entrepreneur will then have more pressing things to do. Don't waive the life insurance requirement at a closing. The entrepreneur may seem to be in no rush to get the policy. What if four weeks after you invest, he or she has a heart attack, but there is no insurance policy? Be tough at a closing. Do not waive material items.

CLOSING FEES

Lawyers can spend considerable time on the actual closing itself. Many hold a preclosing the day before the actual closing. This dress rehearsal, as well as the actual event, can be costly. Envision the lead VC's lawyer, the lawyer of the bank giving a loan, as well as the lawyer for the small business. These three lawyers may charge $750 per hour each. On top these fees are those of the junior attorneys, paralegals, and secretaries, which can run from to $80 to $150 per hour. All in all, the deal is probably being billed at the rate of $3,000–$6,000 per hour.

If the deal is extremely large and complicated and involves additional people, that figure can be multiplied by two or three. But for the moment, assume that the minimum is $2,000 per hour. If the lawyers spend five hours in preclosing and seven hours in the actual closing, this is a total of twelve hours. Twelve times $2,000 is $24,000, just for the preclosing, quite apart from what you will pay for the drafting, research time, and other document gathering.

There is only one way around the expense of closing, and that is to be absolutely ready when a closing date is set. Your lawyer should have reviewed all the documents in detail with the small business lawyer to ensure that when closing occurs and everyone is sitting around the table, everything that is needed to close will be at the table. There will be no last-minute scurrying for any documents and there will be no last-minute changes. If you can impress upon your lawyer that you do not want the closing set until everyone is absolutely ready, you will be doing yourself a big favor. Do not go the closing table prematurely. It will cost a lot of money if you do. What is worse, you will have to do it over again if the investment does not close.

WHAT TO REMEMBER ABOUT LAWYERS

You should remember that lawyers are merely specialists in a specific area and have knowledge of an area in which you do not, namely, the laws that govern business activities. Remember, too, that they are providing a service and that you hire them just as you hire any other employee or advisor. Tell them what you want them to do and you will have a satisfactory relationship with your attorneys.

Also remember that lawyers make money by charging for time and that they are disposed to spend a great deal of time working on something. Most of the problems lawyers work on are not legal problems. They are simply problems that businessmen have left to them to solve. Many business problems turned over to lawyers can easily be solved by two businessmen in a head-to-head discussion.

Before you try to solve a problem from a legal standpoint, be sure you have exhausted all other remedies. Legal solutions are expensive. In one case in New York City, a VC lost $150,000 when the lawyer, who was a member of one of the large prestigious law firms in New York, had been negligent in his closing of the loan and clearly was open to suit. When the venture capital firm looked into suing this lawyer, it found that it would probably have to pay at least $150,000 to do so. The VC was told that he would be lucky if he recouped any of his legal fees, much less the $150,000 that the lawyer had lost for the venture capital firm.

Also remember that the number of lawyers in the United States is higher than ever before. By many counts, there is a surplus of lawyers. If you do not like the lawyer you are working with, find a new one. There are hundreds of good lawyers seeking work with a growing company.

DOCUMENTATION

The lawyer should supply you with a complete original of all the documents collected at closing. They should be packaged by the lawyer into an indexed file that will become the basis for your legal relationship with the company. Make sure your lawyer delivers this package as soon as possible after closing.

10 MONITORING THE INVESTMENT

Investing in a small business has been compared with getting married, and closing the deal is said to be the wedding ceremony. To carry the analogy even further, after the honeymoon is over, the investor and the entrepreneur will have to make a life together. For the next three to ten years, these two individuals will be working together, -not so much on a day-to-day basis but indirectly. However, they will work together enough for it to feel like a full-time relationship.

INVOLVEMENT

Before you make the investment, you will have to determine how much you intend to be involved in the business. Most venture capital investment firms are not passive. Most venture firms are extremely active in the management of companies and have a consulting staff to help perform this task. These consultants may supply marketing expertise to help improve the small business's marketing effort. The VC might also supply production expertise to help with problems in the production area or financial expertise to help with financial matters. Furthermore, the consultants can help with the overall management of the company. And almost always, the VC investor will help with hiring of any top executive for the company.

However, most venture capital firms are not staffed with consultants. Many will not invest in the company unless it has a full management team to run the business on a day-to-day basis. By and large, venture capital firms do not have expertise in marketing, production, or administrative matters. Most managers of venture capital companies are heavyweights in the area of finance and recruiting management talent for their investments. If they have been in business for an extended period of time, they may possess considerable knowledge of business practices.

As an investor, you will need to determine what role you will play in the business. If you want a very small role, be sure the management team is complete so that it will not have to depend on you.

MAJOR POLICY DECISIONS

All major policy decisions about the company should be discussed with the investor and the entrepreneur. Both of you have a vested interest, and you should talk about any major changes. It is very helpful if the entrepreneur describes any major decisions that need to be made in a memo. This memo should be the basis on which the two of you get together and discuss the situation. When entrepreneurs put "major problems" down on paper, they seem to be reduced considerably.

MONTHLY REPORTS

Monthly financial statements are usually required by venture capital firms when they invest in the company, and this is the minimum any investor should require. The importance of timely monthly financial statements is second only to that of timely monthly payments on debts owed to investors. If you are not receiving timely monthly financial statements and a report on the company, you need to visit the company and find out why. It is usually a sign that the company is having more than reporting problems.

You may have heard practically every excuse for not preparing a monthly financial statement. To date, none are worth the breath is takes to utter them. Simply stated, no firm can be managed without accurate and timely monthly financial statements. Any entrepreneur who begins to tell you that he doesn't need them should be replaced. Without regular financial statements, there is no way that an investor can make reasonable decisions about the business's health. Tardy monthly financial statements are a big red flag to every VC.

Not only should these statements be prepared monthly, but they should also be accurate. Every VC has been in an investment in which after the auditors have come in and adjusted the year-end financial statements, the VC had quite a surprise. There are various types of surprises, but the most common one is lower earnings. The most common "big surprise" is a company that will show profits for 11 months and a huge loss for the year, after the accountant has adjusted all of the sales and expense numbers.

The usual reason given for these year-end surprises is inaccurate accounting records for accounts payable and inventory. Also, some entrepreneurs blame the problem on standard cost systems, and as a result have a year-end write-down. Few financial statements do not have adjustments at the end of the year; however, it is the magnitude of the adjustment that you should be concerned about. The reason for any significant change in financial statements at year's end needs to be explained fully. Any entrepreneur who gives the VC a big surprise at year's end, and has not fully prepared the VC in the prior months for large write-offs, has destroyed much of entrepreneur's credibility. When credibility is gone, your investment is definitely in trouble.

MONTHLY WRITTEN REPORT

A monthly written report in letter or memo form stating exactly what is going on at the business is required by almost every venture capital firm. An example of such a monthly report follows:

MEMORANDUM

TO: A. V. Capitalist

FROM: O.K. Entrepreneur

SUBJECT: Monthly Report for October

Attached are the monthly financial statements for the nine-month period ending September 30. The profit-and-loss statement is understated in that our company will probably not pay taxes at the rate of 50% this year because of our net operating loss carried forward from last year. This should put approximately 95% of the pretax dollars to the bottom line.

As we near year's end, it is evident that the next year will be an extremely busy year. Our backlog has increased fivefold over last year. You should also note that inventories have increased approximately 40% more than our forecast. This is due to three very large orders that are now working their way through our production line. We have had to add people to the second shift to make sure that the items come through on schedule. None of these three orders will be completed and shipped by our year's end; therefore, we will start out the year with an extraordinary amount of sales in the first several months.

We have talked to four people since we began looking for a controller to relieve some of the duties of our vice president of finance. However, as of today we have not found a suitable candidate but may be able to find one within the next 10–20 days.

Finally, I am happy to say that the second generation of our product has now been completely designed and developed, and should be ready for introduction into the marketplace within six months at the national convention/trade fair. It will be an important milestone for our company; we introduced our first prototype only two years ago and have since built many of these products. At our next board meeting we may be able to see a second-generation unit.

The monthly report above mentioned several key items, each of which has bearing on the future of the company. It also included a brief discussion of the financial statements, which are fairly self-explanatory. The discussion of the financial statements brought out a point that probably was not obvious to the VC reviewing the financial statement for 10 minutes. It is incumbent upon you to highlight in the monthly report any negative—or in this case, positive—developments.

Board Meetings/Investor Meetings

The company should have regular board or investor meetings so that the investor can hear a verbal report and ask questions of the management. You can keep fairly well informed through financial statements and memos, but a face-to-face meeting two to four times a year is a necessity if you are to keep up with the business. It is important that the small business prepare for these meetings. Management should have an agenda and go through it as though they were holding a formal meeting with their board of directors and stockholders.

The first thing on the agenda should be the financial statements. Every management team should be required to review the financial statements against statements of past periods and projections. If management is presenting a new set of projections, a detailed explanation is in order. In general, the entire meeting should have a financial orientation, rather than a marketing or production orientation. As an investor, you are looking at the numbers, and the numbers speak louder than words. The entrepreneur should tell you how much cash the company has on hand and how much credit in the bank lines.

As part of the meeting, the investor should be taken on an abbreviated plant tour and shown any new improvements that are being made in the company. Other members of the management team should be present at these meetings and should participate in the discussions. An investor should have easy access to all of the individuals on the management team, and each should be questioned during these sessions.

In the early stages of the investment, the entrepreneur should be able to produce a cash reconciliation showing exactly where the money invested by the venture capital group was spent.

OTHER DISCUSSION ITEMS

If the entrepreneur has completed any market research or customer surveys, the results of those should be shared with the investor, especially if there is a significant change from the company's original perception. If the entrepreneur has news about the competition and their activities, this should also be passed along. If suppliers have changed policies or the entrepreneurs have found new suppliers, the investors are normally told of these changes at this time. If the entrepreneur fails to do so, you should ask your own questions about such items.

You may want to ask whether any industry studies or articles about the company or industry in general have appeared in any trade journals and whether you can get copies of them for background information. You will want to ask whether the company has hired any key people or whether it has fired some of the people that you have met before. Hiring a new director of marketing or changing a controller is a material action, and you should look for these changes. You should ask what changes in overhead have transpired and what additions or subtractions have been made, and you should ask for an explanation. If the company is opening additional offices, find out how it justifies this move.

Make sure to find out what kind of capital expenditures have been made since the last time you met. Any material changes in the backlog, either up or down, should be high-lighted in the entrepreneur's discussion. When audit time comes around, make sure you determine when the audit is going to be out; if it is going to be late, find out why. If research and development is going on, ask for completion dates. As an investor, you should make sure the company meets those completion dates. If there is a target date for introducing a product into the marketplace, you should know whether that target date is met. As an investor, you will always be seeking material information about the company in which you have invested. You don't want to be inundated with a huge amount of statistical information, but you need to keep up to date on any material changes in the business or the industry.

You will probably find it helpful to subscribe to the magazines and newspapers in any industry in which you are investing. This way, at least once a month or sometimes every week (in the case of a newspaper), you gather information about the industry in which your company is competing. It keeps you up to date. The more you keep up to date on the business and its industry, the more successful your investments will be.

MAINTAINING GOOD RECORDS

Maintaining records of your investment will be the key to keeping up and understanding the investments you have made in a company. It is imperative that the following records be kept accurately.

LEGAL RECORDS

The legal documents are your bible for every investment. You should have complete files containing accurate statements of all amendments, extensions, conversions, sales, exercises of warrants, and the like. The items in your files should be executed copies of the purchase agreement with all modifications. Any supporting agreements should also be enclosed. In addition, you should have conformed copies of all the securities, corporate charter documents and bylaws, specific documents to which the venture firm is a party, and copies of pledges, voting trust, escrow agreements, and mortgages. Any options or employment benefit plans and any franchises or patents, as well as any legal opinions and other miscellaneous items should also be included. All of these should be bound and indexed for easy reference. If you have not organized your legal file correctly, you will regret it later.

CORRESPONDENCE FILE

You should maintain a general file of correspondence between you and the company. The contents of this file should be arranged in chronological order but do not need to be indexed to specific sections. Instead, tabs can be placed on specific correspondence with meaningful data. The general correspondence file should also include any memos that you dictate to the file to record conversations with the management team. It is extremely helpful to put these notes in the file because they will jog your memory about things that have occurred in the business that you may need to remember in following a company accurately. The memo need not be typed up each time you talk to the entrepreneur. But if you take notes constantly, you will want to record the highlights of the conversation. At the top of the page, write the name of the investment and make sure that you put it in the general correspondence file. This will let you refer back to conversations that you have had with the people at the company and will put you in a better position to judge the progress of the company.

FINANCIAL RECORDING FILE

In addition to the legal file and the general correspondence file, you should keep a file of the monthly financial statements, as well as any annual audits. Other financial information, such as tax returns or flash reports on sales should also go in the file. In addition, there should be both projections and actual statements in the file. This will help you continue to monitor the situation in which you are an investor. You may also want to file in this section the one- or two-page reports supplied by the company as to the financial operations of the business. It may be easier to keep them with the financial information so that you can follow the company's progress without waiting for a lot of correspondence.

BOARD MEETING FILES

If you have been elected to the board of directors or if you are a visiting member of the board of directors on a regular basis, you may want to set up a file that includes all the information that you have been given at board meetings, except for the financial information that you will put in the financial file. This will give you an ongoing file that will help you follow the progress of the company from the standpoint of the board of directors. It may be critical for you to review certain events at the board level to determine whether the company is going in the right direction. For the above reasons, you may need a separate board file. If you are on the board of directors, this separate file will also help you remember what has happened at prior meetings when you attend board meetings.

TRACKING FILE

All venture capital funds track the financial progress of their investments by setting up tracking files. These are nothing more than spreadsheets that contain past key information as well as budget and projected information. When new information comes in, the VC can compare historical and projected information with current information to evaluate the progress of the company and compare budgeted information with actual information to see whether the company is on budget. These tracking files often contain all of the ratios in full so that a VC can quickly see whether the company is having financial operating problems.

Most of the tracking files are kept on computer spreadsheets and are printed out or digitally conveyed at regular intervals for people to review. The files may also be kept in the common files area of a central VC computer where all the members of the venture capitalist firm have easy access.

When financial information is received that is not digital, it is keyed and transferred to the tracking model spreadsheet. This is stored in the tracking model file, which is then used to compute all the necessary ratios and to compare them with past results or projected results. This type of detailed financial information can be extremely useful in monitoring a company and will indicate how strong the operating performance really is.

WARNING SIGNS

Generally speaking, entrepreneurs are unrealistic in evaluating problems. They often fail to recognize the early stages of failure. Entrepreneurs are by nature optimistic. They will cling to their dreams until the doors to their businesses are locked tight and the auctioneers have sold off the last piece of equipment. In all probability, you will have to be the first to react to the warning signals you receive about the business. This is not a difficult task.

These signals of problems are commonly called "red flags." Normally, investors are the first to point out problems and burst the dream bubble of the entrepreneur. As such, you are apt to incur the anger of your entrepreneur. It is in your best interest to seek cooperation from your entrepreneur but at the same time, you should not let an obvious red flag go unnoticed. If you see the problem and your entrepreneur doesn't, you are doomed to have a problem business. Listed below are a number of red flags that VCs often see.

LATE PAYMENTS

If the entrepreneur is late in making payments on a convertible debenture or debts to the bank, the investor will see this tardiness as a very tight cash flow. Some entrepreneurs think it is acceptable not to make payments on investor's debt so that they can use the money as working capital. If the entrepreneur's business is not making payments to you, it is probably not paying other folks, including the IRS, payroll taxes, and suppliers. It is only a matter of time before the day of reckoning will arrive. When you find these early warning signals, make sure you try to become involved in the business early enough to head off any potential problems.

LOSS OF PROFITS

If the monthly financial statements start showing losses, you should become concerned. Losses can be a temporary aberration, but you need to determine that very quickly. Don't listen to the entrepreneur who says the company will be profitable in the next month or quarter. Make sure you go into the details of the problem with the entrepreneur to determine exactly why he or she believes the company is going to improve. Do your own investigation on the numbers, if possible, so you can better understand problem.

LATE FINANCIAL REPORTS

Tardiness in sending out financial reports and other items to the investor is a clear sign that the business is not operating well. Usually financial statements are late because of bad news. Every investor should know that when the statements are late, he or she is likely to get a financial surprise. If financials are late, make sure you contact the person responsible in the firm and find out why. No one can run a business without timely financial statements.

POORLY PREPARED FINANCIAL REPORTS

Sometimes the entrepreneur prepares financial reports quickly but not accurately. Poor reports are unreliable indicators of how the company is doing. They are definitely a red flag to anyone investing in a company. One entrepreneur sent financial statements to the VC that showed the company was marginally profitable. This was good news, because the business had been losing money. Then the VC discovered that several line items, such as rent and interest payments, had been excluded from the statement. What was worse, when the VC added up the expense column, the VC found an error that understated expenses by 20%. The entrepreneur said these were merely minor mistakes, but within six months the company was liquidated.

LARGE CHANGES IN BALANCE SHEET ITEMS

If accounts payable have increased rapidly, you should suspect that the company is not paying its bills. You need to find out why as soon as possible. If inventory has become very large, you should also become suspicious. It means that sales are not keeping pace with production, and the items are ending up in inventory. Similarly, ballooning accounts receivable may mean that the company is unable to collect some of the receivables that have been booked as sales but perhaps weren't sales at all, merely products put out on consignment that will come back at a later date. Certainly, this is a red flag.

UNAVAILABLE ENTREPRENEUR

When your telephone calls to entrepreneurs are consistently not returned, this is a sign of problems. The entrepreneur may be afraid that you will ask questions about the business and find out it is in deep trouble. Another bad sign is the entrepreneur's failure to schedule regular board meetings. This is a clear warning signal to the investor.

LARGE THEFTS

Unexplained large thefts of inventory may be an indication that the entrepreneur is stealing from the company and covering it up by reported theft. More revealing is theft that the insurance company does not cover. This normally means that the entrepreneur is unwilling to pursue the case with the insurance company because investigation by the insurance company is not welcome. An unexplained fire falls in the same category. Entrepreneurs in trouble often try to cover up their problems with fire. In the South, a large fire that destroys a business inventory has been called "selling out to a Northern concern." As the story goes, "good old boys" will insure their assets through a Northern insurance company, then a mysterious fire will wipe out all the inventory, and they will collect from the Northern insurance company.

MAJOR ADJUSTMENTS IN FIGURES

As discussed before, large year-end adjustments of numbers indicate that management is not running the company well. If the company has to write off a large part of the inventory or if the accounting firm is not willing to capitalize some expenses, the impact on the profit-and-loss statement will be disastrous. This type of adjustment is a sure indication that management is not running the company well. This is a very large red flag.

SIGNIFCANT CHANGES IN MANAGEMENT

Because the decision-making process is handled by so few people in a small company, when one of these decision makers leaves, it is a sure sign of trouble. Continuity of management is essential in business, and the lack of it throws a warning signal not only to the investor but also to employees, customers, and other creditors.

You must determine whether an employee has been fired for good cause or whether the departing employee "jumped ship" because it will soon be sinking. If possible, talk to the employee and find out why he or she has left.

MAJOR CHANGES IN SALES AND ORDER BACKLOGS

As an investor, you are probably following the backlog and sales of the company in more detail than the actual financial statement. When you see the backlog declining, this is a sure indication that the company is going to have problems in the future. Increasing backlog may indicate a problem in production or shipping. Decreasing backlog may indicate that the company is having severe problems in the marketplace. Any rapid change in the backlog needs to be explained.

At times, backlog builds up because the price of the product has been cut and the company is having a tremendous problem in meeting the new pricing structure. A big change in gross profit margin can keep sales increasing, but profits will eventually be eroded. Keep your eye on the backlog, because it may mean that the company will have to revise its lead times to meet customer demands. This backlog could ultimately affect sales. It also may mean that the company will have to expand its production capacity to meet the demands of its customers.

INVENTORY CHANGES

Inventory figures can give you a clue as to what is going on in the company. Inventory turnover that is low in comparison with the rest of the industry may indicate that the company's product is not being accepted in the marketplace and that too much money is tied up in inventory. Out-of-stock items, especially on fast-moving products, can be a sure indication of problems on the production side of the business.

Any inaccuracies in inventory are a sure sign that the company is not being run well. Large changes in the records so that they match physical inventory may indicate that the production process and inventory are both being poorly managed. Eventually, these changes in inventory will have to hit the profit-and-loss statement and will harm the company. A properly managed and documented system is the backbone of a good company.

LACK OF PLANNING

Every company needs to budget and plan. A company that does this poorly will surely not survive. A company with a sound planning system will be able to tell where the company is going. When a budget is missed month after month, you should determine the reason. In addition, you should become concerned if you find that the company has failed to meet the goals of its long-range plan. It cannot succeed in the marketplace if it continues on such a course. As a business grows from the entrepreneurial stage, preparation of financial and operating projections becomes more important to the decision-making process. Thus, the business cannot continue to prosper without timely and accurate data.

CHANGES IN ACCOUNTING METHODS

At times, it is necessary for a company to change its accounting methods but at other times, such changes are adopted so that creditors and potential lenders will not detect the problems that are brewing. The key signs to look for here are changes in the depreciation or useful life of units, changes in the method of recognizing income (such as recognizing revenue before the company has had all the performance criteria), and changes in the method of valuing inventory, such as LIFO (last in first out) to FIFO (first in first out) for overhead rate or the amount of scrap rates. Eventually, they all show up on the profit and-loss statement.

LOSS OF A MAJOR CUSTOMER, SUPPLIER, OR LENDER

One of the easiest warning signals to pick up is the loss of a major customer. This is a sure sign that the company is doing something wrong and that it may eventually lose additional customers.

The same is true for suppliers and lenders. When a supplier drops a company or a lender refuses to lend, something is wrong with the company, and it should be a quick tipoff to you that the company is having problems.

LABOR PROBLEMS

It is the duty of management to get along with labor. An entrepreneur should instill in employees the same kind of fervor that he or she feels for the industry and the business. Whenever employees grow dissatisfied or go on strike, management is not doing its job right. Problems in the work force are a sure tipoff that the company is in hot water. Keep your eyes out for labor problems, which are indicated by either a wildcat strike or a loss of employees.

CHANGES IN PRICES AND MARKET SHARE

Declining sales in a booming industry are an obvious sign of problems, but sometimes the clues are more subtle. Sales may be expanding but the company's share of the market may be shrinking. If it is getting less than its fair share in a growing industry, it is having a problem in the marketplace.

Also, if the company drops its price quickly, this probably means that the product is not being received well. Perhaps the product itself is at fault or perhaps it isn't suitable for its target customer.

EXTERNAL WARNING SIGNS

Signs outside the business can also signal trouble. Below are listed some of the common ones to look for.

TECHNICAL CHANGE

New developments and processes may change the way companies compete in the industry. An entrepreneur must be aware of all such changes to determine how they will affect the way that the company does business in the industry. You must determine whether the company has the flexibility to respond to these changes and stay in the market. Each time there is a technological change, the entrepreneur and the investor must determine what they need to do to meet this new challenge.

GENERAL INDUSTRY DECLINE

At times, the industry itself may go into a slump because the major consumer of the product is no longer demanding the number of units it asked for in the past. These general slumps come and go in almost every industry, and you need to determine why the slump has occurred, how long it will last, and what can be done to reorient the company's products so as to take advantage of some other market that may be developing.

GOVERNMENT CHANGES

Many industries are regulated heavily, whereas others are not. Whatever the case, every industry is subject to some regulation. Each time the regulations change, the industry is affected. Government has been known to regulate a company out of business by making it impossible to perform. This has happened several times in U.S. history. For example the Small Business Administration has changed it policies on its lending programs and put some users of the program out of business. You need to keep your eyes open for new regulations that could kill your company and the investment.

RATIO ANALYSIS AS A WARNING INDICATOR

A host of early warning signals can emerge from the analysis of key ratios in a company. These include not only current ratios and the ratios of stockholders to total assets, but also ratios of working capital turnover in debt to equity. All of these factors will give you a clear picture of what is going on with the company.

If receivables turnover (net credit sales divided by the average net traded receivables) begins to change rapidly, you'd better find out why. If daily sales and receivables continue to change, you also need to find out why. Any number of profitability, productivity, and market ratios can be found in a standard textbook on business ratios. Each one of these will give you an indication of what is going on. The sooner you begin analyzing the company in terms of these ratios, the better you will be able to determine what problems a company is having.

OUR PERSONAL FAVORITES OF EARLY WARNING SIGNALS

Here are a number of things that you may not pick up unless you have had years of experience watching for telltale signs.

1. An entrepreneur once said that he had decided to move from Massachusetts to Florida because the weather was much warmer and thought that he could

run the business just as well from Florida. Even the most casual observer will recognize that you cannot run a business from a great distance. Most small businesses need hands-on management. So when an entrepreneur says that the entrepreneur is going to move to a different town, you'd better make sure that the entrepreneur is going to move the business too, or you will have problems. If at all possible, you should keep the entrepreneur from moving.

2. Moving the business or a major plant within the business is perhaps the most dangerous change anyone can make with a small business. The physical disruption alone can affect almost every aspect of the business. Not only do you lose workers, but it often takes six months to a year to resume operations fully in the new location. Don't finance companies that are about to move. It is just too traumatic, and you always end up losing money on businesses that move.

3. Sometimes an entrepreneur will come in and tell you about an investment that the entrepreneur is going into personally. This is always a big red flag. Whenever an entrepreneur puts his or her time and attention into anything else, you can be sure that the business you invested in will suffer. No entrepreneur can run two businesses. If your entrepreneur is going into another business, your business is simply not going to do as well. Use all your persuasive powers to convince your entrepreneur to ditch the idea. Emphasize that the business can make all the money that the entrepreneur ever wants to make. Every time an entrepreneur changes investment objectives, the investor suffers.

4. All too often, an entrepreneur will come into your office one day and suddenly announce, "I am out of money and I cannot meet Friday's payroll." Invariably, the entrepreneur's cash flow projections showed enough money to get along for another year. Somehow the company has gone through all of the money that you and other investors have given it. What is worse,

the entrepreneur inevitably comes in at the last minute and expects the investor to bail out the company. Resist doing this at all costs and make the entrepreneur get through this crisis alone. If you make it easy for the entrepreneur to get out of this situation, it will happen again and again in the future. The second thing to do when you find that the entrepreneur has led you to the brink of disaster is to look for a way out of the investment. Your other option is to fire the entrepreneur and get someone in who is more responsible.

5. Entrepreneurs who are in love with technology and engineering often create problems. They no sooner finish a prototype product than they are ready to develop the next product, even before they have run any profits out of the first one. This will show you that your development people are not marketing people and that you have just invested in the wrong kind of company, a development company. You should always invest in marketing companies. Whenever you find yourself in a development company, try to get out as soon as you can. Development companies are rat holes in which investors dump millions and millions of dollars, never to see a cent in return.

6. An inventor entrepreneur will develop some great products for you. However, the same entrepreneur will also invent products that are unrelated to the business in which you have invested. If you have invested in a company involved with biotechnology, you may find your entrepreneur hot on the trail of the next great solar energy product. Every entrepreneur believes that each product will launch the next great technological revolution. They want to put money into all of these products. This is the wrong type of management team to invest in. Get out of the business or you will lose every nickel you have put in.

This is a personal sample of some of the nutty things that we have run into as investors. Whenever you see these, start working on a way to get out of the deal.

WHY ENTREPRENEURS HAVE FINANCIAL PROBLEMS

When you ask a VC the question, What makes a good company? the VC will always say, "Good management." But in a sense, that goes without saying. If the company shows strong growth and the VC makes money, it had good management. If the company gets in trouble and loses money for the VC, the company had poor management. So what does the VC mean by good management? The VC means that management knows that the problems a small business fears most are: (1) lack of financial monitoring and control and (2) undercapitalization.

THE FINANCIAL CONTROL PROBLEM

Most entrepreneurs can put together a good business plan and solid projections, and can understand the cost of the required capital from banks and VCs. However, only a few will set up a system to monitor progress and analyze the information they are receiving. As an entrepreneur, you should want to know the weekly sales figures. Some in retail operations even want to know the daily figures. Every entrepreneur should be watching the figures closely. When cost figures do not coincide with those projected, find out why. When sales do not match projected figures, find out why. When the projections do not work out precisely, revise the future projections to determine how much capital you are going to need to go where you want.

The most successful entrepreneurs have been "cash flow freaks." These are people who know exactly what is going on in their companies from a numerical standpoint. They know when they will run out of cash, the so-called drop dead date. They know what they have to do to increase cash flow. When things get rough, they know how much money they need to carry them through the next stage. They know precisely what they are doing in allocating their scarce resources properly. A monthly profit-and-loss statement is almost an afterthought for them. They ride herd on the company's cash on a weekly and sometimes daily basis.

THE UNDERCAPITALIZATION PROBLEM

Undercapitalization has always been a serious problem for small businesses. Too often, the entrepreneur will fail to raise the amount of money needed. The entrepreneur will raise $2 million when the company needs $5 million. The entrepreneur does this so that he or she won't have to give up as much equity to the VC. This approach is shortsighted. Most businesses need more money than originally projected to reach profitability. When the entrepreneur needs the extra money, the VC may charge a high price. Always make sure the business has enough money so that there will not be a difficult moment later.

Smart management recognizes the need to have sufficient capital in the company. It does not tie up excess capital in accounts receivable or inventory. It seeks ways to increase the capital in the company. When the company grows, management knows the company must increase its capitalization. Be a good investor and make sure the management maintains adequate capital for the company.

WHY ENTREPRENEURS HAVE PEOPLE PROBLEMS

Many an entrepreneur can run a company well when it consists of a small, intimate group but cannot manage the business when it begins growing into a larger company. This failure often relates to the selection and management of people. As can be expected, no business can grow and remain a one-person operation, nor can an entrepreneur remain a chief with many Indians. In order for a company to grow, the business must attract top-notch middle management to the team.

There are five basic reasons that many small businesses fail to build a strong middle-management team.

POOR JOB DEFNITION

Senior management often fails to understand precisely what jobs need to be filled. Entrepreneurs are accustomed to dealing with undefined job responsibilities. They expect the team to join in and work. However, as a company grows, specialization becomes important. Certain jobs must be segregated and defined so that suitable individuals can be hired to do those specific jobs. As an investor in the company, you must make sure that management has good job descriptions.

POOR SELECTION PROCESS

Once the job has been defined, top management may use a poor selection process. It is easy, for example, to let "good ole Joe" continue to be controller of the company because he has been the bookkeeper from the beginning or to hire a relative out of loyalty, rather than because of his ability to manage the job that needs to be done. These practices do not ensure strong middle management. As an investor, you need to monitor this.

POOR INCENTIVES TO MANAGEMENT

To attract middle management to your company, you need an effective incentive plan. The members of the entrepreneurial team have a high incentive because they own a large share of the company. Their egos are submerged in the business, and they want to make it a success. New members of the management team won't have the same rewards. To motivate them, top management should consider the various traditional methods of compensating top-notch middle management. These include stock options, stock performance rights, good pension and profit-sharing plans, bonuses based on formulas of sales or accomplishments, and the like. If you do not set up a proper reward system for your middle management people, they will not perform. As an investor, helping to define the reward system is part of your job.

POOR REVIEW PROGRAM

Because middle managers do not get the same satisfaction out of the growth of the company as entrepreneurs, they need to be rewarded through traditional review programs that let them know when they are succeeding and when they are failing. A good review program will give you an early warning of any problems with middle managers. It will also give you an opportunity to correct the problem. You must make sure that the business has a review system that is in concert with the company's incentive system.

POOR DEVELOPMENT PROGRAM

Sometimes a company outgrows the abilities of the initial middle management team simply because the managers are not given a chance to develop their skills through seminars and other educational methods. This situation can be avoided by having all the members of the middle-management team come together to share their ideas and discuss the problems they are having within the company. This interaction permits marketing to become acquainted with what is happening in production and allows finance to understand the problems of marketing better, as well as other aspects of your business. This kind of internal professional development program is necessary for any growing company and should supplement a regular development program. As an investor, make sure the company continues to develop its employees.

WHAT TO DO WITH PROBLEMS

When a company has a severe operating problem, as an investor you will be trying to make one basic decision. Should you try to remove the current management and find a new group to run the company? If you have lost confidence in the management team and this has turned into a crisis situation, removing management might be the best thing you can do for the company. In general, there is a rule in the venture capital community that an entrepreneur only gets one chance. This means that if the entrepreneur screws up and brings the company to a very difficult situation, the VC will try to exercise the legal rights and force the entrepreneur out or sell the business.

In analyzing this situation, you will want to determine the best method of getting back all of your money. You need to minimize your losses. First analyze the earning capacity of the company. Can the problem at hand be solved, and how quickly can it be solved? How much will it cost to carry the company while the problem is being solved? If the problem is solved, will the company be sellable? Before you invest any additional money in the company, you need to analyze the company in the same way you did when you made the initial investment.

Each new dollar that you invest is like a new investment. You must ask the question, What will be my return on investment? Throwing good money after bad money is one of the greatest mistakes investors make. Meeting another payroll just to keep the company alive so you don't have to write off an investment is the easiest way to end up with a lot of money in a bad deal.

Second, after looking at the earnings power, you will have to examine the "bricks and mortar." This means that you must look at the assets of the company to try to see what it would be worth in liquidation. If you move in, liquidate the company, pay off the bank, and have the remaining amount coming to you and other investors, what will you end up with? In doing this analysis, you should look at suppliers who might offset against the inventory, any mechanic's liens that are in place from work that has been done for the company, taxes that could conceivably jump in front of everybody else, and any other creditors that may come out of the woodwork and put a claim on the assets. And don't forget the legal fees, which add up very quickly in a workout situation. Once you have had a chance to review this situation in detail, you will have to choose the "earnings power approach" or the "bricks and mortar approach." When you have decided which road to follow, you will need to stick with it for a while.

WHAT IS YOUR NEXT STEP?

Whenever you have to analyze a company in crisis, the outcome will be less than satisfactory. In fact, most analyses of companies in trouble are inconclusive. Nonetheless, as an investor you will have to make a decision concerning the company in trouble. There are five basic options open to you as an investor.

1. Fix the Problem. To fix a problem, whatever it may be, you are going to have to invest more money in the business to keep it going. You may have to hire additional people or do whatever else is necessary to solve this specific problem and save the company. Most entrepreneurs will plead with an investor to put more money in and go forward with the company and that the end of the rainbow is just around the corner.

In one venture capital situation, the company was in the cement business, which is a very cyclical business based on the demand for housing. In the early 1990s when the housing industry was in shambles, some new projections suggested that a turnaround was about to take place. The entrepreneur and the venture group bought the cement company in the fall and used the capital during the winter to carry the company. By spring, it needed an additional injection of capital, and the equity partners put in additional capital. By the end of the summer, the housing industry had not come forward, and the equity partners were called upon once again to place additional equity in the company to carry it through the winter. Only a few of them put up additional money. By this time, the partners owned approximately 75% of the company and the entrepreneur 25%. When spring came and another capital infusion was needed to carry the company through the summer, the venture partners put up more money and diluted the entrepreneur down again. The expansion of housing starts did not come soon enough, and this time the venture firm sold the company for a pittance, took a few bucks, and left town.

The important thing to remember here is that each new investment opportunity that you are offered should be treated as though you had never had an investment in the company. Don't think about the money you have sunk into the company. If your feelings about a new investment in this company are negative, you should tuck your tail between your legs and walk away like a wounded dog. You should not continue to "throw good money after bad." You should select one of the other alternatives set out below.

2. Sell the Business. Many VCs have gotten out of bad deals by merging them with other businesses. Invariably, it seems that every business is worth more as an operating entity than one that is shut down. This is certainly true of every service-oriented company. Merging the company in which you have an investment with a larger entity that can bring in money and management to the distressed company may be the only way to get your money back.

There was one venture capital situation involving a retail tire store where the alternatives were to inject additional money into the company or sell it. Because the VC had lost faith in the entrepreneur, the only thing to do was to sell the business quickly. As you can imagine, the tire business is made up of leased locations, inventory, and people. Without these three ingredients, you have nothing of value. It was necessary to move quickly and find another tire retailer who wanted to enter the marketplace in which this tire company was located. It was the only way to save the investment.

You will be faced with quite a few situations in which you will want to find a buyer for the company. Before they even go in, some venture capital firms work out a scenario in which they identify companies that would be potential buyers, should the company get in trouble. You may want to do this.

3. Foreclose on Assets. It you were smart enough to make your venture capital investment in this problem company as a loan with an option to buy stock or convertible debenture, you are a creditor in this company, rather than an investor, and you can foreclose against the assets of the company. If the company is not paying you principal and interest as agreed, your loan can be called in default, and you can begin to seize the assets and try to operate the business or sell the assets in a general auction to get your money back. This is a very difficult method of operation, and most VCs do not achieve it successfully.

If you were able to get a secured position on the assets through a UCC-I, you are a secured creditor, and as such you have the option of moving in and foreclosing on the assets. In one venture capital situation, the investment group had to foreclose on the assets of a large radio station and began operating it. One of the main reasons the VC group had to take over the assets was that he previous owner just couldn't get any ads to be played on the station. In operating the radio station, the investors would listen to the radio every day as they drove to meet the payroll. One day as they were driving along, they heard many high-scale advertisements being broadcast. When they arrived they asked the radio disk jockey how he had been able to sell so many good ads. The disk jockey coyly replied, "Oh, I didn't sell any ads, I just like to listen to the ads on the air so I put them on free."

VCs are usually not good operators. As an investor, you may not have the time or the inclination to run the business. On the other hand, you still have the option of holding a foreclosure sale, selling the assets at auction, and taking what money you can get out of that to apply to the money owed you. In the instance above, selling the station would have been the best alternative.

4. Bankruptcy. Some investors now look at bankruptcy as less of a bad place to be, especially if the company has large debts from banks. When the bank begins to move on the assets and foreclose, the only way to salvage anything for the stockholders is to take the company into bankruptcy. The new bankruptcy code is quite lenient toward business owners (it was written for debtors). It allows the creditors to take the company and work with it for a number of months to try to restructure its liabilities and pay them off over an extended period of time.

In one situation, bankruptcy was used to hold off the senior creditor for three years while the company operated as "debtor in possession." This meant that the management team continued to stay in place to run the company and held the bank at bay. The senior creditor was unable to foreclose on the assets, and the company continued to show improvements; in a short time, the company came out of bankruptcy and was able to pay back its debt. This is easily one of the few times this has happened for small businesses in bankruptcy. Usually they get liquidated or the assets are sold to a new group that buys it from bankruptcy.

5. Liquidation. Liquidation has been mentioned along the way, but it is the least desirable of all of the alternatives, simply because it usually doesn't pay off. Sometimes a business that is asset-heavy, such as a paper manufacturing plant, may be worth more dead (liquidated) than it would be as an operating entity. As an operating entity, it is going to continue to lose money. If an investor is placed in this position, the investor definitely needs to seek liquidation of the company's assets to recover as much money as possible. None of these choices are easy. As an investor, your principal concern is to find a way to salvage your investment.

SECRET OF A SUCCESSFUL RELATIONSHIP

Every relationship is based on trust. If you have entered into a financial deal with a company that you do not trust, you have made a grave mistake. You are sure to have some doubts about the firm in the initial months, but if your checking has been accurate, the firm should prove trustworthy. Assuming you both trust each other, there must also be a desire to help each other. The company wants to make money, and you want to make money. You both have a common objective. One should not be making money at the other's expense. You should be on the same level and, therefore, should have a desire to help each other. From time to time, you may be asked to help with various problems encountered by the company. Remember, you are partners.

More than anything, the secret to a successful relationship is the ability to talk to each other and to communicate both the good and the bad news to one another. If two individuals can openly discuss the things they like and dislike about a relationship, as well as tell one another what things are good and what things are bad in a constructive critical approach, the relationship will most likely be a successful one. In turn, the business will probably prosper.

We remember one story of an entrepreneur who was highly motivated, well trained, and an achiever of the first order but was unable to admit failure. This flaw dominated his personality to such a degree that not only did he refuse to admit small errors, but he would not accept the fact that his company had lost $1.75 million at the end of its second year. When he received the audit from a large accounting firm, he would not accept it. He made the accounting firm restate the figures and give him a qualified opinion. The financials showed the company had made a profit and was in good financial condition. The accountants' opinion had a section that said the financials were correct, subject to the adjustments made by the entrepreneur. The entrepreneur presented these financial statements to his board of directors, to his bank, and to his investors. He seemed to think that if he could somehow get through the year without anyone except the accountant knowing his true condition, he would have time to turn the company around and cover up past mistakes. This entrepreneur was unsuccessful in his cover-up, and the company was liquidated. Many people lost a great deal of money.

In relationships with investors, boards of directors, and employees, the players should be open. Save all the conniving and devious actions for the competition, as long as the actions are legal and acceptable in the marketplace where the products are sold.

DEGREE OF INVOLVEMENT BY THE VENTURE CAPITALIST

The amount of time you as a venture capital investor want to spend with the company will depend on a number of factors.

AMOUNT INVESTED

The amount the VC has invested in the company, compared with other investments, will determine how much time the VC spends with the company. This will be a decision you will have to make. If you have invested $500,000 in an early-stage company, you may not spend nearly as much time as if you have had invested several million dollars. The larger the amount invested, the more upset you will be if you lose it. The more the invested funds mean to you, the more attention you will give.

NEED FOR ASSISTANCE

If the company has a management team and does not need assistance, you do not need to spend time with the company. If the company needs a financial adviser or someone to discuss marketing, you may perform that function. The more help the company needs, the more you should be concerned, and the more time you will need to give to the company.

MANAGEMENT'S WILLINGNESS TO ACCEPT ADVICE

If management is willing to accept advice, most investors are willing to give it. If management resists every suggestion, obviously a VC will not waste time making suggestions to management. There is a fine line to walk here. Entrepreneurs should be hungry for advice on major decisions but not on day-today operations.

EXPERIENCE IN CERTAIN AREAS

If you are not experienced in a certain area where the company has a problem, you will not try to advise the company on the matter. If the entrepreneur has good financial information and is a financial whiz, the VC may not try to help with financial decisions.

LEAD INVESTOR

Usually if a VC is the lead investor, the VC will spend more time with the company. This arises from the responsibility to the other venture capital investors. Although the lead VC is under no legal obligation to ensure that the other investors make money, the VC reputation is on the line with the VC's friends. If you are the lead VC, you will have to do a lot of extra work to help keep the others up to date.

DISTRESS OF COMPANY

If the company is in distress, the VC will have to play an active role. Every VC spends time working out problems rather than reviewing new deals. In fact, many VCs say they are not in the venture capital business at all but rather are in the business of working out bad deals. They are always trying to avoid losing their money. It seems that the good companies take care of themselves.

RELATIONSHIP WITH THE ENTREPRENEUR

Often, a strong bond will develop between the entrepreneur and VC. A certain chemistry that exists among people in venture situations draws them together. Great friendships have arisen from these relationships, even in dire circumstances. You will find that many of your greatest friends are the managers of the portfolio companies.

TIME AVAILABILITY

As you know, investing in small companies is very time-consuming. You need to work on the most pressing problems first. If the new investment is a small problem or if it is operating well, you can invest most of your time in solving more serious problems. Make sure the entrepreneur does not interpret your lack of attention as a lack of interest in the company. The amount of time spent on an investment is usually inversely proportionate to the success of the investment. In general, you cannot make a company successful, but you can often save an investment when there is trouble.

TIPS ON MONITORING

There are some basic things that you should try to do as an investor in the company if you want to monitor the company. It is extremely important that you follow some of these suggestions to save yourself from waking up one morning with a serious problem on your hands.

1. Set the Tone on the Way In. When you make your investment, make sure that your entrepreneur understands your objectives and understands that you believe this is a partnership in which you both share a great deal of information about the business. Make sure you set the right tone on the way in to the investment. Exhibit a great deal of interest and enthusiasm for the business, and you will find that the entrepreneur will understand your interest and supply you with plenty of information.

2. Understand the Business and the Products. Make sure you understand what business you are in and what products the company produces so that you do not come across as a complete fool when you are talking to the entrepreneur about the business. The entrepreneur does not expect you to be an expert in the business, but if you do not know one product from the other or continually show little knowledge of the industry, the entrepreneur will conclude you do not have as much interest in the industry and, therefore, will stop giving you information about it. Stay on top of the business and its products so that you can talk knowledgeably with the entrepreneur.

3. Keep Up with the Industry and the Competition. It is also important that you know who the competition is and that you continue to seek information about it. Every time you see information about the competition, clip that piece out and send it to the entrepreneur to show that you are keeping up with what is going on in the business. If there is a study coming out on the industry, try to read it and share your thoughts about the industry with the entrepreneur. By being an informed investor, you will be sure to gain additional information from the entrepreneur. Be a knowledgeable person, and the entrepreneur will seek you out to discuss the problems of the business and the industry.

4. Subscribe to Industry Magazines. You may not need to join a local trade association to gather the information about the industry, but you will definitely want to subscribe to industry magazines. They may be boring reading from time to time, but one or two articles will come along that will let you know more about the industry than you did before and will be a source of information to discuss with the entrepreneur running the business. Because it is important to keep up with the industry, a subscription to the industrial magazines is a must; joining the trade association is an option.

5. Know the People in the Business. You need to know all of the people in the business in which you have invested. Know the top five or six people; get to know the secretary to the president. Let them become part of your group. At a minimum, write down all of their names, so that when it comes time to meet them again, you will have their names on the tip of your tongue. Do not walk up and say "Hello"; say, "Hello Joe, it's been a long time since we have seen you." Make sure you know the people in the industry, and keep talking to them. If on an occasion that you have a marketing question are unable to reach the president of the company, call the marketing vice president and ask the question. This will let the management team know that you are out there and that you are part of the team. You do not want to be a pest, but you do want to be part of the team.

6. Spend Time with the CEO. The greatest way to obtain information about the company is to spend time with the chief executive officer. It is an unwritten law that the people who do not spend time with the president are not going to know much about the company. The CEO is at the center of all that is going on in the company. If you do not spend time with that person, you are not going to learn much about the company. It is essential that you and the entrepreneur become close friends and go forward to try to make money together.

It is also essential to building the relationship with the CEO that you continue to communicate. You need to praise people when they do things right and criticize when they miss the mark. Help them build a team by praising them when they do a good job. Make specific observations, but always qualify them with, "We are not experts in the business, but . . ." This will let them know that you are not trying to present yourself as a manager or leading authority in the industry, but rather as a person who is greatly concerned about the company and one who is offering friendly advice.

7. Track Performers. Do not ever let up on tracking the performance of a company. It is imperative to keep up with sales and earnings of the company, as well as all of the financial ratios. If you let down your guard in this area, you are apt to wake up with a big surprise one morning, even though you are the best of friends with the CEO. Tracking performance is one of the critical aspects in watching the company grow.

PITFALLS OF MONITORING

The quickest way to blow it as a monitor of a company is to do one of the following.

1. Appear Only When There Is Trouble. If you appear at the company only when it is having problems, you will be considered an enemy and not a friend. Enemies (vultures) appear only when a company is having problems. This is the most often heard criticism of bankers among small business people. Bankers are never available until a problem occurs, then you cannot get rid of them. Although a banker may be satisfied with this kind of relationship, you as an investor cannot be.

2. React to Problems. It is very easy to react to every problem that the company has, rather than being part of the planning process. If you do react each time, you will again be considered an outsider. Be part of the planning process and understand what the company is trying to achieve. When it misses the mark, come down on the company in terms of negative feedback, but do not react emotionally.

3. Second-Guess Management. Being a Monday-morning quarterback is an easy skill. It is easy to second-guess a management team. However, it is hard to dish out negative feedback without looking as though you are second-guessing them. Be sure you do not say, "If we had been in your shoes, we would not have done that." If you are part of the planning team, you were there when the decisions were made. Try to work your way out of problems and not compound them by discouraging management.

4. Pain Factor. Everybody wants the company to make money. You do not want to be so involved in the company that you become a pain to the management. You want to be a plus to the management team, rather than a thorn in its side. As long as management is following the best path for the company, you should try to be part of the team. In times of trouble, praise works better than pain.

VENTURE CAPITALIST OBJECTIVES

During the period of time you are working together with your entrepreneur, you both will have one objective—growth. You want to see the company grow as fast as possible and see it become as large as possible. You want to see sales increase, and you want to see profits improve. Those are your basic objectives in investing in the company.

If the company has grown sharply and is now becoming a large organization, you will start to look toward exiting your investment through a liquidity event. You want to be able to sell part of the investment when the time is right. You receive no bonuses because of the company's growth and success. You receive your rewards when you are able to sell part or all of your investment and make a large profit.

11 THE EXIT

There has always been a love-hate relationship between the VC and the entrepreneur. Most venture capital investors are frustrated entrepreneurs and think that if they could only run the business themselves, they could do it better than the entrepreneur they have backed. On the other hand, most entrepreneurs love their investor on the day they receive an investment, but as the years wear on, they feel they have done all the work and the investor has done nothing to earn the money that the investor has received.

The relationship between the VC and the entrepreneur becomes more strained when the company is operating poorly. At such times, you must step in to try to save your investment, and this usually causes great friction. Whether it is a successful endeavor or one with a great many problems, there will come a day when you will want to exchange your ownership in the company for cash. "Cashing out," as it is called, is a normal end to any investment.

As an investor in a small business, you should make the entrepreneur know that your stock ownership in the company is for sale at any time; it is just a question of price. Every investor should let the entrepreneur know that someday the investor will want to cash out of the equity ownership, and that will be as soon as the price meets with the investor's expectations for the return.

There are six basic approaches to cashing out of an investment. All of these involve various types of companies in various stages of development or trouble.

1. Selling the company
2. Selling the investor's shares back to the company
3. Selling the investor's shares to a new investor
4. Reorganization
5. Liquidation

All of these have a way for the investor to "cash out." They may not always be at the price you want in order to get out, but each provides a unique avenue for an investor to exit from a deal.

EXIT ONE: GOING PUBLIC

One of the greatest methods for cashing out of your investment is to take the company public. In cold hard terms, the public market pays more for a company than almost any other source. Therefore, the public market is the one you are aiming for. As an investor in a public company, you will have the opportunity to cash in some of your chips by selling a portion of your shares to the public, and eventually you may be able to sell them all.

WHEN TO GO PUBLIC

Many brokerage houses in this world can take a company public, but only a handful specialize in public offerings of small and growing companies. Each of these investment banking houses will have its own criteria for taking a company public. The large national brokerage houses will not take a company public unless it needs at least $50 million. Small houses will take a company public for as little as $20 million. Most of the discussions with the brokerage house will center around the earnings of the company for past periods and projected future years. If the company meets three basic objectives—it has good growth in earnings, it is projecting good growth, and it meets the minimum standards of the brokerage houses,—it will be a likely candidate for a public offering. If one brokerage house says that it can't take the company public, the entrepreneur and the investor should scout around until they find one that will do so.

Investors would like to sell some of their shares in the public offering. It is nice to cash in a few dollars when the company has its initial public offering (IPO). However, the number of shares that can be sold in the IPO will be determined by the underwriter. Sometimes the underwriter will not permit any; at other times the underwriter will permit up to 20 percent of the offering to be sold by insiders. Needless to say, if it is a good public offering, the underwriter will come back to some of the investors and ask to buy the shares from the investor to be sold in the secondary market or to have a secondary offering.

Every investor has to review his or her portfolio of investments to determine whether there are business opportunities greater than the investment in the current company. If there are, then obviously the investor should cash in some of the stock holding in the company and invest it in the higher return investment opportunity.

There is also the question of good portfolio management. If you have a number of investments but one business opportunity now makes up a great deal of net worth, you should definitely cash in some of your stock in the initial offering whenever the opportunity presents itself. You should never have too much money in any one investment. Diversity is the best thing possible in an investment portfolio. When the time comes, don't forget to review your situation, and make sure you cash in some stock.

UNDERWRITER'S FEES IN THE PUBLIC OFFERING

A stockbroker will charge a fee for acting as the underwriter on any stock offering. Part of the fees will go to the other stockbrokers who joined in the group selling the stock, but most of the fee will go to the firm you choose to be the underwriter. Underwriter's fees range from 6 percent to 10 percent; 7 percent seems to be standard for an IPO and 5.5 percent for a secondary offering. The higher the risk, the higher the fee. It is possible to reduce the underwriter's fee by giving the underwriter some options to buy stock. All in all, it is very difficult to get the fee below 5 percent.

On top of the underwriter's fee there will be legal fees, printing costs, auditing fees, and a number of fees for writing the prospectus. The point of all of this is that if you have not negotiated to have all fees in any public offering, then as a selling stockholder you will have to bear your pro rata share of the fees. This means that if you sell $10,000,000 worth of your stock, you may end up with only $8,500,000. So the underwriter's fees become an immediate concern of any major investor, as well as anybody selling stock in the offering.

SELECTION OF A BROKERAGE HOUSE FOR A PUBLIC OFFERING

As you begin to talk with various brokerage firms as well as friends, accountants, and bankers, the names of some local and regional brokerage houses will come to mind as possible underwriters for the new issue that you are talking about. As you continue your research, two or three names will keep coming up, and you will eventually start to interview brokerage companies to determine which one should be selected to take the company public.

In selecting a brokerage, you will want one of the most reputable firms. You should look for experienced underwriters in the new issue area. You should look to a brokerage house that has the financial strength to distribute the shares to its clients. You should also determine whether the brokerage firm has good market-making ability. That is, once it sells the stock, someone will have to make a market for the shares to be bought and sold. If the brokerage you are considering is not good in this second area, the stock will surely fall in price after the initial offering.

Stock research can also be a consideration. If the underwriter has a research analyst who is well known in the area, that may help the offering. However, always remember that analysts who work for underwriters have a bias. If the analyst is already following some of your competition, he or she may not be happy about your entry into the capital markets. This could color their coverage of your company. There is also the fact that if you stop giving the brokerage further underwriting business, the analyst may stop writing positive reports about the company you have taken public and will negatively affect the share price. There is no perfect system: *caveat emptor.*

EXIT TWO: SALE TO A STRATEGIC OR FINANCIAL BUYER

The second method of exiting from a venture capital investment is to sell the entire company to a strategic buyer. There are public and private companies that see their prime means of growth as purchasing other businesses. Sometimes these are businesses buying up companies within their industry and sometimes the buyer is a company seeking a way to enter an industry. Selling to a strategic buyer is a very good way of realizing your investment. A buyer will be willing to pay more for the company when all of the stock is available, rather than buying a minority interest or buying when only part of the stock is available. When someone is buying a company, control of that company is a valuable asset to acquire.

In addition, there are financial buyers that may pay almost as much as a strategic buyer. Financial buyers are leverage buyout funds (LBO funds) and other pools of capital looking for good investments. Usually these buyers pay less than the strategic buyers.

Sometimes you can sell only part of the company to a financial buyer. However, remember that trying to sell a minority interest in a company is much more difficult than selling the entire company because it involves selling control. Selling your small interest in a company will be discussed later.

When you sell the entire company, you can be paid for your stock or the assets of the company in several ways. Basically, there are six ways that a company can pay you for your interest in the company. You should understand each of these so that you will be able to negotiate with the buyer of the company to maximize the cash that you will ultimately receive.

SELLING THE STOCK IN THE COMPANY FOR CASH

This is the simplest of all mechanisms; it triggers a capital gain to you and a capital gain tax. Here, you will receive all cash for your investment from a strategic or financial buyer, which usually means there is no need to incur debt on the company in order to facilitate the purchase.

SELLING STOCKS FOR NOTES

Rather than taking cash for your stock, you may wish to take a note from the buyer. That is, the buying company may buy the stock you own in your company by giving you a note that will promise to pay off debt over time. It will pay you cash over a certain period of time, for example, five years. In the buying or selling of the business world, these notes are called "paper." So when buyers ask if you will "take back paper," they mean that they want to give you a note in the place of cash. Although cash is certainly made out of paper, only notes are called paper. Maybe the word *paper* is used here because it suggests something that is worthless. There are certainly many people who have sold their companies and have taken notes in place of cash, and those notes have later become worthless because the buyer ruined the business and could not pay off the notes.

It is common to give notes in order to establish a deferred purchase and give you, the seller, a tax advantage. From a tax viewpoint, you may be able to recognize the income from the sale of the stock as you receive payments on the notes. Most sales are expected to pay some deferred payments for their stock. When it comes time to sell your company for deferred purchase notes, make sure that you know how well secured the notes are. Be sure you understand what you are receiving for your stock or you may end up with a lot of worthless paper.

SELLING STOCK FOR STOCK

There may be certain circumstances where a large public company or strategic buyer wants to purchase your company. Sometimes you can structure this deal in which you would rather take stock in a very large publicly traded conglomerate or a large publicly traded industrial concern for the stock that you own. This will give you a definite advantage in that you do not have to pay taxes until you sell the stock that you receive from the public company. Most of these "stock-for-stock" transactions are tax-free exchanges. You do not have to pay taxes until you sell the shares of the large public company.

Of course, it is more dangerous to take stock in a smaller company. It might even be considered insane for you to swap the stock you hold in your company for the stock of another private company because you have neither equity nor income from the stock you received. Certainly when you are dealing with large companies you should try to obtain registered shares so that you will be free to sell the stock whenever you wish, rather than having to wait for a period of time (usually one year) before you can sell any of the stock and get a capital gains treatment with lower taxes.

Another possibility is to take a dividend-paying preferred stock from a large conglomerate that is convertible into the current conglomerate's common stock. This way, you will have income while you are trying to you decide whether to convert your shares into common stock and sell them. This could be the best of both worlds.

SELLING ASSETS FOR CASH

With the craziness of the tax law, the situation in which the company sells all of its assets to a new buyer and liquidates the company can cost a bundle in taxes. When you sell the company's assets, you trigger a taxable event whereby the company must pay taxes on the gain on those assets before it makes a liquidating distribution to you. In turn, you must pay taxes on the gains that you receive from the company, which means double taxes.

Because of this stupidity in the tax law, it is very difficult to sell assets for cash and liquidate the company that distributed the cash. However, in certain circumstances where the assets are being sold at book value or perhaps even below book value, you can still use the sale of assets for a cash and liquidation scheme. Because you are selling the assets below book value, there is no tax, and the tax comes only when the individuals receive the cash and the liquidations of the company.

SELLING ASSETS FOR NOTES

Sometimes the acquiring company may not have the cash to pay for the assets it is buying from the company you are selling. In this situation, your company may have to take notes secured by the assets being sold as payments. The assets have been sold for notes. These notes will have to be collected. Again you will have to be careful about the type of notes that you are taking for assets. If the notes are paid as agreed, the company may not recognize a gain on the sale of the assets until it actually receives the cash from the notes. Because of the tax law, if the company decides to liquidate and distribute the loans you took in place of cash for the assets of the business, it could be considered a taxable event, and taxes could be due on the amount of the gain that is the difference between the note price and the cost basis you had in the assets of the business you sold. You will want to have a tax lawyer examine any situation in which you are taking notes for assets.

SELLING ASSETS FOR STOCK

In some circumstances, you might sell the assets of the company for stock in the purchaser, particularly if it is a publicly traded company. You could then liquidate the company and distribute the stock of the publicly traded company to the stockholders of the selling company. Because of the tax law, this could trigger two taxable events: (1) tax on the sale of stock or (2) tax when the stock is distributed to stockholders. You could end up with a double tax on an illiquid company, which would not be good tax planning. There seems to be a scenario in which it would make a great deal of sense for you to swap stock for assets when stock is in excess of the depreciated value of the assets. However, if you are selling assets at below book value, you could take advantage of this situation.

OTHER FORMS OF PAYMENT

Many other forms of payment are used in concert with the above six basic structures. One common structure is called an "earn-out." An earn-out means paying sellers an additional amount for the company they have purchased if that company achieves higher-than-expected earnings. In such a situation, the managers of the business would continue to operate it as a division or a wholly owned subsidiary of the buying company. To the extent that the management of the division could increase earnings above the amount projected, the selling stockholders would receive additional payments, based on the percentage of that excess.

As an example, the company that purchased your entrepreneurial company might agree to pay stockholders an additional amount (the earn-out) equal to 25 percent of the pretax income in excess of $5 million for each of the next five years. This would mean that you and the other stockholders would get your prorated share of the cash distributed based on the above formula. Many buyers like to have earn-outs because it gives the buying company the undivided attention of the entrepreneur, who wants to make additional money by getting the earnings of the company higher, even though the entrepreneur is no longer a stockholder.

As a nonoperating partner in a venture capital company, you will have to watch for entrepreneurs who sell their companies, then get significant compensation in the form of consulting contracts or noncompete agreements. You may find yourself in a situation in which a company is willing to buy a company that you wish to invest in but at a significantly lower price than you feel it is worth. You may then find that, in addition to negotiating a low sale price, the entrepreneur had wangled an agreement for an enormous consulting contract for the next five years. In essence, the buying company is paying for the purchase of the stock by agreeing to take on this entrepreneur-turned-consultant for the next five years. The entrepreneur is trying to dip into your share of the real value of the business by taking a large portion of it in the form of a consulting contract. This scenario is particularly troublesome because part of the purchase price is being paid to the seller in the form of a contract, and as an investor you get none of that part of the purchase price.

Your commitment letter and legal documents should contain a provision that would prevent the entrepreneur from doing this. You should pay particular attention to this item and make sure it is in the agreement for the sale of the company in which you have invested.

EXIT THREE: SALE BACK TO THE COMPANY

The tactic discussed in this section is not used frequently in the venture capital community, although we have used it in a large number of exits. This is called a *recapitalization*, or "recap." As an investor, you are prepared to sell everything that you own, and in essence, everything that you have is for sale. Letting the entrepreneur know this can trigger an opportunity for you and the entrepreneur to negotiate a purchase of your equity in the company by the entrepreneur or by the company itself. This can occur when the company has cash or when it can borrow the money from the bank or even other investment companies.

The entrepreneur will have the company buy your stock by borrowing the money from the bank and purchasing it from you. After repurchasing your share, the entrepreneur and any other stockholders will own 100 percent of the company, but the company will have increased its liability in the form of a bank loan. In some circumstances where the company has good cash flow but cannot convince the bank to allow it to borrow additional funds to buy out the investor, it may be necessary for you to sell your equity back to the company through a short-term or medium-term note. Here the investor more or less finances his own buyout.

Remember that in this situation, you are taking paper in a small company, and you want to make sure that the loan you have made to the company is a secure one. At a minimum, you should take collateral in the stock that you are selling to the company so that if the company defaults on its note, at least you will have the stock that you started out with. You will be in no worse a position than just before you sold your stock back to the company.

There are other variations on this idea, whereby you sell the stock back to the company for other assets that you would rather have. For example, you might sell your stock back to the company for the land and building that the company owns. The company would then lease that land and building from you (called a *sale leaseback*). You could probably dream up a number of swaps but they are relatively uncommon in the venture capital world; most VCs want cash.

PURCHASE BY EMPLOYEE STOCK OWNERSHIP TRUST

The vehicle that some entrepreneurial companies use to purchase an investor's stock is an Employee Stock Ownership Plan (ESOP). In this situation, the company sets up an ESOP, and each year has the company make a contribution to that trust based on the employees' payroll. The ESOP takes the place of a pension plan and, in some cases, a profit-sharing plan.

This different type of pension plan must buy stock in the company, and because the company is not selling the stock, it will buy from the investor. The ESOP obtains money through company contributions and, therefore, builds up cash. Because the contributions consist of pretax dollars, the company is retiring your equity position with pretax dollars that are contributed to the ESOP, which in turn purchases your shares. For a quicker transaction, the ESOP can borrow from the bank, then use that money to purchase your stock. The contribution made to the ESOP would retire the debt in the ESOP plan. Because the ESOP receipts are tax deductible to the company, this is a relatively painless way for the company to buy out an investor. However, ESOPs are complicated structures and must be approved by the Department of Labor, as well as tax experts. Anyone contemplating this method of exiting should contact an expert in the field of employee ownership trusts and get good tax advice.

Exit by Puts and Calls

When you negotiated the investment in the entrepreneurial company, you may have set up a formal arrangement that provides for an exit by the investor. These are usually in one of two forms: a put or a call. As noted earlier, a put is the right given to an investor to require the company to purchase his or her ownership in the company at a predetermined price or a predetermined formula. The call provision gives the company the right to purchase the investor's ownership on the same basis.

There are probably as many different put and call formulas as there are minds thinking about how to structure deals. However, there are seven popular ones for you to consider:

1. **Price-earnings ratio (PE).** Probably the most popular is a price-earnings ratio formula that values a company's stock in the same way as the stocks traded on national stock exchanges. The earnings per share are figured for the shares owned by the VC. A popular price-earnings comparable ratio is selected from public stocks in the same industry. That PE ratio is multiplied by the earnings per share of the company to come up with a price per share that the company will pay the VC for the stock he or she owns.

2. **Book value.** A less common formula is based on the book value of the company. It is simple to compute the book value per share for stock owned by the VC. That would be the price the company would pay for the shares owned by the venture capital company. Book

value per share is seldom used because in the early years of a company's development, the company usually has a small book value. It is only in older companies that have been around long enough to establish a realistic book value that this becomes the method of valuing the VC's equity position.

3. **Percentage of sales.** Sometimes it is inappropriate to use the earnings of the company in a price-earnings formula because in the early years of development, particularly in a start-up company, the earnings may be low, due to heavy depreciation or research and development expenses. It may take several years for the company to become profitable. Using pretax earnings may seem to be more appropriate. However, pretax earnings are often held low because of heavy salaries or heavy expenditures for promotion. In such a case, it may be easier for you to take the normal profit before tax as a percentage of sales typical for the industry. You will find statistics on the industry in publications of business statistics. You may find that most companies similar to this one have pretax earnings of 10 percent of sales. It would be simple then to take 10 percent of the company's sales and pretend that number is the profit before taxes. By using this method, you would have determined earnings per share by using the hypothetical profit before taxes. Using the industry price-earnings ratio, one can easily determine what the value of the stock owned by the venture capital company would be worth if the hypothetical earnings existed. This can be the method used for buying back the shares.

Using the percentage of sales formula to value and buy back the shares can be very expensive. If sales are pumped up because advertising has been increased to push sales and market share up, the formula for repurchasing shares will be high. On the other hand, if the formula is based on earnings, the entrepreneur can control the amount of earnings. For example, the entrepreneur might increase advertising to reduce earnings and build a name for the company in the future. By using the earnings formula, the entrepreneur will be reducing the value of the shares. The entrepreneur cannot tamper with sales as easily; therefore, sales become a good indicator of the value of the company.

4. **Multiple of cash flow.** In some industries, cash flow is a more accurate barometer of how the business is doing than are profit-and-loss statements. Using a six-to-ten-times cash flow formula, one can value a company, and it is simple to compute the value of the percentage of the company owned by the VC. The entrepreneur can use this as the method for establishing a price for the stock.

The cash flow formula may work quite well for a stable company but could be extremely expensive in an asset-heavy, LBO situation. For example, in an LBO, the company may have inflated the value of the assets in order to shelter income. However, when heavy depreciation is added back in the calculation of cash flow, the cash flow number will be much higher than the profit-before-tax figure. Therefore, the price you receive for your equity can be artificially high if it is based on cash flow.

5. **Multiple of sales.** The value of some companies in certain industries is based on a multiple of sales. Radio stations traditionally sell at two to three times gross sales. If you determine the value of a company to be 2.5 times gross sales, it would then be simple to compute the value of the investor's percentage of equity ownership. As in the percentage-of-sales calculation above, the multiple-of-sales valuation also means the entrepreneur will be trying to buy back stock in a company that may or may not have earnings. Many investors in the radio business buy a poorly run station on a multiple-of-sale calculation, knowing full well that the station's earnings cannot possibly pay back the investment. The investor who is buying the station must put in enough money to carry the station until its sales and earnings can be increased.

6. **Appraised value.** It is often easy to find a business expert or a stock brokerage firm to appraise the value of the equity ownership held by the investor. The appraisal will probably be based on a combination of some of the items above. Appraisals are usually computed by two methods. First, the value of the company is determined by its earning power, both past and future. This formula is similar to the price-earnings ratio used above. Second, the value of the assets (bricks and mortar) is determined as though they were to be sold at auction as part of an orderly liquidation. From this liquidation, the appraiser subtracts all debts outstanding, and the remaining value is the appraised value. The bricks-and-mortar formula is similar to the book-value calculations, except the liquidation approach includes an appraisal of the assets and a restated new book value, based on their appraised value. When these two figures (liquidation vs. earnings valuation) do not agree, the appraiser usually selects something close to the higher of the two. The appraiser would assume that the highest and best use of the company is to sell all of its assets or to operate it as a going concern.

7. **Prearranged cash amount.** Of course, a simple formula would be to base a put-and-call option on a single cash amount. That is, at the end of three years, the venture capital firm would have the right to require the company to buy its equity ownership position for a certain amount, say, $2 million. Although this method saves a great deal of negotiating and appraising at the end of three years, people find it difficult to agree on a value at the beginning of the investment period.

EXIT FOUR: SALE TO ANOTHER INVESTOR

Sometimes it is possible to find a new investor who will buy your ownership in the company at an attractive price. There may be a circumstance in which the entrepreneur would like to have a working partner, and you could sell your position to someone who would like to become a working partner of the company. In another situation, the entrepreneur might have a close personal friend who has enough money to purchase the position held by you. All of these are rare; it is not often that you will find a passive investor who wants to be a long-term investor in a small company and who is willing to buy the position held by another investor.

CORPORATE PARTNER

Sometimes, when the company has made substantial progress and has a new idea, usually technological, you can find a corporation that would like to be a corporate partner to the small business. This gives you, the investor, an opportunity to sell to the new corporation as a new partner. The corporate partner's objective may be to own all of the company at sometime in the future; therefore, it makes good sense for this partner to purchase a small position in the company.

In addition, the corporate partner may make a better partner in a small business than you, the investor, because the corporate partner will know more about the marketplace and how to produce the product. As an example, a VC once invested in a small company and later brought in a corporate partner that happened to be a large international telecommunications conglomerate. As the small company started to grow, the conglomerate decided it wanted to buy the company. However, the venture capital position was the only one that was for sale, so a bargain was struck, and it was purchased. This gave the corporation an opportunity to see what was going on in the company, and it was later able to convince the entrepreneur to sell out completely.

NEW VENTURE CAPITAL PARTNER

In certain circumstances, it is possible to find another VC or another investor to purchase a position held by an investor. This is different from the financial buyer we discussed above because you are selling only your investment; the entire company is not being sold. For example, the first venture capital partner may be an equity-oriented venture capital fund that invests in early-stage companies. The second investor group may be one that purchases equity in later-stage companies. Although it is unusual, you may be able to sell your stock to a later-stage venture capital company.

At one time, an investor had money in a small advertising company that was having operating problems and not growing at all. The entrepreneur was able to find another venture capital fund that still believed in the new method of advertising. That venture capital fund invested enough money in the small business to buy out our investment. When the company continued to show poor results, a third venture capital fund came in and bought out the second VCs, who had become quite disillusioned. The third venture capital fund was able to attract several more rounds of venture financing. Eventually, this became one of the most profitable public companies backed by venture capital in recent times. As the investor looked back at his inability to ride out the rough storm with the entrepreneur, he could only shed a few tears for not staying with it all the way.

EXIT FIVE: REORGANIZING THE COMPANY

Among VCs and investors, the word *reorganization*, or its more grizzly name, "Chapter 11," has appeared all too often in the venture capital world. Reorganization is a long word for bankruptcy. Reorganization has been used by many small businesses to remove creditors as well as investors. By using Chapter 11 of the bankruptcy code, small businesses can compromise debts and squeeze out stockholders. It is one of the most depressing circumstances an investor can be in. Without question, you are at the mercy of the legal tribunal known as bankruptcy court, which has ultimate authority. A judge can confirm a plan that actually removes the investor as a material stockholder in the company. A bankruptcy judge can "cram down" debt holders into equity positions to the extent that the original equity owner is diluted down to nothing and the new equity holders—the original debt holders—become the owners of the company. A bankruptcy judge has the power to determine that secure debt is really unsecured and that unsecured debt should be "compensated" by stock in the new company.

Companies sometimes go to bankruptcy court. It is not a good place to recover money unless you are a lender, and even then it can be very costly. From an equity investor's viewpoint, bankruptcy is virtually the end of the world. When a company goes into bankruptcy, you can be sure that the original amount of money that you invested into the company will end up being a small pittance in comparison.

It is unwise for any equity investor to attempt to use the bankruptcy court as a means of salvaging an investment. Almost everyone who has tried to do it has ended up paying enormous legal bills and has received much less than they ever expected. One of the iron rules of equity investing is to stay away from bankruptcy.

EXIT SIX: LIQUIDATION

More VCs than you can imagine have made their exits by liquidating companies. If all else fails and the business performs poorly, this may be the easiest way out. One can sell those assets that have some value and take the remaining cash to dissolve the investment in the company. Any number of companies have grown to a certain stage and have then found themselves worth more dead (liquidated) than alive. It is conceivable that the land, building, machinery, equipment, and other assets of the company are worth more in liquidation than the company can possibly earn with those assets.

This scenario can be seen in industries that go through very difficult periods. They may be good, solid businesses for a number of years and have built up assets that are not strictly needed by the business, such as land, building, and certain other nonperishable assets. Then the industry goes through a severe downturn, and the profitability drops substantially. At such a moment, the assets, if sold and invested in a passbook savings account, could be worth more than the business. This is particularly true of companies that experience severe competition from foreign companies. A recent example is the chain-making industry in the United States. Making common-length chains has become a commodity business, and many developing countries have developed chain-making capability. Because their labor content is substantially lower than that of industrialized nations, these countries are able to sell chains in the U.S. market at substantially lower prices than the U.S. companies This lowers the profitability of chain-making companies considerably and has made some of them worth more in liquidation than as going concerns.

For the investor, if all else fails, liquidation may be your most logical answer. At the moment of liquidation, you will be much happier if your investment is in the form of a loan or a debenture than in straight stock because as a creditor you may get more money than a stockholder. You may be forced into liquidating a company and getting the cash from the liquidation (you hope).

Liquidation, on occasion, can be very successful. However, the success is often based on picking a good auctioneer who can auction off the assets in a very competitive manner. Some auctioneers can skillfully work up the audience to the point where a reluctant bidder will step forward and make a cash bid for the business assets. It is quite an exciting moment for the investor when there is a good auction and the cash price of the assets get most of the investment back. Be very careful about the auctioneer and the auctioneer organization you choose to liquidate your company; it will mean the difference between getting out and a big loss.

When You Are in a Workout

Sometimes during the monitoring process, you will realize that something has gone wrong. The projections are not being met, and the company is running out of money. It is hard for the entrepreneur to recognize this because the entrepreneur's personality is entwined in the business and its success, so that when problems begin to develop, you may be the only one to see them. Somewhere along the way, you may recognize that there is a problem in your business that needs to be "worked out." There are many different scenarios of what is wrong, the most common being declining profitability. Being the first to burst the dreams of the entrepreneur and declare the investment in trouble can be dangerous because you may alarm the entrepreneur. By classifying the investment as a workout, it may cause the entrepreneur to overreact.

Workouts don't develop overnight. They develop slowly, and you must recognize the telltale signs. Although a bad loan or investment may take time to develop, you need to treat it as though it were an "on or off" switch. The investment is either a problem or not a problem, and if it is a problem, you need to take appropriate action.

Don't believe that things will get better. Always assume that things are going to get worse, and make sure you understand the consequences. Also know that money is not a cure for all problems. Many an investor has been lulled into putting in small amounts of capital and nursing a losing situation for months and years. The cumulative effect comes in one horrendous write-off when the company is finally liquidated, and the entire investment is lost.

There are no quick fixes in this type of investment business. Meeting the payroll will not fix the company. Selling the company will not happen overnight. There is no way to make a company turn around, get sold, or be cured in a short time. It is a long and arduous task to bring an ailing company back to profitability or get it sold to someone who can.

Your personality and that of the entrepreneur will be wrapped up in the business. It will be hard for either of you to admit that this is a bad investment, and when you do finally recognize it as a bad investment, you may be so upset that you can't think clearly. This is a time when you need to remain calm and think things through. You need to begin working out the problems immediately.

QUICK STUDY

As a first step, you need to have a damage estimate. You need to determine in which of the worst-case assumptions will happen over the next 12 months. Management of the company is rarely clearheaded enough to understand the problem and make the damage assessment. You need to spend the time to come up with that report.

As part of this quick study, you need to ask yourself several questions. Why have sales projections been missed? Do any executive sales people or other employees seem to be making less than their full contribution? Is there excessive spending that could be trimmed away? Is there a real demand for the company's product or services? Does the management have a true understanding of the cash flow?

You may want to have your accountant come in to prepare adequate cash flow projections so that a true estimate of the damage can be computed. Can you pinpoint the root cause of the problem? Once you have completed that quick study, you need to move on to other aspects.

THE BUSINESS PLAN

In the same way that you prepared your original business plan, you need to develop a business plan for the workout. You need to review the business from stem to stem and try to come up with an aggregate business plan that will allow you to move the company from its problem situation to positive cash flow. This business plan should be completed as quickly as possible.

TURNAROUND EXPERTS

You may want to hire a person who is known as an expert in turnaround situations if you don't have time or ability to run the business yourself. There are many people who are turnaround experts in specific industries. You can start by contacting the Turnaround Management Association. However, beware that people who are excellent at turning businesses around are very often not very good at running the business once it is "fixed." Turnaround people have a very specific skill that is good while a business is in trouble. However, once the business is running at a healthy rate, it is time to find a leader who is good at running a growing company.

LIQUIDATION ANALYSIS

When you prepare your business plan, you also need to prepare a liquidation analysis. That is, under an orderly liquidation whereby you sell the assets of the business and pay off creditors, what would the company be worth? To do this, you need to make a reasonable assessment of the assets. Go through all of the items on the balance sheet, as well as assets off the balance sheet, and determine whether they have significant value beyond that listed on the balance sheet or perhaps a lesser value under the liquidation scenario.

You may want to consider putting the company in Chapter 11 if that is the only way to stave off creditors who are making demands on the company.

SAVE YOUR INVESTMENT

During the workout period, you must not be swayed from your main goal: to save the money that you have invested in the company. Sometimes in a workout situation, you can get caught up in saving the jobs of the people employed there, saving the company that you once believed in, or not destroying the hopes and dreams of the entrepreneur. All of these are worthwhile goals, but your first priority is to save your own investment. In this situation, you need to look out for number one only.

12 Finding Good Investments

As chronological sequences go, this chapter should be the first chapter. However, it seemed important that you be able to recognize a good investment before you go searching for one. So we began this book with the determining what is a good investment, following up with the due diligence process, completing the closing process, monitoring the investment and then finally exiting the deal. We now discuss *where* to look for good investments. Venture Capital has become a very mature and saturated market, so distinguishing yourself and your products is essential.

Developing an Investment objective

Before you can establish a marketing approach to finding good investments, you need to develop your own investment objectives. This is not as easy at it sounds. Making money is a very general objective, and although everybody says that they are out to make money, there are thousands of ways to do it. As an investor, you must make some basic choices or you'll be pulled in a thousand different directions. Here are some important areas to review in establishing your objectives.

PURPOSE OF INVESTING

Every time you ask VCs why they are investing, they usually say they are investing to make money for themselves and their investors. But VCs have other desires, as well. For example, some major corporations invest in small businesses in order to have a "window on technology." That is, they want to see what small companies are doing in a certain area of technology. So they invest not only to make money, but also to learn about new technologies.

Other large companies invest in small companies to develop information about an industry so that they can acquire companies in that industry. They also may invest as a prelude to making acquisitions, like a shark taking its first bite before it swallows the whole fish. Some large companies invest for public relations purposes. That is, they try to generate goodwill in the marketplace by investing in some small, community-based companies.

Some people invest to "save the world." They feel that by investing in a small company with a great technology, they will be able to help the world. It may be a new medical product. It may be a new solar generator or alternate energy source that is going to wrest power from the hands of the oil cartel.

When you are looking around for partners to co-invest with, make sure you understand your proposed partner's purpose for investing. If it is not consistent with your own, you should not co-invest. In all likelihood, you will end up at odds in trying to decide where the company should go.

THE TYPE OF MONEY YOU HAVE TO INVEST

Some investors have plenty of equity money to invest in small businesses, and as a result, they can invest in common stock or preferred stock, or they can buy debt in the company. If the investor has equity-type money and plenty of it, there are many alternatives that the investor can provide. On the other hand, if the investor has a strong net worth but not much cash, the investor may be willing to guarantee a debt from a bank to a small business in return for an equity stake in the company. By doing this, the small business gets the money it wants, but it receives the money in the form of a loan, and it has to pay interest on the loan, as well as give some equity to the guarantor.

In another method, the investor may have great credit lines with the bank so that the investor can borrow the money and lend it to the small business. In this situation, the investor has access to debt-type money and needs to use a debt instrument for the investment in the small business so that there is money coming in to service the loan the investor took from the bank. Otherwise, the investor has a negative carry, meaning that the investor has to pay the interest on the loan to the bank and has no income from the investment.

Most VCs have short-term money. The partnership they form to raise the money has a finite life, and their investment must be paid back so they can meet the terms of their partnership. The general term of VC partnership money is five years.

The type of money you have to invest will play a big role in determining what type of investment you are looking for and how you can make money.

STAGE OF DEVELOPMENT

Some investors prefer to be involved in a particular stage of a company's growth. There are many stages of development: seed, start-up, and later-stage. Seed stage is when the business is just an idea. Start-up stage is when the company is just beginning to produce its product. There are later stages, such as second- and third-round financings. These later stages have relatively lower risk than the earlier stages because the company is most likely nearing cash flow positive, where it can carry itself. However, it doesn't give the investor as great a feeling of accomplishment as it would the investor who had invested in the company since inception.

In addition, there are many varieties of turnaround investments, in which the investor finances a troubled company that will need a great deal of work in order to turn it around and make it profitable.

There are also LBOs, in which a group of management people get together and borrow a great deal money and put up some equity to buy a company. This, too, is a special type of investing that takes a different type of investor.

You need to determine the stage of company development at which you wish to invest.

SPECIALTY INVESTING

Some VCs are generalists. They will invest in practically any area of industry and have an appetite for anything from oil wells to high technology. Generally speaking, most investors feel that they must specialize in an area (or areas) in which they have some knowledge so that they can concentrate on finding the best investments in that industry. You too, will need to select a specialty area that you would like to invest in so that you can communicate this to the outside world. It is important to convey a specialty in an area or a type of financing in order to differentiate yourself in the market. Not only has the equity market become very competitive, but you may also be spending time on investments in which you may lack a fundamental understanding. You may also be sorting through a wide variety of investment opportunities, many of which will be a waste of your time.

TIMING OF YOUR INVESTMENT EXIT

Your investment timing may depend on the cycles you think are occurring in the marketplace. If your ultimate objective is to take the company public, you will have to keep a sharp eye on which way you think the stock market is headed. If you are ready to invest in a company but think the stock market is going to be in too difficult a period to have a successful IPO, you may want to curb your appetite for investing in companies that need a public exit. If, on the other hand, you feel that the stock market will be strong in five years, you may want to invest long-term and take the company public in five years.

Another idea is to invest in a company that you can sell to a larger company. When you invest in this mode, you must pick several target companies you think will want to buy the company and try to judge when they might be willing to do so. Your timing is important because a very acquisitive company may, after several years, stop acquiring in order to digest what it has purchased. Timing in this regard will be more difficult to predict, but you should think about timing your exit before you invest. First, you want to decide whether you are investing in the short term or the long term and whether some part of your portfolio is in that time frame. You then want to think about how you will exit—through a public offering, private sale of the company, or some other method that may have to be "Plan B" if those two exits don't work out.

SIZE OF YOUR INVESTMENT

You need to determine the size of your investment, that is, the amount of money you will be willing to risk in any one company. If you decided that you don't want to invest more than $1 million or $2 million, this would place you in some very small companies, and you might find yourself limited to investing to very early-stage companies. This will determine how you are going to invest your dollars.

On the other hand, if you only have a few dollars to invest, you may want to associate yourself with an investment group in which you can bring more to the table than just money. In every big city, there are a number of "angel investment groups" that invest in small businesses. You may want to join one of them. If you have specific expertise in a certain area, don't be shy about letting local venture capital funds know that you have expertise in this area and money to invest. Let them know that you would like to co-invest with them and that you would be willing to do a lot of the work on the due diligence.

GEOGRAPHIC PREFERENCE

You must determine what distance you are willing to go to invest. Are you willing to invest only in your own backyard, or are you willing to board an airplane and fly to see a company? Generally speaking, if you are going to invest in early-stage companies, they should be within a very small circle around the area where you live because usually, early-stage investments take a lot of your time, money, and energy. On the other hand, if you are getting ready to invest in a fairly large third-round financing in which you will not play a major role, time and energy will not be as necessary, and you may be willing to travel a longer distance.

LIQUIDITY PREFERENCE

VCs typically invest in companies that don't have much liquidity, but there are a number of "penny stocks" in which you may want to invest. This gives you the right to sell your stock at almost any time, as long as there is a public market for it. This will give you liquidity, whereas most venture capital investments are illiquid.

Be careful, some small public companies are public for a time but then lose their trading status on the over-the-counter system NASDAQ, because they fail the net worth or earnings tests and get delisted. Stock in delisted companies is hard to sell.

RISK PROFILE

There is a wide spectrum of risk. You can go for a high-risk, high ROI or you can accept a low-risk, low return. Generally speaking, there are some interesting ways to determine how high your risk is going to be, as discussed in previous chapters. You need to determine how much risk you are willing to take and communicate this to the outside world. If you are really interested in taking flyers, you will have a lot of early-stage, start-up investments reaching your desk for money.

ACTIVITY LEVEL

Determine how active you are going to be in the company in which you invest. If you are going to play an active role managing the company, you will be looking for companies that need someone like you to help. The typical ad in the newspaper for companies seeking financing will read, "Active Partner Needed." This might just suit you. If so, you will be looking for a different kind of investment than most VCs. Typically, VCs are involved in management but not in a day-to-day fashion. They are called in from time to time to help out with problems.

It is also possible for you to be a passive venture capital investor. Some VCs play little or no role in the small companies in which they invest. In fact, they make the investment, then more or less sit back and hope that the investment comes out okay. These investors rarely invest in the company a second or third time. They invest once and hope for the best. You will have to follow your own vision here and determine how active you are going to be in any one company. Obviously, you can't be very active in many small businesses or there won't be enough hours in the day.

TIMING OF RETURN

You need to determine when you think you are going to have your money back in any company in which you are going to invest. Most VCs want to invest for five to eight years, whereas others want to invest for only three to five years. Some players will invest for 10 years or more. You need to determine your time horizon for investing in any small business. When you invest, you want to make sure that your time horizon is congruent with that of the small business and the other investors.

Once you have analyzed each of these areas and written down your investment objectives, you will have a much clearer vision of what type of deals you should be looking for.

ORIGINATING INVESTMENT OPPORTUNITIES

Now that you have identified your basic objectives, you need to get the word out about what types of deals interest you.

You should put together a one- or two-page letter that describes what you are interested in and what you are willing to consider, then send it out by e-mail and regular mail. You should set up a Web page to describe your interest. Then you need to circulate it among the various areas that may come into contact with small businesses in need of equity. You may also be able to reach many of them on the internet. However, with all the spam email, it may be harder to get someone to focus on your investment abilities, than getting a letter on their desk. The following describe some sources of investment opportunities.

BANKS

A bank can be of help in a number of areas. First, the lending department will be interested in showing you situations that need equity funds. Banks always have loans that need an infusion of equity. Second, bankers often have small businesses come to them looking for cash. If the commercial banker does not feel that the small business has sufficient collateral to justify a loan, the small business person may then ask the banker to refer any investor who might be a good investment match for the company. Commercial bankers run into a large number of small businesses looking for money and can help you find investments.

The workout department of a bank is also a good place for problem loans. You may find the banker in a very precarious situation, trying to get the bank's money back, and you may be the answer. If you like turnarounds (those businesses that show declining profitability but can be "fixed"), the bank workout department is a good place to visit. It usually knows of one or two companies that are in deep trouble and need some help.

The bank trust department also has tips on businesses for sale, usually because an owner has died and has left his or her small business in the estate. The bank would like to find somebody to buy the business and run it. Bank trust departments are trying to sell these businesses, and you might be the right person at the right time. Make sure the bank trust departments in your town know what you are looking for. Also, the trust officer will be planning people's estates, and if they have decided to sell, they have most likely communicated this to the bank trust department. Even though you may not want to buy the business, you may well be the catalyst and the financial source needed to get the business sold.

ACCOUNTANTS

Small and large accounting firms run into an inordinate number of businesses for sale and many that need money. You may be just the right person to help an entrepreneur buy a business or you may be the right person to help out an entrepreneur who currently owns a business in need of money. Many accountants play the role of investment banker and help small businesses find money from individuals, as well as institutions. You should make sure that you spend time with these accountants.

ATTORNEYS

Attorneys are much like accountants. They spend time with their clients and understand what clients are going through. If an elderly client trying to settle an estate, the word will go out to the lawyer. You can back the existing management in the LBO of the company from the seller. You should communicate your interests to lawyers.

In addition, lawyers work with small businesses that need money because of operating problems or growing pains. They often know about the small businesses in their area that are in need of cash. You should let the lawyer know that you have money to invest in small businesses.

INVESTMENT BANKERS/ STOCKBROKERS

Almost every brokerage firm has a group of brokers known as investment bankers. These are people who work for the brokerage house in a separate area, not buying or selling stocks but acting as brokers on the sale or in the financing of businesses. Every department has a group of specialists in the small business area (sometimes called "middle market") or the merger and acquisitions area, and you should get to know these people because they can help you find investment opportunities. They are compensated by the company paying a fee to the brokerage house.

BUSINESS BROKERS/FINANCIAL BROKERS

There is a rather undefined group of individuals known as business brokers and financial brokers who help small businesses find buyers or investors. These people are similar to investment bankers but do not work for large brokerages. They usually work for themselves or for "boutique" investment banks that specialize in small businesses. Many times, these small brokers help one or two businesses a year find deals, and you may be the perfect fit.

You can locate these people by looking in the Yellow Pages under financial or business brokers. You can also look in the Sunday classified ads of your newspaper under business opportunities. There you will find dozens of business brokers listing businesses for sale. You should contact them and tell them you are interested in investing in small businesses. Ask whether they know of any in which the entrepreneur doesn't have enough money. They will be eager to help you and some of their entrepreneurs get together because they stand to get a fee for selling a business.

Warning: There are many unethical brokers who are rip-off artists. Most have no association with financial sources. Make sure you are dealing with a quality broker who is affiliated in some way with a financial group or have strong recommendations from other businesses previously helped by them. These will be your best brokers.

CONSULTANTS

Good consultants in the area of small business are few and far between. However, many of the big accounting firms have consultants who specialize in this area, and some independent consultants in the marketplace also look at small businesses and try to help them with their problems. You should get to know some of these people and tell them what you are looking for. These consultants often see small businesses that need money and could steer them to you.

CONVENTIONS

Many conventions around the country are oriented toward entrepreneurs and small businesses, as well as venture capital. You should attend these fairs and try to determine whether any of the small businesses participating are worth your investment. Unfortunately, it has been our experience that most of these conventions are not good places to find investments. But who knows, maybe you will find something different in your town!

ECONOMIC DEVELOPMENT ORGANIZATIONS

Every city and even some towns have an economic development organization whose investment officers are on the lookout for small businesses that might relocate in their area or might need help after relocating. Many of these businesses need equity capital, and you could be the person to provide those funds. Determine who these economic development officers are and get to know them. Make sure they know what you are looking for.

INDUSTRIAL AND PROFESSIONAL TRADE ORGANIZATIONS

Most cities have industrial and professional trade organizations to help their small businesses. Get to know these trade associations and let it be known that you have money to invest in small businesses in their industry. Each of these trade associations has contacts throughout their industries, and they often know of small businesses that need money. They will be most happy to send you to the small business and earn "brownie points" from their members.

LOCAL CHAMBERS OF COMMERCE

Like the economic development organizations, your local Chamber of Commerce will know of a lot of businesses in your area. Some of them will be looking for money. Make sure that you want to invest in the area, and get letters and information into their hands so they can pass the word along.

FRIENDS AND ASSOCIATES

In talking to the outside world, you should tell your friends and associates that you are very interested in small businesses and are looking for investment opportunities. They may run across a company looking for investment capital and send them your way.

VENTURE CAPITAL COMPANIES AND LBO FUNDS

Although it is unusual for venture capital companies to syndicate their investments with individuals, it does happen. It usually happens when the individual has special information or abilities in a certain area, and they will want you for your expertise. You should let local venture capital companies know that you are interested in investing in anything they are financing and would gladly play a more active role than they may have time to play. For example, you could sit on the board of directors and provide management with advice. Under that scenario, you will find VCs very interested in hearing about what you are looking for. In addition, every city and town has a local (or sometimes many) organization. You may want to start going to their meetings and introducing yourself to other people in your field.

COLD CALLS

From time to time, you may hear of a small business in the area that sounds interesting. All you have to do is pick up the phone, call the company, ask who the president is, try to get through to him or her, and say you have investment capital and would like to invest in the company. You would be surprised how many cold calls get through when the caller is looking for an investment opportunity in the business. The next time you read about a company, don't say, "I wish I had invested." Call and see whether you can invest.

ADVERTISING AND DIRECT MAIL

Placing advertisements in newspapers, periodicals, and trade journals can sometimes help generate investment opportunities. The advertisement should specify certain requirements, such as the stage of development (for example, start-ups) or the level of investment, so as to ward off nuisance calls. Some venture capital companies have gained tremendous opportunities from such advertisements, whereas others have had very little luck with them. The type of company and the type of investment you are looking for will determine whether you should use advertising. If you are looking for a very narrow investment opportunity such as radio stations, advertising in periodicals that are mailed to radio stations will generate an opportunity list from the radio arena. In addition, direct mail can be used to solicit opportunities from specific business areas, but like advertising, it also generates a large number of nuisance calls.

SUPPLIERS

Sometimes suppliers to a specific industry, such as electronic components, can help you find growing companies that need financing. Many of these suppliers have a vested interest in helping their customers obtain financing. In one such situation, drug wholesalers wished to finance a chain of drug stores that was growing rapidly at the time. It turned out to be a good investment. Similarly, you could select an industry and go to the suppliers in that industry to find investment opportunities.

OTHER GROUPS

There are some other groups you can contact from time to time to let them know you are looking for investments. These include employment agencies that may be recruiting for small businesses and could pass along your message.

Financial planners are another source. They frequently work with the heads of small businesses to plan their estates. They may be able to get through to the CEO when no one else can.

Now and then, the staff of elected officials also hear from small businesses that are looking for money and might be able to send someone in your direction.

Universities, too, at times try to help small businesses and so are involved in the entrepreneurial process. Make sure that they know you are willing to invest in their small businesses.

Regional Small Business Administration (SBA) offices can be a source of small companies seeking venture capital. Most of these are start-up situations, and many of them have contacted the SBA as a last hope. When you contact the SBA office, remember that here you will be seeing last-chance investment opportunities.

PROACTIVITY

To succeed in finding good investments, you must be proactive. You must seek out investment opportunities whenever you can. You cannot sit in your office and hope that good investment opportunities will show up on your desk. Good investments come to those who are looking for them. If you want to be successful in the venture capital investment arena, you will have to hustle. Opportunities will not come into your office by chance.

HANDLING INVESTMENT OPPORTUNITIES

If you want to get a good reputation in the venture capital business, you should have a very quick method for handling the initial inquiries (also refer to Chapter 1). You need to be able to review a business plan or listen to a presentation over the phone and decide immediately whether you have an interest. If instead you ask people to mail in a business plan and leave them waiting for weeks while you ponder to see whether it is a good investment, you will get nowhere in the investment community. A quick "no" is much better than a "maybe" that turns into a "no."

However, quick analysis requires a quick screening process for initial inquiries. The screening list presented here is a condensed version of the entire due diligence process. It contains the key questions that you must ask about the business.

1. What is the business of the company (10 words or less)?
2. What is so great or unique about the business of the company (25 words or less)?
3. Is the management knowledgeable and experienced in this industry?
4. Does the management consist of entrepreneurs, achievers, and aggressive and energetic people?
5. Is the management of top quality?
6. Will you have to hire a new Chief Executive or Chief Operating Officer now or in the near future?
7. Is the company profitable? If not, why not? Is the cash flow positive?
8. What are the historical figures and projections? Note dollars (in thousands) of yearly sales, profit, and cash flow.
9. What is the projected and actual sales growth rate in average percentage per year? Actual percentage? Projected percentage? Is it achievable?
10. Is there a company one can use as a role model? Has anyone else done this before? If so, who?
11. What is the deal you think you can get? What percentage of ownership?
12. How much money will you make? How did you compute this?
13. What collateral will you have? What is the downside risk?
14. Why do you like this situation?
15. What is wrong with this situation?
16. Does this rate as a good deal? Why?

USING BROKERS

Most investors and venture capital firms do not use brokers to help them find investment opportunities. That is, they do not hire investment bankers or brokers to find them deals. Investment bankers are generally hired by companies seeking capital. However, if you do decide to hire a broker to help find investments, there are a number of things you will want to look for.

QUALITIES TO LOOK FOR IN A BROKER

In any business arrangement, you should look into the background of the person you are backing. After all, this person will be working for you and representing your company to the outside world. The broker who meets most of the following qualifications is the one most likely to point you toward good financing opportunities.

Experience. Extensive experience in helping finance business is usually a must. Without such a background, a broker will not understand the problems of a small business. Nor will he or she understand the sources of funds that usually finance small businesses.

Professional. A business broker should be a true professional, one who is knowledgeable about your investment approach and the type of investment that you are looking for. He or she should be working as a broker full time. It is unlikely that any part-time person can assist you.

Credentials. Any broker you have working for you should have a strong financial background. A degree from a recognized business school is a plus. Prior experience as an investment banker or as an employee of a recognized brokerage firm is also a plus. Prior experience in venture capital investment would be even better.

Special Knowledge. If you are seeking investments in high technology or a specialty industry, the broker you are working with must have professional training in that special area.

Without a degree from a technological school and knowledge of the technological area, the broker will not be able to gain the confidence of those in the industry and lead you to a potential investment opportunity.

AGREEMENT WITH BROKER

Your broker may want you sign a written agreement stating that if the small business concern is unwilling to pay his or her fee, you will be responsible for it. Such an arrangement between you and any financial broker should have all the elements of a good contract. Once you have a full, written understanding of the relationship between you and the broker, you will be in a better position to use his or her services. Below are some of the items that your written agreement should contain.

Definition of the Service. In this section of the legal agreement, you should spell out in detail the service to be performed by the broker. Establish what is expected of you in the way of information. You should also clearly state the objective of this arrangement, such as "a venture capital investment of $1 million."

Time Frame. Every legal document should specify the date that the relationship terminates. You should also specify intermediate dates by which certain milestones are to be completed. If either you or the broker fail to meet these intermediate dates, the contract can be canceled by either party. You will be in a position to call the broker and ask what progress has been made. If none has been made, terminate your agreement by letter, stating that you are terminating it because the specified progress has not been made.

Termination Clause. The termination should be subject to written notices from one party to the other party. This clause will state how and for what reasons the agreement can be terminated.

Amount of the Fee. State the amount of the fee in detail. It can be a flat fee that covers all out-of-pocket expenses or it may be a fee plus out-of-pocket expenses. If you are agreeing to the latter, make sure you have in writing an estimate of the out-of-pocket expenses in excess of some named amount.

Reports on Progress. The agreement should state whether any progress reports are to be produced by the broker. Normally, the broker should report to you verbally at least once every week and should frequently give you a written report of the work completed.

Ownership of Work Completed. Any work completed by the broker, such as charts or work on the business proposal, should be owned by you. You have paid for the work; therefore, you should own it. If you do not have this clause in your agreement, any work completed by the financial broker may belong to him or her. If you should terminate this agreement for just cause, the broker may keep everything. This will force you to duplicate a great deal of work.

Nondisclosure Clause. There should be another clause in your agreement specifying that the broker will not disclose any information divulged to him or her to any other persons without your prior written consent. This will prevent the broker, under any circumstances, from passing along information and potentially squeezing you out of a deal you originally found.

Indemnification. The broker should indemnify you in the agreement against any misrepresentations or wrongful doings by him or her while in your service. The broker should also indemnify you against violations of federal and state security laws. If the broker does not indemnify you for actions taken by him or her, your situation could conceivably be misrepresented to someone, and that person could sue you because of the misrepresentation. After all, your broker is your representative.

Complete Agreement. The agreement should state that this is the only agreement that the parties have entered into and that any verbal understandings are null and void. This written agreement should supersede any previous agreements, and all future modifications should be in writing.

SOME TIPS ON DEALING WITH BROKERS

The soundest advice anyone can ever give you is to urge you to check out the broker. Obtain references from the broker and determine whether the broker is legitimate. Call any companies that the broker claims to have helped. Call the presidents of those companies and ask about the broker. Also, ask the broker for some names of companies that the broker was *unable* to help. Contact the president of those companies and ask them why the broker did not succeed. Any information you can develop about this individual will be useful in helping you to decide whether to hire.

FINAL WORD

Now that you have read this book and learned some of the "tricks of the trade," you will have an idea of how to find a good investment, evaluate it, perform due diligence, close it, monitor it, and then exit the deal for a great return. As you can see, it is not an easy process. Thousands of men and women are doing this for a living every day. It takes time, great energy, and superior judgment. But for those of us in the industry, it is great fun. Every day we meet wonderful entrepreneurs and it is rewarding to see them make their businesses become successful and their dreams become a reality.

The venture capital industry and the LBO industry where we work each day are filled with excitement. There are new products and services coming to market, and we get to see them first and decide whether they are ones that will make money. We work on complex buyout transactions that are both taxing and rewarding. Completing a complex buyout is a great achievement.

As investors, we stand at the pinnacle of capitalism, determining which businesses get funded. It is an awesome responsibility and an exciting experience. We represent the branch of capitalism that allocates capital to new and exciting opportunities. For those of you just entering the industry, we welcome you and invite you to come see us. We would like to get to know you and co-invest in some great companies with you.

For all of you reading this book, we wish you happy hunting. May you fine the perfect investment and may it yield you great personal and professional rewards.

A Questions Used in Venture Capital Investigations

Investigation is an arduous task. Some people have a gift for investigating people and businesses, but most of us need help. We need help in organizing our approach. This means putting together lists of questions about the things we should be looking for.

Although no list is complete for every business situation, a long general list is better than no list at all. A general list of questions will obviously not fit the style of every investigator. You must, therefore, develop your own list of general questions, then adapt that list to each different business opportunity. The general list below is only a beginning. You must improve on it by deleting those questions you believe are not important and adding questions that are not on the list.

There are numerous basic areas to investigate. Each one is like a flat stone. You have to turn up each stone to see whether there is a snake under the stone. If you do not turn up each and every stone, you may leave a snake hiding that will come out one day and bite you. You never know which stone might be hiding a deadly snake that could someday kill the business in which you invested. It might be production or it might be finance. To repeat, when investigating business, you should leave no stone unturned.

Think of each of the areas below as a module that you must complete before your investigation is finished. The degree of detail you examine in each module will depend on the stage of development of the business, how much you know about the industry, how well you know the entrepreneur, and many other factors. Below is a guide to begin your search. Some of the same questions can be asked in each area to determine consistency. You need to modify this list of questions to suit your own needs.

I. MANAGEMENT AREA

Most VCs say people are the most important part of any good investment. "Good management" is a key phrase of investors. But whether management is "good" seems to hinge on performance. That is, if the management team has made lots of money for the VCs, it is considered "good management." What is it that makes a VC believe a management team will succeed and therefore be good? What makes a good entrepreneur? Well, a billion pages have been written on these subjects in every type of publication imaginable, from psychology journals to popular self-help magazines. Judging people will be one of your most difficult tasks. Here are some questions to help you start thinking about the key people.

A. Chief Executive Officer (CEO)

1. What achievements has the chief executive had in prior business? In personal affairs? In general? What makes you think the CEO will achieve the established goals in this business venture?
2. What other business ventures has this CEO been in? How successful was he or she? Why was he or she unsuccessful?
3. What is the style of leadership of the chief executive? Will that style be effective in this business?
4. How does the CEO perceive the CEO's role relative to other members of the management team? Is the

emphasis on one individual or on the team effort? Does the CEO believe the CEO is the key player or the team?

5. How well does the chief executive understand the details of this business? Is the entrepreneur a detail-oriented or a concept person? If the CEO does not know the details, who in the team does?

6. Does the CEO know the details of the day-to-day operations of the business? Is the CEO involved in the details or in the big picture? Is the CEO the coach or the coach/quarterback?

7. Is the CEO knowledgeable about all parts of this business, marketing, production, finance, etc.?

8. To what extent does the CEO rely on subordinates or other managers to analyze business operations?

9. Does the chief executive take a lead role in the company's planning efforts or rely on others to do the planning?

10. Is the chief executive innovative in dealing with existing or potential problems?

11. Characterize the CEO in terms of behavior, attitude, and approach to life? What behavior traits does the CEO have?

12. Is the CEO honest? Does the CEO have integrity?

13. When you ask questions about the financials, can the CEO answer them or does he or she defer to others in the business?

14. Is the CEO knowledgeable about the industry? Does the CEO know many people in the industry? Is the CEO a member of the trade organization for this industry?

15. What is the reputation of the CEO in the company, in the community, and in the industry?

16. What is the net worth of the CEO? Is the CEO wealthy outside this business? If so, what will motivate this CEO to make money?

17. What is the age of the entrepreneur? Does the CEO have the energy to run this business?

18. What is the health of the CEO?

19. Is the CEO insurable?

20. What kind of home life does the CEO have? Is it stable? How will it affect the CEO's ability to run the business?
21. What does the CEO want to make in capital gains from this business? How much in salary?
22. There can be only one final decision maker in any company; is this CEO the final decision maker? Is the CEO in control of the decision-making process?
23. Is there a natural successor for the chief executive? Would the company be able to function smoothly without the CEO?
24. Does this CEO have a burning need to achieve at this business?
25. Is the CEO competitive?
26. What achievements are in the CEO's background?
27. Does the CEO have a high energy level?
28. Does this CEO give you straight answers to questions?
29. Does this CEO have a need for autonomy?
30. Does the entrepreneur seek independence?
31. Does the CEO need to dominate every situation?
32. Is the entrepreneur self-confident?
33. Is the CEO persuasive?
34. Does the CEO have a high tolerance for ambiguity?
35. Does the CEO change?
36. Is the CEO able to perceive risk well?
37. Does the CEO take excessive risk?
38. Does the CEO have good verbal ability?
39. Does the CEO have a good personality? Is the CEO easy to get along with or a difficult person to live with?
40. Is the CEO a leader or manager?
41. Does the CEO have a broad and deep knowledge of the industry or the market?

B. Numbers Two and Three in Management

1. Would the people who are second or third in command be able to fill the shoes of the CEO if the CEO should die or be disabled? Why do you believe this?
2. Are there any disagreements between the top executives? What kind of friction exists between them? Can they work as a team?

3. What are the backgrounds of the second- and third-level executives? How do they fit together as a team? Do their backgrounds complement each other? Does each have a specialty?

4. Ask the same questions of other key people as you did for the CEO above.

C. Management as a Team

1. Obtain an organizational chart and job description indicating present management areas of responsibility.

2. How does management experience in the past and the responsibilities of each person in the team compare with present job requirements? How does salary level compare?

3. Are there any gaps in the present management structure? What are the company's plans for remedying these deficiencies? Should they be remedied before an investment is made?

4. Why do you think this team of managers will be successful? Have they worked together in the past?

5. What percentage of ownership or potential ownership does each member of the management team have? What was the amount of their cash payment for shares held? How significant is each person's investment position in the company relative to that manager's overall financial resources?

6. Are there any loans to or from management or key stockholders?

7. Does the company have the right to repurchase shares held by employees if they leave or are fired? For how long does this right continue? Can the company repurchase shares at cost?

8. What are the present salary levels of management?

9. Are there any kinds of incentive compensation?

10. Are there any employment contracts?

11. Have key employees signed noncompete or confidentiality agreements?

12. Is there presently any litigation or other potential liability resulting from management's previous relation-

ship with another company? For example, have any of the management team signed noncompete or confidentiality agreements with their past employers?

13. What changes have there been in the management group in the last three years?

14. How is coordination between members of the management team achieved?

15. How do other members of management feel about the other executives and their management style? How do they feel about the CEO?

16. Does the company have a management development program?

17. How often is performance by members of the management team reviewed? By whom?

18. Is there a strong team spirit in top management? Is there *esprit de corps*?

19. Is there a strong work ethic? Do they work long hours?

D. Organizational Structure and Decision Making

1. Who exercises the principal authority?

2. What are the relative powers of the president, chairman of the board, vice president of marketing, etc.?

3. Are there any functioning committees? What functions do they perform? Who sits on them? How often do they meet? What records are kept?

4. Who are the members of the board of directors? What recent changes have there been in board membership? What are their backgrounds and qualifications? What compensation do they receive? What actual or potential stock ownership positions do they have?

5. What role do board members play in the company? Do they attend board meetings?

6. What is the relationship between management and the board of directors?

7. What role do investors now play in the company?

8. What is management's attitude regarding the function of the board and the investors?

9. What other outside interests influence management's decision making?

10. What are the individual duties, responsibilities, and authorities of each member of the management group? Who defines these? Do written job descriptions exist?

11. Are the basic rules of good organization being adhered to, such as delegation of authority, defined authority limits, defined responsibility limits, simple and flexible organization, separation of line functions and staff functions?

12. Are successful and proven management personnel available to carry out plans or does everything depend on one or two key persons? What happens if a key employee is not available for an extended period?

13. Is there a blend of youth and experience, or are most employees the same age? Do they have the same experience?

14. Are there cohesive lines of authority and communication? Do all parts of the unit work closely together? Is there an integrated approach to all major problems?

15. Does any one individual excessively dominate operations and planning?

16. Have development plans been established for key managers and high-potential employees?

17. What is the strategy for filling key positions? Can internal development alone meet the requirements or will intercompany transfers or outside hiring be required? Are outside consultants used? What has been the company's past experience?

18. Are local laws prohibiting discriminatory hiring and advancement practices being complied with?

19. Is the compensation plan being administered so as to attract and retain top-quality personnel? Are salary levels competitive with industry norms?

20. Does the company have "key man" life insurance and disability insurance on any of its officers?

21. Do any voting trust arguments exist on any of the company's stock?

22. Does the company have a pension plan, profit-sharing plan, insurance plan, stock bonus plan, deferred compensation plan, or severance plan?

E. Questions Relating to Management Characteristics

1. What type of leader is successful in this industry? Is your entrepreneur like them? What type of leader is likely to be successful in this company? Does your entrepreneur fit?

2. What experience does the management team have in this industry?

3. How much energy does this management team have? Are members of management in good health?

4. How creative are they? How flexible are they?

5. How intelligent are they? What schools did they attend? What degrees did they receive? What did they achieve in college?

6. What successes have they had? What have they achieved in their lives?

7. What is the reputation of the management, the board members, and the company?

8. Have any of the officers, directors, or major stockholders been involved in legal proceedings? Criminal proceedings?

9. Has any officer, director, member of the management group, or employee of the company, (including subsidiaries and/or affiliates) ever filed a petition under the Bankruptcy Code or State Receivership, or made any assignment for the benefit of creditors? If so, describe.

10. Has any officer, director, member of management group, or employee of the company (including subsidiaries and/or affiliates) ever been indicted or convicted of any crime other than a minor traffic offense? If so, describe.

11. Has a member of the management team left? If so, why? Contact this person and discuss the company and why he or she left.

12. Are there any actions, lawsuits, or proceedings pending or threatened against the company or any officers or directors? If so, list.

13. Does the company have any management contracts?

14. Do any affiliated transactions exist between the company and any of its officers, directors, or their relatives, other than in their capacity as officers or directors?

15. Have the company, its officers, or its directors had any Securities and Exchange Commission problems or violations in the last 20 years? Also, do any exist at present, or are any pending or threatened?

16. Have any officers or directors violated any federal, state, or local laws (other than minor traffic regulations) in the past 20 years?

F. Corporate Ownership

1. How much of this company does the CEO own? After the financing, will the ownership be enough to motivate the CEO to achieve long-term capital gains?

2. How much of this company does each member of the management team own? After this financing, will they own enough to be motivated to achieve long-term capital gains?

3. How much of the company do the outside/nonmanagement directors own? Are they motivated to achieve long-term capital gains?

4. Do any individuals outside the company own a large percentage of the company? What is their role in the company?

5. Does the company or any of its officers own 10 percent or more of the equity in any company other than the company you are considering?

BASIC INFORMATION YOU NEED TO COLLECT

A. Documentation of the Management Area

1. Management organizational chart.

2. Details of management stock ownership.

3. Detailed resumes (including past experience, salary and promotion history, and academic qualifications)

and business and personal references for each key member of management and each department head.

4. Information on the CEO's family life, children, physical impairments, illnesses, and other personal data.
5. Copies of any employment agreements, noncompete agreements, or agreements with respect to the repurchase of shares owned by management.
6. Copies of any incentive compensation plans.
7. Copies of any litigation material.
8. Management checks:
   a. Personal reference
   b. Former employers of management
   c. Former employees of this company
   d. Former investors, shareholders, or business partners
   e. Retail credit reports
   f. Daily litigation reports
   g. Bishop's report
   h. Dun & Bradstreet on past business
   i. Past trade creditors
   j. Past suppliers
11. At least five business and three personal references for each key member of management. Business references should correspond to most recent job, as indicated on resume.
12. The characteristics of the CEO and each of the members of the management team.
13. A complete list of the total compensation to the officers of the company including salary, commissions, bonuses, fees, prerequisites, loans, advances, autos, club fee, pension, profit sharing, and other. What does each person cost the company?

B. Management Reports

1. What management reports are received by top management?
2. Which management reports are used by top management to "run the business?"

3. Does top management get performance reports on each functional area?

4. Do members of management receive sufficient, timely, and accurate reports so they know what is going on in the business?

C. Strengths and Weaknesses

1. List the five strengths of the CEO.
2. List the five strengths of the management team.
3. List the five weaknesses of the CEO.
4. List the five weaknesses of the management team.
5. What are the three greatest risks of backing this management?
6. What do you like or dislike about the CEO? About management?

D. Summary Analysis

1. In a very few words, how do you feel about the CEO? About management?
2. Can this CEO make this business plan happen with this management team? Why do you believe this?
3. Are you willing to bet real money on this CEO and this management? Would you bet your career or job on this CEO and management?

II. PERSONNEL AREA

Personnel or human resources are a vital part of any company's long-range plan. Every company needs to put in place compensation systems that will motivate its employees to make the company successful. A company that ignores its personnel area will probably fail. Top management's ultimate task is to select and retain good people. You must determine that the company you are reviewing has a good personnel plan.

A. Corporate Organization

1. Does the company have a complete organizational chart for each division?
2. Are there job descriptions for each person in the organization?
3. Is there a complete list of officers and directors?
4. Is there a complete list of stockholders?
5. Is there a complete list of employees?
6. Is the organization consistent in its short- and long-range objectives?
7. Are savings available through consolidations or other restructuring?

B. Employee Compensation

1. Is there a list of all officers, directors, department heads, and other employees whose compensation exceeds $30,000/year?
2. What is the date and percentage wage increase of the latest general pay raise for all employees?
3. List the average salary and hourly wage level for the three categories consisting of officers, supervisors, and other employees. Is the average for each higher, the same as, or lower than it is for other local firms in the area and for the competition?
4. Does the company have a written procedure for determining beginning salaries, raises, promotions, etc.? Who sets these policies?

C. Pension Plan

1. Does the company have a pension plan? If so, obtain a summary.
2. Is it fully funded? Through what date? Who is the actuary?
3. Do any Employee Retirement Income Security Act (ERISA) violations exist? If so, describe.
4. List the contributions for each of the past five years.
5. Is the plan overfunded so that termination of the plan will trigger a return of the surplus to the company?

D. Profit-Sharing Plan

1. Does the company have a profit-sharing plan? If so, obtain a summary.
2. Have all disbursements been made to the plan for the past year? If not, describe.
3. Can the plan be terminated at any time at the discretion of the company?
4. List the contributions for each of the past five years. Are they excessive?

E. Bonus Plan

1. Does the company have a bonus plan for any of its employees (including Christmas)? If so, describe.
2. Obtain a list of the bonuses paid last year. Are they excessive?

F. Other Employee Benefits

1. Describe medical and sick leave benefits and policies. Also determine the number, type, and cost of claims over the past three years, and specifically identify any significant open claims.
2. Describe vacation/holiday policies.
3. Describe stock option or related equity incentives.
4. Describe policies related to travel and entertainment expenses.
5. Describe policies related to the use of automobiles, airplanes, limousines, boats, etc.
6. Comment on escalation clauses or expectations, if any, within current fringe benefit programs. Expected higher levels of benefits and/or inconsistencies with the buyer should be highlighted.

G. Special Compensation Arrangements

1. Do any employment contracts, noncompete contracts, termination agreements, or other special employee agreements exist? If so, list.
2. Why does the company have such arrangements?

3. Who has signed these agreements? Who determines who must sign the agreements?

4. Who is responsible for obtaining these agreements?

H. Payroll Records

1. Obtain a copy of the weekly and monthly payroll record or printout for salaried, hourly, full-time, and part-time employees. Identify the codes, departments, supervisors, and officers.

2. What payroll records exist for each employee? Why are they maintained?

I. Employee Books/Manuals

1. Does the company have a corporate policy handbook for the employees? If so, obtain a copy.

2. Does the company have an employee benefits handbook? If so, obtain a copy.

3. Does the company have a standard operating procedure manual for all departments and/or job functions? If so, review.

J. Union

1. Has a union represented any employee groups during the past 10 years? If so, describe.

2. Is any union activity threatened or pending? If so, describe.

3. Does the company have a formal anti-union plan in existence? If so, review.

K. Work Stoppage

1. Has the company had a work stoppage for three hours or longer because of strikes, equipment failure, inventory shortages, or other reason during the past five years? If so, describe.

2. Has the company been threatened with work stoppage during the past three years?

L. Training Program

1. Does the company have a formal training program for its employees? If so, describe.
2. If no formal program exists, describe the procedure for training new employees and transferred employees.
3. Who is responsible for assuring that the company has a well-trained group of employees?
4. Describe the extent to which the employees in each department have been cross-trained to reduce problems when employees are absent.

M. Attitude and Morale

1. Has the company ever conducted an attitude/morale survey? If so, obtain a copy of the results.
2. If not, does the company plan to have one?
3. In touring the facilities, what did you think of the attitude and morale of the employees?
4. Is there a strong work ethic among the employees? Is there a team feeling, an *esprit de corps*?

N. Record Maintenance

1. Review the company reporting procedure for maintaining records regarding:
   a. Hiring of new employees
   b. Employee evaluations
   c. Employee transfers
   d. Employee promotions/demotions
   e. Employee compensation changes
   f. Employee reprimands
   g. Employee disciplinary actions
   h. Employee training
   i. Employee tardiness
   j. Employee absenteeism
   k. Employee terminations
   l. Procedure for building legitimate cases for employee termination
   m. Union organization activity

14. Review several actual employee files.

15. Review personnel files for all officers, directors, department heads, and supervisors.

O. Reports 1.

1. List the reports originating within the personnel department for other areas of the company and their value.

2. List the reports generated by outside personnel that you receive and their value to you.

P. Hiring Procedure

1. Review in detail your procedure for soliciting, interviewing, screening, evaluating, conducting reference and credit checks, and hiring new management personnel and other new employees.

2. Does the company use lie detector tests? Honesty evaluation tests?

Q. Motivation

1. What specific methods and techniques has the company found and applied to motivate hourly employees? Salaried employees? Can you quantify the effectiveness of each?

2. What monetary rewards are given for outstanding performance?

3. How is performance measured and used to communicate to employees?

R. Employee Litigation

1. Has employee litigation action occurred in the past 24 months, or is any threatened or pending now? If so, describe.

2. Why have some employees been fired and why have they sued?

S. Regulatory Agencies

1. Has the company experienced any regulatory problems or complaints within the past 24 months with any local, state, or federal agency? If so, describe.
2. Is the company in compliance with all federal, state, and local laws and with all rules and regulations of the agencies and commissions thereof, including but not limited to safety and health, consumer products safety, environmental (air, water, waste treatment, land)? Is any threatened or pending? If so, describe.

T. Consultants

1. Has the company used any outside consultants within the past five years regarding any aspect of the company's personnel? If so, describe. Get copies of any reports.

U. Key Nonexecutive Personnel Department 1.

1. Are the critical functions staffed with well-qualified people?
2. Are there special personnel or skill needs, e.g., related to technology, marketing, or manufacturing (short or long term)?
3. What are the plans to respond to skill needs or technical obsolescence?
4. Is there or will there be an excess of manpower in some functional areas?
5. Can excess people be retrained for other positions within the organization if the need arises?

BASIC INFORMATION

A. Documentation

1. The personnel manual given to each employee.
2. The company's rating for unemployment and Worker's compensation.
3. A complete organizational chart.
4. Job descriptions for various key jobs in the organization.

5. List of officers and directors.

6. List of the percentages of stock owned by all stockholders and the amounts paid for their ownership.

7. Payroll listing by employee showing what each person makes.

8. Copy of pension and profit-sharing plans plus their financial statements.

9. Copy of any employment contracts.

10. Copy of noncompete and nondisclosure contracts.

11. Union contracts.

12. Personnel procedure manual.

13. Written statement about any outstanding personnel or employee problems or suits.

14. Copy of the stock option plan.

15. List of all people with stock options, the number of options held, and the price of the options with the expiration date.

B. Personnel Reports

1. Obtain copies of reports used by the personnel department to "run" the department.

2. Obtain copies of reports given to top management.

3. Obtain a copy of the budget used in the personnel department.

C. Ratio Analysis

1. Calculate the average salary over time by dividing the total payroll by total number of employees. This will tell you how much the average payroll has gone up per employee over time.

2. Calculate the average salary per employee by division such as sales, production, etc. This will show which divisions have high labor cost. Divide total payroll expense for that division by the number of employees in the division.

3. Calculate total payroll as a percentage of sales by dividing total payroll and benefits by net sales. This can show you whether labor costs are going up, relative to sales.

4. Calculate benefits as a percentage of sales by dividing benefits by total payroll. This will tell you whether benefits are going up.

5. Calculate employee turnover by dividing the total number of employees who left in a year by the average number of employees. This will measure the stability of the work force and perhaps reflect how satisfied employees are.

6. Calculate management per employee by dividing number in management by total number of employees. This can tell you whether the organization is "management top-heavy."

7. Calculate sales per employee by dividing net sales by number of employees. This can give you a measure of efficiency.

D. Major Strengths and Weaknesses

1. Identify the company's five major strengths in personnel.

2. Identify the company's five major weaknesses in personnel.

E. Summary Analysis 1. In a very few words, how do you feel about the personnel situation?

2. Can the personnel policies of the company produce a winning team? Can they motivate the employees to win?

3. Are you willing to bet real money that this group of employees, working under these personnel policies, will be successful? Would you bet your career or job?

III. MARKETING AREA

The study of marketing is the study of how the outside world (external to the company) sees the company and how the company sees the outside world. Your task is to try to see the outside world as the entrepreneur's company sees it, then to compare that view with your own investigation of the outside world and how it sees the company. Your analysis should begin by looking at the marketing people.

MARKETING PEOPLE

In this section you are trying to understand who the marketing people are. It is a short list, and you should ask these questions of personnel and management.

A. The Marketing People

1. Who is the head of marketing?
2. What is the background of the head of marketing?
3. How long has the head of marketing been working for the company?
4. What is the head of marketing's salary? How is it divided into commissions and base salary?
5. Who are the top 10 salespeople for the organization?
6. What are their backgrounds?
7. How long have these individuals been part of the company?
8. What salary and commissions have they received in the past 12 months?
9. What has been the sales volume of each individual during the past 12 months?
10. What has been the sales quota for each of these individuals during the past 12 months? Did they make that quota?
11. What is the sales quota for each of these salespeople in the future? How does this compare with the projections?
12. What is your basic appraisal on a scale of 1 to 10 of each of the salespeople, including the head of marketing?
13. What is the approximate age of each person in the sales force? How much energy do they have? How achievement-oriented are they?
14. Perform the same analysis of management here as was used in the management area above.

B. Personnel and Organization

1. How many people are involved in the marketing function?
2. How many sales offices are there? Where are they located? How large a geographical area is served by each one? How many and what kinds of people are employed at each one?
3. What volume of sales is required to support the expenses of each sales office?
4. What is the number of people at each level?
5. What is the average wage or salary rate at each level?
6. What are the most recent annual sales production and compensation figures for salespeople? For sales managers?
7. What is the sales compensation plan? How does this compare with competitive plans?
8. What other benefits or forms of compensation are provided?
9. What is the relationship between past performance levels and performance levels required by projections?
10. What is the availability of required personnel?
11. How are hiring and firing decisions made?
12. How are employees trained? What is the cost of training?
13. How is productivity measured? How long does it take a salesperson to become self-sustaining?
14. How are incentives provided for salespeople? Are sales quotas used? How do quota levels compare with sales forecasts?
15. What are the procedures for promotions and raises?
16. How frequently and in what fashion are performance appraisals made and communicated to employees?
17. What has the rate of turnover been for each kind of employee?
18. Describe specifically the techniques and/or methods by which the marketing department motivates its employees and representatives.
19. List the name, years with the company, and reasons for termination for all salespeople and representatives

who have resigned or were terminated during the past three years.

20. Perform the same analysis of marketing personnel that was used in the personnel area above.

C. Documentation of Marketing Personnel1.

1. Obtain resumes of the marketing people.
2. Check the background of key marketing people.
3. Obtain an organizational chart from marketing.
4. Examine a typical personnel file to see how the procedures examined above are documented.

PRODUCTS

For each product, describe it in the terms set out below:

A. Product Description and Product Features for Each Product

1. What does the product do for its user? How does it work? What need does the product fill for its user? Is the need real, created, or imagined?
2. Give a complete physical and functional description of the product.
3. Does the product have any proprietary features?
4. Is the product or any aspect of it patented? When does each patent expire? How important is the patent to the success of the business?
5. What service goes with the product? Is the service the key to the sale?
6. Does a written procedures manual exist for the marketing department? If so, get a copy.
7. If one exists, is it followed closely?
8. Is it current? What is the date of last review?

B. Product Pricing

1. How is the product priced? What does management consider before making a pricing change?
2. How do prices compare with competitive products; end-user price, distributor price, original equipment manufacturer (OEM) price, etc.?

3. What have been the past price trends for this and other products?
4. What are expected future price trends? Why?
5. Will engineering and other features of this product make it more competitive or less competitive as these trends develop?
6. How are pricing decisions made? Who establishes the prices for each product? What is the rationale for the present pricing structure?
7. Describe the process you follow in establishing prices for your products.
8. Who is authorized to sell products at a price that differs from the approved price list? Who can discount?
9. How often are price changes reviewed?
10. Which products are the most profitable for the company?
11. What is the relationship between product profitability and incentives for salespeople?
12. How do pricing policies and structure compare with those of the competition?
13. What has been the price movement in relation to frequency of occurrence, magnitude of occurrence, elasticity of demand, and sales promotion?
14. What is the industry's ability to meet current and future product demand?
15. Does management believe cost increases could be passed on? Why?
16. Is the company sensitive to industry price changes?
17. Is there a price leader? Which company? Describe the circumstances.

C. Product Life and Reliability

1. When was each product introduced? When have major changes been made?
2. What stage of life cycle is the product in: new, emerging, mature, declining?
3. What is the estimated useful life of the product, stated in months or years?
4. What engineering changes are planned? What will be the effect on product cost and performance?

5. How reliable is the product? Give mean time to failure or some other specific statistical measure. Determine how this measure was arrived at. Compare this measure with the competition.

6. Is the product a standard product or does it require customizing? What is the cost of the basic product vs. the typical customization cost? How is the purchaser charged for customization? Can the product be mass-produced?

7. Is quality the key to the sale of the product?

D. Product Warranty

1. Describe your present warranty policy.

2. What was the warranty expense for each of the past three years?

3. What is the amount of the company's present warranty reserve? Is it adequate?

E. Product Development

1. What new products are planned for the company and what are the dates when they will be available to sell?

2. Does the company have any missing product to complete the product line? If so, describe.

3. What products are needed?

F. Promotion

1. What are annual advertising expenditure levels?

2. What is the advertising policy?

3. How does this relate to overall marketing strategy and objectives?

4. What other kinds of promotion are utilized?

5. What is the rationale for the overall mix of promotional activity?

6. How are the results of advertising and other promotional expenditures evaluated?

G. Product Packaging

1. What kind of packaging does the product have? Is the packaging a part of the promotion?
2. What is the cost of the packaging? Does the packaging cost more than the product itself?
3. What overall image is the package trying to project in the eye of the receiver? Is it well executed?
4. How could the packaging of the products be enhanced?

H. Documentation of Products

1. Sales literature describing product features and applications.
2. Technical literature describing product design and functioning.
3. Picture of product.
4. Copies of any patents or patent applications.
5. Samples of the products.
6. Copy of the procedures manual for the marketing department.

CUSTOMER DESCRIPTION

A. Customer Analysis

1. Who are the customers? What industry groups are they drawn from? What are the overall trends of this consumer? Is the buyer an individual or a corporation?
2. What is the procedure for making a buying decision?
3. How long does the purchase decision process take?
4. What are the key variables in the buying decision? Price, service, product features (enumerate), reputation of selling company, credit terms, delivery speed, or relationship with salespeople?
5. Are buying decisions affected by advertising or sales promotion?
6. What is the degree of brand loyalty among customers? How is it measured or determined?
7. What methods are used to lock customers in?

8. What would be required to persuade the user of a competitive product to switch?
9. How much would a product switch cost the customer? What other inconveniences would be involved?
10. Why does the customer buy this product? What problem does it solve? What need does it fill? Does it save cost, improve efficiency, etc.?
11. Is this product a luxury item or a necessity?
12. What alternatives does the customer have? Are these substitutes for this product?
13. What factors affect the customers' need for this product? What would cause an increase in need? What would cause a decrease?
14. How are the needs of the customers or the makeup of the customer group changing? What are the reasons for the change?
15. Does the company have any contracts or special arrangements with the major customers, including consignments? If so, describe.
16. Has the company lost any major customers in the past two years, or is the company about to lose any? If so, describe.
17. What is the influence of overall business conditions on demand for the company's products? What is the importance of disposable income, consumer income, industrial production levels, population growth, and other broad economic trends to the company's business?
18. How important is personal selling to this customer? How good does the salesperson have to be?

B. Customer Complaints

1. List the five most common complaints received from the customers regarding the product.
2. List the five most serious or costly complaints received from the customers regarding product.
3. List the five most common complaints received from the customer regarding service.
4. List the five most serious or costly complaints received from the customer regarding service.

5. Describe the procedure for handling complaints.
6. Does the company have a monthly or cumulative complaint summary list? If so, review.

C. Customer Credit

1. Who establishes the credit limits for customers?
2. Describe the credit approval process.
3. Does the company have any special credit arrangements with customers? If so, describe.
4. What role does the marketing department have in the account collection process?
5. What are the normal terms of sales?
6. Are any sales invoices over $10,000? Are any under dispute?

D. Documentation

1. Obtain copies of any marketing studies, newspaper articles, magazine articles, etc., describing overall dimensions and configuration of markets and the customer.
2. List the 10 largest customers by dollar sales volume and the 10 largest customers by unit volume. Obtain the names, addresses, and telephone numbers of the largest customers.
3. Obtain a complete customer list.

CUSTOMER SERVICE

1. How is the company service function organized? Who does the service manager report to? How many people work in the service area? How are they recruited, trained, compensated, reviewed, etc.? What is personnel and salary structure within the department?
2. How many service offices are there? What is their relationship with the sales and marketing offices? How is the responsibility for customer relationships divided between these two groups? How is management responsibility divided?
3. What are the service requirements for each product? Can third parties be used to provide service for any

products? What cost/performance tradeoffs are involved in the choice between using the company's service department and a third party?

4. How important is service capability to the customer? What are the customer's most frequent service demands—repair of equipment, replenishment of usable supplies, etc.?

5. How is the customer charged for servicing? Is this a profitable operation for the company? If not, why not? What volume or other requirements are necessary in order to break even or turn a profit?

6. What are the logical follow-on products from a service standpoint? Can service personnel be used to provide service for other companies on a third-party basis?

7. How many employees are in the C/S department?

8. Who performs C/S work? Company employees, service reps, both?

9. Is there a C/S manual?

10. Describe the C/S operation.

11. List your 10 major C/S problems.

12. What is the amount of the C/S budget for this year?

13. Describe the extent of product warranties and guaranties provided.

14. Does the company contract out any customer services/work? If so, describe the terms. Provide the names, addresses, telephone numbers, and contracts of contractors.

COMPETITIVE ANALYSIS

A. Competition

1. Who are the major competitors at present? Are there any expected new entries or other potential competitors?

2. What is the financial strength of the present competition?

3. What new entries are expected in the market?

4. What are the present and expected future competitive shares of market?

5. What is the relative ease of entry into the field? What are the capital and other requirements for entry? What

is the importance of intangibles such as lead time, goodwill, patents, etc.? What are the barriers to entry in this industry?

6. How does the company compare with competition in each of the following categories: product features and capabilities, product price, present market share, marketing capability, production capability, financial resources, financial management, R & D capability, overall management strength, other strategic advantages?

7. If possible, construct a chart indicating the degree of competitiveness with each significant competitor on a 1–3 scale where 1 = superior, 2 = competitive, 3 = below average or not competitive.

8. Compare the company's product with that of the competition, stressing uniqueness of this company's product.

9. List the features and functions of all the products in the marketplace, and then check off those for each of the company's products and each of the competition's products.

10. Compare the company's price points against the competition's price points.

B. Documentation

1. Obtain a list of the company's competition with names, addresses, and telephone numbers.

2. Obtain product literature on the competitors.

3. Obtain annual reports and other literature on the competition.

INDUSTRY ANALYSIS

A. Industry Structure

1. What is the number of companies in the industry by size and category, national and international?

2. To what degree is the industry concentrated in one or a few companies?

3. Which way are mergers and acquisitions trending? Are they vertical, horizontal, or in some other mode?

4. What is the trend of business failures or successes? Are there a lot of failures? What are the causes of the failures?
5. How is the industry structured in terms of geographical location, product lines, channels of distribution, pricing policies, degrees of integration, and types of customers?
6. What are the various barriers to entry by new companies into this industry?

B. Size and Nature of Market

1. How big is the overall market, both domestic and international? List the total dollar size of the market at present by each product category.
2. What is the overall market annual growth rate for each product category, both for the past three years and projected for the next three years?
3. What is the source of the information for questions 1 and 2 above?
4. How is the market segmented geographically, by type or size of customer, by application, etc.? How is growth expected to be distributed among market segments?
5. What is the source of data on market size, growth rate, and market shares?
   a. Information supplied by company?
   b. Independent consultant's research report?
   c. Published data from other sources?
4. How were market estimates and other market data arrived at (market research methodology)?
5. What degree of reliability is attached to each market size estimate, growth rate projection, and market share estimate?
6. What are expected future trends in the market? Greater concentration of market share? More price competition? Why?
7. What are normal terms of sale?
8. What is the sale/lease ratio? How long is a typical lease? Are leases normally full payout leases?
9. Is this market typically a seasonal or cyclical one? Why?

C. Industry Growth

1. What are the annual growth rates for the industry for the past ten years?
   a. What has the sales growth been each year?
   b. What has the profitability of the companies in the industry been each year?
   c. How has market share changed?
4. What are the estimated annual growth rates for the industry for the next 10 years?
   a. What is the sales growth in dollars and in percentage increase for the next 10 years?
   b. What are the profit projections for the next 10 years in total dollars and percentage of increase?
   c. What market share changes are anticipated for the industry?
4. What factors will affect growth in the future? Analyze each of the following:
   a. What are the demographic changes?
   b. What are the general economic trends?
   c. How will disposable income affect the industry?
   d. How will interest rates affect the industry?
   e. How will the composition of the industry change with respect to new business or failing businesses?
   f. How will the market size change?
   g. How will the market share change for each of the companies?
   h. What technological innovations are apt to spur growth?
   i. What production design changes will enhance productivity and perhaps spur growth?
   j. What economies of scale in the industry are likely to affect growth?
   k. What pricing differentials will occur, and what products will be priced differently?
   l. How will imports from foreigners affect the growth of the industry?
   m. How will exports of the product affect the growth of the industry?

   n. How will advertising and other forms of market development affect growth?
   o. What governmental factors affect the industry? Will there be government demand for the product?
   p. How will government regulations affect the industry?
   q. How will government fiscal policy in general affect this industry?
   r. How will consumer buying power change and affect this industry?
   s. What environmental considerations could change the growth patterns of this industry?

D. Competition

   1. What is the strategy for other companies in the industry?
   2. What competition will this industry have from substitute products from other industries?
   3. To what extent will trade practices and cooperation among businesses change this industry?
   4. What barriers to entry may change to increase competition?
   5. What key factors in success may change and allow the competition to get ahead?

E. Customers of the Industry

   1. List all the major industries in which this product is sold.
   2. Estimate the health and welfare of these industries in the future.
   3. What major impacts on the industries to which these companies sell will change this industry directly or indirectly?
   4. Has there been any significant growth in new customers in the past five years?
   5. Has there been a trend toward integration of customers in this industry?
   6. Does this industry depend on a few key customers?

F. Suppliers of the Industry

1. List all the major industries from which this company must buy its products.
2. How have the industries from which this company must purchase products changed over the past five years?
3. What is the outlook for the suppliers of this industry over the next five years?
4. Has there been any significant growth in new suppliers for this industry for the past five years?
5. Has there been a trend in forward integration of suppliers during the past five years?
6. Does this industry depend on a few key suppliers?

G. Labor of the Industry

1. Is the supply of skilled labor adequate for this industry?
2. Are the pay rates in this industry competitive with those of other industries? Are people leaving to join other industries?
3. Have there been any recent union negotiations in this industry?
4. Have there been any new labor contracts or renewals in this industry? What were the results of the settlement and negotiations?
5. To what degree is the industry as a whole unionized?
6. How influential is the union as a whole in the industry?

H. Government Regulation of the Industry

1. To what extent is the company regulated by the government? You should describe this in detail.
2. What regulatory agencies are responsible for regulating this industry?
3. Is there a trend toward more government regulation in this industry?
4. Are there any unique reporting requirements by this industry to government agencies?

I. Patents, Trademarks, Copyrights, and Other Intellectual Properties1.

1. Are any patents, trademarks, and copyrights important to the company's line of business?
2. To what degree do these patents, trademarks, and copyrights determine which company in the industry will succeed?
3. Are there any "household names" in this industry?

J. Cyclical Factors

1. What cycles does the industry go through?
2. What are the determinants of the cycle?
3. How easy is it to predict a cycle upturn or downturn?

K. Industry Associations and Trade Periodicals

1. Is the company a member of any trade or industry association? If so, list the name, address, phone number, and association manager.
2. Is the company represented at any trade shows? If so, list.
3. Is the company represented at any conventions? If so, list.
4. List the names of the three most important trade periodicals in the industry.

L. Documentation of the Industry

1. Obtain current periodicals, newspaper clippings, trade association releases, and company-prepared documents that will assist you in understanding the industry.
2. Obtain information from standard employee reports, value line surveys, Moody's Manual Extracts, and security research reports that will help you understand the industry.
3. Obtain government data and publication and census studies that provide background information on the industry and the competition.

4. Learn the trade associations for the industry and contact them to obtain industrial information.

5. Determine who the experts are in the industry and contact them for additional information.

MARKETING STRATEGY

A. General Strategy

1. What are overall objectives in the marketing area? What are the top three objectives?

2. How are the objectives to be implemented? What are the details of the strategy?

3. What marketing effort is required? Is this a new product that requires extensive customer education and training?

4. Does the product replace a competitor's product or is it a new installation? If both, record the percentage of sales in each area.

5. Who does the marketing force consider to be the strongest competitors?

6. Obtain available sales breakdowns by territory, product, customer, industry, product end use, domestic, international, etc. How do these compare with overall market segments? With future expected sales?

7. Obtain historical and projected percentages of sales to OEMs, distributors, and end users.

8. What are the strengths and weaknesses of any OEMs or distributors?

9. How are potential customers identified? How are leads developed? What is the ratio of leads called to leads qualified? What is the ratio of leads qualified to leads closed?

10. What are the average dollar and time requirements to close a sale? How do these compare with projected sales levels and marketing expenses?

11. What is the size of a typical order? What has been the trend? What are the reasons for this trend?

12. What is the frequency and amount of repeat or follow-on orders? How many of the company's sales have been made as a result of follow-on orders?

13. What has been the trend in the rate of monthly orders?

14. What is the size and quality of present backlog? How much is released to production and shippable within six months to one year? How does this figure compare with projections?

15. How is backlog split between orders from existing customers and orders from new customers? How does this compare with projection assumptions?

16. What is the present geographical dispersion or concentration of product installations? How many installations are there per sales office and per service office? How is this ratio expected to change in the future?

B. Sales Projections

1. What input does marketing have in assisting the company to establish budgets and forecasts?

2. How often are these budgets and forecasts reviewed?

3. If they exist, review them for the past three years for degree of variance from actual.

4. What does marketing think the results will be for this year? By product line or individual product, project sales for the next five years.

5. Why will sales go like this projection?

6. What backlog does the company have by product or product line? What has it been in the past? Is it increasing or decreasing? Why?

C. Advertising and Public Relations

1. Obtain the name and address of the advertising firm that the company employs.

2. Does the company have a written advertising program for this year? If so, obtain a copy.

3. What was the company's advertising expenditures for this year and each of the past three years?

D. Documentation

1. Obtain a copy of the marketing plan.
2. Determine who put the plan together.
3. Obtain promotional literature of this company for the future.

DISTRIBUTION OF THE PRODUCT

1. How many distributors are used by the company? How many salespeople per distributor?
2. How are distributors selected?
3. What is the availability of qualified distributors?
4. What is the geographical distribution of distributors?
5. What were the most recent annual volumes by each distributor?
6. How are distributors compensated?
7. What other products does the distributor sell?
8. What percentage of each distributor's sales do company products account for?
9. How does each distributor's compensation on company products compare with its compensation on the other products it distributes?
10. Does the distributor purchase products from the company or merely take a commission for selling products?
11. What credit terms are extended to the distributor?
12. How are the financial capabilities of distributors determined?
13. What sales support and other services (maintenance, customer financing, etc.) does the company provide for distributors?
14. How do distributors sell the products?
15. How does the company ensure a consistent sales approach by different distributors?
16. What are the other details of any distributor marketing agreements? Obtain a copy.

17. What is the rationale for use of a distributor organization versus direct sales force or other type of marketing arrangement?

18. Under what conditions would a change in distribution methods be justified?

BASIC INFORMATION

A. Documentation of Marketing

1. Copy of written marketing plan.
2. Historical data on sales breakdowns.
3. Historical data on order rates and trends.
4. Data on backlog size and analysis.
5. List of sales and service offices by location.
6. Complete price list and service charge information for all products.
7. Copies of any promotional or sales literature.
8. Organizational charts and salary structure for marketing group and service group.
9. Copy of representative distributor agreement(s).
10. Copy of typical service or maintenance contract.
11. Copy of any OEM contracts.
12. Customer list, including several references to contact.
13. Complete distributor list and names to contact.
14. List of reports generated by the marketing department.
15. Charts or graphs used by the marketing department.
16. Sales projections by product.
17. Make sure you obtain the documentation items above under separate sections in the marketing area.

B. Marketing Reports

1. Obtain copies of the reports used by marketing to "run" the department.
2. Obtain copies of marketing reports given to top management.
3. Obtain a copy of the budget used by marketing to govern spending in that department.

C. Ratio Analysis

1. Calculate sales per salesperson by dividing total sales by the number of salespeople. This will measure the salesperson's productivity.
2. Calculate selling expense as a percentage of sales by dividing selling expenses by sales. This will measure the cost related to obtaining a sale.
3. Calculate salaries and commissions as a percentage of sales by dividing total salaries and commissions by total sales. This will tell you what percentage of total sales accounts for payroll and will give you an indication of the human cost of a sale.
4. Calculate gross profit per salesperson by dividing gross profit by the number of salespeople. This will let you measure the ability of salespeople to contribute to company gross profit.
5. Calculate gross profit as a percentage of marketing expense by dividing gross profit by total marketing expense. This will give you a measure of the effectiveness of marketing in gross sales dollars.
6. Calculate marketing expense as a percentage of sales by dividing marketing expense by sales. This will give you a measure of the cost of the marketing programs compared with the amount of sales generated.
7. Calculate discounts as a percentage of sales by dividing total discounts by total gross sales. This will indicate the discounts the company must be giving in order to accomplish sales.
8. Calculate returns as a percentage of sales by dividing total returns in dollars by total sales before returns. This will give you a measure of customer satisfaction and the quality of the product.

D. Strengths and Weaknesses

1. Identify the five major strengths the company has in marketing.
2. Identify the five major weaknesses the company has in marketing.

3. Are any of these weaknesses so great that the company cannot overcome them?
4. What could go wrong in marketing?

E. Summary Analysis

1. In a very few words, how do you feel about the marketing of the company?
2. Can the people operating the marketing section of the company accomplish their objectives?
3. Will this marketing strategy win?
4. Are you willing to bet real money that this group of marketing people will develop and execute a successful marketing strategy?

IV. PRODUCTION AREA

The production area is a view from within the company. It's a review of how the company sees itself. It involves the production of the product or service and the value added by the company. Your task here is to determine the value added and how well the company performs. As usual, you need to understand the people before you dive into the production process.

A. Production Management

1. Who is the person in charge of production?
2. What is the background of the person in charge of production?
3. Does this person have the background and experience necessary to manage the production process?
4. Ask the same questions about production management that you asked in the management area above.

B. Personnel and Organization

1. Obtain or assemble an organizational chart for production personnel.
2. What is the total number of employees? How many employees are there at each level?

3. What is the average wage or salary rate at each level? What other benefits or forms of compensation are provided?

4. What is the availability of each type of employee in areas where the company operates?

5. How are hiring and firing decisions made?

6. How are employees trained? What is the cost? How long does it take?

7. How is productivity measured? Are any incentive plans in effect?

8. How are promotion and raise decisions made?

9. How frequently are performance appraisals made? How are these communicated to employees?

10. What has the turnover rate been for each kind of employee?

11. What is the general appearance and attitude of workers?

12. If the company has several plants, answer questions for each plant.

13. What is the number of employees who report to top production management?

14. Does the company have any training manuals?

15. Describe the selection and training procedure for new supervisors and for hourly employees. Who does the training?

16. Identify the key production positions. What personnel backup does the company have for each?

17. What specific techniques does the company use to motivate employees?

18. How does the company specifically measure employee productivity and efficiency?

19. Review several completed employee evaluation forms. Do they seem to be in order?

20. Has the company experienced any problems with the Equal Employment Opportunity Commission during the past 12 months?

21. Review the written wage rate schedule for employee positions. What was the date of last revision?

22. Are the wage rates for the company high, low, or average in relation to the industry? In relation to the area? How does the company know this?

23. What is the date of the last general increase for all production employees?

24. Ask management to describe its five major personnel problems.

25. Does the company have a formal procedure for reporting employee absences, reprimands, promotions, transfers, etc., to personnel?

26. Does the company have an operating procedures manual for its various production departments? Review. Is it current and do the employees strictly adhere to it, or is it a nominal one? What is the date of the last revision?

C. If Union

1. How many employees are unionized?
2. What is the union?
3. When does the present contract expire?
4. Have there been any strikes in the past?
5. How are grievances handled?
6. How many grievances are outstanding?
7. What is the general status of union relationships?
8. Who is the union leader?

D. If Nonunion

1. Have there been any recent attempts to unionize employees?
2. What methods were utilized?
3. What was the outcome?
4. Are any additional efforts expected?
5. What specific plan has the company implemented to reduce the possibility of the employees becoming unionized?

E. Staff Meetings

1. Do you have regularly scheduled meetings with all supervisors? When?
2. What regularly scheduled meetings does the company have for department heads?

PRODUCTION PROCESS

A. Production Facilities

1. Where is each plant located? Describe the location and construction. Estimate the remaining useful life. Evaluate its condition.
2. Is the plant leased or owned?
3. What is the mix of products produced there?
4. What is the production capacity of each plant? What is the throughput for each production line? At what capacity is the plant operating?
5. What are the reasons for the present distribution of production capacity? How does it relate to customer distribution and shipment requirements? To raw material and labor supply requirements?
6. What is the replacement value for each plant? How does this compare with book value and liquidation value?
7. How much and what kinds of insurance are carried on each plant? How does this compare with replacement value?
8. Is there a mortgage on the plant? How much? Have there been any recent appraisals? What was the basis of the appraisal—replacement value, liquidation, etc.? Obtain a copy.
9. How old is the existing plant? What condition is it in?
10. What are the annual maintenance expenditure requirements? Are they expected to increase significantly as the equipment gets older?
11. What are the present maintenance procedures and replacement policies?

12. What is the estimated useful life of the plant and major pieces of equipment? How do these compare with depreciation rates?

13. Does the company have a formal preventive maintenance (PM) program in effect? If so, review the program, including equipment maintenance scheduled for last month and this month. Are the PM records current? Make sure you review the repair record and program for the critical pieces of equipment.

14. Who is responsible for PM?

15. Does the company prepare a monthly PM report? If so, who gets a copy? Review it.

16. Does the company anticipate any major repair or reconditioning work on its equipment in the next 12 months? If so, review items and amounts. Have these been included in the company's capital expenditure budget for this year?

17. Does the company need any new capital equipment items and/or production space during the next 12 months that will cost in excess of $5,000? If so, review the items and amounts. Have these been included in the company's capital expenditure budget for this year?

18. Assuming the company had no money constraints, what pieces of equipment would the company replace? What new equipment items would the company add to improve efficiency?

19. What equipment bottlenecks exist that limit the plant from increasing production?

20. What pieces of equipment can cause a production stoppage for a period of three hours or more if they fail to function properly? What plan exists if that situation occurs?

21. Is the equipment sufficiently modern so the company is not at a competitive disadvantage?

22. What is the company's capitalization-versus-repair expense policy?

23. Does the company have surplus or idle buildings or equipment valued at $5,000 or more. List.

24. Does a formal procedure exist for approving capital expenditures? If so, review. What is the company's ROI hurdle rate for new equipment? What is the payback period?

25. What alternate use could the physical plant be used for? Is it a one-use plant?

26. Is the company's plant and equipment in good repair?

B. Manufacturing Process

1. Obtain a plant layout sketch.

2. Is production a continuous process or a batch process?

3. What is the length of each production cycle? What are the setup times and costs for each one?

4. What are the key segments of the manufacturing process? What is the unit throughput rate for each one? How many employees are there in each segment?

5. Which segment is the bottleneck at present? What would be required to increase the throughput of the segment? What would be the next bottleneck?

6. Is the production flow generally efficient? How could it be improved? How does this operation compare with other manufacturing operations in the industry?

7. Is the manufacturing process labor-intensive? What is the number of employees per sales dollar? What is the labor content per sales dollar?

8. To what extent is the production process now automated?

9. What is the capital investment per sales dollar? What is the value of equipment leased by the company for production use? What is the investment per sales dollar, including the value of leased equipment?

10. Are any computers or other electronic processing equipment used in the production process? What kinds? Where are they located? What functions do they perform? How much downtime has been experienced with each piece of equipment? What kind of backup system is available? How much production downtime has been experienced as a result of electronic equipment failures?

11. Is any of the production equipment highly specialized or custom-made?

12. Are there any backups in the event of failure of key elements? How long would it take to obtain replacement parts or equipment?

13. How much flexibility is there to shift production within each plant? Between plants?

14. To what extent could additional parts of the manufacturing process be automated? What would the capital requirements be? What would be the effect on overall product costs? On labor utilization? On labor content of product cost? On production flexibility? What other considerations are involved?

15. Are there any plans at present to replace or add equipment? Are they reflected in the budgets prepared by the company?

16. What kind of manufacturing process exists?
    a. Mass production or job shop-oriented?
    b. Product or process structured flow?
    c. Production to order or for stock?

17. Have the key components of the manufacturing process been identified?

18. Nature of operations:
    a. What are the major operations and their sequence (e.g., component fabrication and machining, component assembly, final assembly and testing)?
    b. What is the relationship of the cost of each operation to total product cost?
    c. What percentage of total factory floor space is used for each major operation?
    d. What is the degree of mechanization and automation for each major operation (highly automated machinery, semiautomatic, etc.)?

5. To what extent are finished products and components standardized?

6. What programs exist for increasing standardization and ensuring quality control?

7. What are the major components of total production cycle time?

8. Productivity:
   a. What are the current trends in manufacturing productivity?
   b. Are there indications of technical obsolescence?
   c. Does product design restrict the selection of the manufacturing process?
   d. Is the design conducive to an efficient manufacturing process (safety, degree of accuracy, etc.)?
   e. What degree of integration exists between product and manufacturing engineering?
6. Has the efficiency of this process been compared with that of competitors in the industry?
7. Does the plan layout appear efficient?

C. Complexity

1. How many component parts and raw materials are used in the production process? What are the annual requirements for each one? How are parts lists updated?
2. How many parts or components are available from only one supplier?
3. What are the lead times for critical components? Are they handled differently from routine inventory times?
4. What is the inventory reorder procedure? Is it computerized? How are usage rates monitored and matched with lead times?
5. Is any consideration given to reorder costs and carrying costs in determining the optimal time and amount of reorders?
6. Is there an identifiable trend in the recent relationship between inventory levels and order positions?
7. How are suppliers selected? Are current supplier relationships satisfactory? Are trade payables up to date? How often do suppliers fail to deliver on time? What effect has this had on production schedules? Obtain lists of supplier references.
8. What have price trends for components been? What are expectations?

9. Are any of the raw materials used by the company dependent on a harvest each year? What percentage of raw material costs do these items account for? What have recent (three years') price trends been for these materials? How does the company control the risks associated with the price fluctuation of these materials?

10. What are the inventory control procedures? Are inventory requisitions used? Is there a separate, enclosed area for inventory?

11. How often are physical inventories taken?

12. Trace the flow of raw materials from purchase to final product and document at each stage.

13. Visually examine the work-in-process areas. How do inventory levels appear to compare with book value? Do they contain any unfinished products that should be written off?

14. How is production coordinated with sales activities?

15. How much and what kinds of scrap or waste are generated by the production process? How is it disposed of?

16. What pollution control standards is each plant subject to? How are they expected to change over the next five years? What federal and local enforcement commissions exist? What is the company's current status with respect to pollution control requirements? How will future needs be met? Are any capital expenditures required? Are they included in the budget? Verify company status with appropriate agency officials.

17. What Occupational Safety and Health Administration (OSHA) requirements is each plant subject to? What has the company's record been with respect to past OSHA inspections? What fines have been paid by the company as a result of OSHA inspections? Have violations been corrected?

18. How are production operations monitored? How does the production manager identify potential problem areas and inefficiencies? Does the monitoring system have a numerical base? How are these numbers generated?

D. Energy Requirements

1. What kinds of fuel does the company use? How much of each kind?

2. Where are energy supplies obtained? What companies supply energy? Do firm contracts or other commitments exist? Are there any questions about suppliers' ability to meet commitments?

3. Is the company or any of its suppliers subject to allocation regulations? What is the effect of these regulations on the company's ability to maintain or increase production levels?

4. What is the physical proximity of the company to raw material sources and sales markets? How are raw materials and finished goods presently transported?

5. What are the company's annual transportation expenses? How would a slowdown or reduction in transportation services affect the company's operations? Does it have any contingency plans in the event that one of these occurs?

E. Quality Control

1. What procedures does the company have for testing incoming raw materials and component parts?

2. What are the quality standards for each key component and material?

3. What has been the company's experience with each supplier of key components or materials?

4. What happens to parts or shipments that do not meet quality standards?

5. At how many points in the production process are tests made for quality or performance? What happens to items that do not meet tests? Can they be recycled? Are they disposed of? What is the average failure rate at each test point?

6. What do the final test and QC procedures consist of? What is the average failure rate for products in final test? What happens to rejected products?

7. Does the company employ any full time QC people?

8. Who is in charge of the QC area?
9. How are the QC standards established?
10. Can the company match up product returns and can the QC inspector or production shift?
11. Describe in detail the company's QC programs, and obtain a copy of the QC procedures manual.
12. Is there a specification sheet for each product?

F. Engineering

1. What is the size, organization, and salary structure of the engineering department?
2. Who does the engineering section report to? What is its function within the overall corporate strategy?
3. What specific projects is the engineering group now working on?
4. How are engineering projects organized and monitored? How are efficiency and productivity measured?
5. How are engineering time schedules established? What is the past record with respect to completion of engineering projects within scheduled times?
6. How are cost budgets established? How are costs monitored and controlled? What is the past record of performance versus budget?
7. What is the relationship with production operations?
8. How are engineering change orders originated and implemented? Trace the cycle for an engineering order.

G. Regulatory Agencies

1. Is the company in compliance with all federal, state, and local laws and with all rules and regulations of the agencies and commissions thereof, including safety and health, consumer products safety, environmental (air, water, waste treatment, land)? Is any action threatened or pending?

H. Subcontract Work

1. Is any work subcontracted to others?
2. What problems are they having?

3. Is there a second and third source for this subcontracting work?

4. Are any critical parts obtained from a single subcontractor?

5. Is the subcontractor owed a lot of money?

6. Is the subcontractor a stockholder of this company?

I. Inventory

1. Is the current level of inventory at optimum levels? If not, describe. Who establishes the optimum inventory level?

2. What is the optimum inventory level for finished goods and raw materials?

3. Does the company have any inventory items that require delivery lead times in excess of 30 days? If so, list.

4. Do inventory items have only a single source of supply? If so, list.

5. Are any items in inventory obsolete, outdated, out of style, subject to markdown, etc.? If so, describe.

6. What was the inventory turn last year?

J. Production Stoppage

1. Has the company experienced a production stoppage of three hours or more during the past 24 months for any reason? If so, describe.

2. Is there a possibility that production will be stopped in the future? If so, from what?

K. Production Costs

1. Does the company have a detailed worksheet for determining direct labor costs? Indirect labor costs? Review.

2. Is a standard cost system used?

3. When was the date of the last standard cost revision?

4. How does the company monitor and control various costs of production?

5. Specifically, how does it use the information generated to keep costs under control?

6. What are the present and historical product costs? Obtain a complete list of labor and material costs, indirect costs, amount of overhead allocation, and other components of product cost, if any.
7. What are expected future costs? How do they compare in each category? What are the reasons for expected changes in costs?
8. What are the principal materials used in manufacturing each product? Where are they obtained? How many suppliers are there for each one? What are expected usage levels over the next three years? Obtain a list of suppliers to confirm availability and pricing of materials.

L. Production Level

1. How is the weekly/monthly production schedule established?
2. Is a copy of the monthly unit production summary for each of the past 12 months available? Obtain a copy.
3. How many shifts/day is the company now operating?
4. What is production capacity if we assume that no new plant and equipment are added? At what percentage of capacity is the company operating?

PURCHASING, SUPPLIERS, SHIPPING, AND RECEIVING

A. Purchasing

1. Analyze purchases for the last year. Make a list of the 10 largest suppliers during the past year. Get their names, addresses, telephone numbers, and the person to contact.
2. Are there any inventory items for which less than two suppliers are available?
3. Do any contracts exist between the company and any suppliers?
4. The company's objective is to maintain inventory levels to support how many months of production?

5. Do any inventory items have delivery lead times in excess of 30 days?
6. What are the normal credit terms from suppliers?
7. Does the company take purchase discounts?
8. How often are physical inventories taken? Describe the procedure.
9. Who establishes the specifications for items purchased?
10. What is your purchase requisition/approval procedure? Obtain a requisition.
11. Is there a procedural manual for purchasing? If so, review. Is it current? Does the company strictly adhere to it, or is it a nominal one?
12. What system is in place for reducing the possibility of internal theft?
13. Has the company experienced any inventory shortages exceeding $1,000 in the past three years? If so, describe.
14. Is there a formal system of reorder quantities and reorder levels or does the company use an informed approach based on communication received from production foremen, review of bills of materials generated for work orders, and review of raw material inventory records? Describe.
15. Obtain a copy of the company's purchasing procedures or, if not available, determine through discussion with management the informal procedures that may exist.

B. Suppliers

1. List the basic raw materials used in the manufacturing process.
2. List all suppliers who furnish 5 percent or more of the total material purchased for any of the facilities listed previously for the past three years and next three years. List the name, address, type of material, unit price, total purchased, and special terms.
3. Determine the economic condition of the suppliers' industry, including competitive structure and the related possibility of significant raw material shortages, interruption of deliveries, or price fluctuations.

4. List and describe any long-term supply contracts and/ or reciprocal buying agreements.

5. Summarize intracompany/intercompany purchases.

C. Receiving

1. Is there a procedures manual for receiving goods and services? Is it strictly followed? If not, describe. Also, give date of latest revision.

2. Describe the procedure for receiving goods and services. How are requisition and receiving tickets reconciled? Receiving hours?

3. Is a receiving ticket signed and completed for every item received?

4. Who is authorized to sign receiving tickets? To accept returned damaged goods or unacceptable goods?

5. What system is followed to ensure that items received are properly recorded in the company logs?

6. What system is in place to reduce the possibility of internal theft?

7. Describe the procedures for determining that the goods and services received meet the specifications and quality of those ordered.

D. Shipping

1. Is there a procedures manual for shipping products? Review.

2. Who signs the shipping tickets and how does the accounting department know the goods were shipped?

3. Does the customer sign the shipping ticket to prove the merchandise was received? If not, what record is there that it was received?

4. What checks and balances does the company use to reduce the possibility of theft?

5. Who is responsible for shipping cartons?

6. Describe the methods of shipping—consumer carrier, UPS, company trucks, etc.

E. Efficiency Analysis

1. Does the company use any of the following methods for improving efficiency? If so, how is it working out?
2. Control of inventory using "ABC," zero inventory, and/or "just in time" inventory techniques.
3. Setup and production line time reduction studies.
4. Plant utilization and layout studies.
5. Obsolescence reviews.
6. Long-term supplier contracts.
7. Responsibility accounting for inventory and scrap.
8. Value engineering (input from purchasing in decisions made by engineering regarding the components of new products).
9. Parts standardization.
10. Establishment of a cycle counting program.
11. Reduction of engineering change notices.
12. Purchasing reviews (e.g., usage vs. substitution, competitive bidding, approved vendor list, etc.)
13. Vendor evaluation procedure (quality, timeliness, price).
14. Establishment of a routing system.
15. Time and motion studies.
16. In-line vs. batch manufacturing.
17. Make or buy analyses.

BASIC INFORMATION

A. Documentation of Production

1. Organizational chart and salary structures for production and engineering personnel.
2. Copies of any union contracts and negotiation dates.
3. Plant layout sketch for each plant.
4. Diagrams of manufacturing process and production flow.
5. Copies of any recent appraisals of plant.
6. Useful life schedules for plant and major equipment.
7. Historical data on inventory trends.
8. List of supplier references.
9. Historical data on cost trends.

10. List of pollution agency officials to contact.
11. Copies of any fuel supply or transportation contracts.
12. Historical data on quality control test results.
13. Resumes on management of production.
14. A complete description of each physical plant or facility in terms of land acreage, building, square feet, cost assessed value, approved value, insured value, size, age, expansion dates, capabilities to expand leases, etc.
15. Copies of any appraisals.
16. Copies of any leases.

B. Production Reports

1. Ask for a copy of any management reports generated outside of the production area that the company receives and have someone explain their value.
2. Ask for a copy of any management reports generated in the production area and have their value explained to you. Who receives copies?
3. Is a written shift report made out at each shift change? Review it.
4. Is there a production log report? Review it.

C. Ratio Analysis

1. Compute the hours needed to produce a unit by dividing direct labor hours by unit produced. This will measure the units of labor it is costing for each unit produced and will measure employee productivity.
2. Calculate labor cost as a percentage of total production cost by dividing labor costs by total production costs. This will measure the proportion of labor cost to the total production cost to give you an idea of the labor content in the production process.
3. Calculate material costs to total production costs by dividing cost of material by total production cost. This will measure the proportion of the production costs in the material side.
4. Calculate manufacturing overhead to total production costs by dividing manufacturing overhead by total pro-

duction costs. This will measure the proportion of the total production costs and those consumed in manufacturing overhead.

5. Idle time percentage can be calculated by dividing the total idle time by total available direct labor hours. This will measure the efficiency the company is achieving in keeping all employees busy.

6. Calculate the direct labor hours as a percentage of total factory hours by dividing direct labor hours by total hours of factory personnel. This will measure the amount of support personnel needed to complete the production process as opposed to the direct labor hours needed.

7. Calculate the percentage of hours worked on overtime by dividing overtime hours worked by total hours worked. This will measure the overtime and the percentage needed to complete the work and will indicate how well the employees are being scheduled.

8. Calculate machine utilization by dividing productive machine hours used by total available hours. This will measure the efficiency of the equipment utilization as well as scheduling of the machines.

9. Calculate scrap rate by dividing the number of units scrapped by total units produced. This will measure the company's efficiency in producing good usable units without scrapping any of the pieces.

D. Strengths and Weaknesses

1. Describe the company's five major strengths in production.

2. Describe the company's five major weaknesses in production.

E. Summary Analysis

1. In a very few words, how do you feel about the production process.

2. Can management carry out the production plan?

3. Can the personnel involved in production be a winning team? Can the production people be motivated to be winners?

4. Are you willing to bet real money that this group of production employees working under this production situation will be successful? Would you bet your career or your job?

V. RESEARCH AND DEVELOPMENT

A. Management and Personnel

1. Who is head of R&D? What is that person's background? Why was that person chosen?

2. What backup does the company have in R&D management?

3. Does this person like being in R&D?

4. What is the size, organization, and salary structure of R&D department?

5. Who does R&D report to? What is the function of R&D within overall corporate strategy?

6. Ask the same questions of research as you did for the management and personnel areas above.

B. Questions

1. How are projects chosen for R&D?

2. What marketing studies are completed before an R&D project is funded?

3. What specific projects is the R&D section presently working on? What are the timetables for their completion?

4. How are R&D tasks organized and monitored? How is productivity in this area measured?

5. How are time schedules established? What is the past record with respect to the completion of projects within scheduled time periods?

6. How are cost budgets established? How are costs monitored and controlled? What is the past record of performance versus budget?

7. To what extent do future revenues projected in the present business plan depend on the results of R&D efforts?

8. How do budgeted cost and time requirements compare with successful efforts at developing similar products? What are the reasons for any projected variance?

9. If a formal R&D program has been adopted, what is the amount of its budget for this year and each of the past three years?

10. What specific projects are presently in progress? Why were they chosen? Who made the decision to proceed?

11. Has any formal market research been completed for any of the projects? Describe.

12. What outside consultants have been used?

13. Is the company involved in any basic research, such as "what is electricity"?

14. How is the secrecy of R&D projects ensured?

15. Describe the company's procedure for capitalizing and expensing R&D activities.

16. Who does R&D report to?

17. What reports does R&D generate and who receives them? Have someone explain their value.

18. What is the estimated remaining life span of each of the company's major products? What is the company doing to sustain its past growth?

19. Does the company own any patents or have any patents pending? If so, learn the value and importance of patent positions.

20. Does the company produce any goods under patent licenses? If so, describe.

C. Major Programs

1. Describe the major programs completed during the past five years in terms of what they cost the company and the estimated benefit the company has received from the program.

2. Describe the major programs in progress now and estimate the costs that have been incurred to date. Esti-

mate the amount of money it will take to complete the project. Estimate the time it will take to complete the project. Estimate the benefits that will accrue to the company as a result of this project.

3. Describe in detail the proposed projects that are to be undertaken by the company, the costs it will incur, and the time it will take to complete them. Also estimate the benefits that the company will derive from completing these R&D projects.

4. List any significant products recently developed and/or underway by the competition.

5. Compare the industry expenditures for R&D with those of the company, as well as those of competitors in the industry. Review the percentage of the expenditures for R&D as a percentage of sales during the last five years and try to determine why there have been any major variations.

6. What is the status of patents and trademarks regarding new products?

7. Are all of the company's proprietary rights protected by patents and trademarks?

8. Determine the current historical levels of R&D and the variations in those numbers. Determine why any R&D projects have been deferred or why costs have increased.

9. Evaluate the facilities and laboratories used for R&D. How convenient are they for management supervision? How related are they to the production process? What input does marketing have in R&D?

10. To what degree are those people involved in R&D "in touch" with the consumer or the marketplace that will ultimately buy the product?

11. To what degree are those involved in R&D desirous of conducting "basic research," rather than developing products that can be brought to the market in the near term?

BASIC INFORMATION

A. Documentation

1. Organizational chart and salary structure.
2. Resume of the head of R&D.
3. List of projects underway and those planned.
4. Marketing studies supporting the decision to produce a product.
5. A copy of the budget used by the R&D team to govern spending in that department.

B. R&D Reports

1. Determine which reports are prepared by the R&D department for managing the R&D process and obtain copies.
2. Determine which reports have been prepared and given to top management and obtain copies.
3. Determine from top management which reports it uses to manage the R&D process.

C. Ratio Analysis

1. Calculate the percentage of gross sales to R&D spent by dividing R&D expenditures by total gross sales. This should give you an idea of what percentage of sales is being plowed back into R&D.
2. Calculate the percentage of employee expenses as a percentage of total employment expenses by dividing the payroll for R&D by total payroll for the company. By analyzing the human side of R&D, you can obtain an understanding of the human cost of R&D.

D. Strengths and Weaknesses

1. Identify the five major strengths the company has in R&D.
2. Identify the five major weaknesses the company has in R&D.
3. What are the three critical aspects of this production process?

E. Summary Analysis

1. In a very few words, write down how you feel about the R&D at the company.
2. Determine whether the people operating the R&D section can accomplish their objectives.
3. Will this R&D strategy win? Is it the right product at the right time?
4. Are you willing to bet real money that this group of R&D people will develop the next great product for this company?

VI. FINANCIAL AREA

Your financial investigation of the business will complement the work you have completed in the previous sections. All the qualitative investigation in the previous areas must now be verified by quantitative measures. Although it is difficult to restate your findings in numbers, it is just what you must do. In this case, if you can't count it, it doesn't count.

BASIC INFORMATION

A. Management, Personnel, and Organization

1. Who is responsible for this section? Who are the people who will operate the financial side of this business? You should perform the same analysis of the key people here that you did in the management area above.
2. What are the size, organization, and salary structure of the finance section? You should ask the same question about personnel here that you asked in the personnel area above.

B. Management Reports

1. What financial reports are provided to the CEO and the top management?
2. Who is responsible for the management reports?

3. Are they prepared on time or are they late and useless?

4. Are the reports accurate or filled with errors?

5. Are performance reports prepared for all major areas of accountability? Do these reports relate actual performance to plans and budgets? Is adequate information provided to manage effectively and make informed judgments?

6. Describe the interface of subsidiaries, divisions, and departments with corporate headquarters concerning centralized reporting requirements.

7. Describe how the financial and management reporting systems work.

C. Budgeting and Controls

1. What are the company's budgeting procedures? How often are budgets assembled? Are they modified on an interim basis?

2. How are budget figures derived? What supporting schedules are available? What is the lowest unit component of the budget? Obtain or assemble a chart indicating the profit and cost centers on which the budget is based.

3. Does the company utilize a "top-down" budgeting process wherein goals are established by management? If not, how are corporate objectives integrated with the budgeting process?

4. Is the budgeting process an interactive one that allows for feedback and coordination between top management and line managers?

5. How has historical performance compared with budgets?

6. What kind of variance analysis does the company use? How does this help to improve its budgeting process?

7. How is overall coordination between budgeted goals and operations achieved?

8. How often is performance relative to budget measured?

9. What kind of accountability procedures does the company employ? Who is held responsible for deviations from budget? What corrective procedures are utilized?

D. Cash Management

1. What is the amount of cash flow handled by the company each month?
2. How many collection accounts does the company have?
3. How many depository bank accounts does the company have? What is the average amount of cash in accounts?
4. What is the average amount of collected cash that is in the "float" and unavailable for company use?
5. What procedures does the company utilize to minimize the transfer time for collected cash balances?
6. How many cash disbursement accounts does the company have?
7. Who is authorized to make payments of company funds and what amounts are they authorized to disburse?
8. What procedures are utilized to ensure proper adherence to disbursement limits and authorization procedures?
9. Does the company take advantage of discounts when available? What procedures are utilized to avoid loss of discount due to late payments? What is the effective annual cost of funds when the discount is not utilized?
10. What is the minimum amount of cash balances that the company needs to maintain for transaction purposes? How was this amount determined?
11. How much is kept in short-term marketable securities? How are the amounts and maturities of the marketable securities determined?

E. Receivables Management—Credit and Collection Policy and Procedures

1. What percentage of the company's sales is on a credit basis?
2. What are the normal credit terms?
3. How do these terms compare with the competition?
4. What are the reasons for the credit terms being established?

5. What credit information and credit analysis does the company use to determine the eligibility and amount of credit for individual customers?

6. How are credit extension procedures coordinated with sales activities?

7. How frequently is customer credit information updated?

8. What is the dollar amount and number of orders that have been declined for credit reasons? How are these divided between existing customers and new customers?

9. Does the company have a historical analysis with respect to the dollar amount and number of accounts on which credit losses have been incurred?

10. What percentage of sales have credit losses amounted to in each previous year? How does this compare with present and projected levels of bad debt expense?

11. How are delinquent accounts identified and monitored? How often are accounts receivable aging schedules prepared?

12. How long are accounts permitted to go unpaid before being considered delinquent?

13. What collection procedures does the company employ? What are historical and projected costs of collection?

14. What portion of the company's credit and collection procedures utilize electronic data processing techniques?

F. Inventory Management and Control

1. What procedures are utilized to minimize the cost of funds tied up in inventory?

2. How is this coordinated with the production manager's need for maximum flexibility? What are the tradeoffs between these two? Is the company able to quantify them?

3. How is the responsibility for inventory control divided between finance and production?

G. Investment Management

1. What capital budgeting procedures does the company employ?
2. Who makes the order decisions for production equipment and machinery?
3. What is the minimum acceptable investment return on capital items?
4. To what extent is leasing utilized? How are lease-versus-purchase decisions evaluated?
5. What is the amount of capital expenditure budgeted for the coming year? How is this different from past years?

H. Debt Management

1. Who is the company's lead bank? How many banks does it have relationships with?
2. Who in the company is responsible for banking relationships? Investment banking? Financial public relations?
3. Can all debt be assumed in the case of an asset purchase or liquidation? State restrictions on debt assumptions, if any.
4. What assets, if any, are pledged as collateral against the liabilities?
5. Does the company have an analysis of short-term borrowing patterns for the past five years (minimum and maximum levels, average amount, weighted average interest rate, etc.), and how does it compare with the cyclical nature of sales, inventory, and production levels? Indicate interest rate and security required, if any.
6. Is there any "off-balance-sheet" financing and if so, obtain a summary of terms and restrictions.

I. Documentation

1. Organizational chart and salary structure.
2. Chart indicating cost and profit-center structure.
3. Number and location of cash collection points and depository accounts.
4. Credit analysis forms.
5. Historical data on credit approvals and credit losses.

6. Copy of auditor's "management letter."

7. Copy of company operating manual indicating control procedures to be utilized—cash, credit, receivables, inventory, etc.

8. A complete history of all previous financings indicating date, amount, type of instrument, and price.

9. A complete list of all shareholders.

10. A complete description of the company's present capitalization.

11. A list of all common stockholders, the number of shares they hold, the price paid, and the date acquired.

12. A list of all options or warrants.

13. A list of all preferred stock.

14. A list of all convertible debt.

15. a list of equity repurchase agreements such as puts, calls, and rights of first refusal.

16. A list of restrictions placed on equity securities.

17. A list of any stock owned by management and other major stockholders (10 percent or more) pledged.

18. A list of any restrictions against the company repurchasing any of its equity.

19. A list of treasury stock, how and when acquired, price, and reasons for acquisition.

20. A description of the circumstances under which the company has ever filed SEC registration.

21. The corporate policies and procedures manual, if any, so that you can broadly assess comprehensiveness and determine how compliance with these policies and procedures is enforced.

22. Independent accountants' memoranda on accounting procedures and internal controls for the past three years.

23. Internal audit department reports for the past three years and management response thereto.

24. A copy of the most recent aging schedule

25. A list of all banks with whom the company maintains a borrowing relationship by bank name, location, type of credit, maximum size, terms of commitment, interest rate, collateral, and other significant terms.

26. Copies of loan agreements and indentures.
27. Descriptions of financial covenants with latest compliance computations and auditor's/officer's certifications attached.

ANALYSIS OF FINANCIAL OPERATIONS

A. Accounting Policies

1. Have there been any significant changes in accounting principles, policies, or estimates over the past three years?
2. Are any accounting policies unique to the company's industry?
3. What are the accounting policies that differ from industry practice, and represent alternative methods where other preferable methods exist, or are excessively conservative or aggressive?
4. Are the interim financial statements prepared on a basis consistent with that of the annual report? Describe any differences.
5. Are there any proposed accounting pronouncements or government regulations that may `have a significant impact on the company?

B. Accounting Methods and Costing Practices

1. What accounting procedures does the company use with respect to the recognition of revenue and expense? How does revenue and expense reporting compare with cash flows?
2. Are there any deferred costs or other intangible assets on the company's balance sheet? Over what period are they amortized? Obtain both amortization amounts and the amount of increases in deferred costs before amortization for the last three years.
3. What inventory valuation method does the company use? Has there been any recent change in inventory accounting practices? What was the effect of this change on reported earnings and net worth?

4. When was the book value of inventory last reconciled with the present market value of inventory? Is any information available on the age of items presently in inventory?

5. How is inventory divided between raw materials, work in progress, and finished goods? What have recent trends been with respect to the amount of inventory in each of these categories?

6. How are work in progress inventory levels monitored? When was work-in-progress inventory last evaluated? How are work-in-progress or other inventory adjustments accounted for?

7. How are product costs established? Does the company utilize a job-order costing system or a standard costing system? Trace the flow of paperwork involved in establishing product costs and the relationship between paperwork and the manufacturing process.

8. Are burden rates used for indirect manufacturing expenses? How are burden rates determined? What is the rationale?

9. How are overhead expenses allocated to productive departments?

10. What depreciation method is used for fixed assets? Is the same method used consistently? What is the rationale for any difference in methods?

11. Have there been any recent changes in depreciation methods? What was the effect on reported net income?

C. Leverage Analysis

1. What are the average historical turnover rates for inventory, receivables, and accounts payable? How do these compare with projected levels?

2. What is the relationship between working capital needs and sales expansion based on these three turnover rates? That is, what is the effect of a $1 increase in sales on working capital needs?

3. What is the relationship between capital required for fixed assets and sales expansion?

4. What is the minimum feasible increment in the expansion of production capacity?
5. What is the incremental sales volume required to break even on incremental production capacity?
6. What is the incremental profit at full capacity?
7. What is the gross margin on sales?
8. What is the incremental pretax profit on a $1 increase in sales? How does this relationship change as volume increases?
9. What are the fixed and variable components of marketing costs and other overhead expenses?
10. Can these relationships be expressed as mathematical equations or put into chart form?
11. How does each expense category in past financials and projections compare with the sales figures suggested by this analysis?
12. What are the front-end costs required for an expansion of the marketing effort? How long does it take to recover these costs?

D. Lease Analysis

1. What percentage of the company's products is leased?
2. What is the typical term of a lease? Is it a full-payment lease?
3. How many months of lease payments are required for full recovery of product costs? Of products plus marketing and financing costs? Of full list price?
4. Does the company have any third-party leasing agreements at present? How many times monthly rental does this agreement call for? How are lease payments beyond this amount divided between the company and the leasing company?
5. What are the cash requirements for financing the company's leased products over the period for which projections have been provided? How are they to be financed?
6. What is the projected "if sold" value of equipment to be leased? What multiple of monthly rental is used?
7. How does the present value of any leases compare with current market prices?

E. Energy Intensiveness

1. What percentage of operating costs is accounted for by energy purchases? What portion of this is used directly in the manufacturing process?
2. What is the outlook for energy supplies in areas where the company operates?
3. Are any major customer groups significant energy users?
4. Is the processing of any raw materials heavily dependent on energy?
5. What ability does the company have to pass increased costs on to its customers without losing market share?

F. Impact of Inflation on Operations

1. Where FIFO is used to value inventory, has the company estimated the impact of restating costs based on current prices (i.e., elimination of "inventory profit") for each product line in order to determine the real gross profit?
2. Have sales price increases during the past year (and projected for the next year) been enough to offset the increase in costs? Has the gross profit percentage been maintained?
3. If depreciation or rental expense was calculated on the estimated replacement cost of property, plant, equipment, and leases rather than on the book value, what impact would this have on net income?
4. If interest on all long-term debt was at a current rate rather than the existing rate, what impact would it have on net income?
5. How does the company manage each of the following to ensure that current inflation is taken into account:
   a. Sales price increases to pass through increased costs?
   b. Speed in billing receivables, the use of lockboxes in key geographical areas, discount policy, and collection efforts?
   c. Fixed assets: financing methods, major replacement or expansion needs, appropriation proce-

dures, and increasing/decreasing fuel costs on older, less efficient facilities?

d. Accounts payable and accrued liabilities: deferral of payments, cash discount policy, and pension and tax payment timing?

e. Labor costs: competitiveness of wages, influence of unions, pension-funding assumptions, and impact of possible relocation?

f. Frequent review of insurance coverage?

G. Documentation

1. Actual historical profit and loss, cash flow, and balance sheet, together with supporting schedules and list of assumptions.
2. Copies of recent audited statements and audits for the past three years.
3. Security and Exchange Commission reports 10K, 10Q, and proxy, if public company.
4. Copies of any bank loan agreements.
5. A list of all shareholders by number of shares and price paid.
6. Company chart of accounts and accounting policy manual.
7. Copies of typical lease agreements.
8. A summary of significant accounting policies and procedures.
9. Auditor's reports and management's representation letters for the past three years. Did any issues or events result in other than an unqualified opinion?

FINANCIAL STATEMENT ANALYSIS

A. Financial Statement Records

1. Does the company have monthly financial statements for the past 36 months?
2. Are there annual audited statements for the preceding three years?

3. Are any interim financial statements for the past months older than one month?
4. Are there individual financial statements for each major business segment, product line, or geographical location?
5. Does the company have a prospectus, annual report, or other SEC filings?

B. Assets

1. Cash:
   a. What are the names and checking account numbers of all disbursement accounts?
   b. What has been the average cash balance in each account for the last year?
   c. Have all bank accounts been reconciled? Have unusual reconciling items been properly explained?
4. Receivables:
   a. What is the recognition policy for recording revenues and establishing receivables?
   b. What are the credit terms given to purchasers?
   c. Describe the collection of accounts receivable.
   d. What is the discount policy?
   e. What is the returns policy?
   f. Which receivables are discounted or factored, and with whom, cost, terms, purpose, etc.?
   g. List all major receivables for amounts over 20 percent of the total.
   h. Are there accounts receivable that represent conditional sales?
   i. Does the company have a list of accounts receivable 30, 60, and 90 days old? Obtain an explanation of why accounts receivable over 90 days have not been collected. Are those over 90 days worthless?
10. Notes Receivable:
   a. Is there a list of notes receivable indicating the details, such as interest rate, terms, etc.?
   b. Why was each material note receivable incurred?
   c. What is the company's bad debt reserve policy?

    d. What is the bad debt experience for the past three years and most recent interim period?

    e. Is the reserve balance adequate?

    f. Is there a list of receivables for the past three years?

7. Investments:

    a. Is there a list of all marketable securities by original cost and carrying value?

    b. Why does the company hold these securities?

3. Inventories:

    a. What is the breakdown for each major component, such as raw material, work in progress, and finished goods, by each product line?

    b. What is the location of inventory (on hand, in transit, at outside warehouses, etc.)? Is it owned, on "bill and hold," or on consignment? Is it pledged as collateral for outstanding borrowing?

    c. Is labor and overhead counted in the dollar amounts for inventory? What are the percentages of material, labor, and overhead in inventory?

    d. How was the value placed on inventory? Is it market value, replacement value, or cost?

    e. How was the physical inventory that you saw on your tour?

    f. How are the inventory accounting records? Do perpetual inventory records exist?

    g. What are the dates of the last physical inventories? What were the amount and nature of adjustments? Are there book-to-physical reconciliations and analyses?

    h. What parts of the inventory are identified as excess, slow-moving, or obsolete? How is such inventory identified?

    i. How is realizable value of the inventory determined?

    j. What have the write-downs been for the past three years and most recent period?

    k. What are the seasonal inventory requirements?

    l. Is a standard or actual cost system used for inventory?

m. How is job costing accomplished?

n. What costs are included in overhead, and what overhead allocations are made to inventory?

o. What capacity assumption is made about absorbing overhead costs into inventory?

p. How are returns, overruns, and scrap costs calculated?

q. Have variances been significant if a standard cost system is used? What have the variances been by product line for the past three years.

r. How reliable is the inventory valuation procedure?

s. Are there open long-term contracts? If so, what are their prices, terms, profit recognized, and total estimated cost? Have there been any variations in the open contracts?

20. Property, Plant, and Equipment:

a. For each piece of land and building held, list the following: location, description, cost, current value on balance sheet, current market value, and liens.

b. For each piece of equipment list the following: location, description, age, cost, book value, estimated market value, and liens.

c. What significant plant, property, and equipment additions have occurred during the past three years? Are there any projects currently under construction or committed to?

d. Is there a list of all significant leasehold improvements, including original cost, accumulated amortization, and the period of amortization?

e. What is the accounting policy for depreciating capital assets? What changes have occurred in the policy during the last three years?

6. Does the company have a description and explanation of how other assets arose, capitalization and amortization policy, liens, and appreciation for each of the following: goodwill, deferred charges, R&D, organization costs, contract rights, patents and trademarks, and names?

C. Liabilities

1. Accounts Payable:
   a. Which companies constitute 5 percent or more of the current total accounts payable or accounted for 5 percent or more of the average annual balance during the past year?
   b. What are the regular and unusual credit terms (such as value discounts or extended payment terms) that exist with the companies listed?
   c. Are discounts taken on normal credit terms?
4. Accrued Liabilities:
   a. What are the accrued liabilities outstanding and how did they arise?
   b. Have all items been accrued? Look at professional fees, employee benefits, payroll, taxes, vacation pay, claims, severance and retirement benefits, warranty costs, pension liabilities, and utilities.
3. Look at the notes payable. Does the company have a payee, description, interest rate, date, original amount, current amount, payment schedule, and explanation of why each note was incurred?
4. Look at the long-term liabilities. Does the company have a payee, description, interest rate, date, original amount, current amount, payment schedule amount, and explanation of why each was incurred?
5. Do any defaults or violations exist in any of the company's corporate obligations, including loan agreements, notes, leases, etc.?

D. Stockholder Equity and Net Worth

1. Does the company have a list of all classes of stock in terms of type, shares authorized, shares outstanding, voting rights, liquidation preferences, dividends, terms of warrants and options outstanding, major owners, date acquired by major owners, major owner cost basis, market price range, and special terms?
2. Does the company have a complete shareholders' list?

3. What activity has occurred in treasury stock for the past three years?

4. Does the company have any stock option or purchase plans? If so, obtain details concerning each.

5. Do any restrictions exist on any of the company's common stock?

6. Do any preemptive rights exist on the company's stock? If so, list the dates and findings.

7. Do any options or rights of first refusal exist on any of the company's common stock?

8. Does the company have more than one class of stock?

9. Does the company have any stock purchase warrants, options, subscriptions, convertible instruments, contracts, or agreements for issuance of common stock, puts, calls, or other equity-related instruments?

10. Does the company have any treasury stock?

OTHER ASSETS AND LIABILITIES

A. Unrecognized Liabilities

1. Is there a current review for unaccrued and unrecorded liabilities performed by the company?

2. Are there any truth-in-advertising problems?

3. Are there any product liability claims?

4. Are there adequate reserves for warranties?

5. Are there service guarantees?

6. Are there any employee-related deficiency letters issued by governmental agencies?

7. Are there any OSHA, EEOC, or other employee violations? What actions has the company taken to resolve them?

8. Are there any employee occupational hazards inherent in the industry, such as "black lung" found in coal mining?

9. Is the company a member of a pension plan, and if so, have the funded and unfunded benefits been calculated?

10. Is the union due compensation for a planned plant shutdown?

11. Does the company have any unfunded pension costs or plans?

12. Have any environmental regulation violations or warnings been given to the company? If so, what actions does the company plan to take to resolve them, and what will the related cost be?

B. Contingent Liabilities and Commitments

1. Does the company have a list of all leases by description, years remaining, minimum annual payment, maximum annual payment, escalations, adjustments, renewals, and options to purchase?

2. Does the company have a list of the capital lease payments due for the next three years and the computed interest to derive the present value of such future lease payments? Has such amount been reflected as a liability? How have the related assets been reflected?

3. How does the present value of capital leases compare with their fair market value?

4. Are there sublease terms?

5. Has the company been involved in any significant litigation in the past three years? Is it threatened by pending or unsettled claims? Does the company have a list and description of the nature of those claims and the current status?

6. Are there any legal problems or potential litigation presently facing the industry (such as the asbestos industry), and if so, what effect might this have on the company?

7. Are there any potential antitrust problems?

8. Does the company have a list of all loans for which the company is a guarantor? What is the financial condition of the related companies?

9. Do subsidiary loans, guarantees, or exchange laws restrict dividend payments to the parent company?

10. Has the company promised to do other things or made any type of performance guarantees? What warranty guarantees exist?

11. Has the company entered into any guarantee to buy or sell merchandise? Are there contractual agreements to buy other companies? To sell or merge this company?

12. Does the company have any contingent liabilities, including but not limited to warranties, patent infringements, loss contracts, compensation for services, contracts subject to termination or renegotiations, etc.?

13. Does the company have a list of all open contracts? Describe the nature and potential cost, including informal agreements.

C. Undervalued Assets

1. Does the company have any patents, trademarks, copyrights, or licenses that are undervalued?

2. Does the company have a priority process that others would pay to know?

3. Does the company have undervalued real estate or equipment?

4. Are inventories understated?

5. Is the pension and profit-sharing plan overfunded? Can money be taken out?

TAXES

A. Federal Income Taxes

1. In general, what are the applicable federal, state, and local income, property, excise and other taxes paid by the company?

2. What examinations have been conducted by federal tax authorities?

3. What is the last year examined by the government?

4. What are the amounts of deficiencies and nature of adjustments in last years that were examined?

5. Have the results of the above reviews been reflected in the current reserve for taxes?

6. What is the status of the current examinations?

7. What are the tax years open and closed to future tax authority examination?

8. What tax loss carry-forwards does the company have? Describe the amounts by year of expiration. Identify the type (i.e., net operating loss, capital loss, ITCs, FTCs, R&D credit, etc.)
9. Describe any special industry tax considerations, such as depletion allowances, special credits or deductions, etc.
10. Can the company reconcile the effective income tax rate to the statutory tax rate for the past five years?
11. What are the deferred tax provisions for the past five years?
12. What are the current income tax requirements compared with the current income tax reserve?
13. What are the components of the deferred income tax reserve? Are they reasonable, and what are the future cash requirements?
14. Is the company current on all taxes owed (FICA, income, real estate, etc.)?

B. State and Local Taxes

1. Have state and local tax returns been filed for the past three years?
2. Have there been any state tax audits?
3. What are the amounts of the deficiencies or adjustments in the past three years?
4. Have the results of the above reviews been reflected in the current reserve for taxes?
5. Have federal deficiencies been reflected in state and local tax reserves?
6. Does the company have state tax carry-forwards? If so, what are the amounts by year of expiration and type?
7. Is the company complying with regulations regarding sales tax and payroll tax collection and remittance?

C. Tax Planning and Preparation

1. Is the company's tax planning adequate?
2. Has the company taken advantage of all potential tax savings?

3. Are aggressive interpretations adequately reserved for?

4. Does the company maintain adequate tax basis records?

D. Other Tax Considerations

1. Are there any other significant tax planning considerations of interest? Include potential tax savings not currently achieved but that could be achieved, e.g., LIFO, accelerated depreciation, installment sales, accelerated pension or other expensing, etc., or proposed legislation that may adversely affect the company.

E. Buyout Specials Tax Questions

1. Does the company have an analysis of the tax basis of assets being acquired and an estimate of the fair value of the assets being acquired and liabilities assumed? What is the estimated recapture tax liability, assuming that such is triggered? Consider the following:

    a. Depreciation

    b. Tax credits

    c. LIFO inventory reserves

    d. Research and development

    e. International, FSC, or DISC earnings and profits

    f. Previously expensed items, e.g., supplies, tools and dies, etc.

7. Are there deferred intercompany gains or nondeductible writeoffs that may result in additional taxes?

8. What is the expected transaction effect on net operating loss and tax credit carryovers?

9. What are the expected benefits of a taxable versus nontaxable transaction?

10. Has the present value of step-up benefits been compared with the recapture and related tax liability cost?

11. What expense items can be added back to the income statement because the owner has been taking out excessive compensation? Consider:

   a. Salaries
   b. Bonuses
   c. Pension and profit sharing
   d. Loans
   e. Airplanes
   f. Expense accounts

F. Documentation of Taxes

1. Copies of federal and state tax returns for the last three years.
2. Evidence that federal withholding taxes have been paid.

OTHER SECTIONS

A. Data Processing

1. What is the data processing equipment configuration?
2. Does the company have a description of the financial systems that have been computerized, i.e., sales, inventory, accounts receivable, accounts payable, payroll, general ledger, and projections, etc.?
3. Is the information produced by the computer accurate, reliable, and useful?
4. Does the company plan to make more extensive use of computerization? If so, describe areas in which computerization will be expanded.
5. Describe the computer facilities by type of machine, ownership, date installed, location, and application. Are facilities adequate for the company's needs?
6. Is an outside computer utilized?
7. How do users perceive the EDP function? How do user and EDP department perceptions differ? How effective is communication between EDP and user personnel?
8. Does the company have a recent evaluation of the EDP function with significant weaknesses, problems, and/or opportunities noted?

B. Insurance

1. Does the company have a list of policies in force on its property? If so, describe significant conditions, benefits, and frequency of review.

2. Does the company have a self-insurance plan?

3. What claims have been filed over the past five years?

4. What is the estimated replacement cost of assets held?

5. Is there adequate coverage for contingent liabilities?

6. Are there significant unaccrued costs on incurred but not reported claims?

7. Are increased premiums anticipated as a result of unfavorable trends or the need for increased coverage?

8. Are significant retroactive premium adjustments anticipated?

9. Does the company have life insurance on its key officers? Does it have disability insurance for the key officers?

10. What other insurance policies are in force, e.g., product liability, medical, etc.?

C. Long-Range Budgetary Planning

1. Do the managers develop the objectives and plans for their areas and communicate them to the appropriate personnel?

2. Does the budgeting system monitor the accuracy of forecasts? Are there explanations of major variations (actual vs. budget) on a current basis and over the past three years?

3. Does the company have a contingency plan in the event that actual results will vary significantly from the budget?

4. Is profitability of individual business units and product lines monitored? Are financial ratios, controllable expenses analyses, contribution to overhead analyses, direct costing, and other performance techniques employed?

D. Procedures and Organization Manuals

1. Does the company have procedures and organizational manuals? If so, provide a brief description, including the use of these manuals and personnel responsible for preparation.

ANALYSIS OF PROJECTIONS

A. Basic Assumptions

1. How were the projections and the assumptions put together? Are they realistic?
2. How much should they be discounted?
3. Has an accountant reviewed the numbers and assumptions?
4. Why do you believe they are achievable projections?
5. When you compute basic ratios in the projections, are they consistent? Does gross margin change year by year?
6. Are basic ratios consistent with industry figures? If not, why not?
7. How do these assumptions and projections differ from past projections?
8. Has the company achieved its projections in the past? If not, why not? If not, will it achieve its projections in the future?
9. Is there a model for this kind of growth in this industry, or are we being pioneers here?
10. Are there significant details in the projections to make them believable?
11. Is there enough reliable information behind the assumptions to make them believable?

B. Projected Financial Statement Analysis

1. On what methodology is the forecasted growth based (e.g., regression analysis, trend projection and extrapolation, economic or industry indicators, market studies, management estimate)?

2. Are the assumptions concerning sales growth (volume and price), gross margins, working capital requirements, operating expenses, capital expenditures, and financing requirements and terms reasonably based on historical results, trends, industry, and overall business expectations?

3. Do the basic financial ratios (i.e., profit to equity and sales to assets) indicate that projected levels of growth are feasible without significant infusions of outside capital or changes in historical financial ratios? If not, how will increased financing, faster asset turnover, and improved profit margins be accomplished?

4. Identify and describe any items that may not be recorded at fair market value:

   a. Lease agreements
   b. Long-term receivables
   c. Plant, property, and equipment
   d. Inventory
   e. Intangible assets, patents, copyrights, computer software
   f. Distribution agreements, customer lists, licenses
   g. Pension obligations and assets
   h. OSHA, EPA, and other regulatory deficiencies
   i. Severance costs (anticipated layoffs)
   j. What are customer lists, licenses, franchises, easements?
   k. Net-of-tax valuation adjustments (resulting from different tax vs. accounting valuations)

12. Identify potential future earnings adjustments:

   a. Excessive expenses incurred to reduce tax liability, i.e., personal expenses, excessive owner compensation, etc.
   b. Functions performed by parent for which no cost has been allocated
   c. Salary adjustments required for a more competitive wage or other employee benefit requirements
   d. Expected changes in material or other costs

    e. Incremental depreciation and amortization charges resulting from expected asset/liability revaluation, other effects of asset/liability revaluations

    f. Different tax provision due to new ownership structure and tax basis

    g. Cost savings from elimination of duplicate facilities, overhead, and "synergy"

    h. Reduction in interest income from excess cash

    i. Expected sales of facilities

10. What are the anticipated industry changes/trends in accounting principles and effect on present and future operations?

C. Sensitivity Analysis

1. What effect does variation in key assumptions underlying financial projections have on profit and loss, cash flow, and projected balance sheet? Look at key assumptions: inventory and receivables turnover rate, gross margin on products, amount of sales expense required, rate of market penetration, variation in sales/lease ratio, variation in product mix, delay in production buildup, etc.

2. What are realistic best-case and worst-case projections?

3. Was a computer model used for this analysis?

4. Can the results be expressed in graph form?

D. Risk

1. What is the probability that the company can meet its projections?

2. What major obstacles does the company have to overcome and what is the probability that it will?

3. What time pressures are management members under and can they meet them?

4. Can you structure the investment as a debt instrument? As a secured debt instrument?

5. What collateral is available for your investment?

6. If the company is liquidated, what will you get?

7. Can the company be sold if it gets in trouble? Is there a ready buyer?

8. Who will put up more cash if the company needs it?

E. Return

1. What is the valuation placed on the company under present investment terms? Pre-money and post-money? How does this value differ from other companies in this industry?

2. What are the best-case and worst-case expected returns and your most likely projections (vs. the company's)?

3. What are the ROI, IRR, or NPV calculations based on your projected cash returns? Is this return sufficient for the risk you must take?

4. What return will the entrepreneur enjoy if the company meets projections? Other investors?

5. What is the probability that you will make the stated return?

BASIC INFORMATION

A. Documentation of Finance

1. Be sure you obtain the documents listed under documentation in other sections above.

2. Obtain a detailed schedule of the use of proceeds for the first six- to twelve-month period for one to three years.

3. Obtain profit and loss and cash flow projections for the next three to five years, together with supporting schedules.

4. Obtain a complete list of all the assumptions used by management to make projections and budgets.

5. Obtain a sensitivity analysis of management's projections so that you can understand them.

6. Obtain a complete written analysis of the return of the investment or internal rate of return on this business proposition.

B. Financial Reports

1. Obtain copies of reports used by financial people to "run" their department.
2. Obtain copies of reports given to top management by the finance department.
3. Obtain a copy of the budget used in the finance department to control costs.

C. Financial Ratio Analysis

1. Gross margin percentage can be calculated by dividing gross profit by sales.
2. Profit margin percentage can be determined by dividing net income before taxes by net sales.
3. Return on equity can be determined by dividing net income by total shareholder equity.
4. Return on assets can be calculated by dividing net income by average total assets out during the year.
5. The current ratio can be calculated by dividing current assets by current liabilities.
6. Quick ratio can be calculated by dividing current assets minus inventories by current liabilities.
7. To calculate the working capital as a percentage of assets, divide working capital by total assets.
8. Liquidity ratio can be calculated by dividing total assets by total liabilities.
9. Debt equity ratios can be computed by dividing total debts outstanding by total stockholders' equity.
10. A similar ratio is total liabilities to stockholders' equity, which can be computed by dividing total liabilities by stockholders' equity.
11. The working capital to net sales can be computed by dividing net sales by working capital.
12. Debt coverage ratio is calculated by dividing earnings before interest and taxes by total annual debt service.
13. Cash flow debt coverage ratio is calculated by dividing earnings before interest and taxes plus depreciation by interest and principal due on all of the company's debts.

14. Percentage fixed charges of earnings is calculated when you divide the fixed charges by earnings before interest and taxes plus fixed charges.

15. Cash flow cycle can be calculated by dividing receivables plus inventory by the cost of goods sold.

16. Calculate the receivables cycles by dividing net credit sales by average trade receivables.

17. The past due index is calculated by dividing total receivables past due by total receivables.

18. Calculate the bad debt expenses as a percentage of sales by dividing bad debt expenses by total credit sales.

19. Inventory turns can be calculated by dividing cost of goods sold by the average inventory outstanding in a year.

20. Percentage of cash flow to total assets can be calculated by dividing net cash flow by total assets.

D. Strengths and Weaknesses

1. Identify the five major strengths the company has in finance.

2. Identify the five major weaknesses the company has in finance.

3. What could go wrong in the finance area?

E. Summary Analysis

1. In a very few words, how do you feel about the finance side of the business?

2. Can the financial people managing this company be a winning team? Can the finance people be motivated to succeed for the company?

3. Are you willing to bet real money that this group of financial employees working under the financial policies of this company will be successful? Would you bet your career or job that they can make it happen?

VII. REFERENCE AREA

You still need to develop many other pieces of information. Some of it is general information, and some is specific and can be obtained from various references. This is where you go outside the company to verify what you have learned about the company.

A. General

1. What is the exact corporate name and address?
2. Where (what state) and when was the company incorporated?
3. What are the states in which the company is qualified to do business?
4. Where are the minute books, bylaws, and certificate of incorporation?
5. List any predecessor organization or prior names of the corporation.
6. List corporate organizations—subsidiaries, divisions, and branches. Give names and locations and describe operations. Draw a box chart to show relationships.
7. What is the fiscal year end for the company?
8. What is the Standard Industrial Classification Code for this company?
9. What is the IRS Employee Identification Number?
10. Have you reviewed the corporate minutes for the past three years?
11. Have you reviewed all past business plans? Operating plans? Marketing plans?
12. Does the company have any subsidiaries?
13. Does the company have any shareholder agreements?
14. Does the company need approval of any entity other than the board of directors regarding this financing?

B. Miscellaneous Questions for Management

1. Are there any actions, lawsuits, or proceedings pending or threatened against the company or any officers or directors? If so, list.
2. Is any broker entitled to a commission on this financing?

3. Do any defaults or violations exist in any of the company's corporate obligations, including loan agreements, notes, leases, etc.?

4. Is the company current on all taxes owed (FICA, income, real estate, etc.)?

5. Is the company in compliance with all federal, state, and local laws and with all rules and regulations by agencies and commissions thereof, including but not limited to safety and health, consumer product safety, and environmental regulations (water, sewer, air, land) that are relevant to the ownership of its properties or operation of its business?

6. Are there any restrictions on any of the company's common stock?

7. Do any corporate guaranties exist?

8. Has the company acquired any operating entities or products within the past five years? Any divestitures?

9. Have any officers or directors violated (other than minor traffic laws) any federal, state, or local laws in the past 20 years?

10. Do any options or rights of first refusal exist on any of the company's common stock?

11. Does the company have any stock purchase warrants, options, subscriptions, convertible instruments, contracts, or agreements for issuance of common stock, puts, calls, or other equity-related instruments?

12. Does the company need approval of any entity other than the board of directors regarding this financing?

13. Has the company experienced any union-organizing activities during the past five years?

C. Reference List

1. Bank: List the bank name, address, telephone number, and account officer for any bank the company has done business with for the past five years.

2. Other Institutional Lenders: Provide the same information as in item 1 for lenders who have loaned the company $100,000 or more.

3. Accounting Firm: List the firm name, address, telephone number, and account manager for any accounting firms the company has used in the past five years.

4. Law Firm: List the firm name, address, telephone number, and individual attorney for any law firms the company has used in the past five years.

5. Suppliers: List the supplier names, addresses, telephone numbers, and contact people for the company's 10 highest volume suppliers and for 10 others.

6. Customers: List the customer names, addresses, telephone numbers, and contact people for the company's 10 highest volume customers and for 10 others.

7. Competitor: List the competitor names, addresses, telephone numbers, and chief operating officer names for the company's five strongest competitors and for five others.

8. Independent Sales Representatives: List the firm name, address, telephone number, and representative name for any independent sales representative organization.

9. Independent Service Representative: List the firm name, address, telephone number, and representative's name for any independent service representative.

10. Directors: List the names, addresses, and telephone numbers of all directors.

11. Officers: List all names, home addresses, and home telephone numbers of all officers.

12. Principal Stockholders: List the name and address of every stockholder owning more than 5 percent of the company's common or preferred stock or anyone who has an option to buy more than 5 percent.

13. Dissenting Stockholder: List all dissenting stockholders.

14. Investment Banker: Get the names of all those used; call them and discuss the company.

15. Institutional Industry Analysis: Get the name of the person in any large Wall Street brokerage house who follows this industry.

16. Industry Consultants: Obtain the names of industry consultants or "gurus" who are quoted frequently and are knowledgeable about this industry.
17. Trade Associations: Obtain the names of trade association executives in this industry.
18. Trade Publications: Obtain a list of trade publications in this industry and any newsletters covering this industry.
19. Venture Capital Investors in the Industry: Find out who else has invested in this industry.
20. Public Companies: Obtain public information on the public companies in this industry.
21. Financial or Business Broker: Obtain the name, address, and telephone number of any broker involved in this transaction.

D. Questions to Manufacturing Representatives

1. What products do you represent for the company?
2. How long have you been its representative?
3. What other products not made by the company do you represent?
4. How many of the company's products did you sell during the past 12 months? What does that represent in dollars?
5. Does the company have high-quality products? Do the customers like the products?
6. Have you had complaints about the products? If so, what kind of complaints?
7. How does the product compare in quality with competitor's products in the market?
8. Is the product priced right? Is it too high or too low, compared with the competitor's prices? What price do you think the product should have?
9. Can you continue to sell the product? How many units can you sell in the next 12 months (dollar volume)?
10. How has the company treated you as a rep? Does it give you good support?

11. Has it paid commissions on time? How long does it take the company to pay commissions?

12. What changes would you like to see the company make?

13. What do you think of the management of the company?

E. Questions to Lawyers

1. Who is the lawyer? How long has he or she been on this client's work?

2. Are there any suits against the company outstanding?

3. Are there any suits against the company in the last two years?

4. Are there any potential suits against the company?

5. Has the company filed suits against others that are still open?

6. Has the company filed suits against others in the last two years?

7. Does company plan to file suits against others?

8. Are there any product liability suits or problems?

9. Are there any union suits or legal problems?

10. Are there any patent suits or problems?

11. If there is a suit, specify the following:
    a. Maximum settlement amount
    b. Minimum settlement amount
    c. Most likely settlement amount
    d. When it will be settled
    e. The nature of the suit
    f. Whether the suit has merit

7. Is the company in compliance with all federal, state, and local laws and with all rules and regulations by agencies and commissions thereof, including but not limited to safety and health, consumer products safety, and environmental agencies (water, sewer, air, land) that are relevant to the ownership of its properties or operation of its business?

8. Are there any legal problems whatsoever?

9. What do you think of management?

F. Questions to Accountants

1. Verify the numbers in the audit on assets, sales, and profits.
2. Was a management letter issued? If so, get a copy from the accountant or management.
3. Are the books and records in good condition for easy audit or do they need improvement?
4. Are adequate controls in place to foil misuse of funds?
5. How long have they been the auditors?
6. How long has the individual auditor been handling or working on the annual audit?
7. Is the financial officer good?
8. Is the company having operating problems?
9. Have accountants started this year's audit? If so, are there any material negative items?
10. Are there any significant or material changes in the numbers set out by management and the final audit, such as:
    a. Disagreement over inventory value?
    b. Disagreement over quality of accounts receivable?
    c. Disagreement over work in progress and cost of goods sold?
    d. Other material differences?
5. Did anything come to your attention during the audit that would indicate the company is having operating problems?

G. Questions to Suppliers

1. What do you supply the company?
2. What is the annual dollar volume you supply?
3. What credit limit do you have for the company?
4. Do you anticipate any shortage in the items you supply to the company?
5. How promptly are you paid by the company? Is payment ever a problem?
6. Have you ever shipped the company anything COD?
7. What do you like about the company?

8. How would you describe your relationship with the company? How are you treated as a supplier?
9. Will you continue to supply the company?
10. Any other comments?

H. Questions to Customers

1. What products have you purchased from the company? How long have you been buying from the company?
2. How long ago did you purchase the company's product?
3. What is your current outstanding order? Confirm this with the company's backlog of orders. Also confirm that the order in the backlog will be shipped in the next 30, 60, or 90 days.
4. Are you a repeat user?
5. Do you like the product?
6. Has the company's product lived up to the quality that you had originally perceived? Does the product perform as well as you expected?
7. Have you ever been shipped faulty goods? What happened?
8. Has the company lived up to the service representations it made to you before you bought the product?
9. Was the product overpriced or was it a bargain?
10. Do you think the product has brand-name recognition?
11. Have you purchased products from competitors of the company or other manufacturer brand names similar to the company's product?
12. How does the company's product compare in quality to products of competitors that you have either purchased or considered?
13. Do you intend to buy from the company again?
14. Estimate how much you will purchase in the next 12 months.
15. What changes would you like to see the company make in the product?
16. What do you think of the people with whom you had contact in the company?
17. Any other comments?

I. Questions to Landlords

1. How long have you been renting to the company?
2. How many square feet does it rent from you?
3. Where is the rental property located?
4. What is the monthly rental for the property?
5. How timely are the payments?
6. Have you ever had to contact the company for failing to pay the rent?
7. What condition is the property kept in?
8. Would you rent to the company again?
9. Who is your contact?
10. Any general comments?

J. Questions to Advertisement People

1. How long have you been advertising for the company?
2. How often does the company advertise?
3. What is the average cost of its advertising?
4. Do you have a standing order?
5. What is the average cost of its advertising?
6. How timely are its payments?
7. Have you ever had to contact the company for failing to pay?
8. Will you continue to run its ads?
9. Who is your contact?
10. Any general comments?

K. Questions to Banker

1. How long has the company been banking with this bank?
2. Who did it bank with before?
3. How long has this bank officer been the company's loan officer?
4. What amount of credit (high and low) has the bank extended to the company?
5. What is the collateral for the loan?
6. Does the company pay as agreed? Has it ever been in default on a loan?

7. Has the company ever asked for credit and been denied? What was the amount?
8. Does the company have operating problems?
9. Is the management good?
10. Do company people "live the high life?"

B ACTUAL DOCUMENTS

WHAT DO ACTUAL COMMITMENT LETTERS AND LEGAL DOCUMENTS LOOK LIKE?

The following documents are actual documents used in a financing, except that they have been broadened in concept to include many of the standard "boiler plate" items used by most VCs. After reading these documents, you will be well prepared for the ones you receive from the entrepreneur. All documents are for fictitious companies and people. The following documents are covered in this appendix:

- Commitment letter for a loan with options for stock on Ace Electromagnetic, Inc.
- Legal Document 1: Loan Agreement on Ace Electromagnetic, Inc.
- Legal Document 2: Promissory Note on Ace Electromagnetic, Inc.
- Legal Document 3: Stock Purchase Warrants on Ace Electromagnetic, Inc.
- Legal Document 4: Stock Purchase on Ajax Computer Genetics Corp.
- Legal Document 5: Exhibits to Stock Purchase on Ajax Computer Genetics Corp.

Commitment Letter

Venture Capital Corporation
123 Main St.
McLean, VA. 22101

J. B. Entrepreneur, President
Ace Electromagnetic Incorporated
123 International Drive
McLean, Virginia 22102

Dear J. B.:

The Management of Venture Capital Corporation (Venture) has approved a loan to your company (the Company) in the amount of $3,000,000.

1. The approval was based on the following representations made by you:

   1.01 The Company is a corporation in good standing in Virginia. You will provide Venture with a Certificate of Good Standing and a copy of the charter, bylaws, and minutes of the organization of the Company.

   1.02 The Company is primarily engaged in the business of manufacturing electromagnetic equipment.

   1.03 There are no lawsuits against the Company or against its directors or its officers personally, nor any you know of that may be contemplated. If there are any suits outstanding or contemplated, your attorney will provide Venture with a letter stating the nature of such suits and a copy of the suits. You will provide Venture with a copy of all lawsuits you have filed against others.

   1.04 The Company is current on all taxes owed and, in this regard, you will provide Venture with a copy of the last three years' tax returns for the Company.

   1.05 You have presented financial information showing that the Company, for the 12-month period just ending, had: sales of $850,000 and pretax loss of $25,000; assets of $600,000; liabilities of $300,000; and a net worth of $300,000.

1.06 The money borrowed will be used as follows: A. $100,000 to pay First National Bank. B. $100,000 to pay accounts payable. C. $100,000 to pay fees and working capital.

1.07 Upon completion of Venture's loan, you will have approximately the following assets:

- Cash, $100,000.
- Accounts receivable, $100,000.
- Machinery and equipment, $100,000.
- Land and building, $100,000.
- Other assets, $300,000.

1.08 With regard to leases, you will provide Venture with a copy of every major executed lease.

1.09 The information presented to Venture is correct, and you believe the projections presented to Venture are reasonable.

1.10 You will pay no brokerage fees, legal fees, or other fees on this loan without Venture's written approval, and you will indemnify Venture against all such fees.

1.11 During the past 10 years, none of the directors has been arrested or convicted of a material crime.

2. The terms and conditions of the loan shall be:

2.01 A loan of $3,000,000 for six years at 11 percent per annum, paid monthly on the first of each month.

2.02 The loan shall be interest only for the first 36 months and, beginning with the 37th month, you will pay principal and interest sufficient to amortize half of the loan over the remaining 36 months. All principal and interest outstanding at the end of six years shall be due and payable in full as a balloon payment.

2.03 The loan may be prepaid at any time in whole or part, with a prepayment penalty of 3 percent in the first year and 2 percent in the second year.

2.04 Take-down of the loan shall be $3,000,000 at closing.

2.05 Other terms standard for such loans.

2.06 In connection with this financing, Venture shall receive at closing separate options to purchase stock in the Company. Cost of the options to Venture will be $100. These options, when exercised by Venture and the other investment company, will provide stock ownership in the company of 25 percent at the time of exercise. The exercise price will be $100. The options will expire 10 years from closing. Venture will share pro rata in any redemption of stock by the Company.

2.07 There shall be an "unlocking" provision whereby if there is a bona fide offer to purchase the Company and Venture wishes to accept the offer and you do not, then you shall acquire Venture's interest on the same terms or sell the Company.

2.08 There shall be a "put" provision whereby any time after five years from closing, Venture may require the Company to purchase its options or the resulting stock at the higher of the following:

- Ten percent of sales for the year just ended times a price/earnings ratio of eight, less Venture's debt times 25 percent.
- Ten times cash flow for the year just ended, less Venture's debt times 25 percent.

2.09 Venture shall have full "piggyback" rights to register its shares any time the Company (or its management) is registering shares for sale, and such registration of Venture's shares shall be paid for by the Company.

3. Collateral for the loan shall be:

3.01 A second deed of trust on the land and building of the business, subordinated as to collateral to a mortgage of approximately $1,000,000, on terms acceptable to Venture.

3.02 A first secured interest in all of the tangible and intangible assets of the Company, including but limited to inventory, machinery, equipment, furniture, fixtures, and accounts receivable.

3.03 Pledge and assignment of all the stock of the Company and assignment of leases listed above.

3.04 Personal signatures and guarantees of you and your spouse.

3.05 A life insurance policy on your life for $3,000,000 with the policy assigned to Venture and with Venture as the loss payee to the extent of its loan.

3.06 Adequate hazard and business insurance, which shall include federal flood insurance if your business is located in a designated federal flood area. All such insurance shall be assigned to Venture, and Venture shall be listed as the loss payee to the extent of its interest. In this regard, you will supply Venture with a list of all business insurance, and such insurance and coverage shall be acceptable to Venture.

4. Conditions of the loan are:

4.01 Provide Venture with monthly year-to-date financial statements in accordance with generally accepted accounting standards (including profit and loss and balance sheet) within 45 days of the end of the month.

4.02 The president of the Company will provide Venture with a certificate each quarter stating that no default has occurred in the Loan Agreement.

4.03 If requested in writing, provide Venture with an annual certified audit within 90 days after the year's end from an accounting firm acceptable to Venture.

4.04 Before each year end, provide Venture with projections of the next year in the same format as the financial statements.

4.05 Within 30 days after they are filed, provide Venture with a copy of all documents filed with government agencies, such as the Internal Revenue Service, Federal Trade Commission, and Securities and Exchange Commission.

4.06 There will be no change in control of the Company, nor will there be a change of ownership without Venture's written approval.

4.07 Management will not sell, assign, or transfer any shares it owns in the Company without the written approval of Venture.

4.08 The Company will maintain in accordance with generally accepted accounting principles:

- A current ratio of one to one.
- Sales of $5,000,000 per year.
- Sales of $300,000 per month.
- Sales of $1,000,000 per quarter.
- Net worth of $1,000,000 or more.

4.09 The Company will have board meetings at least once each quarter at the Company's business offices. Although a Venture representative will not serve on the board, a Venture representative will have the right to attend each meeting at the Company's expense, and Venture shall be notified of each meeting at least two weeks before it is to occur.

4.10 The Company will pay no cash dividends, and the Company will not sell any assets of the business that are not part of the regular course of business without Venture's approval.

4.11 The Company will not expend funds in excess of $1,000,000 per year for capital improvements and the like.

4.12 You will live in the general Northern Virginia metropolitan area.

4.13 The Company will not pay, loan, or advance to any employee money that, in total, is in excess of $250,000 per year without the written approval of Venture. If (1) the Company is in default for nonpayment to Venture or any senior lien or (2) the Company is not profitable for any quarter, then the Company will not pay, loan, or advance to any employee money that, in total, is in excess of $200,000 per year without written permission of Venture.

4.14 The Company will not pay any brokerage fees, legal fees, or consulting fees in excess of $50,000 per year without the written permission of Venture.

4.15 Other conditions standard for such loans.

4.16 You will pay all closing costs and recording fees, which include all attorney's fees. You may use any attorney to draw the legal documents; however, they must be reviewed and approved by Venture's counsel. A simple review by Venture's counsel will not incur a fee; however, if the work done by Venture's counsel is beyond a simple review, a fee will be charged, and the fee will be paid by you.

4.17 In connection with this financing, Venture will receive a $60,000 fee. Upon acceptance of this commitment letter, you will pay Venture $15,000 of this fee and the remainder at closing. Should closing not take place owing to the fault of Venture, then the fee will be returned, less out-of-pocket expenses; otherwise, it is forfeited.

5. This commitment is conditioned on the following, which, if not attained, will make Venture's commitment void:

5.01 Acceptance by you of this letter and the return of one copy to Venture fully executed by you, with the fee set out in 4.17 above, within 15 days.

5.02 Closing on the loan before the year's end.

5.03 All legal documents being acceptable to Venture.

5.04 A favorable credit check of you and your business and no material adverse occurrences before closing.

5.05 A favorable visit by Venture to your business.

Sincerely,
A. V. Capitalist
President

VENTURE CAPITAL CORPORATION

AGREED: ACE ELECTROMAGNETIC, INCORPORATED

By: _____DATE: _____

J. B. Entrepreneur, President

_____DATE: _____

Personally: J. B. Entrepreneur

LEGAL DOCUMENT 1

Ace Electromagnetic, Incorporated
McLean, Virginia

LOAN AGREEMENT

WHEREAS, Venture Capital Corporation, a Virginia corporation (hereinafter "Venture") has committed under terms of a letter of _____(date) to lend to Ace Electromagnetic, Incorporated, a Virginia corporation (hereinafter "Company") the sum of Three Million dollars ($3,000,000);

WHEREAS, the Company will issue VENTURE Stock Purchase Warrants (hereinafter "Warrants") for a total of twenty-five percent (25%) of the common stock of the Company.

NOW, THEREFORE, the Company and Venture agree as follows:

I. PARTIES

This Agreement shall bind and accrue to the benefit of the Company and its successors, the undersigned shareholders of the Company, Venture, and any subsequent holders of the Note, Warrants, or the stock issued thereunder (collectively referred to herein as "Holders"). The Note issued hereunder may be held by different persons, as may the Warrants. The terms of this Agreement as of the day the Company receives notice that a new party is holder of a Note or Warrant shall be binding between the Company and such new party, regardless of modifications that may subsequently be made between the Company and another holder.

II. LOAN

The Company will borrow and Venture will lend the sum of Three Million Dollars ($3,000,000) to be repaid according to the terms of the Promissory Note of even date herewith, (hereinafter "Note").

III. USE OF PROCEEDS

The Company will use the proceeds of the loan only to fund commercial electromagnetic operations, with approximately One Million Dollars ($1,000,000) to repay a line of credit at the First National Bank, One Million Dollars ($1,000,000) to pay accounts payable, and One Million Dollars ($1,000,000) for fees and working capital.

IV. COLLATERAL

The Note and the Holders' rights herein shall be secured pari passu against the collateral below, provided that future advances in addition to the original Three Million Dollars ($3,000,000) advanced to the Company shall not be considered in determining the secured parties' shares from sale of collateral. In regard to the items in subparagraph 2, the Company grants Holders a security interest to attach when the Company has signed this instrument and acquired rights in the property and when Venture has made whole or partial disbursement of loan funds to the Company, the Company's designated payee, or an escrow agent. Although other parties may become holders of the instruments secured hereby, all security interests of record will remain in the name of Venture Capital Corporation, which will hold such interests in trust for the benefit of all Holders. The collateral shall be as follows:

1. A second mortgage on the Company's real estate in the Commonwealth of Virginia, subject to a first mortgage to a financial institution according to terms of a separate instrument;

2. A second security interest in the furniture, fixtures, machinery, equipment, inventory, contract rights, licenses, and all tangible and intangible personal property of the Company, subject to credit lines from financial institutions;

3. Assignment of accounts receivable and pledge of all the outstanding stock of the Company, subject to bank lines of credit according to the terms of separate Agreements therefore;

4. Collateral assignment of the policy number 1234567 issued by ABC Life Insurance Company insuring the life of J. B. Entrepreneur in the amount of Three Million Dollars ($3,000,000);

5. Personal guarantees of Mr. and Ms. Entrepreneur according to the terms of a separate instrument.

V. Representations and Warranties

To induce Venture to enter this transaction, the Company represents and warrants that:

A. It is duly incorporated, validly existing, and in good standing under the laws of Virginia, having Articles of Incorporation and Bylaws (all of the terms of which are in full force and effect) as previously furnished to Venture; it is not and does not intend to become an investment company or passive investment vehicle;

B. It is duly qualified to conduct business as proposed by it and is in good standing as a foreign corporation in all states in which the nature of its business or location of its properties requires such qualification;

C. It has full power and authority to enter into this Agreement, to borrow money as contemplated hereby, to issue the Warrants and upon exercise thereof to issue the stock pursuant thereto, and to carry out the provisions hereof; it has taken all corporate action necessary for the execution and performance of each of the above (including the issuance and sale of the Warrants, the reservation of shares of stock, and the issuance thereof upon the exercise of the Warrants); and each document above named will constitute a valid and binding obligation of the Company enforceable in accordance with its respective terms when executed and delivered;

D. The authorized capital stock of the Company is as set forth below, and all such stock has been duly issued in accordance with applicable laws, including federal and state securities laws;

E. The list of officers and directors of the Company previously submitted is complete and accurate; all representations made by the Company, its officers, directors, shareholders, or guarantors in any instrument described in this Agreement or previously supplied to Venture in regard to this financing are true and correct as of this date; and all projections provided are reasonable;

F. The Company has no debts, liabilities, or obligations of any nature, whether accrued, absolute, contingent, or otherwise arising out of any transaction entered into or any state of facts existing prior hereto, including without limitation liabilities or obligations on account of taxes or government charges, penalties, interest, or fines thereon or in respect thereof except the debts to be paid off by the use of proceeds of this loan, and debts on open account; the accounts payable and the debts to be paid herewith have not changed materially since the date of the June financial statement previously submitted; the Company does not know and has no reasonable grounds to know of any basis for any claim against it as of the date of this Agreement or of any debt, liability, or obligation other than those mentioned herein;

G. The Company has not been made a party to or threatened by any suits, actions, claims, investigations by governmental bodies, or legal, administrative, or arbitrational proceedings, except as set out in the Company counsel's letter (hereinafter "litigation letter"); neither the Company nor its officers nor directors know of any basis or grounds for any such suit or proceeding; there are no outstanding orders, judgments, writs, injunctions, or decrees or any court, government agency, or arbitrational tribune against or affecting it or its properties, assets, or business;

H. Since the date of the Venture commitment letter, the Company has not suffered any material adverse change in its condition (financial or otherwise) or its overall business prospects, nor has the Company entered into any material transactions or incurred any debt, obligation, or liability, absolute or contingent, or sustained any material loss or damage to its property, whether or not insured, or suffered any material interference with its business or operations, present or proposed; and there has been no sale, lease, abandonment, or other disposition by the Company of any of its property, real or personal, or any interest therein or relating thereto, that is material to the financial position of the Company;

I. The Company has duly filed all tax returns, federal, state, and local, that are required to be filed and has duly paid or fully reserved for all taxes or installments thereof as and when due that have or may become due pursuant to said returns or pursuant to any assessment received by the Company;

J. The Company is not bound by or party to any contract or instrument or subject to any charter or other legal restriction materially and adversely affecting its business, property, assets, operations, or condition, financial or otherwise;

K. Except for matters set out in the litigation letter, the Company is not in breach of, default under, or in violation of any applicable law, decree, order, rule, or regulation that may materially and adversely affect it or any indenture, contract, Agreement, deed, lease, loan Agreement, commitment, bond, note, deed of trust, restrictive covenant, license, or other instrument or obligation to which it is a party or by which it is bound or to which any of its assets are subject; the execution, delivery, and performance of this Agreement and the issuance, sale, and delivery of the Warrant and other documents will not constitute any such breach, default, or violation or require consent or approval of any court, governmental agency, or body except as contemplated herein;

L. Neither the Company nor any of its officers, directors, partners, or controlling persons is an "Associate" of Venture, as such terms are defined in section 107.3 of the Regulations as amended promulgated under the Investment Company Act of 1940, nor an "Affiliated person" of Venture, as such term is defined in section (a)(3) of the Investment Company Act of 1940 as amended;

M. To the best of the Company's knowledge, it has complied in all material respects with all laws, ordinances, and regulations applicable to it and to its business, including without limitation federal and state securities laws, zoning laws and ordinances, federal labor laws and regulations, the Federal Occupational Safety and Health Act and regulations thereunder, the Federal Employees Retirement Income Security Act, and federal, state, and local environmental protection laws and regulations;

N. There are no material facts relating to the Company not fully disclosed to Venture; no representation, covenant, or warranty made by the Company herein or in any statement, certificate, or other instrument furnished to Venture pursuant hereto or in connection with the transaction contemplated hereby contains or will contain any untrue statement of or omits to state a material fact necessary to make the statement not misleading;

O. The Company is primarily engaged in the business of commercial electromagnetic manufacturing and is not a franchise;

P. The Company for the twelve (12)-month period ending January 31, 1983 had: sales of Eight Hundred Fifty Thousand Dollars ($850,000); pretax loss of Twenty-Five Thousand Dollars ($25,000); assets of Sixty Thousand Dollars ($600,000); liabilities of Three Hundred Thousand Dollars ($300,000); and net worth of Three Hundred Thousand Dollars ($300,000);

Q. After disbursement of the subject loan, the Company will have approximately the following assets: accounts receivable One Million Dollars ($1,000,000), machinery and equipment One Million Dollars ($1,000,000), land and building One Million Dollars ($1,000,000), other assets Three Million Dollars ($3,000,000);

R. Copies of leases provided are true and correct;

S. During the past ten (10) years, no officer or director of the Company has been arrested or convicted of any criminal offense.

VI. AFFRMATIVE COVENANTS

Until the Warrants are exercised and the Note repaid in full, the Company will:

A. Promptly make all payments of principal and interest as due under the Note and furnish from time to time to each Holder all information it may reasonably request to enable it to prepare and file any form required to be filed by Holder with the Securities and Exchange Commission or with any other regulatory authority;

B. Forward or cause to be forwarded to Holders its monthly accounting balance sheet and profit-and-loss statement within forty-five (45) days from the end of each month;

C. Forward or cause to be forwarded to Holders its final year end accounting balance sheet and profit-and-loss statement within sixty (60) days of such accounting year end, which if demanded by a Holder in writing shall be prepared at Company's expense by an independent outside accounting firm acceptable to a Holder, according to generally accepted accounting principles uniformly applied;

D. Maintain a net worth of Five Million Dollars ($5,000,000) or more and a level of current assets (which shall be reflected in its books in accordance with generally accepted accounting principles), such that the amount of such current assets shall equal or exceed the amount of current liabilities; maintain sales of at least Five Million Dollars ($5,000,000) per annum, One Million Dollars ($1,000,000) per quarter, and Three Hundred Thousand Dollars ($300,000) per month, as reflected on its books in accordance with generally accepted accounting principles uniformly applied;

E. Provide to Holders in writing each quarter the certification of the President of the Company that no default has occurred under the Warrants, Note, or this Agreement, or any debt or obligation senior to the debt of the Holders hereunder; or if any such default exists, provide Holders with a statement by the President of the Company as to the nature of such default;

F. Maintain such shares of its common stock authorized but unissued as may be necessary to satisfy the rights of the Holders of the Warrants;

G. Perform all acts as required under the Warrants, including without limitation, the reissue of replacement Warrants to a Holder upon loss or destruction;

H. Permit any authorized representative of any Holder and its attorneys and accountants to inspect, examine, and make copies and abstracts of the books of account and records of Company at reasonable times during normal business hours;

I. Notify Holders of any litigation to which the Company is a party by mailing to Holders by registered mail within five (5) days of receipt thereof, a copy of the Complaint, Motion for Judgment, or other such pleadings served on or by the Company; and any litigation to which the Company is not a party but which could substantially affect operation of the Company's business or the collateral pledged for this loan, including collateral securing any guarantees, by mailing to Holders by registered mail a copy of all pleadings obtained by the Company in regard to such litigation, or if no pleadings are obtained, a letter setting out the facts known about the litigation within five (5) days of receipt thereof, provided that the Company shall not be obliged by this paragraph to give notice of suits where it is a creditor seeking collection of account debts;

J. Prior to each accounting year end, provide Holders with projected financial statements for the coming year, in the same format as used for item C above;

K. Hold a meeting of the Board of Directors of the Company at least once each quarter; give Holders at least two weeks' prior notice of such meeting; allow one representative designated by each Holder to attend such meeting at Company's expense;

L. Maintain all-risk hazard insurance on its assets, with mortgagee clause in favor of Holders, in such reasonable amounts and forms as required by Holders, to include federal flood insurance if any assets be in a designated flood plain; and supply Holders with a list of existing coverage prior to closing;

M. Give Holders notice of any judgment entered against the Company by mailing a copy to Holders within five (5) days of entry thereof;

N. Take all necessary steps to administer, supervise, preserve, and protect the collateral herein; regardless of any action taken by Holders, there shall be no duty upon Holders in this respect;

O. Within thirty (30) days of filing, provide Holders with copies of all returns and documents filed with federal, state, or local government agencies, including without limitation the Internal Revenue Service, Federal Trade Commission, and Securities and Exchange Commission;

P. Maintain an original or a true copy of this Agreement and any modifications hereof, which shall be available for inspection under subparagraph H above.

VII. NEGATIVE COVENANTS

Until the Notes are repaid and the Warrants exercised, the Company will not without the prior written consent of all the Holders:

A. Declare or pay any cash dividend of any kind on any class of stock; make any material change in its ownership, organization, management, or the manner in which its business is conducted; authorize, issue, or reclassify any shares of capital stock except as required under the Warrants;

B. Become a party to any merger or consolidation with any other corporation, company, or entity;

C. Make expenditures for capital improvements or acquisitions in any fiscal year in excess of One Hundred Thousand Dollars ($100,000);

D. Make loans, advances, or wage payments, including salaries, withdrawals, fees, bonuses, commissions, direct or indirect in money or otherwise, to any officer, director, shareholder, partner, or employee in excess of Two Hundred Fifty Thousand Dollars ($250,000) per year, or One Hundred Fifty Thousand Dollars ($150,000) per year if there is a default under this Agreement;

E. Transfer, sell, lease, or in any other manner convey any equitable, beneficial, or legal interest in any of the assets of the Company except inventory sold in the normal course of business, or allow to exist on its assets any mortgage interest, pledge, security interest, title retention device, or other encumbrance junior or senior to Holders' liens except for liens of taxes and assessments not delinquent or contested in good faith;

F. Permit any judgment obtained against the Company to remain unpaid for over twenty (20) days without obtaining a stay of execution or bond;

G. Incur any declared default under any loan Agreement pertaining to another debt of the Company;

H. Pay or incur any brokerage, legal, consulting, or similar fee in excess of Fifty Thousand Dollars ($50,000) per year;

I. Create or incur any debt other than that incurred hereunder, trade debt, or short-term working capital debt normally incurred in the ordinary course of business;

J. Incur any lease liability or purchase any additional life insurance from business income or assets;

K. Become a guarantor or otherwise liable on any notes or obligations of any other person, firm, corporation, or entity, except in connection with depositing checks and other instruments for the payment of money acquired in the normal course of its business.

VIII. INVESTMENT COVENANT

By accepting a Warrant, the Holder thereof represents, warrants, and covenants that it is an "accredited investor" within the meaning of section 4(6) of the Securities Act or an "accredited person" within the meaning of Rule 42 of the Securities Act, or acquiring the Warrant and any stock issued thereunder for its own account for investment and not with the view to resale or distribution thereof except in accordance with applicable federal and state securities laws. Upon exercise of any conversion rights under the Warrant, this representation, warranty, and covenant shall be deemed to have been given with respect to the stock received.

IX. Fees, Expenses, and Indemnifcation

The Company shall reimburse Holders for reasonable expenses according to the terms of the commitment letter. The Company shall pay, indemnify, and hold any Holders of the Warrants and Note harmless from and against any and all liability and loss with respect to or resulting from any and all claims for or on account of any brokers and from finder's fees or commissions with respect to this transaction as may have been created by the Company or its officers, partners, employees, or agents; and from any stamp or excise taxes that may become payable by virtue of this transaction or the issuance of any stock or modification hereunder. Venture warrants that it has not contracted to pay any such fees.

X. Unlocking

If at any time after five (5) years from the date of this Agreement, the Company or its shareholders receive a bona fide offer to purchase the assets of the Company or an equity interest in the Company, then the party receiving such offer (hereinafter "offeree") will submit a copy of the offer and such information pertinent thereto as it may have to the Holders of the Warrants or the shares issued thereunder within three (3) days of receipt of said offer. Within ten (10) days of receipt of said copy, each Warrant Holder will indicate in writing to the offeree its approval or disapproval of the offer. If a Holder approves the offer, then the offeree shall, within twenty (20) days thereafter or such shorter time if provided in the offer, accept or reject the offer. If the offeree rejects the offer, then simultaneously with such rejection it shall be bound to purchase the approving Holder's Warrants or resulting stock in the Company under the same terms and conditions that such Holder would have received under the offer. If a Warrant Holder fails to communicate timely approval or disapproval, the Company may construe such failure to indicate disapproval.

XI. "PUT" RIGHTS

Beginning five (5) years from the date of this Agreement and ending ten (10) years from the date of this Agreement, Warrant Holders may by written demand require the Company to purchase its Warrant or the shares of stock issued hereunder at a price of thirty-five percent (35%) of the higher of the following sums:

(a) Ten Percent (10%) of the Company's sales for the fiscal year immediately preceding the year of the demand times a price earnings ratio of twelve (12), less the aggregate principal balance of the Note on the day of demand; or

(b) Ten (10) times the Company's cash flow for the fiscal year immediately preceding the year of the demand, less the aggregate principal balance of the Note on the day of demand.

XII. DEFAULT

A. If any of the below-listed events occurs prior to maturity of the Notes, then a default may be declared at the option of any Holder without presentment, demand, protest, or further notice of any kind, all of which are hereby expressly waived. In such event, the Note Holder shall be entitled to be paid in full the balance of any unpaid principal of its Note plus accrued interest and any costs thereof, including reasonable attorneys' fees, and to any other remedies that may be available under this Agreement, the Warrant, the Note, or any applicable law:

1. Occurrence of any default provision as set out in the Warrants or Note;

2. Any material representation made by the Company in writing herein or in connection herewith that is untrue and remains so for thirty (30) days after written notice to the Company thereof;

3. Failure of the Company to comply with the covenants in this Agreement and such failure continuing for a period of ten (10) days after receipt of notice thereof from any Holder of the Note;

4. The Company's assignment for the benefit of creditors; admission in writing its inability to pay its debts as they become due; filing of a voluntary petition in bankruptcy; adjudication as bankrupt or insolvent; filing of any petition or answer seeking for itself any reorganization, arrangement, composition, readjustment, liquidation, dissolution, or similar relief under any present or future statute, law, or regulation pertinent to such circumstances; filing any answer admitting or not contesting the material allegations of a petition filed against the Company in any such proceedings; seeking or consenting to or acquiescing in the appointment of any trustee, receiver, or liquidator of the Company or of all or any substantial part of the properties of the Company; or the Company or its directors or majority shareholders taking any action initiating the dissolution or liquidation of the Company;

5. The expiration of sixty (60) days after the commencement of an action against the Company seeking reorganization, arrangement, composition, readjustment, liquidation, dissolution or similar relief under any present or future statute, law, or regulation without such action being dismissed or all orders or proceedings thereunder affecting the operations or the business of the Company being stayed; or a stay of any such order or proceedings thereafter being set aside and the action setting it aside not being timely appealed;

6. The expiration of sixty (60) days after the appointment, without the consent or acquiescence of the Company, of any Trustee, receiver, or liquidator of the Company, or of all or any substantial part of the

properties of the Company without such appointment being vacated;

7. The Company being declared in default under an Agreement in regard to the debts described in paragraph VI E above;

8. Any guarantor or undersigned shareholder of the Company failing to comply with the terms of his or her undertakings to Holders;

B. No course of dealing between a Holder and any other party hereto or any failure or delay on the part of the Holder in exercising any rights or remedies hereunder shall operate as a waiver of any rights or remedies of any Holder under this or any other applicable instrument. No single or partial exercise of any rights or remedies hereunder shall operate as a waiver or preclude the exercise of any other rights or remedies hereunder;

C. Upon the nonpayment of the indebtedness under the Note or any part thereof when due, whether by acceleration or otherwise, a Note Holder is empowered to sell, assign, and deliver the whole or any part of the collateral for the Note at public or private sale, without demand, advertisement, or notice of the time or place of sale or of any adjournment thereof, which are hereby expressly waived. After deducting all expenses incidental to or arising from such sale or sales, Holder may apply the residue of the proceeds thereof to the payment of the indebtednesses, under the Notes, subject to the terms of paragraph XIII below, returning the excess, if any, to the Company. The Company hereby waives all right of appraisement, whether before or after the sale, and any right of redemption after sale. The Company shall have the right to redeem any collateral up to time of a foreclosure sale by paying the aggregate indebtedness under the Notes;

D. Holders are further empowered to collect or cause to be collected or otherwise to be converted into money all or any part of the collateral, by suit or otherwise, and to surrender, compromise, release, renew, extend, exchange, or substitute any item of the collateral in transactions with the Company or any third party, irrespective of any assignment thereof by the Company and without prior notice to or consent of the Company or any assignee. Whenever any item of the collateral shall not be paid when due, or any part thereof has become due, Holders shall have the same rights and powers with respect to such items of the collateral as are granted in respect thereof in this paragraph in case of nonpayment of the indebtedness, or any part thereof, when due. None of the rights, remedies, privileges, or powers of the Holders expressly provided for herein shall be exclusive, but each of them shall be cumulative with and in addition to every other right, remedy, privilege, and power now or hereafter existing in favor of the Holders, whether at law or in equity, by statute or otherwise;

E. The Company shall pay all expenses of any nature, whether incurred in or out of court, and whether incurred before or after the Notes shall become due at their maturity date or otherwise (including but not limited to reasonable attorneys' fees and costs) which Holders may deem necessary or proper in connection with the satisfaction of the indebtedness under the Notes or the administration, supervision, preservation, protection of (including, but not limited to, the maintenance of adequate insurance), or the realization upon the collateral. Holders are authorized to pay at any time and from time to time any or all of such expenses, add the amount of such payment to the amount of principal outstanding, and charge interest thereon at the rate specified in the Notes;

F. The security interest of the Holders and their assigns shall not be impaired by a Holder's sale, hypothecation, or rehypothecation of a Warrant or Note or any item of the collateral, or by any indulgence, including, but not limited to:

1. Any renewal, extension, or modification that a Holder may grant with respect to the indebtedness of any part thereof, or

2. Any surrender, compromise, release, renewal, extension, exchange, or substitution which a Holder may grant in respect of the collateral, or

3. Any indulgence granted in respect of any endorser, guarantor, or surety. The purchaser, assignee, transferee, or pledgee of the Warrants, Notes, collateral, any guaranty, or any other document (or any of them), sold, assigned, transferred, pledged, or repledged, shall forthwith become vested with and entitled to exercise all powers and rights given by this Agreement to Holders, as though said purchaser, assignee, transferee, or pledgee were originally named in this Agreement in place of the Holders.

XIII. NOTICE

All notices or communications under this Agreement of the Warrants or Notes shall be mailed, postage prepaid, or delivered as follows:

To Venture: 123 Main Street, McLean, VA 22101

To Company: Ace Electromagnetic, Incorporated

123 International Drive

McLean, VA 22102

or to such other address as shall at any time be designated by any party in writing to the other parties.

XIV. ENTIRE AGREEMENT

The Warrants, the Note, and this Agreement and the documents mentioned herein set forth the entire Agreements and understandings of the parties hereto in respect of this transaction. Any prior Agreements are hereby terminated. The terms herein may not be changed verbally but only by an instrument in writing signed by the party against which enforcement of the change is sought.

XV. Controlling Law

This Agreement shall be construed in accordance with and governed by the laws of the Virginia.

XVI. Headings

The headings of the paragraphs and subparagraphs of this Agreement and the Warrants and Note are inserted for convenience only and shall not be deemed to constitute a part of this Agreement or the Warrants and Note.

IN WITNESS WHEREOF, the undersigned hereby affix their hands and seals on the year and day first above written.

Ace Electromagnetic, Inc.
By:_____
J. B. Entrepreneur
President

Venture Capital Company
By:_____
Venture Capitalist President

Promissory Note

$3,000,000

FOR VALUE RECEIVED, the undersigned Ace Electromagnetic, Incorporated, a Virginia corporation (hereinafter "Company") promises to pay to the order of Venture Capital Corporation, a Virginia corporation (hereinafter "Holder") the principal sum of Three Million Dollars ($3,000,000), together with interest as set out herein, at its offices in the District of Columbia or such other place as Holder may designate in writing.

INTEREST

From date of advance and thereafter until repayment, interest shall accrue hereunder at the rate of eleven percent (11%) per annum.

PAYMENTS

Payments shall be due on the first day of each month after the day of this Note. Through the first thirty-six (36) full calendar months after the date hereof, payments shall be for interest only in the amount of Twenty-Seven Thousand Five Hundred Dollars ($27,500.00). Thereafter until maturity, payments shall be in the amount of Forty-Two Thousand Five Hundred Twenty Dollars ($42,520) per month.

MATURITY

The entire indebtedness hereunder shall become due and payable in full six (6) years from the date of this Note.

PREPAYMENT

Payment of any installment of principal or interest may be made prior to the maturity date thereof without penalty. Such prepayments shall be applied against the outstanding principal in inverse order of maturity.

DEFAULT AND ACCELERATION

   A. If any of the below-listed events occur prior to maturity hereof, then a default may be declared at the option of the holder without presentment, demand, protest, or further notice of any kind (all of which are hereby expressly waived). In such event, the Holder shall be entitled to be paid in full the balance of any unpaid principal amount plus accrued interest and any costs including reasonable attorney's fees, and to any other remedies that may be available herein in the Loan Agreement or under any applicable law:

1. Failure to pay any part of the indebtedness hereof when due;
2. Occurrence of any default as provided under the Loan Agreement pertaining hereto.

B. No course of dealing between the Holder and any other party hereto or any failure or delay on the part of the Payee in exercising any rights or remedies hereunder shall operate as a waiver of any rights or remedies of the Holder under this or any other applicable instrument. No single or partial exercise of any rights or remedies hereunder shall operate as a waiver or preclude the exercise of any other rights or remedies hereunder.

C. Upon the nonpayment of the indebtedness, or any part thereof, when due, whether by acceleration or otherwise, Payee is empowered to sell, assign, and deliver the whole or any part of the collateral at public or private sale, without demand, advertisement, or notice of the time or place of sale or of any adjournment thereof, which are hereby expressly waived. After deducting all expenses incidental to or arising from such sale or sales, Holder shall apply the residue of the proceeds thereof to the payment of the indebtedness, as it shall deem proper, returning the excess, if any, to the Company. The Company here by waives all right of appraisement, whether before or after sale, and any right of redemption after sale. The Company shall have the right to redeem any collateral up to the time of a foreclosure sale by paying the aggregate indebtedness.

D. Holder is further empowered to collect or cause to be collected or otherwise be converted into money all or any part of the collateral, by suit or otherwise, and to surrender, compromise, release, renew, extend, exchange, or substitute any item of the collateral in transactions with the Company or any third party, irrespective of any assignment thereof by the Company, and without prior notice to or any consent of the Company or any assignee. Whenever any item of the collateral shall not be paid when due or otherwise shall be in default, whether or not the indebtedness, or any part thereof, has become due, Holder shall have the same rights and powers with respect to such item of the collateral as are granted in respect thereof in this paragraph in case of nonpayment of the indebtedness, or any part thereof, when due. None of the rights, remedies, privileges, or powers of the Company expressly provided for herein shall be exclusive, but each of them shall be cumulative with and in addition to every other right, remedy, privilege, and power now or hereafter existing in favor of Holder, whether at law or in equity, by statute or otherwise.

E. The Company will take all necessary steps to administer, supervise, preserve, and protect the collateral; and regardless of any action taken by Holder, there shall be no duty upon Holder in this respect. The Company shall pay all expenses of any nature, whether incurred in or out of court, and whether incurred before or after this Note shall become due at its maturity date or otherwise (including but not limited to reasonable attorneys' fees and costs) that Holder may deem necessary or proper in connection with the satisfaction of the indebtedness or the administration, supervision, preservation, protection of (including, but not limited to, the maintenance of adequate insurance), or the realization upon the collateral. Holder is authorized to pay at any time and from time to time any or all of such expenses, add the amount of such payment to the amount of principal outstanding, and charge interest thereon at the rate specified herein.

F. The security rights of Holder and its assigns shall not be impaired by Holder's sale, hypothecation, or rehypothecation of this Note or any item of the collateral, or by any indulgence, including, but not limited to:

1. Any renewal, extension or modification that Holder may grant with respect to the indebtedness of any part thereof, or

2. Any surrender, compromise, release, renewal, extension, exchange, or substitution that Holder may grant in respect of the collateral, or

3. Any indulgence granted with respect to any endorser, guarantor, or surety. The purchaser, assignee, transferee, or pledgee of this Note, the collateral, any guaranty, and any other document (or any of them), sold, assigned, transferred, pledged, or repledged, shall forthwith become vested with and entitled to exercise all the powers and rights given by this Note as though said purchaser, assignee, transferee, or pledgee were originally named as Holder in this Note.

DEFNITIONS

The term *indebtedness* as used herein shall mean the indebtedness evidenced by this Note, including principal, interest, and expenses, whether contingent, now due or hereafter to become due, and whether heretofore or contemporaneously herewith or hereafter contracted. The term *collateral* as used in this Note shall mean any funds, guarantees, or other property rights therein of any nature whatsoever of the proceeds thereof that may have been, are or hereafter may be hypothecated directly or indirectly by the undersigned or others in connection with, or as security for the indebtedness or any part thereof. The collateral and each part thereof shall secure the indebtedness and each part thereof.

IN WITNESS WHEREOF, the undersigned has caused this Note to be executed and its seal affixed on the day and year first written above.

SEAL

Ace Electromagnetic, Incorporated

BY:_____

J. B. Entrepreneur
President

Attest:_____
J. J. Smith
Secretary

THE SECURITIES REPRESENTED HEREBY HAVE BEEN
ACQUIRED IN A TRANSACTION NOT INVOLVING ANY PUB-
LIC OFFERING AND HAVE NOT BEEN REGISTERED UNDER
THE SECURITIES ACT OF 1933. SUCH SECURITIES MAY
NOT BE SOLD OR TRANSFERRED IN THE ABSENCE OF
SUCH REGISTRATION OR AN EXEMPTION THEREFROM
UNDER SAID ACT.

LEGAL DOCUMENT 3

Ace Electromagnetic, Incorporated
McLean, Virginia

STOCK PURCHASE WARRANTS

I. Grant

Ace Electromagnetic, Incorporated, a Virginia corporation (hereinafter "Company") for value received,
hereby grants to Venture Capital Corporation, a Virginia corporation, or its registered assigns (hereinafter
"Holder") under the terms herein the right to purchase
that number of the fully paid and nonassessable shares
of the Company's common stock such that, upon exercise and issuance of stock hereunder, the Holder will
hold twenty-five percent (25%) of the outstanding common stock of the Company. On the present date, such
number is One Thousand Seven Hundred Twenty-Four
(1,724) shares.

II. Expiration

The right to exercise this Warrant shall expire ten (10)
years from the date hereof.

III.   Exercise Price

The exercise price of this Warrant shall be One Hundred Dollars ($100.00).

IV.   Effect of Redemption

Regardless of the above provision, if the Company shall redeem or otherwise purchase for value any of its shares of common stock prior to issuance of shares under this Warrant, the Holder shall be entitled to receive hereunder the same number of shares it could have received had the redemptions or purchases for value not occurred.

V.   Exercise Procedure

This Warrant may be exercised by presenting it and tendering the purchase price in tender or by bank cashier's or certified check at the principal office of the Company, along with written subscription substantially in the form of Exhibit I hereof;

The date on which this Warrant is thus surrendered, accompanied by tender or payment as hereinbefore or hereinafter provided, is referred to herein as the Exercise Date. The Company shall forthwith at its expense (including the payment of issue taxes) issue and deliver the proper number of shares, and such shares shall be deemed issued for all purposes as of the opening of business on the Exercise Date, notwithstanding any delay in the actual issuance;

VI.   Sale or Exchange of Company or Assets

If prior to issuance of stock under this Warrant the Company sells or exchanges all or substantially all of its assets, or the shares of common stock of the Company are sold or exchanged to any party other than the Holder, then the Holder at its option may receive, in lieu of the stock otherwise issuable hereunder, such money or property as it would have been entitled to receive had this Warrant been exercised prior to such sale or exchange.

VII. Sale of Warrant or Shares

Neither this Warrant nor other shares of common stock issuable upon exercise of the conversion rights herein have been registered under the Securities Act of 1933 as amended or under the securities laws of any state. Neither this Warrant nor any shares when issued may be sold, transferred, pledged, or hypothecated in the absence of (i) an effective registration statement for this Warrant or the shares, as the case may be, under the Securities Act of 1933 as amended and such registration or qualification as may be necessary under the securities laws of any state or (ii) an opinion of counsel reasonably satisfactory to the Company that such registration or qualification is not required. The Company shall cause a certificate or certificates evidencing all or any of the shares issued upon exercise of the conversion rights herein prior to said registration and qualification of such shares to bear the following legend: "The shares evidenced by this certificate have not been registered under the Securities Act of 1933 as amended or under the securities laws of any state. The shares may not be sold, transferred, pledged, or hypothecated in the absence of an effective registration statement under the Securities Act of 1933, as amended, and such registration or qualification as may be necessary under the securities laws of any state or an opinion of counsel satisfactory to the Company that such registration or qualification is not required."

VIII. Transfer

This Warrant shall be registered on the books of the Company, which shall be kept at its principal office for that purpose, and shall be transferable only on such books by the Holder in person or by duly authorized attorney with written notice substantially in the form of Exhibit 11 hereof, and only in compliance with the preceding paragraph. The Company may issue appropriate stop orders to its transfer agent to prevent a transfer in violation of the preceding paragraph.

IX. Replacement of Warrant

At the request of the Holder and on production of evidence reasonably satisfactory to the Company of the loss, theft, destruction, or mutilation of this Warrant and (in the case of loss, theft, or destruction) if required by the Company, upon delivery of an indemnity Agreement with surety in such reasonable amount as the Company may determine thereof, the Company at its expense will issue in lieu thereof a new Warrant of like tenor.

X. Loan Agreement

This Warrant is subject to the terms of a Loan Agreement dated this date between the Company and the Holder, a copy of which is on file and may be examined at the principal office of the Company in McLean, Virginia during regular business hours.

XI. Unlocking

The Holder or its registered assigns shall have certain unlocking rights, as set out in the above-mentioned Loan Agreement.

XII. "Put" Rights

Beginning five (5) years from today and ending ten (10) years from today, the Holder may by written demand require the company to purchase this Warrant or the shares of stock issued hereunder at a price of twenty-five percent (25%) of the higher of the following prices:

- Ten percent (10%) of the Company's sales for the fiscal year immediately preceding the year of the demand times a price earnings of eight, less the aggregate principal balance of the Note on the day of demand; or
- Ten (10) times the Company's cash flow for the fiscal year immediately preceding the year of the demand, less the aggregate principal balance of Note on the day of demand.

XIII. Registration

If the Company shall at any time prepare and file a registration statement under the Securities Act of 1933 with respect to the public offering of any class of equity or debt security of the Company, the Company shall give thirty (30) days' prior written notice thereof to Holder and shall, upon the written request of Holder include in the registration statement or related notification such number of Holder's shares as Holder may request to be sold on a one-time basis; the Company will keep such notification or registration statement and prospectus effective and current under the Act permitting the sale of Holder's shares covered thereby to be sold on a time-to-time basis or otherwise; such inclusion, in any event, shall be at no cost to Holder and shall be at the sole cost and expense of the Company; in the event the Company fails to receive a written request from Holder within thirty (30) days after the mailing of its written notice, then the Company shall treat such failure with the same force and effect as if Holder's failure to respond constituted notice to the Company that Holder does not intend to include its shares in such registration statement or notification; the foregoing shall not apply to a registration relating to securities of the Company covered by an employee, stock option, or other benefit plan; in connection with any notification or registration statement or subsequent amendment to any such notification or registration statement or similar document filed pursuant hereto, the Company shall take any reasonable steps to make the securities covered thereby eligible for public offering and sale by the effective date of such notification or registration statement or any amendment to any of the foregoing under the securities or blue sky laws of Virginia; provided that in no event shall the Company be obligated to qualify to do business in any state where it is not so qualified at the time of filing such documents or to take any action that would subject it to unlimited service of process in any state where it is not so subject at such time; the Company shall keep such filing current for the length of time it must keep any notification, registration statement, post-effective amendment, prospectus, or offering circular and any amendment to any of the foregoing effective pursuant hereto; in connection with any filing hereunder, the Company shall bear all the expenses and professional fees that arise in connection with such filings and all expenses incurred in making such filings and keeping them effective and correct as provided hereunder and shall also provide Holder with a reasonable number of printed copies of the prospectus, offering circulars and/or supplemental prospectuses or amended prospectuses in final and preliminary form; the Company consents to the use of such prospectus or offering circular in connection with the sale of Holder's shares; in the event of the filing of any registration statement or notification pursuant to this Agreement or document referred to herein that includes Holder's shares, Holder shall indemnify the Company and each of its officers and directors who has signed said registration statement, each person, if any, who controls the Company with the meaning of the Securities Act, each underwriter for the Company and each person, if any, who controls such underwriter within the meaning of the Securities Act, from any loss, claim, damage, liability, or action arising out of or based upon any untrue statement or any omission to state therein a material fact required to be stated therein or necessary to make the statements therein not misleading, furnished in writing by Holder expressly for use in such registration statement or required to be furnished by Holder.

XIV. Covenants of the Company

The Company covenants that until this Warrant is exercised or expires, it will:

(a) Reserve authorized but unissued One Thousand Seven Hundred Twenty-Four (1,724) shares of its common stock or such additional number of such shares as necessary to satisfy the rights of the Holder;

(b) Not pay any dividends in cash or in kind unless written authorization is received in writing from the Holder;

(c) Furnish the Holder consolidated financial statements of the Company, which statements shall include and be rendered as follows:

1. Monthly year-to-date financial statements within forty-five (45) days after the close of the last previous month, which statements shall include a balance sheet and a statement of profit and loss for the period in question, and

2. If requested in writing by Holder, within sixty (60) days after the close of each fiscal year a balance sheet and a profit-and-loss statement of the Company relating to such year, certified by a firm of independent public accountants of recognized standing in McLean, Virginia and approved by the Holder, accompanied by any report or comment of said accountant made in connection with such financial statements, and with a copy of all other financial statements prepared for or furnished to the Company.

(d) The President of the Company shall certify on each statement furnished to the Holder that no default exists hereunder, or, in the event a default does exist, the President shall submit his or her statement of such default;

(e) Maintain an office in the McLean, Virginia, area, at which its books and records will be kept and notices, presentations, demands, and payments relating to this Warrant, the Note, and the Loan Agreement may be given or made;

(f) Maintain books of account in accordance with generally accepted accounting principles;

(g) Permit the Holder through its designated representative to visit and inspect any of the properties of the Company, to examine its books and records, and to discuss its affairs, finances, and accounts with and be advised as to the same by the officers of the Company at such reasonable times and intervals.

XV. Investment Covenant

The Holder by its acceptance hereby covenants that this Warrant is, and the stock to be acquired upon the exercise of this Warrant will be, acquired for investment purposes, and that the Holder will not distribute the same in violation of any state or federal law or regulation.

XVI. Laws Governing

This Warrant shall be construed according to the laws of the District of Columbia.

IN WITNESS WHEREOF, Ace Electromagnetic, Incorporated, has caused this Warrant to be signed on its behalf, in its corporate name, by its President, and its corporate seal to be hereunto affixed and the said seal to be Attested by its Secretary, as of this 31st day of January, 1983.

Seal: Ace Electromagnetic, Incorporated
By:_____
J. B. Entrepreneur, President
Attest: _____
J. J. Smith, Secretary

LEGAL DOCUMENT 4

Ajax Computer Genetics Corp.
123 International Drive
McLean, VA 22102

Venture Capital Corp.
125 Main Street
McLean, VA 22101

Dear Sirs:

STOCK PURCHASE AGREEMENT

You have informed us that, subject to certain conditions, you are prepared to subscribe for and purchase, at a price of Ten Dollars ($10.00) per share, Two Hundred Fifty Thousand (250,000) shares (the "Shares") of our authorized but unissued Common Stock, One Dollar ($1.00) par value (the "Stock"). In this connection, we hereby confirm our Agreement with you as follows:

1. Representations and Warranties.

    ("Ajax" or "we") is a corporation duly organized and validly existing in good standing under the laws of the Virginia and is duly qualified to transact business as a foreign corporation under the laws of Florida and California, the only jurisdictions in which the nature of the business currently transacted by us requires such qualification.

    1.1 The authorized capital stock of Ajax consists of One Million (1,000,000) shares of the Stock, all of one class, of which there are outstanding on the date hereof Nine Hundred Seventy-Two Thousand Five Hundred Fifteen (972,515) shares, and Seven Thousand Eight Hundred (7,800) shares are reserved for issuance pursuant to options held by key employees of Ajax and subsidiaries. Other than the shares (1) so reserved for stock options and (2) the shares being purchased by you.

    1.2 Ajax has no subsidiaries, nor does it intend to establish any subsidiaries.

    1.3 There have been furnished to you the consolidated financial statements of Ajax as of and for the years just ending. These financial statements are complete and correct, and present fairly the consolidated financial condition of Ajax and the consolidated results of their operations as of the dates thereof and for the period covered thereby. Such financial statements have been prepared in accordance with generally accepted accounting principles applied on a consistent basis throughout the periods involved, subject to any comments and notes therein. Since the year end there has not occurred any material adverse change in the consolidated financial position or results of operations of Ajax, nor any change not in the ordinary course of business.

1.4 There are no actions, suits, or proceedings pending nor, to Ajax's knowledge, threatened, before any court, agency, or other body that involves Ajax, wherein Ajax is a defendant.

1.5 This Agreement and the issuance and sale of the Shares pursuant hereto have been duly authorized by appropriate and all required corporate action; such issuance and sale and Ajax's compliance with the terms hereof will not violate Ajax's articles of incorporation, bylaws, any indenture or contract to which Ajax is a party or by which it is bound, or any statute, rule, regulation, or order of any court or agency applicable to Ajax; and the Shares when issued and sold as provided herein will have been duly and validly authorized and issued, fully paid and nonassessable.

2. Covenants.

We covenant and agree with you that:

2.1 Prior to your purchase of the Shares, we shall provide to you, your agents, and attorney access to the same kind of information as is specified in Schedule A of the Securities Act of 1933 (the "1933 Act"), and shall make available to you during the course of this transaction the opportunity to ask questions of, and receive answers from, ourselves and our officers necessary to your satisfaction to verify the accuracy of such information.

2.2 For a period of at least two years following the Closing Date, we will not apply more than twenty percent (20%) of the proceeds from the sale of the Shares to the business of any new products without the concurrence of all members of our Board of Directors who have been nominated by you pursuant to Section 2.3 or elected thereto pursuant to Section 5.4.

2.3 As long as you and your affiliates own combined a total of at least ten percent (10%) of the outstanding voting securities of Ajax, you and your affiliates together shall be entitled to nominate a total of two (2) persons for election as members of our Board of Directors and, if they are so nominated and legally qualify to serve in that capacity, our Board of Directors will support their election.

2.4

(a) If, at any time while you or your affiliates (collectively "you") hold any of the Shares, we shall decide to register with the Securities and Exchange Commission any issue of Stock (other than a registration of shares solely for the purpose of any plan for the acquisition thereof by our employees or for the purpose of a merger or acquisition), we will give you written notice of such decision at least twenty (20) days prior to the filing of a registration statement and will afford you upon your request the opportunity of having any Shares then held by you included in the registration if the request is made within ten (10) days after receiving such notice, to the extent and under the conditions upon which such registration is permissible under the 1933 Act and the Rules and Regulations of the Securities and Exchange Commission; provided, however, that we may exclude such Shares from a registration statement filed by us to the extent that, in the opinion of the managing underwriter of the issue being registered, the inclusion of such of the Shares or of more than a designated portion thereof would be detrimental to the public offering pursuant to such registration, and to the further extent that such exclusion is made applicable to sales by all holders of outstanding Stock, pro rata in proportion to their holdings. In the event in any registration we offer you the opportunity to sell such of the Shares that you propose to register to underwriters on a "firm commitment" basis (as opposed to a "best efforts" basis), you shall, as a condition of your participation in the registration, accept an offer to sell such of the Shares to the underwriters if the managing underwriter so requires or, in the alternative, agree not to sell such of the Shares pursuant to such registration within such reasonable period (not exceeding One Hundred Twenty [120] days) as may be specified by the managing underwriter to enable those underwriters to complete their distributions; and in any event, shall enter into an Agreement with us and such underwriter containing conventional representations, warranties, and indemnity provisions. You will comply with such other reasonable requirements as may be imposed by the managing underwriter to effect the offering and an orderly distribution of the shares, including your acceptance of the same offering price as shall be accepted by us for the Stock being sold by us pursuant to such registration statement. All expenses of such registration applicable to Shares offered by you shall be payable by us, to the extent permitted by Securities and Exchange Commission Rules or policy, except for your pro rata share of the underwriters' discounts and commissions.

(b) Our obligation to accord you the right to register Shares pursuant to paragraph (a) shall apply to each and every registration that may be effected by us following your purchase of the Shares, except if at the time you shall otherwise be, both as to time and amount, free to sell all the Shares held by you. Without limitation, for the purpose of this paragraph (b), you shall be considered to be free, both as to time and amount, to sell all the Shares held by you if all such Shares may be sold within a period of ninety (90) days pursuant to Rule 144 promulgated under the 1933 Act.

In the event that any registration statement relating to any Shares shall be filed and become effective pursuant to any of the foregoing provisions of this Section 2.4, then at any time while a prospectus relating to such of the Shares is required to be delivered under the 1933 act, but later than nine (9) months after the effective date of such registration statement, we will, a your request, prepare and furnish to you a reasonable number of copies of such prospectus and of such registration statements as may be necessary so that, as thereafter delivered to purchasers of any of the Shares, such prospectus shall comply with Section 10 of the 1933 Act.

In the event that any registration statement relating to any Shares shall be filed pursuant to this Section 2.4, we will use our best efforts to qualify such of the Shares for sale under the laws of such jurisdiction within the continental United States as you may reasonably request and will comply to the best of our ability with such laws so as to permit the continuance of sales of dealings in such of the Shares thereunder. The filing fees with respect to such jurisdictions requested by you shall be payable to you. We shall not, however, be obligated to qualify as a foreign corporation or file any general consent to service or process under the laws of any such jurisdiction or subject ourselves to taxation as doing business in any such jurisdiction or qualify under the securities laws of any jurisdictions that we reasonably deem unduly burdensome.

2.5 If the sale and purchase of the Shares shall be consummated, we will pay the reasonable fees and disbursements of your special counsel in connection with this Agreement and the transaction contemplated herein and, in addition, will pay to you a fee of Twenty Thousand Dollars ($20,000.00) for services in connection herewith.

2.6 We shall indemnify you and any of your affiliates against any claim for any fees or commissions by any broker, finder, or other person for services or alleged services in connection herewith or the transaction contemplated hereby.

3. Representations and Agreements of Investors.

By accepting this Agreement you confirm to us that:

3.1 You and your officers have such knowledge and experience in financial and business matters that you and they are capable of evaluating the merits and risks of your investment in the Shares.

3.2 You represent that you will acquire the Shares for investment and without any present intention of distributing or otherwise reselling any of them.

3.3 You understand that the Shares will be "restricted securities" as that term is defined in the Rules and Regulations of the Securities and Exchange Commission under the 1933 Act and accordingly may not be reoffered or resold by you unless they are registered under the Act or unless an exemption from such registration is available, and you consent that any certificates for the Shares may be legended accordingly.

3.4 You represent that you have no knowledge of any fees or commissions due in this transaction, except those fees set forth in 2.5 above and any fee that may be due and payable to JMB Investment Bankers (Brokers).

4. Closing.

   Subject to the terms and conditions hereof, the purchase and sale of the Shares shall take place at our office in McLean, Virginia the last day of this month, at 11:00 A.M. (the "Closing Date") by our delivery to you of a certificate or certificates for the Shares, registered in your name, and your payment to use of the purchase price therefore by wire transfer to our account with The First National Bank.

5. Conditions.

   Your obligation to take up and pay for the Shares on the Closing Date shall be subject to the following conditions:

   5.1 Our representations and warrantees herein shall be true on and as of the Closing Date as though made on such date; we shall have performed all of our covenants and Agreements herein required to be performed on or before the Closing Date; and we shall have delivered to you a certificate to such effects, dated the Closing Date and executed by our President or Executive Vice President.

   5.2 There shall have been delivered to you a letter dated the Closing Date from our accountants to the effect that, (i) nothing has come to their attention that would require them to withdraw or modify their annual report on your consolidated financial statements as of and for the two years just ending; and (ii) they have performed a review of the interim consolidated financial statement of Ajax as of and for the three months ending, in accordance with the standards established by the American Institute of Certified Public Accountants. Such a review of the interim financial statements consists principally of obtaining an understanding of the system for the preparation of interim financial statements, applying analytical review procedures to financial data, and making inquiries of persons responsible for financial and accounting matters. It is substantially less in scope than an examination in accordance with generally accepted auditing standards, the objective of which is the expression of an opinion regarding the financial statements taken as a whole. Accordingly, no such opinion is expressed.

5.3 There shall have been delivered to you a favorable opinion, dated the Closing Date, of our general counsel, J. P. Paul, Esquire, as to the questions of law involved in Sections 1.1 through 1.4 and 1.5 and covering such other questions of law as you or your special counsel may reasonably request.

5.4 There shall have been elected as a member of our Board of Directors, subject to the purchase and sale of the Shares, your President, A. V. Capitalist.

5.5 The certificates, accountants' letter, and legal opinion delivered on the Closing Date shall be deemed to fulfill the conditions hereof only if they are to your reasonable satisfaction and to that of M. S. Smith, your special counsel for the purpose of this transaction.

6. Miscellaneous

6.1 All notices required or permitted by this Agreement shall be in writing addressed, if to us, at our address appearing at the head of this letter and, if to you, as this letter is addressed. Either party may, however, request communications or copies thereof to be sent to different addresses, and you may direct us to pay any dividends on the Shares to a bank in the United States for your account.

6.2 All representations, warranties, and covenants made by all the parties herein shall survive the delivery of and the payment for the Shares.

6.3 This Agreement shall be binding upon and inure to the benefit of the parties hereto and their respective successors and assigns.

6.4 This Agreement shall be construed in accordance with, and the rights and obligations of the parties hereto shall be governed by, the laws of the Commonwealth of Virginia, U.S.A.

6.5 This Agreement supersedes any prior Agreement, written or oral, between the parties hereto or their affiliates regarding the subject matter hereof.

6.6 In the event the closing described in Section 4 hereof has not taken place by mid-year, this Agreement shall terminate unless the parties agree in writing to further extend the same. In the event of termination, all rights, duties, and obligations of each of the parties shall cease and terminate, and this Agreement shall be considered cancelled and of no effect or validity thereafter.

If the foregoing accords with your understanding of our Agreement, please sign and return to us the enclosed copy of this letter.

AJAX COMPUTER GENETICS CORPORATION
By:_____
J. B. Entrepreneur, President

ACCEPTED: VENTURE CAPITAL CORPORATION
By:_____
A.V. Capitalist, President

LEGAL DOCUMENT 5

SCHEDULE A: EXHIBITS TO STOCK PURCHASE AGREEMENT

1. Ajax (the "Company") is a Virginia corporation with its principal office at 123 International Drive, McLean, Virginia, 22102.

2. (A) Exhibit 1A enclosed herewith is a copy of the Annual Report of Ajax for the fiscal year just ending, and included in said report under the same date, is a copy of the Certified Audit of the Company made by its current accounting firm for the above fiscal year. (B) Exhibit 1B enclosed herewith is a copy of the preliminary unaudited Financial Statements of Ajax of the one month just ended. A list of Officers and Directors of the Company and their addresses is enclosed as Exhibit 2.B hereof.

3. J. B. Entrepreneur, the President of the Company, is the sole owner owning ten percent (10%) or more of record and beneficially of stock of the Company.

4. As of this date, J. B. Entrepreneur owns of record and beneficially Two Hundred Thousand (200,000) shares of stock of the Company.

5. The Company is not a holding company and has no subsidiary corporations.

6. Ajax has Two Million (2,000,000) authorized shares of stock, all common, with a par value of One Dollar ($1.00) per share, and presently issued and outstanding there are Three Hundred Thousand (300,000) shares of stock. In addition thereto, there are options to purchase One Hundred Thousand (100,000) shares of stock issued to and held by existing employees. The company has a stock option plan with One Hundred Thousand (100,000) remaining unissued shares.

7. See Exhibit 3 pertaining to a list of Stock Options outstanding that have been granted to employees of the Company.

8. The Company intends to sell not less than Fifty Thousand (50,000) shares of stock in this private placement at an offering price of Ten Dollars ($10.00) per share. The Company may sell additional shares of stock to a secured venture capital firm at a price of not less than Ten Dollars ($10.00) per share, which transaction would take place in the near future if consummated.

9. Proceeds of the private placement will be used as follows; One Million Dollars ($1,000,000) in research and development, One Million Dollars ($1,000,000) in plant expansion, and Five Hundred Thousand Dollars ($500,000) in salaries and working capital.

10. For the year-end period just ending, the Company paid salaries, bonuses, and director's fees to J. B. Entrepreneur in the amount of Two Hundred Fifty-One Thousand Dollars ($251,000). For the current fiscal year, J. B. Entrepreneur is being paid a base salary of Two Hundred Fifty-One Thousand Dollars ($250,000.

11. The net book value per share of Ajax is Five Dollars ($5.00) as of the year just ended. The Company anticipates receiving the entire net proceeds, with the exception of commissions and legal expenses that might be incurred under 12 below, derived from the sale of the securities being offered at Ten Dollars ($10.00) per share.

12. Commissions being paid for services rendered in the sale will be Twenty Thousand Dollars ($20,000) to the Venture Capital Corporation.

13. The Company has: (A) Employment Contract with J. B. Entrepreneur entered for a period of five (5) years providing for annual compensation of not less than Two Hundred Fifty Thousand Dollars ($250,000). (B) The other basic contracts that the Company has are for leases for office space where it maintains its offices in McLean, Virginia.

14. Enclosed herewith is Exhibit 4, a copy of the Articles of Incorporation together with all Amendments thereto of Ajax, and Exhibit 5, a copy of the existing Bylaws of the Company.

C LIST OF TRAITS FOR ANALYSIS OF PEOPLE

Use this list to crystallize your thinking about an entrepreneur. After you have gotten to know him or her, go through the list and circle the adjectives that best describe the entrepreneur. After you have been in the investment for a while, go back and select traits again. Very likely, they won't be the same. You may want to rate your entrepreneur and the team every quarter. This is one of the qualitative methods of tracking an investment.

ADJECTIVE	DEFNITION
accomplishing	successful, bringing to completion
accurate	correct, clear-cut, beyond doubt
achieving	accomplishing, persevering, striving
active	energetic, lively, dynamic
adaptive	able to adjust, fits in, flexible
adventuresome	daring, willing to take chances
affiliative	associated, connected, a joiner
aggressive	forceful, assertive
ambitious	enterprising, striving, eager
apologetic	sorry, regretful, makes excuses
apprehensive	fearful, worried, afraid

ADJECTIVE	DEFINITION
approval-seeking	wanting acceptance and praise
carefree	free of worry or responsibilities
charitable	generous, kind, giving
comforting	soothing, relieved, consoling
competitive	seeking to win, ambitious, achieving
concerned	aware, caring, interested
conforming	compliant, obedient
conservative	moderate, prudent, cautious
consoling	offering solace, cheering up
creative	imaginative, inventive, innovative
cultured	refined, showing gentility, taste
defenseless	protective, shielded, careful
dependent	needing aid or assistance
distant	remote, inaccessible, removed
educated	knowledgeable, informed, cultured
egotistic	self-centered, individualistic
empathetic	aware of another, compassionate
energetic	inexhaustible, vigorous
envious	resentful, discontented, jealous
fun-loving	playful, carefree, spontaneous
goal-oriented	seeking success and achievement
good-natured	amicable, pleasant, happy
guarded	kept safe, protected, watched over
hard-working	eager, responsible, go-getter
help-seeking	looking for assistance or comfort
honest	truthful, respectable, sincere
hospitable	welcoming, warm, receptive
humble	reserved, self-conscious, modest
idealistic	daydreamer, imaginative, visionary
impatient	excitable, unable to wait
independent	self-reliant, autonomous
individualistic	one-of-a-kind, independent

ADJECTIVE	DEFNITION
innovative	creative, new, original
insecure	inadequate, unsure, shaky
intellectual	rational, smart, quick-witted
jealous	envious, vigilant, fearful
joking	witty, wisecracking, jesting
kind	gentle, considerate, warmhearted
knowledgeable	exhibiting knowledge or intelligence
law-abiding	tends to obey the law
leadership	has the capacity to lead
liberal	tolerant, generous, unrestrained
likeable	pleasant, enjoyable, attractive
loving	affectionate, devoted, caring
loyal	steadfast, faithful, devoted
meek	humble, submissive, patient
meticulous	extremely careful, scrupulous
neighborly	friendly, amicable, familiar
nurturing	nourishing, supporting, fostering
obedient	compliant, amenable, dutiful
open-minded	aware, unbiased, receptive
optimistic	hopeful, positive, enthusiastic
outgoing	sociable, friendly
passive	submissive, compliant, inactive
persistent	determined, persevering, stubborn
pessimistic	gloomy, negative, depressed
playful	impish, mischievous, frivolous
pleasure-seeking	seeking gratification or delight
precise	clearly defined, exact
protective	defended, guarded, careful
quick-thinking	bright, perceptive, alert
quiet	still, silent, not talkative
religious	pious, scrupulous, devout
reserved	restrained, self-controlled, shy

ADJECTIVE	DEFNITION
responsible	accountable, trustworthy
rigid	stiff, unchanging, inflexible
sarcastic	joking in a biting or cynical way
secretive	covert, underhanded, concealed
seeks attention	wanting to be noticed
seeks recognition	wanting to be praised
self-blaming	guilt, fault finding
sensitive	perceptive, touchy, nervous
serious	grave, earnest, weighty
silly	lacking good sense, frivolous
sincere	true, honest, natural
socially striving	seeking respectability
status-conscious	attentive to position and wealth
stealing	thieving, dishonest
striving	contending, exerting effort
suspicious	doubtful, distrustful, showing uncertainty
sympathetic	comforting, understanding
talkative	chatty, always speaking
tidy	neat, orderly, clean
trusting	confident, committed
truthful	honest, trustworthy
uncaring	lacking in warmth or sympathy
unconventional	unusual, not the norm, rebellious
virtuous	pure, moral, good
warm	friendly, sincere, cordial
wary	cautious, watchful, on guard
wise	profound, judicious, sensible, prudent
yielding	deferring, relenting, gives in

D EVALUATION OF AN ENTREPRENEUR BY AN INDUSTRIAL PSYCHOLOGIST

Name: J. B. Entrepreneur
By: Industrial Analysis, Inc.
Chicago, IL

SUMMARY AND RECOMMENDATION

J. B. Entrepreneur possesses many outstanding qualities for a chief executive officer's position. J. B. is intelligent and empathic, so he will receive good feedback from subordinates. J. B. is open and flexible enough to use that feedback in a constructive way, making use of the ideas and suggestions of people.

Further, J. B. does possess reasonably strong persuasive motivation. Because the chief executive officer often is in a situation in which he or she must persuade, e.g., dealing with the board, with unions, with department heads, etc., this ability to persuade can be extremely valuable. Finally, on the plus side, J. B. is extremely well organized, and although he does not love detail, he is an individual capable of both planning and organizing his own work exceptionally well and planning, organizing, coordinating, and following up on the work of others.

J. B.'s only real drawbacks relate to his aloofness and his somewhat inconsistent assertiveness. As to the former, despite the fact that J. B. has exceptionally good empathy and is able to understand people very well, he does tend to keep them at a distance. J. B. is a bit cool and aloof, so he could be perceived as cold and uncaring, despite his real understanding of subordinates.

It is very important that J. B. be made aware of this and that he work to warm up his relationships to convey the notion that he does understand people in order to do the most effective job. As to the latter, there are many occasions in which J. B. can be strongly assertive, but there are other times when he may back down inappropriately and not push strongly enough for his point of view. J. B. is not by any means unassertive, but more consistency here would help a great deal.

In short, J. B. is definitely an individual who can handle a chief executive officer's responsibility for the firm. Some improvement in the two weaker areas discussed would allow him to perform on an exceptionally good level.

Ego-drive

This person's ego-drive is moderately strong. J. B. does have to some extent the inner personal need to persuade others. J. B. is somewhat challenged when he is convincing other people, because he does enjoy the conquest of others, both for its financial rewards and for his own sense of achievement. However, persuading others does not gratify him in the same personal way it would if his ego-drive were more intense.

Note: Ego-drive is the inner need to persuade another individual as a means of gaining personal gratification. The ego-driven individual wants and needs the successful persuasion as a powerful enhancement of his or her ego. His or her self-esteem is enhanced by successfully persuading another and diminished when he or she fails to persuade. Ego-drive is not ambition, aggression, energy, or even the willingness to work hard. The ego-driven individual wants and needs to persuade, not primarily for the practical benefits that might be gained, i.e., money, promotion, or other rewards, but more importantly, for the feeling of satisfaction that comes from the victory. Successful persuasion, then, is the particular means through which the ego-driven individual gains pleasure and ego gratification.

EMPATHY

J. B.'s empathy is above average. He has good ability to relate effectively to others, accurately sensing their ideas and reactions. J. B. is able to understand objectively another person's point of view and to use this knowledge to good advantage. J. B. is thereby able to make adjustments in his own behavior in order to deal most appropriately with another person.

This good empathy gives him the ability to deal sensitively with others, thus developing good relationships with them.

Note: Empathy is the ability to sense accurately the reactions of another person. Empathy is the capacity to recognize the clues and cues provided by others in order to relate effectively to them. Empathy is not sympathy. Sympathy involves overidentifying with another person, thereby losing sight of one's own objectives. Sympathy can block the ability to deal effectively with others. The individual with empathy is able accurately and objectively to perceive the other person's feelings without necessarily agreeing. This invaluable, indispensable ability to get powerful feedback enables the individual to adjust his or her own behavior appropriately in order to deal effectively with others.

GROWTH

J. B.'s empathy provides the key to his ability to learn and adapt to new situations. J. B. is quite intelligent, and this, linked with his empathy, enables him to grow steadily in the understanding and performance of his job. J. B. is an open, flexible human being who is not only capable of learning and growing, but also welcomes challenges and adapts readily to new methods and ideas.

Thus, his potential for growth personally and on the job is excellent in terms of both his motivation for growth and his ability to achieve growth.

Note: The ability to learn and grow requires considerably more than the possession of good intelligence. It requires the combination of native intelligence with sufficient empathy and flexibility to permit an individual to use his or her intelligence to acquire new ideas and formulate new methods. In many cases, even people with well above average intelligence lack the capacity to grow because they use their intelligence rigidly to defend and justify their preconceptions, rather than genuinely to seek or accept new approaches. On the other hand, many individuals with only average intelligence have the potential for growth because their openness, flexibility, and empathy permit them to make full use of the abilities they do have to acquire new knowledge and skills. Thus, for an individual to have good growth potential, he or she should combine native intelligence with the openness and flexibility to seek and acquire new ideas and integrate and utilize them in day-to-day life and work.

LEADERSHIP

This person's leadership ability is reasonably good. J. B. has some ability to be assertive and is capable of exhibiting real strength on some occasions. However, J. B. does not have the consistent overall assertiveness possessed by most strong leaders, so he might tend to vacillate in a leadership role.

His empathy, intelligence, overall flexibility, and genuine interest in people will most often allow him to lead effectively. Some improvement in his assertiveness and in his willingness to act strongly and decisively, combined with the important assets J. B. does possess, would give him all the attributes of a good leader.

Note: Leadership is the ability that enables an individual to get other people to do willingly what they have the ability to do but might not spontaneously do on their own. Leadership implies that an individual has a special effect on others that commands their respect, admiration, or affection and causes them to follow that individual. In other words, leadership consists of getting a positive response from others and utilizing that response to bring about a desired attitude or course of action.

This implies a certain amount of assertiveness in the sense that the leader projects some part of his or her personality or will on others. It does not mean aggression, force, or coercion. Whether the leader influences by personal example, persuasion, or empathic feedback, he or she wins others over by influencing their willingness to act, rather than by forcing their compliance. The good leader strives to become aware of the abilities of subordinates or associates, so as to guide them toward only goals that they realistically are capable of attaining.

DECISION MAKING

J. B.'s leadership capacity is further enhanced by his ability to balance a strong sense of responsibility with enough impulsiveness to permit him to make decisions on his own. J. B. is willing to risk the possibility of occasionally being wrong by acting quickly and positively when necessary. J. B. is not likely to be wrong too often because he has sound judgment and the ability to sense how his decisions will affect others.

Further, J. B. possesses the intelligence and flexibility to learn from any mistakes he might make and to adjust his future behavior. Rarely will J. B. make the same mistake a second time.

Note: The competent decision maker possesses a strong sense of personal responsibility and the willingness to make quick decisions where called for. His decisions must be thoughtful and should be based on knowledge of all the available data and possible consequences of his action. On the other hand, J. B. must be willing to take the risk of occasionally being wrong in order to act with the speed and decisiveness that many situations require. The overly impulsive decision maker is likely to make decisions too quickly without sufficient thought about their long-range implications. The overly cautious individual is likely to be so fearful of being wrong that he or she would prefer not to act at all rather than to take that risk, so he or she may miss many opportunities owing to this indecisiveness. The ideal decision maker, therefore, combines thoughtfulness and responsibility with courage to act, even to take a risk, with the intelligence and flexibility to make generally sound judgments and to learn from any mistakes he or she might make.

DELEGATION

J. B. is very well able to delegate responsibility to others. He is not so consumed with his own drive that he has to do everything. Rather, J. B. derives a good deal of satisfaction from the achievements of others, so he is willing to allow them to do their own jobs, to grow, and to achieve their own successes.

J. B. is, moreover, well able to assess correctly the ability of another to do a particular job, so he can make good judgments as to the advisability and appropriateness of delegating a specific responsibility.

In short, J. B. possesses the prime requisites of a good delegator. J. B. combines the willingness to delegate with the ability to do so appropriately.

Note: The ability to delegate effectively involves the capacity to judge whether another person can perform a task, the ability to evaluate correctly whether it is advantageous to let this person do it, and the willingness to let this person try. The capable delegator is an individual who, although he or she may personally be as well or better able to do a certain job, realizes that keeping the work may involve the inefficient use of his or her time or ability and possibly interfere with the development and best utilization of others. There are two types of individuals who strongly resist delegating:

1. The highly impulsive, ego-driven individual who wants the gratification of doing the job and who is convinced that he or she can do it faster and better than anyone else.

2. The overly cautious perfectionist who fears that no one will do the job as carefully and responsibly as he or she will. Good ability to delegate combines the willingness to allow others to do a job with the capacity to assess accurately their ability to do so.

DETAIL ABILITY

J. B. dislikes detail work but probably can handle it competently when necessary. J. B. is likely to be restless if he is continually confronted with routine tasks or jobs that are repetitive in nature.

Although J. B. will always see detail as a chore and as the least desirable aspect of any job, his sense of responsibility is sufficient to motivate him to do what is necessary despite these feelings. J. B. possesses the self-discipline to allow him to deal with the details when necessary to complete a job.

Note: The ability to handle detail requires that combination of personality dynamics that enables an individual to organize work in a systematic way. It also enables him or her to deal effectively with activities that are repetitive and structured. At one extreme, a person with too deep-seated a need for personal organization and structure may tend to become so overly involved in day-to-day detail that he or she may lose sight of the real meaning of the activity. At the other extreme, a person may be so impatient and intolerant of order that he or she will be undisciplined in the planning and execution of his or her work. This lack of self-management could hamper the individual, even in functions not normally requiring a great deal of detail involvement. The individual with good ability to handle detail enjoys, or at least is comfortable with, order or structure and yet is not so enmeshed in detail that he or she loses sight of the broader picture.